The Contemporary
Comic Book Superhero

Routledge Research in Cultural and Media Studies

**19. The Contemporary Comic
Book Superhero**
Edited by Angela Ndalianis

The Contemporary Comic Book Superhero

Edited by
Angela Ndalianis

 Routledge
Taylor & Francis Group
New York   London

First published 2009
by Routledge
270 Madison Ave, New York NY 10016

Simultaneously published in the UK
by Routledge
2 Park Square, Milton Park, Abingdon, Oxon, OX14 4RN

Routledge is an imprint of the Taylor & Francis Group, an informa business

Transferred to Digital Printing 2009

Typeset in Sabon by IBT Global.

Library of Congress Cataloging in Publication Data
Ndalianis, Angela, 1960–
    The contemporary comic book superhero / edited by Angela Ndalianis.
      p. cm. — (Routledge research in cultural and media studies ; 19)
    Includes bibliographical references and index.
    ISBN 978-0-415-99176-6
    1. Comic books, strips, etc.—United States—History and criticism.   2. Heroes in art.   3. Heroes in literature.   I. Title.
    PN6725.N33 2009
    741.5'352—dc22
    2008019470

ISBN10: 0-415-99176-5 (hbk)
ISBN10: 0-415-87841-1 (pbk)

ISBN13: 978-0-415-99176-6 (hbk)
ISBN13: 978-0-415-87841-8 (pbk)

This one's for Athanasios, my dad—
thanks for giving me my first superhero comic book.

Contents

PART II
"We Act Normal, Mom! I Want to Be Normal!": Superbodies, Identities, and Fans

PART III
"I'm Just a Puppet Who Can See the Strings":
Revisions, Retellings, and Auteurs

Figures

Acknowledgments

Most of the essays in this book began their existence as papers presented at the *Holy Men in Tights! A Superheroes Conference*, which was held at the University of Melbourne in June 2005. One outcome of that conference was the anthology *Super/Heroes: From Hercules to Superman* (edited by Wendy Haslem, Angela Ndalianis, and Chris Mackie, New Academia Publishing: Washington, 2006), which evaluates the social function and formal characteristics of the hero and superhero in contemporary, ancient, and multiple media contexts, examining its continuities, transformations, and cultural significance. The current anthology focuses instead on the comic book superheroes and their occasional journeys into film and television. The conference was an inspiring event that provided an environment for like-minded experts on and followers of the superhero to meet and generate ideas. One of the ideas was this anthology. Many heartfelt thanks go to all of the paper presenters and participants. I'd like to also acknowledge the support of the University of Melbourne in granting a Publication Grant in support of the publication of this book.

The Marvel and DC Comics images published in this book appear under the Fair Use agreement, as does the panel from Joe Sacco's *Palestine;* thanks go to Marvel Entertainment, DC Comics, and Fantagraphics Books for their support. The images from *Miracleman* are also reprinted under this agreement; however, copyright acknowledgment has not been credited because the current status of *Miracleman*'s ownership is not resolved (and the legal battle between Todd McFarlane and Neil Gaiman continues).

Finally, thanks go to all of those wonderful, creative people in the superhero comic book world who have given us 'readers' such immense pleasure.

Part I

"That's the Problem With You Readers, You Know All the Plots"[1]

Time, Genre, and Narration

1 Comic Book Superheroes
An Introduction

Angela Ndalianis

One of my earliest memories is of being a little girl of about three years old: lying on the floor on my stomach, with feet swinging rhythmically to a nonexistent beat, I'd flip excitedly through the pages of my superhero comic books (courtesy of my pop-culture-enlightened dad), looking up occasionally to allow my face to be bathed by the calming rays of the television screen. Many decades have passed, but not much has changed—well, perhaps now I tend to prefer wallowing in the latest adventures of my superheroes while propped up by pillows in the comfort of my bed. The thrill of eagerly turning each page remains as intense as it was when I was a young girl, but now I also have the advantage of being able to read and even understand the funny scribbles in the boxes and bubbles that are scattered across the pages. Since those early days, my tastes and interests shifted and developed, adjusting, especially since the 1980s, to the darker, more maladjusted hero types: the Preacher, the Invisibles, Hitman, the Punisher, Swamp Thing, John Constantine—they all occupy a special space on my ever-growing bookshelves, but my favorite has never wavered. It was Batman when I was three and it's Batman today. I took him into my life and let his mysterious and dark brand of heroism cut deep into my being. The arrival of the television series in the 1960s further convinced me that this man in tights (not glaringly colored and tasteless spandex like those of Superman or Spiderman) really did exist out there somewhere. How could this complex, brooding being that affected me in such real ways not be real? (As a kid I repressed the extreme campiness of the TV show—hell, I thought camp was a place your parents sent you when they wanted you out of the house for a week!) Perhaps, like Fox Mulder, I still want to believe.

Heroic narratives have a history that's as old as that of the establishment of human socialization. This major cultural construct began before Hercules slew the Nemean lion with his bare hands or Odin killed the giant Ymir, and often reflects the social need for extraordinary action. Hero myths contain universal elements and have a continued presence in cultural memory, yet they're dynamic beings who shift and metamorphose to accommodate themselves to specific eras and historic-cultural contexts. Fast forward to 2008. Thanks to global dissemination and the cross-media phenomenon that drives entertainment media, the hero in his and her superheroic dimensions has reached a level of popularity never witnessed before. Finding forms of expression in comic books like *Catwoman, The Authority* and *Ultimate X-Men*, the television series *Smallville,* and the enormously successful *Heroes,* online computer games like *City of Heroes*, theme park destinations like the *Marvel Superhero Island* at Universal Studios' Islands of Adventure, and the *Spider Man*, *Batman,* and *Superman* blockbuster extravaganzas, the superhero has become part of the wider cultural consciousness. Even historic figures have made a comeback as superheroes in examples like the runaway 2005 blockbuster film *300*, which is an adaptation of the Frank Miller graphic novel (which is, in turn, an adaptation of the 1962 film). Depicting the battle at Thermopylae, which was fought by the Spartans as they held off the invading Persian army into Greece, King Leonidas of Sparta (who comes complete with cape) comes across as an old-school Batman who suffered greatly to create his superheroism. (Being the product of Spartan parents—and therefore a descendant of Hercules—I'm especially pleased about this new addition.)

The comic book aesthetic or, more specifically, the superhero comic book aesthetic, has been overtly present in film and television over the last five years or so. In addition to seeing comic book heroes like Superman, Batman, Iron Man, the Hulk, and Wonder Woman represented in these media spaces, films and television series have adopted and adapted comic book styles to add a stamp of legitimacy to their fictional worlds. Michael Cohen has written about the earlier example of *Dick Tracy* (Warren Beatty 1990), which attempted to meticulously "capture the aesthetic of a comic in a live-action film" through the strategy of "cartooning" (Cohen 2007, 131, 201). Extending the innovative "cartooning" effects that had been introduced in *Who Framed Roger Rabbit* (Robert Zemeckis 1988) two years earlier, the mise en scene (special effects, sets, makeup) and cinematography succumb to the logic of the cartoon world in an effort to produce an "aesthetic of artifice" that's absent from lived reality. More recently, however, this process of cartooning has been replaced by a more explicit comic book aesthetic. In *Sin City* (2005), for example, Frank Miller and Robert Rodriguez extend the cartooning strategy (a strategy that Zack Snyder also adopted for *300*), combining it with the dramatic metamorphosis of 'live' action sequences into comic book images; these images aim at capturing the powerful, still, and abstracted environments and characters of Frank Miller's original comic book world. This obsessive drive to incorporate a comic book style into the live action film is also expressed, albeit in an alternative way, in the television series *Heroes*. In Season One, the character Isaac Mendez's precognitive visions are concretely manifested as both fan-collectible, limited edition comic-style paintings and the comic book series *9th*

Figure 1.1 The Cheerleader—one of the more popular characters in the *Heroes* television series. © NBC/Universal TV/The Kobal Collection.

Wonders! (which is read by characters in the show); the series also has its own online comic book back story spin-off, *Heroes Evolutions*, which is downloadable monthly from the NBC *Heroes* Web site (http://www.nbc.com/Heroes/). In addition, the 'real' artist responsible for these comic book images is Tim Sale, the artist who collaborated with the writer Jeph

Loeb on the comic book classics *Batman: The Long Halloween, Batman: Dark Victor,* and *Superman for all Seasons.* Jeph Loeb also happens to be co-executive producer of *Heroes.* Like many recent and soon to be released examples of superheroes in a moving-image format, since its release in 2006 *Heroes* has adopted the comic book aesthetic in an attempt to prove its authenticity or status as superhero text. Yet, despite the proliferation of sophisticated, hi-tech (and not so hi-tech) illusions of superbeings across a variety of media, it's the comic book medium that remains at the forefront of public consciousness as *the* superhero medium *par excellence.*[2] This is, after all, where audiences were first introduced to the original superman in tights.

Superman's origins and associations with what Richard Reynolds calls the 'man-god' are well-rehearsed. Like Moses, he was sent off as a baby by his parents on a journey that would save him; and like a god, he appeared from the heavens in order to offer salvation to humanity on Earth. When Superman made his otherworldly presence felt on our planet Earth in 1938, he also brought with him the possibility of a utopian reality. As Scott Bukatman (2003) and Adnan Morshed (2004) have argued, during this time, written across the body of the superhero were the "utopian aspirations" of the modern city (185). The New York World's Fair of 1939–1940 took important steps in forging a relationship between science and society: it showcased a new urban landscape that figured the utopian possibilities of technology and science. Appropriately, on the opening night, Albert Einstein switched on the lights that would bring life to the fair's motto: "Designing the World of Tomorrow." Like, Superman—the Man of Tomorrow—the New York World's Fair created a vision of a world in which "science could become a way of life and utopia would be near" (Rydell 1993, 111). In addition to showcasing the latest in technological advances, which included Voder, a synthetic human-speech device by AT&T; Rotolactor, an automatic cow-milking machine; television sets by RCA, GE, and Westinghouse; and Elektro, a walking and talking robot by Westinghouse (Kuznick 1994, 341), it was the representation of a City of the Future that attracted the crowds by the millions. It was at the fair that the plans of industrial designers like Norman Bel Geddes set the foundations for cities that would be riddled with massive freeway systems, cars, and soaring skyscrapers. In the Futurama "Highways and Horizons" exhibit sponsored by General Motors, viewers sat high above a utopian city of the future while a motorized belt moved them around the miniature metropolis. As they looked down on a thirty-six-thousand-square-foot model city of superhighways and skyscrapers designed by Geddes, through speakers built into the backs of their seats, a narrator asked the audience to imagine how the traffic and housing problems of the present United States would be solved through these technological and industrial wonders by the year 1960. The souvenir pins, which were intended as a memento that reflected the fair's theme, "Building the

World of Tomorrow," appropriately read "I have seen the future" (Morshed 2004, 74). As Morshed makes clear, the birth of the superhero in the guise of Superman had a great deal to teach the designers of the 1939 World of Tomorrow. Not only did the new superheroes Superman, Wonder Woman, the Flash, Sandman, and Batman all visit the fair within the fictional spaces of the *New York World's Fairs Comics* of 1939–40, but a 'live' Superman also made public appearances as part of 1940's Superman Day (Morshed 2004, 196). More appropriately, Morshed draws attention to the fact that the Futurama exhibit deliberately placed the viewer not only at a vantage point of height but also of flight: "Bel Geddes had his protagonist—the Futurama's spectator—literally fly to an American utopia" (2004, 77). The exhibit was, in fact, typical of the era's obsession with flight as representational of a new mode of being.

At stake in all these projections was a new type of 'aerialized' spectatorship and, consequently, the possibility of new modes of architectural and urbanistic imagination. The fantastic idea that the view from above would somehow facilitate the process of designing the ideal future city became an enduring fascination among utopian architects, planners, and science-fiction writers (Morshed 2004, 80). Like the cult figure of the aviator, especially as embodied in the persona of the American Charles Lindberg, the comic book superhero joined other popular icons of the time—Buck Rogers and Flash Gordon—in representing the eugenicist concept of the New Man, which had gained popularity since the early 1920s, and found new expression in the fair of 1939 (Morshed 2004, 82). Projecting social Darwinism into a yet to be seen future, many of these superbeings conquered the laws of gravity, physics, and biology: "physically evolved, and standing on a high moral ground, the New Man was projected as the harbinger of a Future Western industrial society" (Morshed 2004, 82).

It comes as no surprise that this quasi-scientific rationale went hand in hand with more esoteric associations. Paralleling this scientific logic, the superheroes were also granted mythological and religious justification. Figures like Superman, who flew so gracefully in the skies and who biologically embodied humanity's scientific advancement of flight through technological means, also came to be associated with the heavens. He became, and has continued to be, the superhero whose image most connotes that of godlike savior. A darker version of Superman (an alternative savior) soon followed in 1939 in the shape of Batman, the self-made superhero who would rely increasingly on science and technology to craft his identity and abilities. In the late 1930s, the skies opened and a little bit of Heaven fell to Earth. The birth of Superman in 1938 heralded the Golden Age of comics, and with it the arrival of a superhero whose image reflected the great gods and hyperhumans of a mythic past. Superman, Batman, Captain America, Wonder Woman—they were the stuff of legend. The superbeings of Mount Olympus and Asgard had spread their arms to embrace new geographies and alternate temporal zones. Realizing (within the world of fiction) the theme of the New York World Fair's Futurama exhibit of 1939, the early superheroes arrived in order to "build the World of Tomorrow." They offered hope to a despairing humanity that had lost faith in the civilization embodied by urban life.

The World of Tomorrow finally arrived, bringing with it new superheroes as well as revamped old ones—the Dark Knight, Watchmen, Punisher, Preacher, the Invisibles, Sandman—and a fissure of immense proportions began to rip across the Earth's surface, bringing with it not gods but armies of super (and delightfully addictive) devils. The comic book superheroes have multiplied and, in the process, become more complicated. Clear demarcations of a moral order have blurred and become confused; super-creatures of the night have multiplied, and the comic books are riddled with vigilante figures who not only take the law into their own hands and whose status as symbolic facilitators and embodiments of civilizing processes[3] are seriously questioned. Mythic tropes introduced by the superheroes of the late 1930s and 40s still exist, but since the groundbreaking revisions introduced by Frank Miller and Alan Moore in the late 1980s, they have also become increasingly inverted, questioned, and all out parodied. In the hands of writers like Garth Ennis, Grant Morrison, and Warren Ellis, the traditional superhero image is scrutinized, deconstructed, reconstructed, and ridiculed.

One example will, perhaps, suffice. Garth Ennis's infectiously diabolical characters, from his superpowered prostitute (The Pro) to his anti-superhero cowboys (Frank Castle, Jesse Custer, John Constantine, and Tommy Monaghan), are men and women *without* tights. In his *Preacher* series (in which he collaborated with artist Steve Dillon), Garth Ennis introduced his special creation, the renegade Reverend Jesse Custer, to the world. One day, while Jesse's giving his weekly sermon in the small Texas town of Angelville, the demon spawn Genesis flies to Earth from the heavens above, possessing Jesse's body, and blowing up his church in the process. No plot summary could do justice to the hysterically funny, deeply intelligent, and highly blasphemous series; suffice it to say that Jesse decides to take on God Himself, who's decided to abandon his post as overseer of all creation. Drawing on influences as varied as the Bible, the western, the vampire subgenre, and the American Gothic, Ennis creates an uncanny story space that defamiliarizes the superhero tradition, pushing its codes deep into the hell zones that threaten to unleash the apocalypse in Jesse Custer's world. In other examples, like his stint on *The Punisher*, Ennis tackles the superhero head on. In *The Punisher* story "Does Whatever a Spider Can" (#2, 2001) the Punisher uses Spider Man (while he's unconscious) as a human punching bag that blocks the blows thrown at him by an enraged, genetically altered Russian hit man. But this

Figure 1.2 Wolverine experiencing a bit of Punisher love. *The Punisher*, #17 2002, Marvel Knights.

is a Russian hit man with a difference—in addition to having three hearts and a gorilla's lungs, he's also been granted enormous boobies courtesy of a militant organization. Spidey may face humiliation after humiliation, but it's the stories in which X-Men's Wolverine (one of the most successful and popular superheroes in the Marvel universe) crosses paths with the Punisher that are truly inspired, offering a radical take on the superhero tradition by parodying the bejesus out of Wolverine's 'superness.' In "Vertical Challenge" and "Aim Low" (#16–17, 2002) the Punisher and Wolverine have intersecting interests in bringing a reengaged mob of 'little people' to their brand of justice. Being a man who prefers to work alone (and knowing that Wolverine has super-repairing powers), Frank Castle, alias the Punisher, stalls "the ol' Canucklehead" first by blowing his face off with a rifle so that only bone and eyeballs remain, then by allowing the little people mobsters to capture him and removed his lower limbs, which the Punisher then follows by blasting the Wolverine family jewels to kingdom come with a rifle at close range. The comedy of horrors is finally wrapped up when the Punisher drives a steam roller over Wolverine's body as he crawls dejectedly across the ground in an effort to escape (Figure 1.2). "And," proclaims the Punisher as he exits, "people say I have no sense of humor."

What do we do with these radical transformations of superhero representations? Is it the case, as writers like Reynolds, Coogan, Lawrence, and Jewett and Klock inform us, that shifts in the genre, its characters, and narratives have much to tell us about the social order in which they were produced? If we're dealing with mythic layers as outlined by the anthropologist Claude Levi-Strauss, then perhaps the refusal to reproduce the codes of epic hero types and grand narratives of moral order in the universe marks a radical turning point in human history. If, as Levi-Strauss suggests, myths give order and narrative structure to the way humans contemplate the world around them, then maybe the world around us has descended into an abyss from which there is no exit. Then again, maybe these new brand of heroes are simply a sign not of social reality but of generic reality in the process of metamorphosis. In *Sunset Boulevard* (Billy Wilder 1950) the writer Joe Gillis exclaimed with great wisdom, "That's the problem with you readers, you know all the plots," and in terms of trying to both attract and maintain a market this can be problem. The superheroes and their stories have grown with the audiences that consume them, and their formulas, conventions, and narrative worlds must alter to follow suit, injecting new, unpredictable, and more challenging characterizations that keep the readers engaged. It is this combination of the fictional and social realities of comic book superheroes that this anthology addresses—with occasional journeys into film and television depictions as they intersect with comic book culture.

The first section of the anthology explores the malleability of the superhero narrative and its conventions. In his essay "'Just Men in Tights': Rewriting Silver Age Comics in an Era of Multiplicity," Henry Jenkins travels a fascinating journey through the history of the superhero genre. Exploring the genre's longstanding relationship with the comic book medium and focusing more specifically on the so-called Silver Age of comics and extending into the current era, Jenkins asks, "What if we stopped worrying and learned to love the dominance of superheroes over the American comics tradition? What would we learn?" What we learn is that the genre has always stretched, ruptured, and often exploded its boundaries in order to reshape its identity to meet the demands of similarly shifting and transforming audiences and cultures. Globalization, the conglomeration of entertainment industries, and the increased reliance of cross-media creations since the early 1980s have further resulted in "transcreations" that not only allow for the migration of one superhero universe into another, or one medium into the next, but also embrace the merger of a variety of generic and medium conventions from multiple national and genre traditions. Through this rampant revisionism and convergence, argues Jenkins, "the superhero genre continually re-invents itself, returning to its past for inspiration but retooling well-established characters, events, themes, and stylistic elements to create novelty and difference." In "The Time of Heroes: Narrative, Progress and Eternity in *Miracleman,*" Paul Atkinson redirects the generic focus to look at the temporal articulations of narrative patterns in the genre. He analyzes the tension that exists between the mythic dimensions of the superhero's past and the modes of narration and articulations of time found in the comic book *Miracleman*, which has his origins in 1954 and underwent a revision in the early 1980s. Implicit in this analysis is the claim that there are a number of interwoven temporal modes in comic book narration. Developing Umberto Eco's analysis of the superhero narrative and its dual relationship to myth and serial form, he argues that Alan Moore consciously deconstructs and manipulates the structural continuity of the story, the intention being to explore the conventions of the superhero genre.

Superhero worlds are the cumulative and ever-expanding outcome of thousands of comics, which are created by hundreds of artists and writers over a period of many decades. In "'Worlds Within Worlds': The Role of Superheroes in the Marvel and DC Universes," Jason Bainbridge examines the function of the superhero, especially as mapped out in the popular Marvel and DC universes. Focusing on the recent Justice League of America/Avengers crossover, which features the first meeting of the two superhero teams from DC and Marvel, Bainbridge suggests that whereas Marvel maintains a connection to the real world, with 'real' locations such as New York, DC favors mythologized cityscapes like Metropolis and Gotham and heroic archetypes like Superman and Batman. Analyzing each universe's response to the real-world events of September 11 2001, the DC and Marvel universes reveal different responses to what it means to be a superhero. Saige Walton also turns to the articulation of the superhero in her essay "Baroque Mutants in the 21st Century?

Re-thinking Genre through the Superhero." Rather than discussing the superhero in terms of a distinct, self-contained genre or as a collection of hybridized generic elements, Walton uses the metaphor of the superhero to understand the inherently baroque play of genre itself. The body of Spider Man as superhero becomes the means by which to explore the cyclical and processlike nature of generic development as the comic book superhero genre slips beyond the parameters of its own medium and into the alternate media territory that is the high concept special-effects film.

The issue of identity is integral to understanding the superhero's *modus operandi*, and the second part of this anthology presents diverging perspectives related to this issue. In "Secret Identity Politics," Scott Bukatman searches for a space and language within the "experience of the real" that can effectively articulate the pleasures that are associated with the more fantastic dimensions of the superhero. In this "search for a rhetoric," Bukatman travels an evocative journey into the visual, kinetic, and performative logic that is integral to both superhero and star performer of the Hollywood musical; and along the way, he unveils the inseparable link that exists between the identity of the author (comic book and academic) and that of the superhero. Turning to the self-reflexive comics *X-Force/X-Statix*, *Capes*, *Powers* and *Astro City*, in "The Superhero as Labor: The Secret Corporate Identity" Greg M. Smith argues that the superhero's attraction to the reader comes from possessing an identity that's a "fantasy of being extraordinary on the inside while continuing to seem ordinary on the outside." Examining the classic dichotomy of the superhero and secret identity, he suggests that many of the secret identities reveal associations with large corporations and, specifically, the "classic corporate secret identity" adopted by superheroes like Superman serve to expose the "monstrous nature of the Organization Man's task." More recently, Smith suggests, comics have brought this corporate theme to the forefront, abandoning the secret identity by focusing instead within the fictional space, on 'selling' the image of the superhero as star icon or marketable franchise; as a result, these comic books highlight what classic superhero comics concealed: "that individual action can never be totally divorced from the corporate self, even in fantasy." In her essay "When Fangirls Perform: The Gendered Fan Identity in Superhero Comics Fandom," Karen Healey turns to what has been perceived as the invisible presence of the female superhero fan, her intention being to erase that invisibility. Analyzing the presentational and language structure of fan sites and blogs online, Healey comes to some fascinating conclusions about the performative aspects of gender that characterize superhero comic book fandom and academic writing about that fandom. Clare Pitkethly continues with the issue of gender and superhero comics in her essay "Recruiting an Amazon: The Collision of Old World Ideology and New World Identity in Wonder Woman." Focusing on Wonder Woman, she outlines how the figure of the Amazon has been appropriated and redefined over time, transforming from an oppositional figure to that of ally to the dominant patriarchal culture. Whereas in the *Iliad*, the Amazon was introduced as an opposing force, to be defeated, and was identified as "the equal of man"; as an ally, Wonder Woman, the Amazon Princess, has become an even more powerful force. Pitkethly argues that she is not just the equal of man, but the equal of Superman, as she fights the battle for justice alongside the world's greatest superheroes in the Justice League of America. In the final essay in the section on identity, Jennifer Dowling's essay " 'Oy Gevalt!': A Peek at the Development of Jewish Superheroines" is concerned with evaluating the evolution of the Jewish superheroes Kitty Pryde (from the *X-Men*), Sabra (from the *Hulk* and *New Warriors* series), Masada (of *Team Young Blood*), and Rebecca Golden, a.k.a. Fathom (of the 'undead' superhero team, the *Elementals*). Dowling traces how the introduction of these new superhero icons heralded further representations of ethnic minorities within the pages of comics; even though all four superwomen were primarily caricatures that resorted to stereotype and clichés. Despite the clichés, these four characters have much to tell us about social anxieties and identity construction, in particular, American anxieties about Jews and Israelis, and Jewish anxieties about world politics and anti-Semitism.

The final part of the anthology more directly explores the reflexive dimensions of contemporary superhero representations: revisions, retellings, and auteurs that sometimes threaten to destabilize the world of superhero mythology. In "Entering the Green: Imaginal Space in *Black Orchid*," Sallye Sheppeard provides an analysis of Neil Gaiman and Dave McKean's *Black Orchid,* which she sees as generating an imaginal space where myth is in process of construction and transition. Its title character originates as human but becomes plant and, as hybrid character, Black Orchid occupies a liminal space that questions, analyzes, revises, and even rejects the traditional tropes of what it means to be superhero. Her search for identity also becomes a search for the identity of the superhero genre in the late twentieth century. In "The Mild-Mannered Reporter: How Clark Kent Surpassed Superman," Vanessa Russell shifts the focus by turning to the comics journalism of Art Spiegelman in *Maus I: A Survivor's Tale* (1986) and Joe Sacco in *Palestine* (1993), which explore the effects of the Holocaust and the impact of the Israeli occupation on Palestinians, respectively. These comics flip the Superman/Clark Kent duality by granting journalists a role in the limelight, in the process undermining the stranglehold that superheroes have had over the comic book format. As Russell explains, the "surpassing of Superman by Clark Kent has enabled both Spiegelman and Sacco to use their comic books to record the extraordinary and ordinary effects of life under war." Steven Zani shifts the direction by tackling Grant Morrison's *Animal Man* comic book series. His essay "It's a Jungle in Here: Animal Man, Continuity Issues and the Authorial Death Drive" focuses on Morrison as one of a number of authors who participated in the revisionist trend of the post-mid-1980s superhero comic book genre. Morrison's Animal Man not only became a vehicle through which to address contemporary political concerns (notably issues of animal rights and ethics), but it became a metatextual platform for discussions of identity construction. Zani concludes that "Morrison's final arguments are that enduring heroism is achieved by constant evaluation of one's self and one's motives, and by constant attention to the process involved in creating, literally writing and drawing, one's own identity." Remaining focused on the subject of Grant Morrison, in "Morrison's Muscle Mystery Versus Everyday Reality . . . and Other Parallel Worlds!" Martyn Pedler is concerned with exploring the surreal site of the superhero body as depicted in examples like *Flex Mentallo*. Morrison's muscular heroes become the means through which to evaluate the "long-standing tradition" that only a superhero fight scene is capable of resolving conflict and ensuring narrative agency. In the hands of Morrison, argues Pedler, superheroes are confronted with postmodern angst and new villains that take the shape of metafictional worlds. Fiction supplants reality and reality frequently enters the world of fiction; time buckles in on itself or multiplies to produce parallel dimensions; and superheroes struggle with ways to put their muscle to righteous use in order to bring order to the universe—and their identities—again. Finally, the anthology comes to a conclusion with "Enter the Aleph: Superhero Worlds and Hypertime Realities." Here, I turn to the television series *Smallville* and argue that it adapts the hypertimeline rationale introduced by Grant Morrison and Mark Waid in their comic books *Animal Man* and *The Kingdom*, using this structure to self-reflexively engage with the Superman mythos. *Smallville* confronts its audience not only with the history of Superman as a cross-media phenomenon, but also challenges *Smallville*'s audience to understand how and why it intersects with the spatiotemporal realities of many other media stories and characters.

NOTES

1. Joe Gillis in *Sunset Boulevard*
2. A sentiment that's reflected in the amazing increase in popularity and attendance of Comic-Con International, which began, in 1970 with 154 attendees and rose in 2007 to over 125,000 participants. See: "Comic-Con International": http://en.wikipedia.org/wiki/Comic_con.
3. For more on superheroes, their moral function, and their origins, see Coogan 2006.

COMIC BOOKS

Ennis, Garth, and Steve Dillon. 1995–2000. *Preacher*. New York: Vertigo.
Ennis, Garth, and Steve Dillon. 2001. *Punisher*, Vol. 4, #2, August. New York: Marvel.

Ennis, Garth, and Darick Robertson. 2002. *Punisher,* Vol. 4, #17, November. New York: Marvel.
Ennis, Garth, and Darick Robertson. 2002. *Punisher,* Vol. 4, #16, November. New York: Marvel.

BIBLIOGRAPHY

Bukatman, Scott. 2003. *Matters of Gravity: Special Effects and Supermen in the 20th Century.* Durham, NC, and London: Duke University Press.
Cohen, Michael. 2007. Dick Tracy: In Pursuit of a Comic Book Aesthetic. In *Film and Comic Books.* Eds. Ian Gordon, Mark Janchovich, and Matthew P. McAllister. Jackson: University Press of Mississippi.
Coogan, Peter. 2006. *Superhero: The Secret Origin of a Genre.* Austin: Monkey Brain Books.
Haslem, Wendy, Angela Ndalianis, and Chris Mackie, eds. 2006. *Super/Heroes: From Hercules to Superman.* Washington, DC: New Academia Publishing.
Klock, Geoff. 2002. *How to Read Superhero Comics and Why.* New York: Continuum.
Kuznick, Peter J. 1994. "Losing the World of Tomorrow: The Battle Over the Presentation of Science at the 1939 New York World's Fair." *American Quarterly,* 46(3), 341–73.
Lawrence, John Shelton, and Robert Jewett. 2002. *The Myth of the American Superhero.* Grand Rapids, MI: William B. Eerdmans Publishing Company.
Morshed, Adnan, 2004. "The Aesthetics of Ascension in Norman Bel Geddes's Futurama" *Journal of the Society of Architectural Historians,* 63, 74–99.
Reynolds, Richard. 1992. *Superheroes: A Modern Mythology.* Jackson: University Press of Mississippi.
Rydell, Robert. 1993. *World of Fairs: The Century-of-Progress Expositions.* Chicago: University of Chicago Press.

2 'Just Men in Tights'

Rewriting Silver Age Comics in an Era of Multiplicity

Henry Jenkins

> *A creation is actually a re-creation, a rearrangement of existing materials in a new, different, original, novel way.*
>
> Steve Ditko (Schumer 2003, 59)

In late 2004, Warren Ellis (*Transmetropolitan, Global Frequency, Planetary*) launched an intriguing project—a series of one-shot comics, each representing the first issue of imaginary comics series. Each was set in a different genre—*Stomp Future* (science fiction), *Simon Spector* (supernatural), *Quit City* (aviator), *Frank Ironwine* (detective). In the back of each book, Ellis explains: "Years ago I sat down and thought about what adventure comics might've looked like today if superhero comics hadn't have happened. If, in fact, the pulp tradition of Weird Thrillers had jumped straight into comics form without mutating into the superhero subgenre we know today. If you took away preconceptions about design and the dominant single form . . . If you blanked out the last sixty years" (Ellis 2005).

Ellis's fantasy, of a world without superhero comics, is scarcely unique. Several decades earlier, Alan Moore's *Watchmen* (1986–87) constructed a much more elaborate alternative history of comic genres (Moore 1987). In a world where superheroes are real, comic fans would seek out alternative genres for escapist entertainment. Moore details the authors, the storylines, the rise and fall of specific publishers, as he explains how the pirates' genre came to dominate comics production. Passages from the imagined DC comic series, *Tales of the Black Freighter*, run throughout *Watchmen*, drawn in a style which closely mimics E.C. comics of the early 1950s. Would a filmmaker conjure up an imagined history of Hollywood in which the western or the musical never appeared? Would a television creator imagine a world without the sitcom? Why would they need to? In both cases, these genres played very important roles in the development of American popular entertainment, but they never totally dominated their medium to the degree that superheroes have overwhelmed American comic book production. In fact, as Gerard Jones and Will Jacobs note in *The Comic Book Heroes*, there was no point from the 1940s to the 1970s, when superheroes represented more than 20 percent of the total product of the American comics industry (Jacobs and Jones 1996), but they have dominated sales charts in recent decades and are now so central to our understanding of the medium that we read their dominance retrospectively across comics history.

In *Understanding Comics*, Scott McCloud demonstrates what we would take for granted in any other entertainment sector—that a medium is more than a genre: "When I was little I knew EXACTLY what comics were. Comics were those bright, colorful magazines filled with bad art, stupid stories, and guys in tights . . . If people failed to understand comics, it was because they defined what comics could be too narrowly . . . The world of comics is a huge and varied one. Our definition must encompass all these types" (McCloud 2004, 2–4). I fully support McCloud's efforts to broaden and diversify the content of contemporary comics. I fear that what I am about to say might well set back that cause a bit. But what interests me in this essay is the degree to which comics do indeed represent a medium which has been dominated by a single genre. After all, nobody really believes us anyway when we say that comics are "more than just men in tights," so what if we accepted this as a starting premise—"you got me!"—and examined the implications of the superhero's dominance over American comics?

Understanding how the superhero genre operates requires us to turn genre theory on its head. Genre emerges from the interaction between standardization and differentiation as competing forces shaping the production, distribution, marketing, and consumption of popular entertainment. A classic genre critic discussing most other media provides a more precise description of the borders and boundaries between categories that are already intuitively understood by media producers, critics, and consumers (Schatz 1981; Solomon 1976). Genre criticism takes for granted that most works fall within one and only one genre with genre mixing the exception rather than the norm. The genre theorist works to locate 'classic' examples of the genre—primarily works which fall at the very center of the space being defined—and uses them to map recurring traits or identify a narrative formula.

Comics are not immune to industrial pressures towards standardization and differentiation, yet these forces operate differently in a context where a single genre dominates a medium and all other production has to define itself against, outside of, in opposition to, or alongside that prevailing genre. Here, difference is felt much more powerfully *within* a genre than *between* competing genres and genre mixing is the norm. The superhero genre seems capable of absorbing and reworking all other genres. So, *The Pulse* (2003–) is about reporters trying to cover the world of the Marvel superheroes; *1602* (2003) is a historical fiction depicting earlier versions of the superheroes; *Spiderman Loves Mary Jane* (2004–) is a romance comic focused on a superhero's girlfriend; *Common Grounds* (2003–2004) is a sitcom set in a coffeehouse where everyone knows your name—if not your secret identity; *Ex Machina* (2004–) deals with the mayor of New York who happens to be a superhero, and so forth. In each case, the superhero genre absorbs, reworks, accommodates elements of other genres, or perhaps we might frame this the other way around—writers interested in telling stories set in these other genres must operate within the almighty superhero genre in order to gain access to the marketplace. And alternative comics are defined not simply as alternative to the commercial mainstream but also as alternative to the superhero genre. As Brian Michael Bendis explains, "In comics, if it don't have a cape or claws or, like, really giant, perfect spherical, chronic back-pain-inducing breasts involved, it's alternative" (Bendis 2000). Yet, to be alternative to the superhero genre is still to be defined by—or at least in relation to—that genre. This chapter will first consider what genre theory can tell us about the persistence and elasticity of the superhero genre, about the genre's historic evolution and current manifestations. It will conclude with a closer consideration of three recent superhero miniseries—*JLA: Year One* (1998), *DC: The New Frontier* (2004–2005), and *Fantastic Four: Unstable Molecules* (2003)—which illustrate some of the strategies by which authors seek to negotiate between the standardization implicit in comics continuity and the diversification desired by contemporary readers. Consider this essay as a set of provisional notes towards a larger project which will deal with the permutations and transformations of the superhero genre in American comics.

FROM CONTINUITY TO MULTIPLICITY

Writing about *Chinatown* in 1979, John Cawelti described a crisis within the Hollywood genre system. Classic genres were being deconstructed and reconstructed, critiqued and parodied, mixed and matched, in films as diverse as *Chinatown* (1974), *Blazing Saddles* (1974), *McCabe and Mrs. Miller* (1971). and *The Godfather* (1972). These films, Cawelti argues, "do in different ways what Polanski does in *Chinatown*: set the elements of a conventional popular genre in an altered context, thereby making us perceive these traditional forms and images in a new way" (Cawelti 1986, 191). What happened to film genres in the 1970s closely parallels what happened to superhero comics starting in the early 1980s. Geoff Klock's *How to Read Superhero Comics and Why,* for example, identifies what he calls the "Revisionary Superhero Narrative" as a "third moment" (after the Golden and Silver Ages) that runs from *Dark Knight Returns* and *Watchmen* (both 1986) through more recent works such as *Marvels* (1994), *Astro City* (1995), *Kingdom Come* (1996), and *League of Extraordinary Gentlemen* (1999), among a range of other examples (Klock 2002). Starting with Miller and Moore, he argues, comic books reexamined their core myths, questioning the virtue and value of their protagonists, blurring the lines between good guys and bad guys, revisiting and recontextualizing past events, and forcing the reader to confront the implications of their longstanding constructions of violence and sexuality. Cawelti's description of what *Chinatown* brought to the detective genre might easily be describing what *Dark Knight Returns* brought to superhero comics: "*Chinatown* places the hard-boiled detective story within a view of the world that is deeper and more catastrophic, more enigmatic in its evil, more sudden and inexplicable in its outbreaks of violent chance" (Cawelti 1986, 189).

Underlying Klock's argument is something like the theory of genre evolution which Cawelti outlines: "One can almost make out a life cycle characteristic of genres as they move from an initial period of articulation and discovery, through a phase of conscious self-awareness on the part of both creators and audiences, to a time when the generic patterns have become so well-known that people become tired of their predictability. It is at this point that parodic and satiric treatments proliferate and new genres gradually arise" (Cawelti 1986, 200). We might see the Golden Age as a period of "articulation and discovery," the Silver Age as one of classicism when formulas were understood by producers and consumers, and Klock's "third age" as one where generic exhaustion gives way to a baroque self-consciousness. Yet, subsequent genre critics have argued for a much less linear understanding of how diversity works within genres. For example, Tag Gallagher notes that the earliest phases of a genre's development are often charged with a high degree of self-consciousness as media makers and consumers work through how any given genre diverges from other and more established traditions (Gallagher 1986). Cawelti himself acknowledges that the forces of nostalgia hold in check any tendency to radically deconstruct existing formulas.

Rather than thinking about a genre's predetermined life cycle, we might describe a perpetual push and pull exerted on any genre; genre formulas are continually repositioned in relation to social, cultural, and economic contexts of production and reception. Genres are altogether more elastic than our textbook definitions suggest; they maintain remarkable abilities to absorb outside influences as well as to withstand pressures towards change, and the best authors working in a genre at any point in time are highly aware of their materials and the traditions from which they came. That said, there are shifting institutional pressures placed on genres which promote or retard experimentation. David Bordwell has described those pressures as the "bounds of difference," noting that even moments in production history which encourage a high degree of standardization (understood in terms of adherence to formulas and quality standards) also are shaped by countervailing pressures towards novelty, experimentation, and differentiation (Bordwell 1985, 110). Bordwell notes, for example, that the Hollywood system always allowed what he calls "innovative workers" greater latitude for experimentation as long as their films enjoyed either profitability or critical acclaim and preferably both. The so-called revisionist superhero narratives similarly reflected a growing consumer awareness of authorship within the medium—in effect offering Bordwell's "innovative workers" greater room to experiment with the existing characters and placing new value on critical response to its product. Historically, comics publishers imposed limits on that experimentation in order to preserve the distinctive identities of their most valuable characters in a system in which multiple writers work on the same franchise and there was constant and rapid turnover of employment. Here, the mainstream publishers loosened those constraints for at least some creative workers. Rather than looking for a period of revisionism, we might better be looking for how far creators can diverge from genre formulas at different historical junctures.

Painting with broad strokes, we might identify three phases, each with their own opportunities for innovation:

1. As the comic book franchises take shape, across the Golden and Silver Ages, their production is dominated by relatively self-contained issues; readers turn over on a regular basis as they grow older. Franchises are organized around recurring characters, whose stories, as Umberto Eco has noted in regard to Superman, get defined in terms of an iterative logic in which each issue must end more or less where it began (Eco 2004). Under this system, creators may originate new characters or totally recast existing characters (as occurred at the start of the Silver Age), but they have much less flexibility once a comic franchise starts.

2. Somewhere in the early 1970s, this focus on self-contained stories shifts towards more and more serialization as the distribution of comics becomes more reliable. Readers have, by this point, grown somewhat older and continue to read comics over a longer span of their lives; these readers place a high value on consistency and continuity, appraising both themselves and the authors on their mastery of past events and the web of character relationships within any given franchise. Indeed, this principle of continuity operates not just within any individual book but also across all of the books by a particular publisher so that people talk about the DC and Marvel universes. The culmination of the continuity era might well have been Marv Wolfstein's *Crisis of Infinite Earths* (1985), a 12-issue "event" designed to mobilize all of the characters in the DC Universe and then cleanse away competing and contradictory continuities which had built up through the years. Instead, as Geoff Klock notes, the "Crisis" led to more and more "events" which further splintered and fragmented the DC Universe but also accustomed comic readers to the idea that they could hold multiple versions of the same universe in their minds at the same time (Klock 2002, 21).

3. Today, comics have entered a period where principles of multiplicity are felt at least as powerfully as those of continuity. Under this new system, readers may consume multiple versions of the same franchise, each with different conceptions of the character, different understandings of their relationships with the secondary figures, different

moral perspectives, exploring different moments in their lives, and
so forth. So that in some storylines, Aunt May knows Spiderman's
secret identity while in others she doesn't; in some, Peter Parker is
still a teen and in others he is an adult science teacher; in some, he
is married to Mary Jane and in others they have broken up, and so
forth. These different versions may be organized around their respec-
tive authors or demarked through other designation—Marvel's Ultimate or DC's All Star lines, which represented attempts to reboot the
continuity to allow points of entry for new readers, for example. In
some cases, even more radical alterations of the core franchises are
permissible on a short-term and provisional basis—say, the destruction of Gotham City (*No Man's Land*, 2000). Beyond the two major
companies, smaller comics companies—Image, Dark Horse, Top
Cow, ABC, etc.—further expand upon the superhero mythos, often
creating books which are designed to directly comment on the DC
and Marvel universes by using characters modeled on comic book
icons (*Battle Hymn*, 2006; *Supreme Power*, 2005–). And beyond
these direct reworkings of the DC and Marvel superheroes, there are
any number of appropriations of the superhero by alternative comics
creators (such as the use of a Superman figure in Chris Ware's *Jimmy
Corrigan, The World's Smartest Kid*, 2000).

In each case, the new system for organizing production layers over earlier
practices so that we do not lose interest in having compelling stories within
individual issues as we move into the continuity era, nor do comics readers and producers lose interest in continuity as we enter into a period of
multiplicity. Even at the present moment, DC remains more conservative
in its efforts to produce a coherent and singular continuity across all of
the books it publishes, and Marvel is more open to multiple versions of the
same character functioning simultaneously within different publications.

Writing in 1991, Roberta Pearson and William Uricchio use the Batman
as an example of the kinds of pressures being exerted on the superhero
genre at a moment when older texts were continuing to circulate (and, in
fact, were recirculated in response to renewed interests in the characters),
newer versions operated according to very different ideological and narrat-
alogical principles, a range of auteur creators were being allowed to experiment with the character, and the character was assuming new shapes and
forms to reflect the demands of different entertainment sectors and their
consumers. They write:

Whereas broad shifts in emphasis had occurred since 1939, these changes
had been, for the most part, consecutive and consensual. Now, newly
created Batmen, existing simultaneously with the older Batmen of the
television series and comic reprints and back issues, all struggled for
recognition and a share of the market. But the contradictions amongst

them may threaten both the integrity of the commodity form and the coherence of the fans' lived experience of the character necessary to the Batman's continued success (Pearson and Uricchio 1991, 184).

The superhero comic, they suggest, may not be able to withstand "the tension between, on the one hand, the essential maintenance of a recognizable set of key character components and, on the other hand, the increasingly necessary centrifugal dispersion of those components" (Pearson and Uricchio 1991, 190). Retrospectively, we can see Pearson and Uricchio as describing a moment of transition from continuity to multiplicity.

DO SUPERHEROES GET EXHAUSTED?

In his *Chinatown* essay, Cawelti identifies three core factors leading to the genre experimentation in 1970s cinema: "I would point to the tendency of genres to exhaust themselves, to our growing historical awareness of modern popular culture, and finally to the decline of the underlying mythology on which traditional genres have been based since the late nineteenth century" (Cawelti 1986, 200). Each of these pressures can be seen as working on the superhero genre during the period that Uricchio and Pearson were describing. Individually and collectively, these forces led to the current era of multiplicity. For example, comics writer Ed Brubaker falls back on a theory of "generic exhaustion" to explain *Gotham Central* (2003–), his series depicting the everyday beat cops who operate literally and figuratively under the shadow of the Dark Knight. Brubaker argues that by shifting the focus off the superhero and onto these everyday men and women, he can up the emotional stakes: "Batman is never going to get killed by these guys, and he's not going to allow them to kill the ballroom of people they're holding hostage. Because Batman, by the rulebook you're given when you're writing it, has to be infallible. He can't get frozen solid and broken into pieces and have Robin become the next Batman. But you can have a Gotham city cop frozen and broken into pieces in front of his partner, and suddenly Mr. Freeze is scary again" (Spurgeon 2002, 91).

Kurt Busiek, on the other hand, has stressed the elasticity of the superhero genre, arguing that superheroes can take on new values and associations as old meanings cease to hold the interest of their readers:

> If a superhero can be such a powerful and effective metaphor for male adolescence, then what else can you do with them? Could you build a superhero story around a metaphor for female adolescence? Around midlife crisis? Around the changes adults go through when they become parents? Sure, why not? And if a superhero can exemplify America's self image at the dawn of World War II, could a superhero exemplify America's self image during the less-confident 1970s? How about the

emerging national identity of a newly independent African nation? Or a nontraditional culture, like the drug culture, or the 'greed is good' business culture of the go-go Eighties. Of course. If it can do one, it can do the others. (Busiek 1999, 7–8)

We can see this process of renewing the core meanings attached to the superhero figure in such recent books as the Luna Brother's *Ultra* (2004–2005), which depicts superheroes as celebrities whose relationships become the material of tabloid gossip magazines (with its central plotline clearly modeled after the Ben Affleck/Jennifer Lopez romance), or *Dr Blink, Superhero Shrink* (2003–), where superheroes are neurotics who need help working through their relationship issues and suicidal tendencies (including a suicidal superhero doomed to disappointment since he is invincible and flies whenever he tries to throw himself off tall buildings). In both cases, we see the genre's building blocks being attached to a new set of metaphors.

Second, Cawelti argues that Hollywood's generic transformations were sparked by a heightened audience awareness of the history of American cinema through university film classes, retro-house screenings, television reruns, and serious film criticism. More educated consumers began to demand an acknowledgment of genre history within the newer movies they consumed. Similarly, Matthew J. Pustz contends that the fan's interest in comic continuity reflected a moment when older comics became more readily accessible through back issues and reissues (Pustz 1999). A focus on continuity rewarded fans for their interest in the full run of a favorite franchise, though it might also act as a barrier to entry for new readers who often found continuity-heavy books difficult to follow. The contemporary focus on multiplicity may similarly reward the mastery of longtime fans but around a different axis of consumption.

More and more, fans and authors play with genre mixing as a way of complicating and expanding the genre's potential meanings. Writing about television genres, Jason Mittell has challenged the claims made by postmodernist critics that such genre mixing or hybridity leads to the dissolution of genre; instead, he suggests that these moments where two or more genres are combined heighten our awareness of genre conventions: "the practice of generic mixture has the potential to foreground and activate generic categories in vital ways that 'pure' generic texts rarely do" (Mittell 2004, 155). Mittell's prime example is the merging of horror and teen romance genres within *Buffy the Vampire Slayer*, but he could just as easily be talking about DC's Elseworlds series, which exists to transform the superhero genre through contact with a range of other genre traditions. For example, *The Kents* (2000) is almost a pure western linked to the Superman franchise through a frame story where Pa Kent sends a box of family heirlooms to Clark so that he will understand the history of his adopted family (Ostrander, Truman, and Mandrake 2000). *Red Son*

(2004) deals with what might happen if the rocket from Krypton had landed in Russia rather than the United States and thus works through how Superman would have impacted several decades in Russian history (Millar 2004). *Superman's Metropolis* (1997) mixes and matches elements from Fritz Lang's German expressionist classic with the Superman origin story (L'Officier, McKeever, and Thomas 1997). As the series is described on the back of each issue, "In Elseworlds, heroes are taken from their usual settings and put into strange times and places—some that have existed, or might have existed and others that can't, couldn't, and shouldn't exist. The result is stories that make characters who are as familiar as yesterday seem as fresh as tomorrow." The Elseworlds books read the superheroes as archetypes who would assert themselves in many different historical and generic contexts; they invite a search for the core or essence of the character even as they encourage us to take pleasure in their many permutations. If we can tinker with his costume, his origins, his cultural context, even his core values, what is it that makes Superman Superman and not, say, Captain Marvel or Captain America? *Speeding Bullets* (1993) pushes this to its logical extreme: fusing the origins stories of Batman and Superman to create one figure—which is bent on using its superpowers to exert revenge for his parents' deaths (Dematteis 1993).

Third, Cawelti reads the genre transformations of the 1970s cinema in relation to a declining faith in the core values and assumptions which defined those genre traditions half a century earlier. Alan Moore made a similar argument for the cultural importance of the revisionist superhero comics: "As anyone involved in fiction and its crafting over the past fifteen or so years would be delighted to tell you, heroes are starting to become rather a problem. They aren't what they used to be . . . or rather they are, and therein lies the heart of the difficulty. We demand new themes, new insights, new dramatic situations. We demand new heroes" (Brown 1986, 1).

This search for "new heroes" is perhaps most spectacularly visible if we examine how the comics industry has responded to the growing multiculturalism of American society and the pressures of globalization on its markets. So, the *Marvel Mangaverse* (2000) series focused on how their established characters would have looked if they had emerged within the Japanese comics industry: the Hulk transforms into a giant lizard and Peter Parker trains as a ninja. Similarly, Marvel released a series of *Spider-Man: India* (2004) comics, timed to correspond with the release of *Spider-Man 2* (2004) in India and localized to South Asian tastes (Figure 2.1). Peter Parker becomes Pavitr Prabhakar and Green Goblin becomes Rakshasa, a traditional mythological demon. Marvel calls it "transcreation," one step beyond translation. Such books appeal as much to "pop cosmopolitans" in the United States (fans who are seeking cultural difference through their engagement with popular culture from other countries) as they do to the Asian market—indeed, *Spider-Man India* appeared in

Figure 2.1 Spider-Man: India, the 2004 retelling of Marvel's Spider-Man by Sharad Devarajan, Suresh Seetharaman and Jeevan J. Kang with Marvel Comics. © Gotham Entertainment Group/Marvel Entertainment.

the United States more or less simultaneously with its publication in South Asia (Jenkins 2006).

At the same time, the mainstream comics industry has begun to experiment with giving alternative comics artists a license to play around with their characters. For example, David Mack, a collage artist, has ended up not only doing covers for Brian Bendis's *Alias* (2001–2004) series but also doing his own run on *Daredevil* (2003). Peter Bagge, whose *Hate* (1990–1998) comics epitomized the grunge influence on alternative comics, was hired to do *The Monomaniacal Spiderman* (2002) in which Peter Parker reads Ayn Rand and gets fed up with the idea that he has any kind of "great responsibility" to look after less powerful people. DC comics, on the other hand, has published a series of *Bizarro* (2001, 2005) collections where alternative artists tell their own distinctive versions of the company's pantheon of superheroes with the framing device that these are what comics look like in the Bizarro world where everything is the exact opposite of Earth. In no other medium is the line between experimental and commercial work this permeable.

REVERSE-ENGINEERING SUPERMAN

The comics continuity, which is taken for granted by both comics critics and fans alike, turns out to be a relatively short-lived chapter in the history of the medium. From the start, the superhero genre emerged through mixing, matching, and mutating genre categories. Arguably, the current phase of multiplicity represents a self-conscious exploration of latent potentials which have been part of the superhero genre from the start, albeit in a context where fans are eager to embrace the diversification of familiar formulas rather than seeing such fragmentation as a threat to the coherence of the fictional universe. As Rick Altman notes, "Genre mixing, it now appears, is not just a postmodern fad. Quite to the contrary, the practice of genre mixing is necessary to the very process whereby genres are created" (Altman 1999, 143). Our current tendency to describe works retrospectively based on the contemporary genre they most closely resemble has the effect of repressing the more complex process by which new genres emerge from existing categories of production. Altman concludes, "The early history of film genres is characterized . . . not by purposeful borrowing from a single pre-existing non-film parent genre, but by apparently incidental borrowing from several unrelated genres . . . Even when a genre already exists in other media, the film genre of the same name cannot simply be borrowed from non-film sources, it must be recreated" (Altman 1999, 34). The superhero comic, in fact, undergoes this process of re-creation not once but multiple times: first, in the early Golden Age, when the superhero genre takes shape from elements borrowed heavily from pulp magazines, and second, in the early Silver Age, when superhero comics reemerge from the generic soup which characterized comic production in the postwar era.

The most common accounts for the emergence of the superhero genre stress the fledgling comics industry's response to the commercial success of Superman. In *The Amazing Adventures of Kavalier & Clay* (2001), Michael Chabon vividly depicts the process by which comics creators sought to reverse engineer Superman to generate new characters: "If he's like a cat or a spider or a fucking wolverine, if he's huge, if he's tiny, if he can shoot flames or ice or death rays of Vat 69, if he turns into fire or water or stone or India Rubber. He can be a Martian, he could be a ghost, he could be a god or a demon or a wizard or a monster. Okay? It doesn't matter because right now, see, at this very moment, we have a bandwagon rolling" (Chabon 2001, 94).

Yet, a somewhat different picture emerges within Gerard Jones's account of early superhero comics. Jones uncovered a handwritten note from Joe Simon and Joel Schuster, the teenage boys who created Superman, suggesting they were rehearsing possible publicity slogans: "The greatest super-hero strip of all time! . . . Speed-Action-Laughs-Thrills-Surprises. The most unusual humor-adventure strip ever created! . . . You'll Chuckle! You'll Gasp! It must be seen to be believed!" (Jones 2004, 115). Superman is already being read against a larger genre tradition ("the greatest super-hero strip of all time!") and at the same time, the comic is being promoted through a diverse range of emotional appeals ("Speed-action-laughs-thrills-surprises," etc.). Siegel and Schuster correctly describe their creation ('the most unusual humor-adventure strip ever created!') as, in effect, bounding over the walls separating various genres. Thomas Andrea has, for example, noted that the superhero figure emerged from a range of different science-fiction and horror texts (Andrae 1987, 124–38). Gerard Jones cites even more influences—including Popeye in the comic strips, the pulp novels of Edgar Rice Burroughs, and *The Scarlet Pimpernel* (Jones 2004, 115–16). We might note the ways that masked heroes from the pulp magazines, including the Shadow, the Phantom, the Spider, and Zorro, modeled the capes and masks iconography and the secret identity thematic of the subsequent superhero comics. The pulp magazines have been described as developing and categorizing many twentieth-century genres, yet the economics of pulp magazine production also meant that the same writers worked within multiple genre traditions and in the many cases, the same story was revised slightly in order to be sold to several different publications (Carter 1977). In early comics, a writer—say, Jack Kirby—might produce work across the full range of pulp genres in the course of his or her career and thus would be able to draw on multiple genre models in their superhero work. The intensity of comics production—new stories about the same characters every month and, in some cases, every week—encouraged writers to search far and wide for new plots or compelling new elements while the openness of comics, where you draw whatever you need, made it cheap and simple to expand the genre repertoire.

The titles of the publications which gave birth to the earliest superheroes have become dead metaphors for later generations of readers who have taken for granted that *Detective Comics* (1937) is where Batman stories are found, *Action Comics* (1938) plays host to Superman, and *Marvel Mystery* (1939–1949) is where the Human Torch first emerged. Yet, each of those titles defines a somewhat different genre tradition. As a result, Superman, Batman, and the Human Torch, while all read as superheroes today, were originally understood in somewhat different contexts.

The Silver Age remapped the relations between the superhero genre and other closely related traditions. The superheroes had been so overused for patriotic purposes during the Second World War that they seemed dated by the postwar era. At the same time, GIs had found comics a lightweight and portable means of popular entertainment and were continuing to read them as they returned home, creating a strong pull towards adult content (Wright 2001). By the late 1940s and early 1950s, superhero books competed with horror, romance, science fiction, western, true crime, jungle adventures, swordplay, and so forth. This push towards more mature content provoked backlash and moral panic (best embodied by Frederick Wertham's *Seduction of the Innocents*) as reformers struggled to make sense of the presence of adult themes in a medium previously targeted to children. The Comics Code cleared away many of those emerging genres, paving the way for a reemergence of the superhero by the end of the 1950s at DC and in the early 1960s at Marvel. Or so the story is most often told.

Yet, again, this story simplifies the ways that the superhero comics of the Silver Age emerged from a more diverse set of genre traditions. As Gerard Jones and Will Jacobs note, for example, the 1950s saw the rise of a range of books like *Challengers of the Unknown* (1958–1971), *Mystery in Space* (1951–1966), *The Sea Devils* (1961–1967), and *Black Haw* (1957–1968); their teams of scientists, soldiers, and adventurers were prototypes for the later superhero teams such as the Justice League, the Avengers, the Defenders, or the Fantastic Four (Jacobs and Jones 1996, 19–32). It is no accident, given DC editor Julius Schwartz's history as a science-fiction fan and as an agent for important writers in that genre, that the first significant superhero to emerge in almost ten years was the Martian Manhunter (Schwartz 2000). When Schwartz began to retool and relaunch such established DC characters as the Flash, Green Lantern, Hawkman, and the Atom, he first tested the popularity of these characters through anthologies which cut across multiple genres: the Flash first appeared in *Showcase* (1956–1970), while the Justice League emerges in *The Brave and the Bold* (1955–1983).

Similarly, Marvel had a distribution contract with DC which limited how many books could be issued each month and somewhat restricted their use of superhero content (Raphael and Spurgeon 2003). The earliest issues of the successful Marvel franchises situate these protagonists in relationship to other genre traditions with the heroes dwarfed on the original *Fantastic Four* (1961–) cover by a giant green monster, with the *Incredible Hulk* (1961–1962) depicted as a "super-Frankenstein" character (Schumer 2003, 82), with *Iron Man* built around the iconography of robots and cyborgs, and Spiderman first appearing in the pages of *Amazing Fantasy* (1962). While these characters today are viewed as archetypical superheroes, they had previously been read–at least in part–in relation to these other genres.

These various franchises carry traces of those other genres even as they are reread within a now more firmly established superhero tradition. Jonathan Letham, for example, writes: "Kirby always wanted to drag the Four into the Negative Zone—deeper into psychedelic science fiction and existential alienation—while Lee, in his scripting, resolutely pulled them back into the morass of human lives, hormonal alienation, teenage dating problems and pregnancy and unfulfilled longings to be human and normal and loved and not to have the Baxter Building repossessed by the City of New York" (Letham 2004). By the same token, as Jason Bainbridge has noted, the two companies which dominated superhero production, then and now, have chosen to pull towards different genre conventions, with DC embracing action-adventure stories with their focus on plot and Marvel embracing melodrama with its focus on character (Bainbridge 2005). What I am describing here as the era of multiplicity exaggerates and extends the generic instability which has been part of the superhero comic from the start. Calling such works revisionist makes no sense because there is not a moment in the history of the genre when the superhero is not under active revision.

HISTORICAL FICTION, FICTIONAL HISTORY

There are so many different forms of generic restructuring going on in contemporary comics that it would be impossible to discuss them all in this essay. I hope to flesh out this argument across an entire book in the not too distant future. For the moment, I will restrict myself to one important way that contemporary superhero comics are playing with genre history in the context of this new era of multiplicity. If one factor contributing to the multiplicity of superhero comics is a growing consciousness of genre history, then it is hardly a surprise that this historical reflection occurs often within the pages of the superhero comics themselves. An important subgenre of superhero comics might be described as a curious hybrid of historical fiction (seeking to understand the past through the lens of superhero adventures) and fictional history (seeking to understand the development of the superhero genre by situating it against the backdrop of the times which shaped it). For example, Alan Moore's *League of Extraordinary Gentlemen* constructs an imaginary genealogy of the superhero team, seeing nineteenth-century literary figures (The Invisible Man, Dr. Jekyll, Quatermain,

Mina Harker, Captain Nemo) as prefiguring the twentieth-century Justice League. Matt Wagner's *Sandman Mystery Theater* (1995–1999) revives an obscure Golden Age protagonist to examine historic constructions of race, gender, and class, resulting in what Neil Gaiman describes as "a strange and savvy meeting between the fictive dreams of the 1930s and the 1990s" (Wagner 2004). Michael Chabon's *Cavalier & Klay* has inspired a series focused on the Escapist (2004–), which not only pastiches comics at a variety of different historic junctures but also has a running commentary situating the stories in an imaginary history of the franchise. As Jim Collins wrote about the Batman comics of the mid-1980s:

> Just as we can no longer imagine popular narratives to be so ignorant of their intertextual dimensions and cultural significance, we can no longer presuppose that the attitude towards their antecedents, their very 'retro' quality can be in any way univocal. Divergent strategies of rearticulation can be discerned not only between different 'retro' texts, but even more importantly, within individual texts that adopt shifting, ambivalent attitudes towards these antecedents. (Collins 1991, 167)

In what remains of this essay, I want to examine three recent attempts to reexamine the Silver Age (*JLA: Year One, DC: The New Frontier,* and *Unstable Molecules*), each representing a somewhat different balance between historical fiction and fictional history, each deploying the "retro" appeal of its caped protagonists to different effect, and each demanding different degrees of knowledge and knowingness on the part of its readers. Here, the current logic of almost unlimited multiplicity builds upon details and events which were well established in the continuity era. Certain events had to occur within these universes—say, the death of Bruce Wayne's father, the destruction of Krypton, or the formation of the Justice League—but we are invited to read those events from different perspectives. The plays with genre and history I am describing are only possible because the "actual" history of these events is well-known to longtime comics readers who want to return to these familiar spaces and have fresh experiences.

JLA: Year One

As Cawelti notes, the wave of revisionism and genre transformation which hit the American cinema in the 1970s was accompanied by enormous nostalgia for Hollywood's past: "In this mode, traditional generic features of plot, character, setting, and style are deployed to recreate the aura of a past time. The power of nostalgia lies especially in its capacity to evoke a sense of warm reassurance by bringing before the mind's eye images from a time when things seemed more secure and full of promise and possibility" (Cawelti 1986, 193). Deconstructionist approaches to genre provoke a sense of insecurity, which in turn makes us long for what is being critiqued.

Cawelti argued, "A contemporary nostalgia film cannot simply duplicate the past experience but must make us aware in some fashion of the relationship between past and present" (Cawelti 1986, 193). Often, this takes the form of exaggerating or transforming those traits which defined genre production in an earlier period.

In his introduction to *Astro City: Life in the Fast Lane* (1999), Kurt Busiek argued for a reconstruction of the superhero genre:

> It strikes me that the only real reason to take apart a pocket watch, or a car engine, aside from the simple delight of disassembly, is to find out how it works. To understand it, so that you can put it back together again better than before, or build a new one that goes beyond what the old model could do. We've been taking apart the superhero for ten years or more; it's time to put it back together and wind it up, time to take it out on the road and floor it, see what it'll do (Busiek 1999, 9).

One author who followed Busiek's call was Mark Waid. Across a series of books, Waid has sought to recapture the spirit of the Silver Age DC comics, tracing the friendship between the Flash and the Green Lantern in *The Brave and the Bold* (2001), mapping the trajectory of the Barry and Iris Allen romance in *The Life Story of the Flash by Iris Allen* (1998), and showing how the Justice League came together in *JLA: Year One*.

When I read Waid's books, I have the sense of returning home—of reencountering the comics I remembered from my boyhood. And that is perhaps the best way to put it since in fact the mode of storytelling here is very different from actual Silver Age comics, having more in common with the ways these characters were fleshed out in our backyard play or in our tree house speculations than anything one would find in the pages of an actual Silver Age comic. As Busiek explains, "The original JLA tales, for all that they are crisply drawn, deftly plotted, and full of inventive twists and turns, were creations of their time—and it was a time that emphasized plot over characterizations . . . Today's readers want their plot twists and bold heroes—but along with that, they also want to get to know their heroes, to see what makes them tick, what goes on beneath the heroic facades" (Busiek 1999). Rather than simply retelling a favorite plot, the book charts a twisty path "through, between, and around existing JLA history, preserving as much of the work of their predecessors as they could, while exploring that history and those character in a new way" (Busiek 1999).

Indeed, Year One books—starting with Frank Miller's influential *Batman: Year One* in the mid-1980s—have a paradoxical mission: on the one hand, they want to strip down encrusted continuity so that they can introduce the classic characters and plots to a new generation, but at the same time, these books are going to be avidly consumed and actively critiqued by the generation of comics readers who grew up with these figures. In many ways, the emotional impact of Year One stories depends on our knowledge of what is to follow (or more accurately, what has already happened in earlier books). To cite a few examples, *JLA: Year One* explores a potential romance between the Flash and the Black Canary, which long-time readers know is doomed, because Barry Allen needs to return to his faithful fiancée Iris and the Black Canary will soon fall under the devil-may-care spell of the Green Arrow. (After all, the Flash was one of the very first superheroes to get married, and we know it wasn't to a woman wearing black leather and fishnet stockings.) Or the book has the boyish Hal Jordon and Barry Allen, fresh from an early success, gush that they will both live to "ripe old ages" (Busiek 1999, 85) cuing the hardened fan to recall how they each died. The book rewards this kind of fan expertise by tossing in background characters without necessarily explaining how they fit within the DC Universe. Most readers will know who Lois Lane, Clark Kent, and Bruce Wayne are; fewer will know Vickie Vale and Oliver Queen, and even fewer, Ted Kord, Maxwell Lord, and Snapper Carr. The book overflows with "first times" including, perhaps, most powerfully the scene when the heroes reveal their secret identities to each other, which works because the readers are all already invested in those alter egos. Year One stories are never about creating first impressions, even though they are often fascinated with documenting the first encounters between various characters.

Waid does critique some of the ideological assumptions which shaped the earlier books, using a press conference, for example, to subject the hero team to some serious challenges about their nationalistic rhetoric and establishment politics. Yet, the criticisms remain mostly on the surface. Waid respects what these men and women stand for and wants those values to be passed along to another generation. Elsewhere, Waid has spoken of his affection for these Silver Age characters and admiration for the men who created them: "I am very reverent towards the characters of the past, but not just because of nostalgia. It's logical; these characters, as interpreted in the forties, fifties, and sixties, sold a hundred times more comics than they sell today. They appealed to a much wider range of readers and were targeted more towards a healthier, younger audience, which we have a potential to reach and grow with. Frankly, the guys back then knew what the hell they were doing and we don't anymore" (Waid 2002). Such affection comes through in running gags and inside jokes—a series of pranks pulled at the expense of the humorless and often perplexed Aquaman, Black Canary's growing frustration with the way that the male protagonists always want to rescue her when she's not in any real distress, or the absurdity of Green Lantern's inability to deal with anything yellow (Black Canary wonders at one point whether this extends to blondes). One of the funniest moments comes when the Martian Manhunter, who has not yet revealed to the group his shape-shifting powers, passes himself off as Superman. His startled and amused teammates, then, want him to imitate a range of other popular culture icons: "Do Yoda!" (Waid 2002, 89).

As the reference to Yoda suggests, Waid has little interest in placing these stories in the historical context of the early 1960s; locating these events within the continuity of the superhero's careers is central to his efforts to revive the spirit of the Silver Age, but situating them in a precise historic period is not. The title of one chapter, "Group Dynamics" (Waid 2002, 52), suggests the book's overarching concern. We watch the superhero team evolve from "a garish gang of well-meaning amateurs" (as Batman calls them on p. 67) into "five brave champions" (as Clark Kent declares in the book's final passage on p. 316), and, in the process, we see special partnerships or leadership styles emerge which we recognize from the classic books. Critics have often stressed DC's distanced and godlike perspective; Waid wants to take us inside their clubhouse. Waid, for example, lets us see the various superheroes' excitement and anxiety about finally having a chance to interact with fellow capes. For some, trusting the other heroes comes easily, while others—notably the Martian Manhunter—have more difficulty letting down their guard. We watch a team of alpha males jockey for position with the Green Lantern convinced he is the leader of the pack when everyone else has long since decided that the Flash has won the right to command.

At the same time, Waid enacts the passing of the torch from one generation to another, primarily through the figure of Black Canary, whose mother held that same identity in the original Justice Society and who has thus grown up thinking of its members as so many aunts and uncles. At the start, Black Canary keeps comparing her new comrades negatively against the original team and the Flash is awestruck by her access to the idols of his youth. Canary discovers that her mother had an affair with another masked hero, damaging her respect for the entire group. By the end, the Justice League seeks the help of the Golden Age characters, the JSA overcomes "any concerns we may have had about handling the baton to you youngsters" (Waid 2002, 315), and Black Canary declares herself liberated from her mother's oppressive shadow.

DC: The New Frontier

Darwyn Cooke's *DC: The New Frontier* depicts the transition between the scientific and military teams of the early 1950s and the Silver Age superheroes who emerged by the end of the decade (Cooke and Stewart 2004). In doing so, Cooke takes a creative risk, centering so much of the book on groups like the Losers, the Suicide Squadron, the Challengers of the Unknown, and the Black Hawks, who are less well known to contemporary readers. Many fan critics have suggested that the first part of the book, dominated by these characters, is less satisfying than the second half, when the Justice League characters come into their own. The climax comes when all of the superheroes of the Silver Age join forces to battle alien monsters. Along the way, however, we kill off many of the characters associated with the previous decade or, in the case of the supernatural figures, they retreat from direct involvement in earthly affairs. The book's first part is fragmented, built up from eclectic materials, since it must deal with the generic diversity in postwar comics, whereas the second part narrows its focus into a tautly drawn superhero comic.

In the opening sections, we see war stories (Hal Jordan's experiences during the Korea War, Lois Lane's perspective as a military correspondent), detective stories (a film noir style interlude as J'ohn J'onzz takes up his secret identity as a beat cop and goes on some of his very first cases), science fiction (the Loser's deaths on a lost world full of dinosaurs, a subplot involving a secret military mission to send men to Mars), and romance (a moonlit date between Hal Jordon and Carol Ferris). Darwyn Cooke captures these genres in lushly colored images—more interested in evoking a mood or a milieu then digging deeply into the characterizations. His artwork borrows little from actual postwar comics, tapping the popular futurism associated with magazine ads and the Technicolor images of Hollywood movies. A chase along the rooftops borrows from the opening of Hitchcock's *Vertigo* (1958), while a wartime sequence in which Hal Jordon finds himself in arm-to-arm combat with a North Korean quotes from Harvey Kurtzman's *Two-Fisted Tales* (1950–1955).

In particular, Hal Jordan (Green Lantern) emerges as a key transitional figure: a hotshot test pilot with a military background, he could easily have served on one of the postwar teams, and yet instead he gains superpowers when he rescues a dying alien in the desert and becomes the Green Lantern. Cooke depicts Jordan through the lens of Tom Wolfe's *The Right Stuff*, starting with a sequence where Hal as a boy tracks down Chuck Yaeger and gets his autograph, which foreshadows his involvement in the aerospace industry and his secret training for a potential space mission (Wolfe 1979). Cooke's Green Lantern evaluates his new powers with the eyes of a test pilot: "It's like my heart's eye come to life—perfect, immaculate, pure—flight. The kind of light that fills your spirit in a way only a dream can . . . I become intoxicated with this glorious new destiny" (Cooke and Stewart 2004, Book Five).

Cooke seeks to resituate the fictional history of the DC superheroes in relation to actual historical personalities and events which would have occurred simultaneous to the release of the original comics. There is a compelling sequence when many of the alter egos of the early DC superheroes and their girlfriends visit Las Vegas, watching an early bout by Cassius Clay and a performance by Frank Sinatra. Another sequence involves a visit to a Motorama trade show where the protagonists admire the wing-tailed automobiles, hinting at the fascination with aerodynamic and streamlined forms that would influence the design of their costumes. In each of these cases, the links are evoked through the visual style rather than directly stated. Superman's battle with a giant robot in postwar Tokyo is represented through screaming neon lights, while Hal Jordon's arrival at Ferris captures the painted colors of the southwestern desert and the wild patterns of 1950s Hawaiian shirts. Acute observers may notice, for example, the Paul Klee prints hanging in the background as the Martian Manhunter watches black and white television in his apartment.

Cooke's fascination with 50s Americana goes beyond matters of style, linking the earlier action teams with the Eisenhower era and the formation of the Justice League with the first stirrings of the New Frontier. If some of the characters—notably Hal Jordon—embody the rugged individualism and square-jawed masculinity one associates with Cold War America (even as he questions the establishment every chance he gets), others struggle with the issues of their times. The Martian Manhunter is constantly investigating how America deals with issues of racial and cultural difference, trying to figure out how much acceptance he would receive if Earthlings knew of his alien origins. At one point, he goes to the movies to see *Invaders From Mars* (1953), hoping to learn what Americans knew and thought about his native planet. Before the film starts, he is intrigued to see the open support for Superman , who makes no secret of his origins on another dying planet: "Lucky fellow. He's from another planet but his face doesn't scare people to death. It must be so easy for him. I can feel the crowd's love for him. It's like that of a parent" (Cooke and Stewart 2004, Book Three). Yet, once he gets into the feature film, he doesn't know whether to laugh or cry: "I could feel their fear of the unknown, their hatred of things that they can't control or understand." Later, he is moved by an Edward R. Murrow–style newscast depicting Steel's attempts to strike back at the Klansmen who murdered his family: "If Americans react this violently to people for a difference in skin color, then I fear they'll never be ready to accept me" (Cooke and Stewart 2004, Book Four).

Similarly, Cooke uses Superman and Wonder Woman to debate America's involvement in Indochina (Cooke and Stewart 2004, Book 2) (Figure 2.2). In a scene which could have come straight from *Apocalypse Now* (1979), Superman has been sent up river to find Wonder Woman. The Amazon has liberated a group of rebel women who have been held in tiger cages and then looked the other way as they slaughtered their captors. We see Wonder Woman surrounded by the revolutionaries, standing atop a table, and lifting a glass to their victories. Superman wants to hold her accountable to U.S. rules which prohibit direct intervention in these women's struggles for liberation. She has been sent there for propaganda purposes, to build up morale or, as she puts it, "hand them a smile and a box of flags," whereas she has taken it upon herself to "train them to survive the coming war" (Cooke and Stewart 2004). When Superman urges her to set a better example, Wonder Woman responds, "Take a good look around. There are no rules here, just suffering and madness" (Cooke and Stewart 2004). Later, when she returns to the United States, she wants to share with Nixon and Eisenhower what she observed, but they have no interest in hearing the truth. She is quickly sent back to Paradise Island.

Figure 2.2 In *DC: The New Frontier* (2004, DC Comics) Wonder Woman and Superman become mouthpieces to debate America's involvement in Indochina. © DC Comics.

Superman is unable to understand why Americans would force her into retirement because he sees truth as central to the American way; the more world-weary Amazon urges him to fight for ideals and not put his trust in any given administration. The debate is a classic one: whether the superhero should act above the laws of any given nation and in pursuit of higher values or be subordinate to earthly authorities even if they have flawed judgments and faulty morals.

The climax links the formation of the Justice League with the emergence of a more youthful and proactive administration as if the superhero alliance could be read alongside the formation of NASA or the launch of the Peace Corps. The final pages weave together Kennedy's "New Frontier" speech, images of superheroes battling evil and rescuing people, and scenes of humans working together to overcome "ignorance, hate and fear." In Kennedy's words, the Justice League embraces not simply a "set of promises" but a "set of challenges," including "uncharted areas of science and space, unresolved problems of peace and war, unconquered pockets of ignorance and prejudice, unanswered questions of poverty and surplus" (Cooke and Stewart 2004, Book Six). If Cooke has previously used the superheroes to question America's cold war and civil rights—era policies, he now uses Kennedy's powerful rhetoric to express the ideals which defined the Silver Age heroes as a product of their times.

If we can see Mark Waid's work as reconstructing the superhero mythos to satisfy contemporary expectations, we might see Cooke as recontextualizing the genre, creating a new awareness of the historical forces which shaped its development. If early Silver Age comics seem strangely isolated from the political debates and social changes of the early Kennedy era— at least on the surface—Cooke suggests the way that they nevertheless embody the ideals and aspirations of that postwar generation.

Unstable Molecules

James Sturm's *Unstable Molecules* is the most radical of these three projects—a fusion of the content of the superhero comics with the thematics and style of alternative comics. As Sturm puts it, "I feel like I went to the Marvel universe, kidnapped some characters, brought them back to my side of the street" (Spurgeon 2004). Like Cooke's *New Frontier, Unstable Molecules* situates the origins of the superhero team, in this case, the Fantastic Four—in its historic context—in the early 1960s. Sturm's book constantly revisits problems of inspiration and origins, never allowing us to have a stable or coherent perspective on the narrative. Whereas Cooke embraced the ideals of the Kennedy era as something to which we should return, Sturm sees the ideals—and lived experiences—of the earlier era as fundamentally inadequate as a basis for heroic action—something to escape from. For all of its play with multiple genres and historical perspectives, *New Frontier* ultimately falls into line with the core genre conventions while *Unstable Molecules* remains, well, unstable. Much as Cawelti wrote about *Chinatown, Unstable Molecules* "deliberately invokes the basic characteristics of a traditional genre in order to bring its audience to see that genre as the embodiment of an inadequate and destructive myth" (Cawelti 1986, 194). If the blurring of the lines between alternative and mainstream comics production is a key factor in the current moment of genre multiplicity, *Unstable Molecules* may be one of the most accomplished and spectacular examples of that process at work.

Unstable Molecules presents itself—from the cover of its first issue forward—as "the True Story of Comic's Greatest Foursome." The cover, designed by Craig Thompson (*Blankets*), combines iconic Jack Kirby–era images of the Fantastic Four with a more realistic, less powerful depiction of Reed Richards. Richards is seated next to an American flag, yet his posture—hunched over, eyes turned upward—is anything but heroic. Other covers similarly contrast the Four as depicted in the comics with the characters as they might be depicted in the pages of an alternative comic.

In the notes at the end of the issue, Sturm sets up his central conceit—that the author stumbled onto yellowing newspaper clippings about Johnny and Sue Sturm while flipping through a family scrapbook, was surprised to discover that the *Fantastic Four* comics had some relation to these actual historical figures, and tracked down documents via the Freedom of Information Act in order to reveal who they really were: "However wonderful the Kirby/Lee version of *the Fantastic Four* was, there was often stringent restrictions upon what could and could not be told. Scripts had to be approved by the Fantastic Four's public relations office and, on several occasions, the U.S. government . . . My intention with this cartoon biography is to revisit the Fantastic Four's beginnings with a historian's eyes" (Sturm 2003, Book One). In a later issue (Book Two), Sue Sturm is described as one of the primary architects of the Fantastic Four's public persona. Strangely, Sturm also provides a fictional bibliography full of nonexistent books studying one or another member of the team and their place in American history. The "real" Fantastic Four were at once unknown and often researched. As Reed Richards remarks in the book's opening, "If anything, I know far less now than when I began. The closer I look, the greater the confusion" (Sturm 2003, Book One).

At some point, it is suggested that Sue Sturm is already part of comic book history—a neighbor, who is a comic book artist, has a crush on her and has used her as an inspiration for the Vapor Girl Comics which run through the story. At other points, it is implied that the Fantastic Four took shape during a riotous party, the emotional climax of this narrative, which was attended by Stan Lee, Jack Kirby, and most of the rest of the Marvel bullpen. At another place, Mantleman, the overweight fanboy who is Johnny's best friend, explains, "In June of 1983, during a particularly manic episode, I was convinced that it was me, not Stan Lee or Jack Kirby, that had created the Fantastic Four. Don't misunderstand me. I knew I didn't draw or write the comic, I just believed that my brain, my memories, were being scanned and used by Marvel" (Book Three). And the issue of inspiration does not end there, since the story (Book Three) also suggests that Betty Friedan's *The Feminine Mystique* was inspired in part by an encounter with Sue Sturm. Sturm thus depicts a world without clear origins or stable truths, a world constructed through quotation, allusion, and delusion.

Interestingly, this sequence about Mantleman's delusions is the only place other than the covers where we see the Fantastic Four in their superhuman form. This story never depicts any heroic aspects of their personalities whatsoever. In an interview with *Comics Journal*, Sturm explains that he was strongly encouraged to link his characterizations more directly to the superhero tradition but found himself unable or unwilling to do so:

> Initially, [Marvel's] Tom [Brevoort] asked me to explore the idea that at some point these people actually get superpowers. And I was trying to wrap my brain around that. Maybe I could do six issues and I'll have them get their powers. And I realized that, the whole conceit is that they never get their powers. These aren't the same people . . . I don't think I can write a superhero book but there is that correspondence with what people imagine they'll become. But really, Sue Sturm is not Sue Storm. They're different but Lee and Kirby's fictional foursome are imbedded in mine, or vice-a-versa (Spurgeon 2004).

Sturm's characters are like the Fantastic Four and may have inspired or been inspired by the Fantastic Four, but at the end of the day, they are not the superheroes who have fascinated comics readers since the 1960s.

What fascinates Sturm is this notion of the superhero team as dysfunctional family; he depicts the four as living in fundamentally different realities with different aspirations and values. In the comics, they are able to work together despite these differences, whereas in *Unstable Molecules* they are unable to understand or even tolerate each other and they are destined to self-combust. As such, they are emblematic of the forces which would fragment and divide America in the 1960s. Johnny Sturm is depicted as a kind of Holden Caufield figure who is awakened by the end of the book when the beat poet whispers in his ear, "Johnny, it is the fiery night and you are a holy flaming flower" in a moment which is ripe with homoerotic overtones (Sturm 2003, Book Three).

Reed Richards is depicted as a cool, distant man who has somehow attracted a much younger fiancé but who never understands or satisfies her desires. Far from elastic, Richards is someone who expects her simply to obey him and put his career above everything else. And by the end of the book, it is clear that he has never fully trusted her, calling her "promiscuous," "amoral," "a harlot," and, perhaps most damningly, "beneath my distinction" (Sturm 2003, Book Four). In the final images, we see Richards contemplating his life through a microscope but unable to understand the "chaotic" forces driving him away from the people he thought he knew and loved (Sturm 2003, Book Four). Professionally, he lacks the intellect or the drive which makes Kirby's Richards one of the greatest thinkers of all time. Instead, he is someone whose research interests are more pragmatic than imaginative: "A theory is only valuable if it has practical applications. Science is about textiles, not time travel" (Sturm 2003, Book One). Even when more or less ordered to give up his own research to contribute to the early NASA program, he is reluctant to embrace a higher purpose.

Ben Grim is, as Richards describes him, "a train wreck of a man"— a down-and-out boxer, a sloppy drunk, a misogynist, and an abuser of women, who makes a move for his best friend's fiancé. At one point, he is trying to convince a Marvel artist that he would be a suitable comics protagonist. Upon being told that Boxer comics don't sell and that horror is the rage, he confesses that his ex-girlfriends all see him as a monster and that he could be depicted as "the Thing from the Black Hole" (Sturm 2003, Book Four). If the Thing who is beloved by comics readers is a gentle man embittered because he is trapped in a monstrous body, *Unstable Molecules* shows him to be a brute even without the rocky form who would be unhappy no matter what happened to him.

Perhaps the most powerfully drawn character is Sue Sturm, who has been neglected in most other versions of the Fantastic Four. She is a young woman who has recently lost her mother and is trying without much success to take on her roles and responsibilities, to mother her brother, who shows her no respect, to integrate into a community of small-minded women, and to hold onto a fiancé who shows her little interest. She struggles to maintain some sense of herself and to preserve some notion of her sexuality while everyone around her is trying to mold her to their expectations. On the surface, she is compliant; underneath, she is beginning to rage. Her conflicting feelings are most vividly depicted through the Vapor Girl comic she is reading throughout issue 2. Sturm juxtaposes images of her showering, shaving her underarms, plucking her eyebrows, putting on a slip, with the more adventuresome images of her comic book counterpart; at the same time, the text of the comic offers ironic commentary on her own feelings—"A second blast will separate her mind from her physical form"; "One final blast and my mind will control Vapor Girl's Body," and so on (Sturm 2003, Book Two). The notes compare her struggle to maintain some sense of identity in these numbing circumstances with the early tremors of second-wave feminism. One might connect R. Sikorak's pastiche superhero comic book images with Roy Lichtenstein's appropriations of images from romance comics of roughly the same era: Lichtenstein's canvases are often read as depicting the banality and emptiness of the world prescribed for middle-class women in an age of domestic containment. It is no wonder that a tipsy Sue Sturm gives in to temptation when a drunken but still attentive Ben Grimm comforts her. She is not, as Reed calls her, "promiscuous" so much as she longs to be "seen" as a woman. There is a precedent for these feelings in Sue's ongoing romantic entanglement with Namor, the Submariner in the Lee-Kirby originals. In the comics, Sue ultimately returns to her husband, but there remains a hint that she sometimes fantasizes about how her life would be different if she had become Queen of Atlantis. Lichtenstein's images work because they are decontextualized, speaking to broader feelings of cultural discontent, whereas the Namor analogy anchors the depicted actions within comics continuity. As Sturm explained, "I think there's a lot for hard-core FF people to get into, but I also think that if you don't know anything about the FF, you might enjoy it just from this 50s domestic drama" (Spurgeon 2004). Either way, we find a Sue Sturm who is deeply unhappy about her invisibility.

Unstable Molecules is much more interested in emotional dynamics than high adventure: the only fisticuffs thrown constitute various forms of domestic violence; dysfunctional families cannot be magically transformed into superhero teams. Lee and Kirby sought to introduce elements of melodrama into the superhero genre, depicting their heroes as imperfect human beings; Sturm and his collaborators pushed that interpretation a bit further, destroying the ties that bind those characters to each other and showing how these same people would have become losers in the real world. It is that core pessimism and skepticism which makes this an alternative comic even though it was published by the most mainstream of companies.

CONCLUSION

I hope the preceding discussion has moved us beyond thinking of revisionism as simply a phase in the development of the superhero genre. We have seen that from the beginning, the superhero comic emerged from a range of different genre traditions; that it has maintained the capacity to build upon that varied history by pulling towards one or another genre tradition at various points in its development; that it has maintained its dominance over the comics medium by constantly absorbing and appropriating new generic materials; and that its best creators have remained acutely aware of this generic instability, shifting its core meanings and interpretations to allow for new symbolic clusters. Through all of that, I have shown that comics are indeed more than "just men in tights."

COMIC BOOKS

L'Officier, Randy, Ted McKeever, and Ray Thomas. 1997. *Superman's Metropolis*. New York: DC.
Millar, Mark. 2004. *Superman: Red Son*. New York: DC.
Moore, Alan. 1987. *Watchmen*. New York: DC Comics.
Ostrander, John, Tom Mandrake, and Timothy Truman. 2000. *Superman: The Kents*. New York: DC.
Wagner, Matt. 2004. *Sandman Mystery Theater: The Face and the Brute*. New York: Vertigo.

BIBLIOGRAPHY

Altman, Rick. 1999. *Film/Genre*. Berkeley: University of California Press.
Andrae, Thomas. 1987. "From Menace to Messiah: The History and Historicity of Superman." In Donald Lazere (ed.), *American Media and Mass Culture: Left Perspectives*. Berkeley: University of California Press.

Bainbridge, Jason. 2005. "Worlds Within Worlds: The Role of Superheroes in the Marvel and DC Universes." Holy Men in Tights! Conference, University of Melbourne, June 2005, Melbourne, Australia.

Bendis, Brian Michael. 2000. *Fortune and Glory: A True Hollywood Comic Book Story*. New York: Oni Press.

Bordwell, David. 1985. "The Bounds of Difference." In David Bordwell, Janet Staiger, and Kristin Thompson (eds.), *Classical Hollywood Cinema*. Madison: University of Wisconsin Press.

Brown, Jeffrey A. 1986. "Introduction." In Frank Miller (ed.), *Batman: Dark Knight Returns*. New York: DC.

Busiek, Kurt. 1999. "Introduction." *JLA: Year One*. New York: DC.

Busiek, Kurt. 1999. "Introduction." *Astro City: Life in the Big City*. New York: Image.

Carter, Paul Allen. 1977. *The Creation of Tomorrow: Fifty Years of Magazine Science Fiction*. New York: Columbia University Press.

Cawelti, John. 1986. "*Chinatown* and Generic Transformation in Recent American Films." In Barry Keith Grant (ed.), *Film Genre Reader*. Austin: University of Texas Press.

Chabon, Michael. 2001. *The Amazing Adventures of Kavalier & Clay*. New York: Picador.

Collins, James. 1991. "Batman: The Movie, Narrative: The Hyperconsciousness." In Roberta E. Pearson and William Uricchio (eds.), *The Many Lives of the Batman: Critical Approaches to a Superhero and His Media*. New York: Routledge.

Cooke, Darwyn, and Dave Stewart. 2004. *DC: The New Frontier*. New York: DC.

Dematteis, J. M. 1993. *Superman: Speeding Bullets*. New York: DC.

Eco, Umberto. 2004. "The Myth of Superman." In Jeet Heeter (ed.), *Arguing Comics: Literary Masters on a Popular Medium*. Jackson: University of Mississippi Press.

Ellis, Warren. 2005. *Warren Ellis's Apparat*, Vol. 1. Rantoul, IL: Avatar Press.

Gallagher, Tag. 1986. "Shoot-Out at the Genre Corral: Problems in the 'Evolution' of the Western." In Barry Keith Grant (ed.), *Film Genre Reader*. Austin: University of Texas Press.

Jacobs, Will, and Gerard Jones. 1996. *The Comic Book Heroes: The First History of Modern Comic Books—From the Silver Age to the Present*. Roseville: Prima Lifestyles.

Jenkins, Henry. 2006. "Pop Cosmopolitanism: Mapping Cultural Flows in an Age of Media Convergence." In Henry Jenkins (ed.), *Fans, Bloggers, and Gamers: Essays on Participatory Culture*. New York: New York University Press.

Jones, Gerard. 2004. *Men of Tomorrow: Geeks, Gangsters and the Birth of the Comic Book*. New York: Basic.

Klock, Geoff. 2002. *How to Read Superhero Comics and Why*. New York: Continuum.

Letham, Jonathan. 2004. "The Return of the King, or, Identifying With Your Parents." In Sean Howe (ed.), *Give Our Regards to the Atomsmashers!: Writers on Comics*. New York: Pantheon.

McCloud, Scott. 1994. *Understanding Comics*. New York: HarperCollins.

Mittell, Jason. 2004. *Genre and Television: From Cop Shows to Cartoons in American Culture*. New York: Routledge.

Pearson, Roberta E., and William Uricchio. 1991. "I'm Not Fooled by That Cheap Disguise." In Roberta E. Pearson and William Uricchio (eds.), *The Many Lives of the Batman: Critical Approaches to a Superhero and His Media*. New York: Routledge.

Pustz, Matthew J. 1999. *Comic Book Culture: Fan Boys and True Believers*. Jackson: University of Mississippi Press.

Raphael, Jordan, and Tom Spugeon. 2003. *Stan Lee and the Rise and Fall of the American Comic Book*. Chicago: Chicago Review Press.

Schatz, Thomas. 1981. *Hollywood Genres: Formulas, Filmmaking and the Studio System*. New York: McGraw-Hill.

Schumer, Arlen. 2003. *The Silver Age of Comic Book Art*. Portland, OR: Collectors Press.

Schwartz, Julius. 2000. *Man of Two Worlds: My Life in Science Fiction and Comics*. New York: HarperCollins.

Solomon, Stanley J. 1976. *Beyond Formula: American Film Genres*. New York: Harcourt Brace.

Spurgeon, Tom. 1999. "Interview with James Sturm." http://www.tcj.com/251/i_sturm.html (accessed May 31, 2006).

Spurgeon, Tom. 2002. "Interview with Ed Brubaker," http://www.tcj.com/263/i_brubaker.html (accessed May 31, 2006).

Waid, Mark. 2002. *Writers on Comics Scriptwriting*. New York: Titan.

Wolfe, Tom. 1979. *The Right Stuff*. New York: Bantam.

Wright, Bradford W. 2001. *Comic Book Nation: The Transformation of Youth Culture in America*. Baltimore: Johns Hopkins University Press.

3 The Time of Heroes
Narrative, Progress, and Eternity in *Miracleman*

Paul Atkinson

There are numerous articles and books that examine the formal organization of time in comic books with the emphasis largely on the most distinctive feature of the medium, the sequence of images on the page. This article also examines the aesthetic and formal properties of the comic book (or sequential narrative) but restricts its focus to the figure of the superhero and in so doing asks what features, on both the level of narrative and visual discourse, are specific to the representation of this type of character. This chapter is still interested in the temporality of the sequential narrative in the comic book, but the focus on the figure of the superhero allows for a more detailed investigation of temporality within this medium. The figure of the superhero both initiates and delimits the examination of the temporal properties of the medium, and consequently the study of this figure allows comic book serialization and visual form to be analyzed in relation to questions about immortality, progress, and the representation of eternity. To examine these issues, I have chosen Alan Moore's *Miracleman* (1982–1992), in particular the first volume, "A Dream of Flying," due to its novel use of a wide variety of stylistic tropes, including its structural foregrounding of temporal themes and the exploration in the diegesis of the relationship between eternity, aging, and becoming. Moore directly attends to the asymmetries of power between humans and superheroes by drawing on classicist assumptions concerning the qualitatively different notions of time experienced by mortals and gods. One of the most innovative features of *Miracleman* (originally titled *Marvelman*)[1] is the incorporation of story elements and stylistic features of the earlier edition (1954–1963) of the comic book which disrupts the usual patterns of serial continuity. Furthermore, Alan Moore's *Miracleman* openly addresses the relationship between superheroes and their historical context, a theme that is also explored in his subsequent works, including *Watchmen* (1987) and *Promethea* (1999–2005).

To establish a point of reference for a detailed discussion of *Miracleman*, and superhero comics in general, it is worthwhile introducing a selective

Figure 3.1 The temporal shift in *Miracleman* is often reinforced by the use of captions. Moore, Alan, Alan Davis, and Garry Leach. 1988. *Miracleman Book One: A Dream of Flying.* Forestville, CA: Eclipse, p. 19.

taxonomy of temporal modes operating within the comic book panel, both visually and diegetically. This is certainly not an exhaustive list and it does not take into account the full complexity of time in still images—an issue that extends across many centuries of painting and drawing—but nevertheless adumbrates the key areas of intersection between narrative and the visual representation of the superhero. There are three main temporal modes in any one comic book panel: the time of the event as an aspect of narrative, progressive historical time, and the implied time of the character's action. The narrative event is clearly situated as part of a series of events that form the narrative whole, that is, to some extent, already complete before the narrative begins. The actual duration of the event is of less importance than the overall logic of the series, with the distinction between before and after functioning as the most important temporal marker. Historical time refers to the placement of the scene within a particular historical period and can be indicated by aspects of the mise-en-scène, including character and setting. In this sense, historical time need not impinge on the action in the scene and serves merely as a backdrop. More importantly, it also refers to the general sense of progression in the comic book series, that is, the degree to which characters develop with respect to their own history. For Umberto Eco, this is the degree to which the characters can "consume" their own future. If the characters do not progress in this way, the narrative remains locked in a present where the future is only tied to imminent narrative action (1979, 111). The time of the character's action is always "implied" because comic books, unlike film, are unable to show actual movement and instead rely on various indices of time such as gesture, framing, speed lines, and the viewer's tacit understanding of the general laws of physics—if the object is suspended in midair there is the assumption that it will fall.[2] These temporal modes are not always easily separated and a single image may include all three, but function differently for each, giving an added complexity to the temporality of event depicted in the panel. For example, in any one panel the gesture of a character may have a timelessness that locates it in an eternal present—a form of continuous present tense—until the reader decides to move on to the next panel, in which case the continuous present tense becomes a past completed action. Physically the image is the same but the temporal mode has changed, from the implied time of the character's action to narrative time, due to a shift in the reader's mode of engagement. This temporal shift is often reinforced by the use of captions, as can be seen in panel 5 of page 19 (Figure 3.1), where the action is closed off by the phrase "During the years we were together we fought the strangest villains of all time" (Moore, Davis, and Leach 1988, 19). Due to its placement, the caption is read after the image is viewed and retroactively changes both the tense and the image's relationship to the narrative. It also isolates narrative elements ("we fought the strangest villains"), which should be distinguished from the semiotically indeterminate image as a whole.

In the analysis of comic book time, there is a tendency to place particular emphasis on the linear and causal structure of the narrative because most comic books are serialized. As a popular medium, the pleasure of the comic book largely derives from the confirmation of expectation and plot redundancy rather than the entropic properties attributed to avant-garde high culture. Umberto Eco applies this approach to *Superman*, arguing that the reader's pleasure is produced in the ability to anticipate what is going to happen. Our anticipation is rewarded when the expected events occur (Eco 1997, 20); however, the expectation must not be too easily met or the pleasure diminishes. Variation is derived through the use of secondary characters, which shifts the emphasis from the repetitive nature of the plot to the reader's ability to discern changes (Eco 1997, 20).

In serialized narratives there is a tension between the stable properties of the character and their milieu and the irrepressible requirements of narrative invention. The complication for the author is to progress the narrative without creating too many "irreversible premise[s]," of which Clark Kent/Superman marrying Lois Lane would be a typical example (Eco 1979, 115).[3] One way of enabling the progression of the series while avoiding irreversible premises is to provide a continually changing explanation of the past. In what Eco calls the "loop-series," the past is revised through the insertion of new narratives that could not possibly fit into the lifetime of the characters ("Innovation" 20). Throughout the history of the Superman comic books, numerous characters are introduced, including the young Superman and Supergirl, and the arrival of these characters is accompanied by complicated plot elements explaining why the characters were hitherto unknown, some involving time travel (1979, 114). The character initiates action and forwards the narrative without being moved closer to their death (115). For Eco, "the loop-series comes to be devised for commercial reasons: it is a matter of considering how to keep the series alive, of obviating the natural problem of the aging of the character" (1997, 20). Through the "loop-series," *Superman* removes the central element of time, the planning towards a future, and the responsibility the character and reader have towards a future (1979, 116).

The narrative of the superhero comic book is generally delimited by what Richard Reynolds calls "serial continuity," which describes the maintenance of the logic of a story line across the series, where the stories are judged in terms of their faithfulness to earlier issues, a process that is policed by the fans (Reynolds 1992, 38).[4] In addition to serial continuity, "hierarchical continuity" assures the place of each costumed hero or villain within a superhero universe based upon a "hierarchy of powers." The strength of one character relative to another cannot be changed without an adequate explanation—Batman could not defeat Superman on a pure battle of strength (Reynolds 1992, 40–41). Hierarchical continuity functions on the level of space and serial continuity on the level of time; together they form the "structural continuity" or the general logic of the comic book universe, which often extends across the various titles of a publisher such as DC or Marvel. Structural continuity includes the relationship between the comic book universe and the "real" world and explains why characters have changed or have not changed despite external, worldly progression (Reynolds 1992, 41, 43). The relationship between narrative time and the external world need not be characterized in terms of historical time as it relates more to the reading experience rather than any great awareness of historical development.

If the comic book title had not appeared for a number of years, the reader would require an explanation for the hiatus in the narrative continuity of the superhero's life. In the case of Moore's *Miracleman*, the return of the comic after a number of turbulent events in its publishing history was accounted for in the diegesis including an acknowledgment of the changed political climate in Britain. The origins of the comic can be traced back to *Captain Marvel*, which began in 1939 and, despite its popularity, ended in 1953 due to a general downturn in the American comics industry and to a dispute between Fawcett publications and National Periodical Publications (which later became DC comics) over copyright—National argued that *Captain Marvel* was too close to their own *Superman* (Khoury 2001, 6). However, the British market remained strong and in 1954 *Captain Marvel* was transformed by Miller publications, through the writer/artist Mick Anglo, into Marvelman, who then uttered the word "Kimota"—atomic spelt backwards—rather than "Shazam" to enact the shift between the superhero and the human alter ego. The comic series ended in 1963 due to waning interest in both *Marvelman* and the *Marvelman Family* (Khoury 2001, 6). *Marvelman* returned in 1982 in the *Warrior* anthology under the imprimatur of writer Alan Moore. In addition to a dispute between Moore and artist Alan Davis, which slowed down the production of *Marvelman*, the publishers of *Warrior* were also sued by Marvel over the use of the name despite the fact that the name was used prior to its adoption in Marvel comics (Khoury 2001, 6). This stopped the publication of *Marvelman* and, because it was the most popular title in the anthology, also led to the end of *Warrior* in 1985; *Marvelman* returned under the new title of *Miracleman* through Eclipse in 1983 (Khoury 2001, 7–8).

In reviving *Marvelman*, Moore recognized the importance of structural continuity to comic book culture and devised an ingenious way of embedding fragments from the early *Marvelman* in the current storyline. In the first issue set in the 1980s, protagonist Mike Moran discovers that he is Miracleman[5] after a confrontation with terrorists at a nuclear plant. He utters the word *Kimota* without understanding the implications of this performative utterance and is transformed into his alter ego, Miracleman. The long extradiegetic absence of the comic book becomes an issue for the protagonist as he learns that he has been suffering amnesia since the 1960s due to a nuclear blast. The reader is aligned with the protagonist and follows him in his pursuit of the truth concerning his identity. Like Mike Moran, the reader is forced to recognize that time has passed and that his body has aged. The amnesia certainly establishes serial continuity with the 1960s British comic book, but Moore further develops the plot to account for other structural discontinuities. The Marvelman of the 1960s is an unreflexive hero whose adventures are little more than schoolboy fantasies and, despite fighting crime, lives in a 60s utopia with his group, the Marvelman family. In contrast, in the 1980s, Marvelman is married and has a job and is fully enmeshed in the quotidian aspects of an imperfect world—the existence of nuclear terrorism is enough to confirm this. The character has not simply aged in the new comic but has undergone an ontological shift: he is no longer suspended in a world where time is limited to narrative events, which can be endlessly cycled and repeated through the loop series, but has entered a world where time is irreversible and progressive. The difference between the two worlds is accounted for using an "it was all a dream" scenario. The reader discovers that Miracleman was a government creation (the ultimate weapon) and the product of a synthesis of alien technology and cloning. This origin story differs from the one presented in the early *Marvelman,* where his powers are the gift of an eccentric scientist called Guntag Borghelm, who presents an image of the scientist as benefactor rather than creator. In Moore's *Miracleman,* this origin story and the 60s utopian life of the Marvelman family are shown to be an illusion created by the chief scientist, Dr Emile Gargunza, to control the new weapons/super-heroes. In the second book, "The Red King Syndrome," Gargunza reveals the source of his inspiration: "One day, in the canteen I chanced upon a flimsy, black and white children's paper, left there by some semi-literate engineer. I picked it up. I read . . . and then, Mrs Moran, I laughed and laughed and laughed" (Moore, Davis, et al. 1990, 57). The figure adorning the cover of Gargunza's comic book is Captain Marvel, and with this reference Moore completes the circuit describing the various phases that lead to the creation of his own *Miracleman.*

The embedded references to the earlier manifestations of the super-hero function as a means of maintaining structural continuity, critiquing superhero utopianism and playing with the postmodern nostalgia for past images stripped of their historicity.[6] Moore deliberately satirizes Miracleman's nostalgic reminiscences of this hallucinatory past through the character of Liz Moran, Mike's wife (Figure 3.1). In an early scene in "A Dream of Flying," Mike recounts how he came to be Miracleman but is interrupted by Liz, who points out the absurdity of the story elements—"Oh, *Mike!* Dicky *Dauntless??* That was his *name??* Come off it! *I*-I'm sorry please go on" (Moore, Davis, and Leach 1988, 19). Her comments prevent the reader from accepting the logic of the earlier period, and from nostalgically indulging in the utopian fantasy of the superhero, by consistently highlighting those aspects of the scene that locate it within the structural logic of Silver Age superhero comics. This is enhanced by a contrast in visual styles where Liz's commentary and the hapless expressions of her husband are shown in a series of small panels intercut with larger panels recounting how Mike Moran came to be Miracleman. These larger panels borrow the visual style of comic books of the sixties: in the background of panel 6, Young Miracleman bends the barrel of a tank in a manner reminiscent of the earlier Hulk comic books, and in the foreground Doctor Gargunza's glasses are broken, mouth distended, and eyes swollen in a way that suggests violence without death, pain, or horror. This is confirmed by the captions, where Miracleman muses that Doctor Gargunza "never did anything really *evil* . . . It was almost as if we were all playing a *game*. A game which *neither* side took entirely *seriously*" (Moore, Davis, and Leach 1988, 19).[7] The separation of the historical present from the indeterminate time of the mythical past is accentuated by the time compression of panel 5 (Figure 3.1), where actions, occurring at slightly different points in time, are combined in a single visual space. The exact duration of the scene is difficult to determine, but the characters' gestures and speed lines give some indication. It performs a similar role to a montage sequence[8] in film but it also bears a structural resemblance to the "monoscenic" narratives on ancient Greek vases and friezes where various aspects of a single moment in time are encapsulated in the single space of the image (Stansbury-O'Donnell 1999, 3). In these images depicting Miracleman's past, the characters are compressed in the two-dimensional frame in a way that connotes precinematic forms of art. The emphasis on frontality and multiple points of perspective can be contrasted with the images from the present, which generally adopt the fixed position of cinematic points of view. The multiple points of view actually serve to remove any one point of view. The past is a collection of events without the specific expression of lived time or actual experience located in a viewing subject. To return to an earlier point, this compression of the past is also manifest on the level of the serial narrative where there is a proliferation of events without character progression. It is a form of epic past that is repeated in the form of a continual restaging but which remains divided from the present.

The opposition between the utopian past and a progressive present is a salient feature of *Miracleman* and is used to highlight the particular problems of representing superheroes as both mythic characters and participants in the everyday. The superhero has many of the qualities of mythological heroes, ossified in an epic past and subject to the necessity of a story that has been told and retold many times before, but they are also part of a contemporary genre that owes much to the novel with its emphasis on human experience and the indeterminate relationship between the present and future. The "mythological character" follows the path of fate and is inflexible in their action, unlike the novelistic character, who is subject to history but also exists as an individual, a human being, with the vagaries this entails (Eco 1979, 109).

The mythological character of comic strips finds himself in this singular situation; he must be an archetype, the totality of certain collective aspirations, and therefore he must necessarily become immobilized in an emblematic and fixed nature which renders him easily recognizable (this is what happens to Superman); but, since he is marketed in the sphere of a 'romantic' production for a public that consumes 'romances,' he must be subjected to a development which is typical, as we have seen, of novelistic characters. (Eco 1979, 110)

The loop series, with its unusual balance of the unchanging figure of the superhero and the timelessness of the quotidian, allows a comic to incorporate both novelistic and epic time. *Miracleman* also negotiates an agreement between the epic past, where all events have already occurred, and the uncertainty of the present but, unlike *Superman*, does not seek to mask their incompatibility in the loop series. Instead, it addresses this issue by exploring the relationship between the historically determined bodies of mortals and the timeless bodies of gods.

In superhero comics, references to Greek and Norse mythology are common. Examples include Wonder Woman's Amazonian heritage, the already mentioned Promethea, the Norse warrior Thor, and the Justice League in which the principles of the United Nations are generally subject to the will of the pantheon. Irrespective of genealogy, it must be noted that superhero comics are not hagiographies, and it would be incorrect to conflate gods and superheroes; indeed, it would be more accurate to call most superheroes demigods, as they have enhanced abilities but maintain a relationship to the quotidian. In general, superheroes are either human (Batman), resemble humans (Superman), or are humans transformed into superhumans (Spiderman, the Hulk). They need not share a lineage with any recognized gods, but they often possess godlike traits. These godlike traits do not include immortality, as superheroes are not directly attributed immortality, as most gods are; rather, they are immortal by default. They are immortal because their bodies are not subject to the usual effects of time and, consequently, there is little direct examination in comic series of what it means to live forever. This is in contrast to continued speculation on the extent of a superhero's powers in terms of strength, speed, and so on. The question of immortality is not commonly addressed in the serialized comic books because the threat of defeat is not usually accompanied by the threat of extinction. Furthermore, to examine the immortality of the protagonist would also raise questions about the agelessness of ancillary characters, such as Lois Lane.[9] There is rarely any examination of ontological questions and difficulties experienced by an immortal interacting with an aging world. What does it mean to live when the body does not bear the scars of age? How is identity constituted for a superhero capable of living through a number of human generations?[10] Since the publication of *Miracleman*, there has been an increased interest in graphic novels which are not often subject to the same rules of continuity and can address issues such as aging.[11]

Moore and his various collaborators are able to address the relationship between immortality and historical time in *Miracleman* because the comic was developed as a complete and discrete narrative built upon a discontinued series. It began as *Marvelman* in the *Warrior* magazine anthology, which allowed a continuing, progressive storyline rather than the three-page adventures reserved for most serialized comics (Moore 2001, 12–13). The comic was eventually collated as a graphic novel which bore all the hallmarks of novelistic progression with a number of "irreversible premise[s]" including the death, birth, marriage, and regeneration of characters. A follow-up series was suggested, but Moore did not adapt the storyline to suit the demands of serialization where characters and character relationships must be maintained for use in future issues. Moore deliberately experimented with the temporal conventions of serialized comic books by inserting the characters in a universe not defined by the rules of serial continuity. Novelistic progression is unusual in the superhero genre. As Reynolds argues, historical continuity, both in the sense of chronological story development and its relationship with both diegetic and extradiegetic historical events, is generally subordinate to the "metatextual structural continuity" or the unity of the mythological universe the superheroes inhabit (Reynolds 1992, 45). There may be careful recording of past battles and relationships in the comic series but without a sense of historical specificity or any permanent change in the character's sensibility. The uncertain relationship between the comic book universe and the actual world inhabited by the writer was integral to Moore's incipient imaginings. The eleven-year-old Moore first conceived of *Marvelman* as a spoof—with the hero forgetting the transformative word—inspired by Harvey Kurtzman's comics in *Mad*, where the superhero was forced to confront "real world logic" (2001, 11–12). Moore thought such confrontation also had many dramatic possibilities, and in his twenties he returned to the idea not as a satire but as a "dramatic" commentary on the fifties superhero (2001, 11).

> I was beginning to see that they [Marvelman comics] could be used for dramatic effect—something quite startling poignant, taking a kind of very innocent and sort of simplistic 1950s super-hero and then dropping him in a much more complex, darker 1980s environment. (Moore 2002, 11)

Throughout his *oeuvre*, Alan Moore has examined how superheroes react to recognizable social conditions and broad historical trends such as Thatcherite economics[12] or Cold War politics. There is also attention to the effects such superheroes would have on an actual city, public, or political structure. For example, in *Watchmen* (1987), the mortal public believes in exterminism (the belief in imminent destruction) because the existence of superheroes makes possible the complete destruction of the world. In *Miracleman*, this belief is justified as London is reduced to ruins in a battle between superheroes, whose power is always in marked contrast to the frail edifices of human civilization. There is no expectation that human life will be spared as even the most ethical superheroes use what is at hand to help them in battle. In book three, "Olympus," Miracleman throws a car with innocent people inside at his nemesis, Kid Miracleman (Johnny Bates) (Moore and Totleben 1990, 83). There are no longer the moral absolutes of the Golden Age of comics, and instead morality is based on harsh consequentialism, where Miracleman is prepared to kill an innocent child for the good of the world.[13]

In examining the temporal modes of the superhero comic book, it is important to separate the movement between the panels from the movement within the panels. There is an overemphasis in many critical works on the function of the gutter as the site of movement and change, which leads to a comparison of the comic book frame to the filmic frame. For example, David Carrier claims that comic books are a midway point between film and painting and extends this analogy to argue that comic book readers function like a projector in film—they add movement to the otherwise still frames (2000, 56). It is true that the reader plays a crucial role in the simulation of motion in comic books, but to compare them to a projector assumes that all movement somehow lies between the frames. Moreover, this claim does not make it clear as to whether the simulated movement is in the imaginary fusion of the panels, comparable to the fusion speed of film, or in the thematic and structural difference between panels. In the former, the comic book panel functions like a film frame and in the latter like a shot. In contrast to this approach, I will focus almost exclusively on the temporal aspects of the single panel and draw out the importance of this to the understanding of the comic book superhero. This approach can be justified because the aspects of time in superhero comics must relate in some sense to the figure of the superhero located in the diegetic and active space of the panel. Extradiegetic features, such as frame and gutter, are external to the character and relate to the general, structural properties of the medium rather than to the specific actions of the superhero or to the conventions of the superhero genre.

The duration of the panel is certainly limited by the implied time of the character's action and the structural features of the image, but unlike narrative painting the time of contemplation and viewing is destabilized by the teleological push of the narrative; the reader feels compelled when viewing any one panel to move on to the next. Narrative time, as has already been noted, is measured by the number of completed actions understood with respect to the narrative whole, and there is a desire on

the part of the reader to seek out in each panel those events which further the narrative. This is complemented by the visual structure of the
page, where the reader is always aware of the succeeding and preceding
panels. It is impossible to read one panel without some impression of the
size, color, and form of the panels surrounding it because the eye glances
across the page as a whole. The present moment (panel) is juxtaposed with
an actual, but not yet articulated, future. This is unlike film, where the
narrative expectancy is not accompanied by an actual visual form because
the images are sequenced in time rather than arranged in space.[14] Furthermore, in comic books it is the reader who lends movement to the narrative
and these prearticulated images are one means of calling the attention of
the reader forward to what is about to happen visually, and consequently
away from the particularity of the present. In other words, the drive of
the visual succession usually overcomes contemplation, where the reader
would continue to gaze at a single image.

Miracleman is remarkable for its interest in the representation of the
superhero as an expression of the eternal—a temporal mode that cannot
be easily accommodated by narrative time. Eternity cannot be represented directly, with the narrative held in an endless moment of contemplation, but it can be invoked through the retardation of narrative time.
There are numerous panels and sequences where this forward movement
is slowed down, allowing the reader to remain for a few extra moments
in the present and outside of the tyranny of succession. Norman Bryson
argues, in relation to the temporality of reception in the plastic arts,
that the time of contemplation in painting is interminable and that an
accompanying inscription or title—the textual correlate to the image—is
the principal mode for transforming inexhaustible contemplation into a
finite and complete moment, meaning, or event. The reader/viewer can
move to another image as soon as he or she has located or determined
the image's relationship to an external narrative through the inscription,
but left to his or her own devices the spectator might prolong contemplation beyond the requirements of instruction. The inscription guarantees
closure; the image must not be allowed to extend into independent life
(Bryson 1981, 4). The comparison of the sequential relation of framed
painting within the space of a gallery to the framed and sequenced articulation of narrative events within the comic book medium is a valuable one. However, despite shared traits, the differences between the
two forms of reader/viewer also have much to teach us. In *Miracleman*,
for example, and superhero comics in general, the text does not always
facilitate the movement to the next panel but can actually retard this
movement through enforced contemplation of a single panel. On the second page of book one, we see Miracleman juxtaposed with his dreaming
alter ego Micky Moran; his body is trailed by motion lines and arches
diagonally across the page (typical indicators of imminent action), but
his gaze is not directed towards a particular object. It is the blank gaze

of someone who recognizes that he or she is being observed and contrasts with the figure of Young Miracleman in the bottom left-hand corner, who looks forward with both eyes and arms at the abandoned space station, the object of their search. Miracleman is presented as an object for contemplation, a god to be marveled at, which is reinforced by the captions that remove him from direct action and accentuate the implicit power of his movement:

> It's a dream of *snow* and of *fireballs*. A dream of death and *numbing vertigo* . . . There is no *fear* at first . . . only the eerie keening of the *wind*, the swirling, silent *blizzard* and the cold, sharp thrill of *altitude* . . . *He* is not alone. Like firebirds in red and yellow, two other figures soar beside him. He cannot see their faces! His *power* courses through his veins like *molten silver*. His *muscles* move with *precise grace* beneath his skin. He knows he is *invincible*. (Moore, Davis, and Leach 1988, 2)

The captions do not exhaust the image by reducing it to a narrative moment but actually extend its duration by directing the viewer across the panel. The figure of Miracleman sits in the nexus of the captions and remains the object of our attention, although we remain aware of the presence of the other characters. The secondary characters are involved in a direct action, but Miracleman is elevated to the level of substance, a status that is confirmed through the use of bold type to highlight the nouns in the captions. He does not act in the world but exists alongside a series of enduring forms (snow, fireballs, and molten silver) and is imbued with enduring qualities, such as "precise grace" and power. Moore uses lengthy explanations and descriptions, which border on purple prose, throughout *Miracleman* to describe the protagonist either in a state of reflection or as a figure deserving of contemplation by the reader. The text situates the protagonist as an object of contemplation by removing them from both the quotidian world and the imperative of narrative succession.

The implied time of the character's action determines the duration of the individual panel and should not, therefore, be confused with the individual film cell which does not discriminate in its replication of the "present." It is always a movement of summation, indicating the articulate range of an action rather than an indiscriminate moment. The time of the panel is more accurately labeled synchronic rather than static because it describes an action or movement rather than an instant.[15] The comic book artist does not create a panel with the disinterested gaze of Muybridge, where the shots are distributed equally according to the time of the machine—a feature also of the cinematic cell—rather, the panels are created around the schematic range of the body and the limits of its physicality. Henri Bergson explains this through the differing modes of representation in classical representational art and modern photography:

Of the gallop of a horse our eye perceives chiefly a characteristic, essential or rather schematic attitude, a form that appears to radiate over a whole period . . . It is this attitude that sculpture has fixed on the frieze of the Parthenon. But instantaneous photography isolates any moment; it puts them all in the same rank, and thus the gallop of a horse spreads out for it into as many successive attitudes as it wishes, instead of massing itself into a single attitude, which is supposed to flash out in a privileged moment and to illuminate a whole period. (Bergson 1944, 361)

The frieze captures the quality or "attitude" of a movement, which cannot be adequately summarized through the depiction of any point in the movement but instead must constitute a key moment, one that can stand in for the whole. For example, the image of a figure crouching would not suffice as the representation of a leap through the air because the coiled figure could be crouching with the intent to leap or crouching after hitting the ground at the end of the leap—the image does not successfully indicate the possible range of the movement. This is of particular importance to comic books due to their use of still images to indicate movement and the artist's relatively slow production time—a cinematographer could produce a range of images at a much faster rate than the comic book artist. The artist must choose a moment that not only depicts an important narrative event but that most adequately summarizes a character's movement over a period of time. In terms of the superhero comic, the gesture and position of the character should not only summarize a movement but express something of the particularity of the superhero, for example, his or her relationship to immortality.

There is an indivisible movement in each panel that can be extracted from the general narrative movement. In other words, there is a comprehensible movement in each panel irrespective of the placement of the panels in a sequence on the page or the event in the causal structure of the narrative. This type of movement is generally invested in living bodies because such bodies are imbued with both a range of possible movements and more importantly with a degree of intention. Intention is usually understood in relation to an object where the body assumes a transitive function; it is judged by its capacity to act on another body. However, in the case of *Miracleman*, there are a range of images in which the active stance of the body implies intentionality, but the subject is not linked to a possible object. The gesture is intransitive and self-enclosed, in that it refers to its capacity to act without placing the body in physical proximity to an object that reflects this movement. In a scene depicting the events immediately following Mike Moran's sudden transformation into Miracleman, there is a clear shift from the transitive to the intransitive (Moore, Davis, and Leach 1988, 8). After his rebirth, Miracleman's first action is to fly outside the atmospheric boundaries of the earth and pronounce "I'm Miracleman . . . I'm back" (Figure 3.2). The gesture, utterance, and location are organized around

Figure 3.2 Miracleman's rebirth. Moore, Alan, Alan Davis, and Garry Leach. 1988. *Miracleman Book One: A Dream of Flying*. Forestville, CA: Eclipse, p. 8.

a common narrative purpose: positing the existence of the superhero in a context in which the purity of his movement is not disrupted by the transient necessities of the human world. The first narrow vertical panel shows Miracleman leaving the nuclear facility accompanied by the phrase "It's over now!" referring to the end of his isolation in a mortal body as well as emphasizing the transition from the material (transient) to the immaterial (eternal). This is further demonstrated in the structure of the panel, with the viewer's gaze guided from the transient materiality of the broken roof to the open area of sky and cloud, an area of boundless movement and possibility. The subsequent panel has Miracleman in a triumphal pose with his arms, torso, and legs tensed. The speed lines describe the trajectory of his movement and enhance the dynamism of the pose. The expression on his face indicates the pure pleasure in unrestricted movement. In the first panel, the body is in profile and the focus is on the upward direction of the movement, but in this panel Miracleman is shown in a frontal view, which accentuates the physical attributes of his body as well as projecting the character towards the viewer. The viewer functions as a limit point to the character's movement, for any further movement would breach the fourth wall or the boundary between diegetic and extradiegetic space. Open space usually indicates the possible direction of a character's movement—as is demonstrated in the first panel—but in the second panel the position of the character is limited by the figure's centrality and the lack of space in the upper sections of the panel. In addition to the layout of the frame, the gesture of the character is intransitive because it does not refer to an object outside of the body. The dynamic elements of the pose combined with the restrictions of the frame and the absence of an object create an image of unmoving movement.

The contrast between transitive and intransitive movement can be likened to Aristotle's distinction between sublunary and supralunary movement. In *Physics,* Aristotle was beset by the problem of positing a primary movement that would serve as the cause of all other movements. This movement cannot act at a single moment on the world, give the world a push and then stand back, but must rather act continuously on all objects. Furthermore, the source of movement cannot move through space, for to do so will change its position and its relationship to other objects in the universe such that it can no longer continuously act upon them or remain "regular." Aristotle's solution was to posit a primary movement in the circumference of the universe that would continuously revolve on its axis but never change place (1984, *sec.* 267^a–267^b). This revolving circumference is the prime mover of the universe because it moves (in the form of rotation) but does not change its position in space (there is no movement of translation), and in terms of time it functions as a representation of the eternal. It is opposed to the sublunary movement within the rotating sphere where time is experienced as becoming and "each thing tries, incessantly, to return through motion to the place that destiny has assigned it" (Lestienne 1995, 8). This comparison to Aristotle might, at first, seem specious as there is no indication by Moore or the other artists that they were concerned with such aspects of movement of time. It is justified, however, in that both Aristotle and the authors of *Miracleman* face a similar problem: how to represent that which is eternal as dynamic and a site or source of movement. In a figurative sense, the gesture in the second panel implies movement, that which changes in time, and yet also represents the eternal due to the balanced position of the body in the frame and its contrast with the transitive movement of the preceding panel. Aristotle's prime mover eternally rotates on its axis and does not require anything outside of itself to justify this movement. It is an image of perfection in the same way that Miracleman finds a basic pleasure in his own body and his independence from the transient and inharmonious becoming of the human world. It is pleasure that requires no other object but itself.

In this respect, this action is similar to Aristotle's conception of God as prime mover who rotates upon his own axis, contemplating his own movement rather than acting upon the world. Such a god is an attractive force that could not engage with the world because this would be a form of debasement—he would be forced to interact with and contemplate that which is of a lower order than himself. The idea of a god separated from the world is central to *Miracleman* because it directly examines the relationship between the eternal and the temporal both on a figurative and narrative level. In terms of the narrative, the character of Miracleman gradually removes himself from the affairs of human beings, and sheds his human alter ego, through his establishment of a utopia on earth. Once this utopia is established there is no longer an active role for the superhero, and in the final book, "The Golden Age" (1992), written by Neil Gaiman, Miracleman is largely indifferent to the world that takes him as its center. Miracleman is a source of attraction rather than a character driving narrative change, and this is the logical consequence of his superheroic traits and his associated separation from the transient world. Alan Moore explores a similar idea in *Watchmen* (1987) through the character of Dr Manhattan, whose powers are so great that he can manipulate matter on an atomic level. The microscopic atomic world, like Aristotle's prime mover, is beneath and beyond the historical world populated by human beings and other animals. Dr Manhattan works on the level of pure ideas which can be applied to an ever-present atomic substance such that all change can be reversed and what disappears can easily be re-created. The utopian vision of *Miracleman* runs counter to most superhero narratives, which rarely examine an existing utopia.[16] Superman has a "fortress of solitude" where his own clear utopian principles can be applied, but he does not extend these principles to the planet as a whole. Matthew Wolf-Meyer argues that superhero comics are interested in the desire to construct a utopian world but only with the acceptance of the "inability to achieve utopia, regardless of rationale" (2003, 501). There are two types of superhero, those who seek to create a utopia and transform human society and those who are intent on preserving the existing political and social structure—in most cases the capitalist hegemony of America (Wolf-Meyer 2003, 501). The conservative superheroes functioning as "agents of the law" are clearly the most common superhero type, and they largely act to curtail the utopian fantasies of the supervillains such as *X-Men*'s Magneto (501). Reynolds argues that in the superhero genre, it is the supervillain who initiates plot changes and forces the hero to react. The villain, with his or her Manichean tendencies, destabilizes the hero's world, and consequently the hero's primary action is to return the world to its proper state (Reynolds 1992, 52). The creation of heaven on earth in the *Miracleman* series removes the need for such supervillains and returns the initiative of narrative change to human individuals, who must now redefine themselves in the presence of an actual god.

Miracleman is an atypical superhero comic, and yet it is one that most directly addresses the ontological status of the superhero and for this reason successfully explores some of the conventions of the superhero genre. Time is central to this examination, for it relates to all levels of the genre and in particular the restraints of serialization where characters are attributed fixed qualities and a limited history. *Miracleman* challenges the conventions of serialization through placing the main characters in a progressive and coherent history rather than in the singularity of the origin story, which does little more than explain a character's motivation. We understand Miracleman through his reflection on his own past and his speculations on an unlimited and unknown future. This leads to a separation of the superhero from the transient lives of the mortals around him, including his own wife, and in the final volume reaches an apotheosis in the form of the creation of utopia on earth. The comic presages this utopianism in the visual style where Miracleman is shown finding pleasure in the purity of his movement rather than in preventing crime or attending to other earthly squabbles. The drive towards utopianism also marks the fundamental mode of engagement for an immortal, who, in accepting the impossibility of death, must also accept the possibility of a life that will never change. *Miracleman* leaves readers with not just a conclusion to its own story but with the end of the superhero genre, where the success of the hero is mirrored in the impossibility of narrative change and development.

NOTES

1. The name of Moore's comic was changed to Miracleman due to a copyright dispute. I will return to this issue later in the essay.
2. Most comic books have actions and characters that defy the common conception of the laws of physics, but this does not undermine this principle. A character's ability to fly, leap, or metamorphose is always regarded as remarkable when judged within a framework in which the laws of physics still apply. The superhero's individual abilities always require explanation to separate them from the actions of nonsuperheroes. Once these anomalies are posited, the superhero is then only required to remain consistent with respect to fixed traits.
3. Eco's article was written before some of the radical developments in the comic book series, including Superman marrying Lois and, of course, the death of Superman. The article does not examine some of the complexities of the comic book series because many of the issues of narrative variation are independent of the figure of the superhero. They may relate to publishing constraints, general generic changes in serialized comic books, responses to

adaptations, and spin-offs, etc. Much of this complexity derives from the need to maintain a character's name over the long duration of publishing history and across media and requires a judgment on the part of the critic as to what constitutes the oeuvre or genealogy. For example, should the critic combine the many comic book series featuring Batman with the television series and films? Should the revisionist graphic novels also be included in the oeuvre? Some readers, fans, and collectors may have shaped their identity in relation to a single character, but many of the texts are written with only scant consideration of earlier manifestations. It is up to the critic to make a judgment as to whether or not the various series featuring a particular character should hold more than a nominal relationship. In this article, the focus is restricted to those temporal qualities that pertain directly to super-heroes—immortality, eternity, etc., which are addressed by Eco—rather than broader questions of serialization. It also focuses on Moore's response to conventions of superhero comics posited in a period prior to what Nda-lianis refers as to the "neo-baroque" elements of serialization. For an imagi-native and detailed discussion of serialization more generally, see Angela Ndalianis, "The Neo-Baroque and Television Seriality," in *Previously On: Approaches to the Contemporary Television Serial*, ed. Lucy Mazdon and Michael Hammond (Edinburgh: University of Edinburgh, 2005); and Jim Collins, "Batman: The Movie, the Narrative, the Hyperconscious," in *The Many Lives of the Batman: Critical Approaches to a Superhero and His Media*, ed. Roberta E. Pearson and William Uricchio (New York: Rout-ledge, 1991).

4. This type of continuity is also central to soap opera narratives, but in comic books there is greater opportunity to judge inconsistencies due to the ready availability of back issues, which function as a permanent record (Reynolds 1992, 38).

5. I will henceforth use the name Miracleman and reserve Marvelman for a discussion of the early British comic.

6. In regard to this latter point, Jameson argues our postmodern historical sensi-bility has been reduced to a desire for disconnected images (1982, 150).

7. The text is bold in the original.

8. In this respect, the image is a synoptic narrative where a series of actions, in different temporal moments, are included in a single image without the repetition of individual characters (Stansbury-O'Donnell 1999, 6).

9. The agelessness of serialized characters is not restricted to comic books but to any genre that does not depend on actors. *The Simpsons* (1989–) makes numerous references to the ahistorical nature of its narrative and impossibil-ity of combining and correlating the numerous events that befall the family.

10. In this respect, while many superheroes may share the burden of immortality with vampires, there is considerable difference between superhero comics and vampire narratives in that the duration of the vampire's life and the burden of immortality are key themes. Even in the serialized vampire televi-sion programs, such as *Angel* (1999–2004) and *Buffy* (1992–2003), there is a continued interest in Angel and Spike's past as well as Buffy's relationship to the line of slayers.

11. There have been a range of graphic novels or comic serials that have also addressed these issues since *Miracleman*, such as Alex Ross's *Kingdom Come* (1996), Frank Miller's *Dark Knight Returns* (1985–1986), and Rick Veitch's *Brat Pack* (1992).

12. In the third volume, "Olympus," Miracleman ridicules Margaret Thatcher through making it clear that she will have only a minor role in the new Brit-ain (Moore and Totleben 1990, 98).

13. Miracleman kills the young Johnny Bates to prevent his return as Kid Miracleman, an act that mirrors Miracleman's brutal killing of a puppy whose alter ego is a vicious uberdog in the second volume, "The Red King Syndrome."
14. Film does use foreshadowing in the form of flash-forwards, but in this case the images are actual, that is, they are visible within the frame. Sound, however, can perform a function similar to that of the comic book page where an off-screen sound alerts the viewer to what will appear in a subsequent frame.
15. Jakobson, in a critique of Saussure, argues the word *synchrony* should not be used to denote static elements but rather the contained dynamism of the present moment: "If a spectator is asked a question of synchronic order (for example, 'What do you see at this instant on the movie screen?'), he will inevitably give a synchronic answer, but not a static one, for at that instant he sees horses running, a clown turning somersaults, a bandit hit by bullets" (1985, 12).
16. Matthew Wolf-Meyer argues that science-fiction novels, unlike superhero comic books, examine already constituted utopias and then proceed to investigate dystopic elements (2003, 500–1).

COMIC BOOKS

Gaiman, Neil, and Mark Buckingham. 1993. *Miracleman: The Golden Age*. London: Eclipse.
Moore, Alan, Alan Davis, and Garry Leach. 1988. *Miracleman Book One: A Dream of Flying*. Forestville, CA: Eclipse.
Moore, Alan, Alan Davis, John Ridgeway, et al. 1990. *Miracleman Book Two: The Red King Syndrome*. Forestville, CA: Eclipse.
Moore, Alan, and John Totleben. 1990. *Miracleman Book Three: Olympus*. Forestville, CA: Eclipse.
Moore, Alan, Dave Gibbons, and John Higgins. 1987. *Watchmen*. New York: Warner.

BIBLIOGRAPHY

Aristotle. 1984. *The Complete Works of Aristotle*. Ed. Jonathon Barnes. Princeton, NJ: Princeton University Press.
Bergson, Henri. 1944. *Creative Evolution*. New York: Random House.
Bryson, Norman. 1981. *Word and Image: French Painting of the Ancien Régime*. Cambridge: Cambridge University Press.
Carrier, David. 2000. *The Aesthetics of Comics*. University Park: Pennsylvania State University Press.
Eco, Umberto. 1997. "Innovation and Repetition: Between Modern and Post-Modern Aesthetics." In *Reading Eco: An Anthology*, edited by R. Capozzi. Bloomington: Indiana University Press.
Eco, Umberto. 1979. "The Myth of Superman." In *The Role of the Reader: Explorations in the Semiotics of Texts*. Advances in Semiotics. Bloomington: Indiana University Press.
Jakobson, Roman, and Krystyna Pomorska. 1985. "Dialogue on Time in Language and Literature." In *Roman Jakobson: Verbal Art, Verbal Sign, Verbal Time*, edited by K. Pomorska and S. Rudy. Oxford: Basil Blackwell.
Jameson, Frederic. 1982. "Progress Versus Utopia; or, Can We Imagine the Future?" *Science Fiction Studies* 9(2): 147–58.

Khoury, George. 2001. "Introduction." In *KIMOTA! The Miracleman Companion*. Edited by J. Morrow and J. B. Cooke. Raleigh, NC: TwoMorrows.

Lestienne, Rémy. 1995. *The Children of Time: Causality, Entropy, Becoming*. Translated from the French by E. C. Neher. Urbana: University of Illinois Press.

Moore, Alan. 2001. "Revival and Revelation." Interview with George Khoury. In *KIMOTA! The Miracleman Companion*. Edited by J. Morrow and J. B. Cooke. Raleigh, NC: TwoMorrows.

Reynolds, Richard. 1992. *Superheroes: A Modern Mythology*. London: B. T. Batsford.

Stansbury-O'Donnell, Mark D. 1999. *Pictorial Narrative in Ancient Greek Art*. Cambridge: Cambridge University Press.

Wolf-Meyer, Matthew. 2003. "The World Ozymandias Made: Utopias in the Superhero Comic, Subculture, and the Conservation of Difference." *Journal of Popular Culture*, 36(3): 497–517.

4 'Worlds Within Worlds'

The Role of Superheroes in the Marvel and DC Universes

Jason Bainbridge

INTRODUCTION

The Marvel and DC universes constitute the two largest and arguably longest-running examples of world building in any media. They are the products of thousands of comics, artists, and writers over seventy- and sixty-year periods, respectively, and home to dozens of the world's most recognized brands, including Superman, Batman, Spider-Man, the Hulk, and the X-Men. Superheroes are central to any consideration of popular media's thinking about concepts of heroism and justice because the superhero has spread beyond comics to be taken up by popular culture more generally as *the* exemplar of justice. The superhero appears in film franchises ranging from comic book adaptations like *Daredevil* (2003), *Ghost Rider* (2007), *Superman* (2006) and the *Spider-Man* (2002–), *X-Men* (2000–), and *Fantastic Four* (2005–) sequels, to genre films like *The Matrix* (1999), *The Incredibles* (2004), and (arguably) *Harry Potter* (2001–), to television series like *Buffy the Vampire Slayer* (1997–2003), *Alias* (2001–2005), *Smallville* (2001–) and *Heroes* (2006–). At the time of writing, this trend shows no sign of abating, with *Iron Man, Wonder Woman, Batman: the Dark Knight,* and *The Incredible Hulk* all in production or about to be released.

To date, superheroes have largely been excluded from academic study. With the notable exceptions of Reitberger (1972), Pearson and Uricchio (1991), Reynolds (1992), Pustz (1999), Goulart (2000), Brooker (2000), Klock (2002), Wright (2001), and Rogers (2004), most studies that do exist are more concerned with the comic book as an art form (for example, Steranko 1970; Eisner 1970; McCloud 1994; Harvey 1996) than as social commentary. Primarily, superheroes are viewed as a kind of adolescent wish fulfillment, the perfect revenge/control fantasy, in that they offer us a view of power without the constraint of law. But this does not mean that they should be dismissed out of hand. Because they are wish fulfillment, a study of superheroes is therefore also a study of the perceived deficiencies in society and what "being heroic" necessarily entails.

While it is clear that superheroes undergo numerous rewritings and revisions, forever placing their identity and role in the world in "crisis," I argue that the way the DC and Marvel superheroes were *originally* structured and conceived continues to inform their responses to real-world issues like the terrorist attacks on September 11, 2001, and to each other, as in the *JLA/Avengers* intercompany crossover. To better understand how these heroes are constructed and what relationship they have with their wider societies, this essay compares and contrasts the role of the superhero in the DC and Marvel universes by focusing on the universes that these companies have created, the way they distinguish themselves from each other (as competitors), and the implications of instances when their worlds collide.

BACKGROUND

The DC Universe is the product of National Allied Publications (NAP) in 1935, one of the few publishers to be offering comics like *New Fun Comics* (February 1935) and *New Comics* (December 1935), with original (as opposed to reprinted newspaper strip) material (Benton 1989, 101). The Universe gains its title from one of its earliest comic books, *Detective Comics* (March 1937), an anthology title produced as a result of a partnership between NAP head Malcolm Wheeler-Nicholson and printing plant owner Harry Donenfield. *Detective Comics* therefore referred not only to the anthology of private-eye stories but also to the enterprise between these two men, that, after Wheeler-Nicholson was bought out and several more changes of name, would eventually be contracted and formalized as DC Comics, Inc. in 1977 (Benton 1989, 102). The idea of the DC Universe coalesced into being with the first appearance of Superman (*Action Comics 1,* June 1938), Batman (*Detective Comics 27,* May 1939), and a slew of like-minded superheroes, culminating in the creation of Wonder Woman in 1941 (*All-Star Comics 8,* November 1941). Confirmation that everyone existed in the same universe came with the publication of *World's Finest Comics* (Summer 1941), featuring Superman and Batman together on the cover.

The universe was further refined with Superman and Batman adventuring together (*Superman* #76, May–June 1952 and 1954 on in *World's Finest* #71, July–August), the formation of superhero groups like the Justice Society of America, the Justice League of America and the Teen Titans, revelations concerning the future in *The Legion of Superheroes*, the existence of multiple Earths (reconciling the existence of Golden and Silver Age variations of the same character), and, finally, the streamlining of the entire universe in 1986's *Crisis on Infinite Earths,* leading to the production of a prestige format series *The History of the DC Universe,* which provided the blueprint for the "current" DC Universe.[1]

Perhaps mindful of the fact that other superheroes were being put out of business by DC (between 1939 and 1940 lawsuits—and the threat of lawsuits—based on copyright infringement ended the careers of a slew of "Superman imitators," amongst them Fox's Wonderman and Superman's main rival, Fawcett's Captain Marvel), Marvel's first line of "superheroes" could in no way be confused with DC's. For a start, they didn't wear costumes. The Human Torch was a synthetic man who burst into flame on contact with oxygen. The Sub-Mariner was an angular looking Atlantean/ human hybrid who battled crime in nothing but a pair of trunks. What's more, they were decidedly unheroic. The Torch and Sub-Mariner had flirtations with crime, the latter so much so that he would reemerge as a villain throughout the sixties. And Captain America, the closest thing Marvel had to a "traditional" superhero, was draped in the colors of the American flag and clearly defined as a "super*soldier*." He was a symbol of the American military, fighting fascism in the thirties, communism in the fifties, and terrorism in the thousands.

The Marvel Universe derives its title from the first comic published by pulp publisher Martin Goodman, *Marvel Comics* #1 (November 1939), a direct response to DC's superhero comics, which Goodman saw as eroding his pulp empire. In the 1960s the company (after calling itself Atlas and Timely) would become Marvel Comics, after this debut issue. The idea of a Marvel Universe emerged as early as 1941 (*Human Torch* #5, Fall 1941) with a lengthy battle between the Human Torch and the Sub-Mariner beginning a long tradition of heroes meeting, fighting, and reconciling. But it was with the rebirth of an interest in superheroes twenty years later, and again as a response to DC Comics (most particularly the popularity of their "superteam," The Justice League of America), that the Marvel Universe truly came into being with the publication of *The Fantastic Four* #1 (November 1961). Closely followed by Spider-Man, the Hulk, Iron Man, and Thor, the Marvel Universe benefited from the unified vision of its architects—Stan Lee, Jack Kirby and Steve Ditko[2]—whose crossovers and guest appearances (especially during 1963) quickly created the idea of a cohesive universe. The return of Namor in *Fantastic Four* #4 (May 1962) and Captain America in *The Avengers* #4 (March 1964) only confirmed that this was indeed the same Marvel Universe that had commenced with the Sub-Mariner and Human Torch back in 1939.

THE SUPERHEROES

Archetypes

We can understand the DC superheroes as part of the heroic tradition, directly informed by the "monomyth" to which Joseph Campbell refers (Campbell 1971 [1949], 3–49); Superman, Batman, and Wonder Woman could just as easily be Hercules, Orpheus, and Athena (from mythology) or Doc Savage, the Shadow, and (maybe) the Golden Amazon (from the pulp magazines that preceded comics). In many respects Superman, Batman, and Wonder Woman represent a condensation of the heroic archetypes.

Visually their formfitting costumes, the body suits that comic artists call "long underwear," link them to this heroic tradition. As Daniels notes: "[they are] in effect the nude figure in action. The reader responds with the unconscious understanding that gaudily colored near-nakedness is the proper attire for fictional characters enacting dreams and fantasies, as did the ancient gods" (Daniels 1991, 17). In action, too, the DC superheroes are what we may term "premodern" or "sacred." An alien god, an Amazon princess, and a personification of justice, all premodern in the sense that they promote themselves as divine figures of retribution, offering both the promise of transcendent justice in place of equality (enabled by their superpower) and physicality in place of rationality (accentuated by their formfitting costumes) as conduits to truth (beating, sometimes literally, the truth out of the villain).

This premodern ideal of law is notable in that its objective is crime control (where the individual rights of the Joker or Lex Luthor are suspended for the greater social good) rather than due process (ensuring the fair and equal treatment of Luthor and Joker). It is therefore protective of community (Metropolis and Gotham) rather than individual (Luthor and Joker's) rights.[3] In comic books the defeat of the villain replaces the confession of the suspect or the delivery of the verdict as the moment of catharsis, providing both resolution and a sense of justice, superheroes often congratulating themselves or being congratulated afterwards for getting "results." In comic books, then, it is the final battle between superhero and supervillain, the rooftop struggle of Batman and the Joker, the underground confrontation between Superman and Luthor, which provides some sense of narrative closure, bypassing the court system and the police with a batarang, some heat vision, and the promise of more excitement in the next issue.[4] Justice is therefore interventionist and legal institutions undermined and to some extent ignored; prisons cannot hold Luthor, psychologists cannot cure Joker, and Commissioner Gordon relies on Batman (hence the batsignal). The superhero becomes the only reliable repository of justice.

Connections to the sacred are made clear in a number of ways: in figures like Wonder Woman (who is steeped in mythology and carries the golden lasso of Gaea that forces her captive to tell the truth) and Captain Marvel (with his catchphrase of "SHAZAM!"[5]) and in stories like *Kingdom Come* (1996), with its references to biblical scripture and imagery of the DC heroes as akin to gods waging war on Earth. Even apparently science-based heroes, like Green Lantern and the Flash, reach back to premodern ideas—the Guardians of the Universe (an omnipotent race of alien "gods") and the mythical "Speed Force"—for the source of their powers.

Melodramatic protagonists

Despite the Marvel Universe's pulp origins, the Marvel heroes do not map as easily onto these archetypes,[6] as again, seeking to differentiate their heroes from DC's, Stan Lee and his collaborators looked to other sources. Character design, for example, came from horror literature. In creating the Hulk, Lee admits "wouldn't it be fun to make a superhero out of—a monster!" (Lee and Mair 2003, 120–21), referencing the sympathetic monsters of *Frankenstein* and *The Hunchback of Notre Dame* and the idea of a monster having a secret identity from *Dr. Jekyll and Mr. Hyde*. This idea carries over not only to the monstrous-looking characters, like the Thing and Nightcrawler, but to a variety of characters who derive their power from horror tropes—being exposed to science or mutation—that I explore in greater detail below.

The idea of a large and well-developed supporting cast came from radio and television serials. As Lee states (in the creation of Spider-Man's frail old Aunt May): "when working with a colorful cast of comic book characters, they mustn't be depicted in a clichéd way. Most of the fun was coming up with surprising twists and turns. In fact, one of the best rules of thumb was, create the kind of characters that would work well in a dramatic television series" (Lee and Mair 2003, 133). Therefore, whereas Superman had a sidekick (Jimmy Olsen), a girlfriend (Lois Lane), and an employer (Perry White), the Marvel superhero works as part of an ensemble cast that doesn't fit as easily into stock character types. Daily Bugle publisher J. Jonah Jameson is indicative of this, simultaneously Peter Parker's boss, Spider-Man's enemy, and a sympathetic character in his own right. Moreover, the stories themselves were serial in nature (as opposed to DC's generally episodic fare), continuing from issue to issue and sometimes crossing over with other comic titles. This effectively means that the Marvel Universe is a serial narrative that has been running for over forty years.[7] Most significantly though, Marvel storytelling came from melodrama. Some elements of melodrama (most particularly the triangle for Superman's affections formed by Lana Lang and Lois Lane) had always been part of comic book writing, but they were usually reserved for the supporting characters. This was arguably the first time that the protagonists, the individual superheroes, were themselves melodramatic.[8]

Peter Brooks, in *The Melodramatic Imagination* (1976), outlines the elements of melodrama, which include moral polarities and schemes; extreme states of being, situations, actions, and emotions; inflated and extravagant expression; overt villainy that manifests itself in dark plots, suspense, persecution of the good (by the villain), and the final reward of virtue. In other words, melodrama involves different combinations of at least five constitutive elements: moral polarization, overwrought emotion, pathos, nonclassical narrative mechanics, and sensationalism (Singer 2001, 37)—all elements that clearly map onto the Marvel Universe.

In melodrama there are usually six different roles: the protagonist, their helpers, the villain, his henchmen, the judge/father figure, and an authority figure (such as a doctor). The villain and henchmen are morally evil roles, providing a stark contrast to the other roles, which represent virtue. Plots are based on Manichean conflicts between pure goodness and pure evil where audience appeals are made to negative emotions directed against the villain (like hatred, fear, vindictiveness) and positive emotions towards the protagonist (sympathy, pity, compassion). The villain is driven by a morally negative motivation such as ambition, avarice, anger, jealousy, or lust (Smith 1973) and thus propels the narrative by investigating and manipulating the passively displayed protagonist (Jacobs 1993, 123), the villain causing the "primal scene" that places the protagonist's virtue and happy existence in peril. This narrative, where the passive victim does not act, but is instead acted upon (Heilman 1968), maintains the euphoric illusion that we are innocent victims of a hostile world (Smith 1973) by focusing on the protagonist's suffering whereby virtue undergoes unbearable trials and endures extremes of pain and anguish (Brooks, 1976).

Certainly, if we take Spider-Man as the template for Marvel stories (and it is arguable that many if not all Marvel characters follow Peter Parker's lead of having a problem, some difficulty dealing with their powers, and villains who are often more politically and/or physically and/or financially powerful than them[9]), we can see several of these melodramatic themes at work. Issues of Spider-Man frequently put Parker through "unbearable trials" and "extremes of pain and anguish," none more famously than *Amazing Spider-Man* #33 (February 1966) wherein Spider-Man is trapped in a tunnel under tons of rubble while trying to rescue his Aunt May. For eight pages Spider-Man strains to lift the rubble while being haunted, in Daniels's terms, by "visions of the uncle he failed and the aunt he was sworn to save" (Daniels 1991, 129). Other famous melodramatic offerings include the kidnapping and murder of Spider-Man's (then) girlfriend Gwen Stacy by the Green Goblin, being drugged and buried alive by (suicidal) Kraven the Hunter, and being hunted by the psychopathic symbiote Venom. In each case Parker is acted upon by the greed, jealousy, and anger of the villain in question, eliciting sympathy for Parker from the reader.[10] In pitching the character of Peter Parker, Lee called him "a teenager with all the problems, hang-ups, and angst of any teenager. He'd be an orphan who lived with his aunt and uncle, a bit of a nerd, a loser in the romance department, and who constantly worried about the fact that his family had barely enough money to live on. Except for his superpower, he'd be the quintessential hard-luck kid" (Lee and Mair 2003, 127), in other words, a great melodramatic protagonist—save for the fact that melodrama's protagonists were generally female.

As Brooks notes, in melodramatic plays the virtuous role is often represented by a young female who demonstrates the stereotypical feminine qualities, such as weakness, passivity, and muteness, muteness in the sense that her message will require elucidation or interpretation by somebody else (Brooks 1976). In those rare moments when the melodramatic protagonist is male, he is often young and the story is about the boy becoming a man, the narrative thus being resolved when he achieves independence and thus his masculinity. Perhaps this is one way of understanding why comics scholars like Daniels see the Marvel superheroes as "challeng[ing] the very concept of the super hero. Spider-Man was neurotic, compulsive and profoundly skeptical about the whole idea of being a costumed savior. The Fantastic Four argued with each other, and The Hulk and Thor had problems with their alter egos, but Spider-Man had to struggle with himself" (Daniels 1991, 95). In making their heroes melodramatic protagonists, Marvel effectively "feminized" their heroes (along traditional melodramatic gender binaries) by placing them in the melodramatic protagonist's role of the good, passive victim. They disguised this "feminization" by simultaneously reinforcing hegemonic masculinity through bodily performance (Gerschick and Miller 1994) and the masculine values of strength, activeness, speed, virility, stamina, and fortitude (Murphy 1990, 94) that become the basis of superheroic abilities.

The Marvel superhero also deepens melodrama. In place of muteness we have something virtually unique to the comic medium, thought balloons, that invoke the soliloquies of *Hamlet* (Daniels 1991, 95). In place of Manichean dichotomies, shades of grey like J. Jonah Jameson and the Punisher, who sit uncomfortably between hero and villain. In the Green Goblin, a confusion of melodramatic roles where the villain (the Green Goblin) is also the judge/father figure (Norman Osborn). And rather than waiting to be liberated, the protagonist (in the tradition of the male melodramatic protagonist) must achieve his independence through action— usually through the application of his superpowers to the problem at hand. Consistent with melodrama's typical happy ending, the superhero, against all the odds, overcomes the danger and the villain receives his comeuppance. The story ends with the public recognition of the superhero's virtue (public in the sense that the reader recognizes it because the authority figures in the text only rarely do) and the eradication of evil to reward the virtuous.

Marvel superhero narratives therefore retain melodrama's historic purpose of providing instruction for people by demonstrating good models of behavior and moral sentiments (Hyslop 1992). They draw on morality plays like *Everyman* (Lee and Mair 2003, 129), for example, in Spider-Man's famous quote "with great power comes great responsibility." But, again, they go further than conventional melodrama (Hyslop 1992, 66) by coupling these moral pronouncements with modern interrogations of more ambiguous notions of heroism represented by characters like Wolverine, the Punisher, and Daredevil. Here, then, alternative models of behavior are advanced and debated, and it is left to the reader to decide which, if any, are appropriate. Marvel and DC narratives vary, then, in that DC's heroes impose their ideas of heroism in a very premodern way, as if they have a divine right, a conduit to the truth and justness of their role. Marvel heroes must work through their heroism—a heroism which is based in ideas of individual advancement, of enduring trials and emerging, virtue restored, at the other end. This results in a number of significant differences between the two sets of superheroes.

The Secret Identity

The DC superheroes' use of the secret identity follows the pattern established by pulp characters like the Shadow (who became Lamont Cranston) and comic strip characters like the Phantom (who became Kit Walker). But importantly these were disguises the heroes themselves wore. The Shadow and Phantom replaced their costumes with another costume, the tuxedo of Cranston, the overcoat and dark glasses of Walker. Clark Kent and Diana Prince are disguises (almost stereotypes) the alien Superman and Wonder Woman adopt to pass as normal in society. Even Bruce Wayne, while being a real person who becomes the Batman to avenge his parents' deaths, becomes a performance, a collection of affected manners that creates "Bruce Wayne the millionaire playboy"; the true Bruce Wayne is the brooding face beneath the cowl of the Batman.

Implicit in each of these identities is a form of social critique. As the character Bill (David Carradine) in Quentin Tarantino's *Kill Bill Volume Two* (2004) (paraphrasing Jules Feiffer (2003 [1965] at 13) notes:

> Superman didn't become Superman. Superman was *born* Superman. When Superman wakes up in the morning he's Superman. His alter-ego is Clark Kent. His outfit with the big red 'S'—that's the blanket he was wrapped in as a baby when the Kents found him. Those are his clothes. What Kent wears—the glasses, the business suit—*that's* the costume. That's the costume Superman wears to blend in with us. Clark Kent is how Superman views us. And what are the characteristics of Clark Kent? He's weak. He's unsure of himself. He's a coward. Clark Kent is Superman's critique of the whole human race.

Contrary to Bill's claim (that in this sense Superman is unique), we can extrapolate that Bruce Wayne, the airheaded socialite, may be how Batman views his contemporaries or Diana Prince how Wonder Woman views the place of women in America. Of course, one cannot generalize for every DC hero, but even DC's later stable of stars, like Green Lantern, the Flash, and Green Arrow, are shown to survive the loss of their "secret identities" (Barry Allen to Wally West, Hal Jordan to John Stewart to Guy Gardener to Kyle Rayner to Hal Jordan again, Oliver Queen to Connor Hawke). Indeed, the entire substitution of one character for another that marks the end of the Golden Age of comics and the beginning of the Silver Age is predicated on that fact—what else links Alan Scott's Green Lantern (a magic-based character in a cape) with Hal Jordan's (a 'Lensman'-like science fiction hero in a bodysuit) but the "Green Lantern" identity? It is therefore the DC superhero (the Flash, the Green Lantern) that is required, not the man beneath the mask.

But the hero who continues to function according to a premodern code now sits somewhat at odds in a modern world. Clearly, as the superhero genre has developed, the neat binaries of good and evil, law and justice have been deconstructed, replaced by competing distinctive worldviews, different conceptions of the revenge/control fantasy that comic books are predicated upon—ranging from those with a respect for the rule of law (like Superman) to proactive superhumans who take the law into their own hands (like the Authority).[11] A recent issue of *Batman* (#617) highlights the difficulty premodern heroes have with the changing nature of their world as Batman begins a more serious relationship with on-again, off-again nemesis Catwoman (Selina Kyle), revealing to her that he is Bruce Wayne and allowing her into the Batcave, much to the chagrin of current Robin, Tim Drake:

> If Tim has one character flaw, it's that he still sees the world in blacks and whites. Good and evil wear very different masks in his eyes. He's getting old enough to accept that there are 'grays' [sic] in every situation. We may not like them, but it's part of what we do. And my relationship with Catwoman is, at best, gray. So . . . when Tim asked the obvious question, 'Do you trust her?'—I gave him the obvious answer. 'I wouldn't have told her I was Bruce Wayne unless I didn't.' (*Batman* #617, Loeb and Lee 2003)

The idea of a premodern superhero is problematized by the fact that each superhero maps out a different relationship to law and to "being heroic," usually without judgment from the author. Some books (*Squadron Supreme*[12] [1985–1986], *Kingdom Come, Watchmen* [1986–1987]) play on this tension; the monumental miniseries *Watchmen,* for example, is driven by the contrasting views of its superhero characters: "Rorschach's fiercely moral view of the world . . . the Comedian's fiercely cynical view of the world . . . Dr Manhattan's kind of quantum view of the world in which cynicism and morality really don't have a part [and] Ozymandias . . . an enlightened human . . . fiercely intelligent . . . he believes that it's the individual man taking responsibility for his circumstances that can change the world" (Moore quoted in Khoury 2003, 113). As Moore goes on to explain, "They're all different worldviews, and there is no central one. The whole point of the book is to say that none of these characters is right or wrong . . . it's up to the reader to formulate their own response to the world—sort of—and not to be told what to do by a super-hero or a political leader or a comic-book writer for that matter" (Moore quoted in Khoury 2003, 114).

More troublingly, Brad Meltzer's miniseries *Identity Crisis* (2004) reveals that the Justice League themselves, like their *Squadron Supreme* counterparts, "brainwashed" supervillains to "clean [them] up a bit" (*Identity Crisis* "House of Laws" #2), dismaying the current generation of superheroes and leading to some (predictably) tragic results. The premodern superhero therefore becomes a hero in crisis, unable to reconcile his or her brand of interventionist justice with the modern world.

The Victim of Modernity

In contrast, the Marvel heroes are "real" people. Peter Parker becomes Spider-Man, Bruce Banner becomes the Hulk, and Matt Murdock becomes Daredevil. And this act of becoming is a twofold process. First there is the scientific accident that creates the superhuman, the radioactive spider bite, the gamma bomb, the radioactive isotope. Second there is the assumption of the superheroic role: Peter Parker puts on the costume of Spider-Man, Bruce Banner "gets angry" and turns into the Hulk, and Matt Murdock puts on the costume of Daredevil. Here then is the complete reverse of the DC hero. Peter Parker dresses up as Spider-Man; Peter Parker is not the disguise that Spider-Man wears.

In each case the superhero is a real person—Peter Parker, Bruce Banner, Steve Rogers—affected by "modernity." They are, in effect, the dark side of modernity, the production of weird comic book science. In his study of horror, *Danse Macabre* (1986 [1981]), Stephen King links Marvel's monsters to present-day incarnations of horror:

> Where for every superhero such as Spiderman [sic] or Captain America, there seem to be a dozen freakish aberrations: Dr Octopus . . . The Sandman . . . and most ominous of all, Dr Doom, who has been so badly maimed in his Twisted Pursuit of Forbidden Science that he is now a great, clanking cyborg who wears a green cape, peers through eyeholes like the archers' slits in a medieval castle, and who appears to be literally sweating rivets (King 1986, 51).

Despite King's claim that "superheroes with elements of monstrosity in their makeup seem less enduring" (King 1986, 51), his idea that Marvel characters may be the modern-day incarnations of monsters is certainly true of many of the heroes. Stan Lee has called the Hulk the modern-day Jekyll and Hyde (Lee and Mair 2003, 151). The Fantastic Four and the X-Men are both products of genetic mutation (one externally triggered, the other internal). Even Peter Parker has grappled with the undesirable effects of that radioactive spider bite (briefly growing extra arms and becoming a Man-Spider). All of these problems spring from the "Twisted Pursuit of Forbidden Science" that King describes (1986, 51), the undesirable side effects of modern science. It is also interesting to note that when the origin stories of these heroes are revised (for a movie, or cartoon series, or revamp) the science is continually updated so they are doomed (always) to be the dark side of modernity. Peter Parker's radioactive spider becomes a product of recombinant DNA and a meditation on the horrors of genetic engineering (in the *Ultimate Spider-Man* series). The injury that prompts Tony Stark to don his Iron Man armor changes from the weaponry of Vietnam to weaponry he helped create during the Gulf War.

This, then, is the modern superhero, modern in the sense that they are the flipside of modernity, produced by scientific accident or genetic mutation, a very different kind of superhero to the DC avatar of justice. Indeed, the term *Marvels* (coined by Kurt Busiek and Alex Ross in their seminal fully painted series *Marvels*) seems far more apt—scientific marvels just one step removed from the horrors of Doctors Frankenstein and Jekyll. Even Thor, the most premodern and mythological of Marvel's characters, is forced to submit to modernity—trapped in the mortal Dr. Donald Blake. In the Marvel Universe the premodern, the sacred, the mythological are replaced with science and technology, an idea that has been there from the beginning in Jack Kirby's mesmerizing artwork that blurred science and magic in images like the Cosmic Cube, Ego the Living Planet, the scientific mythology of Asgard, and the towering figure of Galactus—the technologically advanced alien God of the Marvel Universe.

Distance

This premodern/modern idea carries over into the formation of the universes themselves. In the DC Universe, the cities of the superheroes are themselves archetypes rather than real places. Superman's city is Metropolis, Batman's is Gotham, Flash has Central City, Green Lantern Coast City, Wonder Woman Paradise Island. In this sense the DC superheroes are one step removed from the real world, and this is underlined diegetically as well in the heroes' need for a hideout or otherwise secret base—Superman in his Fortress of Solitude, Batman in his Batcave, the Justice League in their satellite or watchtower—all promoting the sense that they are watching over us (like gods) from a distance. Justice necessarily comes from above.

This is also commented upon directly in Mark Waid and Alex Ross's *Kingdom Come* (1996), depicting a world (twenty something years into the future) where supervillains have either retired or fled and the impending Apocalypse is revisioned as a superhuman war raging between superheroes with competing ideologies. The series sees a clash between the ideologically opposed forces of Magog and his Justice Battalion, vigilantes who kill those who oppose them; Batman and the more youthful "human" heroes who want to bring these vigilantes to justice; and Superman and Wonder Woman, the former having lived in isolation following the world's acceptance of Magog and his ilk, the latter adopting a more militant stance. Following a monumental battle and decisive action by the United States to eradicate the superhuman "threat," Superman unites the remaining superheroes with a promise to the rest of the world that "we will no longer impose our power on humanity. We will earn your trust . . ." (*Kingdom Come Book* #4). *Kingdom Come* therefore acknowledges the divide between the DC Universe and its heroes and overcomes that divide by having the superheroes go out into the world to "earn humanity's trust" as delegates to the U.N. and involved in urban development and renewal, as artist/creator Ross sees it: "superheroes needed to live among normal folk" (Ross 2000).

In keeping with their portrayal of real people as superheroes, Marvel's heroes are very much based in the real world. New York is home to Spider-Man and the Fantastic Four, to the Avengers and Captain America. Daredevil watches over Hell's Kitchen. Dr. Strange lives in Greenwich Village. The Hulk briefly took over one of the Florida keys. They are part of the real world rather than the world being based around them.[13] They do not have secret headquarters (the Fantastic Four are in a skyscraper in New York; the Avengers' base is public knowledge) and therefore do not maintain a distance between themselves and their universe.

September 11, 2001

Just as there has been a profound shift in notions of law, cultural studies, and race since the events of September 11, 2001, so has there been a corresponding change in the depiction of superheroes. As writer Mark Millar notes:

> Comics have led the way in terms of the cultural shift that took place after the devastation of September 11th and the more intelligent and adult approach to story-telling we've been experiencing across all forms of media ever since. In an industry that was built on cartoon violence, it's ironic that we were the first to discover this new humanity in our work and it's perhaps why we've found a whole new generation of readers who had never picked up a comic book until now . . . comics discovered a brand new realism and an evangelical adult audience . . . Radicalised by events a new generation of writers and artists are tackling themes and subject matter nobody else could even afford to contemplate. In my own work, I've enlisted Captain America and a squadron of Marvel Comic's most famous household names into George W. Bush's homeland security initiative and used them to comment on the erosion of American civil liberties [in Marvel's *The Ultimates*]. In the recently released *Superman: Red Son*, I've used the metaphorical notion of a Soviet Superman taking over the world as a means to criticise the over-reaching and unethical US foreign policy . . . reaching right back to our roots as political cartoonists. . . . (Millar 2003, 110)

Interestingly, the aforementioned differences in what being a superhero means informed each universe's response to September 11. Being based in New York, the Marvel Universe's heroes directly commented on and interacted with the event, primarily in *Amazing Spider-Man* #36 (writer J. Michael Straczynski, artist John Romita Jr.) and the relaunching of *Captain America*.[14] As Romita Jr. puts it:

> Spider-Man is a part of New York City and New York City is a part of Spider-Man. It's only natural that he should confront the tragedy

... The World Trade Center Towers are ... were ... a part of New York City, not Metropolis or Gotham City. The majority of Marvel's characters are based in New York, and the Twin Towers were depicted numerous times in the past. Visual acknowledgement of the destruction should be considered. (Romita Jr. 2004, n.p.)

Amazing Spider-Man #36 deals with the aftermath of the World Trade Centre attacks, a series of scenes of Spider-Man and other heroes helping rescue workers, with a running monologue by Spider-Man. Even a collection of the Marvel Universe's greatest villains (absent any would-be terrorists like the Red Skull) briefly appear, to look horrified at what has happened. Spider-Man's monologue reinforces the fundamental strength of the human spirit (highlighting this by briefly depicting the passengers trying to take back their plane) and reframing this event as another melodramatic trial that we can get through, that we can overcome. As he puts it: "We stand blinded by the light of your unbroken will." Marvel superheroes' heroism is located in individual advancement, the "get back to work" ethos expressed in (then) Mayor of New York Rudy Giuliani's speech following the attack. In the following months Marvel pursued the storyline—with Captain America rededicating himself to the war on terrorism (revealing his secret identity to the world in the process)—and metaphorical analogies in the pages of *The Avengers* (Kang's war on Washington, the Red Skull's infiltration of the government) and *The Ultimates* (with their "persons of mass destruction").

The DC Universe, however, remained one step removed from the tragedy. Indeed, in an amazing piece of synchronicity at the time of the terrorist attacks, the DC Universe was itself embroiled in a company-wide crossover known as the Imperiex War (commencing in *Superman* #153, February 2000). The metaphor, even if unintentional, remains profound—in place of terrorists we have an alien "embodiment of entropy" (Beatty 2002, 94), Imperiex, setting out to destroy the earth as part of a larger plan to destroy the universe and start it anew; in place of Osama Bin Laden, a mysterious foreigner (General Zod, "ruler of the war-torn European republic of Pokolistan" [Beatty 2002, 105]) scheming against the West and in place of George W. Bush as forty-second president of the United States, former Superman villain Lex Luthor (*Superman: Lex 2000* #1, 2001). Indeed, the parallels become clearer as the storyline runs on: Luthor's towers are brought down, the heroes suffer terrible personal losses (Wonder Woman's mother is killed, Aquaman appears to die), Superman goes into mourning and Luthor uses the war as an excuse to curtail civil liberties while scoring high approval ratings for his leadership. As this is a metaphor, an ending could be written where Superman takes charge (transcendent interventionist justice again), Imperiex is destroyed, and the heroes are victorious, simultaneously validating the DC Universe's idea of heroism and the idea that there must be distance between their heroes and the real world (both diegetically and extradiegetically).

This is underscored by the fact that DC's only direct engagement with September 11 was in the form of a tribute book (*9–11—The World's Greatest Comic Book Writers and Artists Tell Stories to Remember, Volume 2*), with all proceeds from the book's sale going to various relief organizations. The stories are a mixture of true tales of heroism, reflections on the tragedy, and stories featuring DC heroes. It is notable that two of the latter openly acknowledge this distance between the DC heroes and their world; in one, Superman struggles to get out of his comic book to assist those affected by the tragedy, lamenting the fact he is fictional. In the second, a young boy imagines that had the JLA been here, the tragedy would have been averted. Both then draw on this notion of distance that the DC heroes cultivate—at no time do we see the events of September 11, 2001 occur in the DC Universe; indeed, the young boy's dream of the JLA saving the day confirms that the events of September 11 are incongruous in a universe where superheroes can and must intervene to save the day.

Both universes successfully engage with the themes of 9/11 (loss, terrorism, civil rights) either directly (the Marvel Universe) or through metaphor (the DC Universe), and they each resolve it in terms of their

Figure 4.1 Cover to *JLA/Avengers 3* by George Perez (2005). DC Comics.

individual ideas of heroism, be they individual advancement (Marvel) or transcendent interventionist justice (DC). The differences in these positions were then directly commented upon less than two years later in the landmark crossover miniseries *JLA/Avengers* that, for the "first" time, brought the premiere superhuman teams of both universes together.[15]

JLA/Avengers

The complex plot involves the attempts of rogue scientist Krona to discover the "ultimate truth" (Busiek and Perez 2004, 21), the secrets of creation, placing both universes in jeopardy. During the series, characters visit each universe and the universes are briefly combined, enabling each side to comment on the other.[16] The DC Universe's the Flash's first glimpse of the Marvel Universe is of the persecution of a mutant child (Busiek and Perez 2004, 46). The rest of his team are exposed to Dr. Doom's brutal rule of Latveria, the Hulk in Michigan, and the Punisher in New York. Despite saying they will not intervene, Batman actually does engage the Punisher, characteristic of the DC Universe superheroes' notion of interventionist justice. But it is Superman who becomes the primary spokesman for the JLA's view of the Marvel Universe, again endorsing the DC superheroes' interventionist view when he says:

> This world. This world! It's lush, it's alive . . . there are heroes here too, from what we've discovered. How can they allow this? How can they stand for it? Don't they care?" (Busiek and Perez 2004, 46)

And again:

> If those were its [this world's] heroes I'm not impressed. Not with their world and not with their achievements. I'm not. (Busiek and Perez 2004, 51)

Similarly, the Marvel heroes are amazed that in the DC Universe "they do honour their heroes well here . . . they have a museum to a super-speedster" (Quicksilver) and "idolize their heroes" (Scarlet Witch), prompting Captain America (Marvel's voice of discontent) to say:

> Justice—this isn't justice! Look around . . . this is their city. It wasn't built by men. They must own this world, like little tin gods—demanding the public's adoration instead of protecting its freedoms! Don't you feel it? It's sour—it's wrong. (Busiek and Perez 2004, 56–57)

In this case Captain America labels the DC mode of heroism at worst tyrannical and at best, self-congratulatory. While Quicksilver applauds the fact that "heroes are respected not hounded" (Busiek and Perez 2004, 80), Captain America likens the DC superheroes to "high-and-mighty stormtroopers . . . fascist overlords" (Busiek and Perez 2004, 60) who "strut like peacocks [and] expect to be worshipped" (Busiek and Perez 2004, 144). When Batman is surprised by the appearance of the Captain's ally, the Thing, Captain America is quick to defend him, saying: "Ben Grimm may not be sleek and elegant, like the heroes over here, mister. But he's one of the finest men I know" (Busiek and Perez 2004, 89). In each case Captain America highlights the fact that heroism (in the Marvel sense) should be about individual advancement rather than the imposition of justice, with the Thing, of course, serving as the perfect example of the melodramatic Marvel superhero. Superman sees the Avengers' problem as not being able to "inspire the populace" (Busiek and Perez 2004, 79), and while Aquaman interjects, claiming he doesn't envy the Avengers as "the heroes here seem less powerful, in general, than at home. And their world's stacked against them. So it seems like they've got to fight amazingly hard just to keep things on an even keel," Superman responds, "Maybe they may need to fight harder than we do . . . but it's clear they're not fighting hard enough" (Busiek and Perez 2004, 98–99).

Eventually the heroes join forces against Krona, and on the eve of battle Captain America and Superman admit to doubts about each one's personal brand of heroism:

Superman: "I'll confess—I do worry, sometimes, about doing too much. Denying humanity freedom of choice. . . ."
Captain America: "That's what made it sting, isn't it? [sic] That deep down, we both worry it might be true. In my case, that as hard as the Avengers fight . . . I fear sometimes it may never be enough." (Busiek and Perez 2004, 181)

Again the distinction is drawn between the imposition of justice and individual advancement, heroism on the large and the small scale. With Krona beaten and in parting the heroes find common ground:

Superman: "Captain. Whether we fear we do too much—or not enough—"
Captain America: "We keep trying."

But perhaps there is another more significant commonality here. Krona, the common foe of both the Avengers and the JLA, is described as "a scientist. A seeker of knowledge. I search for the secret of creation, and the truth of what existed before" (Busiek and Perez 2004, 67), a search that puts both universes in jeopardy. Krona (being a scientist) and Krona's search (for scientific knowledge) are therefore seen as dangerous, part of these comic books' ongoing critique of modernity.

Figure 4.2 Cover to *Avengers/JLA 2* by George Perez (2004). DC Comics.

Is the Superhero Postmodern?

Both universes, both sets of superheroes, then, are navigating what I would term a "postmodern" relationship to modernity, "postmodern" in the sense that they both advance different ways of resolving the contradictions and problems with modernity. Following the DC model, modernity is rejected in favor of a premodern transcendent justice. Following the Marvel model, the traumas of modernity are highlighted and worked through to reach a compromise. In each case superheroes and their "super natures" are crucial to exploring this new relationship.

The name of the "first" superhero, Superman, comes from Nietzsche's term *Ubermensch,* coined in 1883 for an individual whose creativity transcends ordinary human limitations. From the start, then, superheroes' "super nature"—their X-Ray vision or ability to fly or great mental acuity—sets them at odds with the rationality of modernity. This reached its apotheosis in the Silver Age of comics where the superhero comic actively begins challenging the rationality of science. Early appearances of *The Flash,* for example, explore faster than light superspeed, time travel, absolute zero producing mirages (like extreme heat), elements and alchemy, "camera mirrors" (which hold and project images), and talking gorillas (*Flash Archives, Volume 1*).

Marvel Comics took this even further. What began as extrapolations on science became full-blown assaults on the nature of reality—subterranean kingdoms, negative zones and microverses, parallel Earths, alien Gods and divergent streams of humanity like Mutants, Eternals, and Deviants culminating in the sustained attacks of Jack Kirby's Fourth World stories (debuting in *Superman's Pal Jimmy Olsen*, #133, October 1970—a Marvel mythology for the DC Universe) and more recent independent examples like "The Dreaming" in Neil Gaiman's *Sandman* (1989–1996) and the "Immateria" in Alan Moore's *Promethea* (1999–2005).

Superheroes therefore take more than just the "super" prefix from Nietzsche, for they challenge, as Nietzsche (1968) did, both notions of truth and the status quo, most obviously in subversive texts like Frank Miller's *The Dark Knight Returns* or Alan Moore's *V for Vendetta* (both pitting individual "superheroes" against totalitarian governments) but also more subtly in the way the superhero challenges the rationality of modernity by presenting a world founded on irrationality, be it the capabilities of the title character (i.e., a man who can fly) or the locations they visit (i.e., a subterranean world existing beneath the Earth's crust). In so doing, the superhero presents an alternative or corollary to modernity, a process of estrangement by which to critique the present system whether in the factual framework of September the 11th or the fictional assaults of Imperiex and Krona. Such an interrogation of modernity suggests two things. First, it suggests that modernity is limited; it is only one of what Lyotard (1984) would term "the grand narratives" or ways of seeing the world open to us. Second, it represents an attack on the notion of absolutes—be it truth, law, or justice. Where is truth in a universe subject to the whims of Krona? Or a multiverse of Earth-Ones and Earth Twos? The superhero therefore becomes another way of suggesting that rationality is stifling—and limiting.

Both the DC and Marvel universes advance different notions of heroism. The former is premodern, invoking a transcendent and interventionist justice. The latter is melodramatic, involving working through trauma to restore virtue. But both follow the comic tradition (established as far back as the first appearance of the Yellow Kid in 1896) that comics can provide serious social critique; in this sense the wish fulfillment embodied in the superhero becomes a way of interrogating the problems with modernity.

NOTES

1. The existence of a common universe is primarily important for commercial reasons. It allows for the property to be clearly branded as a corporate product (e.g., the DC Universe) rather than the product of an individual (e.g., Bob Kane's Batman). Furthermore, it enables the franchise to be developed (through multiple series on the same character, team-up series between characters, spin-offs, crossovers, etc.) and encourages the acquisition of a range of titles to get the 'complete story' or to 'complete the set.' The common

universe also gives the superhero more power. Given the seriality typical of comics, such self-contained (nonconflicting) worlds and the heroes who inhabit them can weave their way into a fan's life far more effectively than discontinuous adventures that do nothing to develop either the heroes or their worlds. The DC Universe, for example, can become a completely immersive experience, a secondary world accessible through a variety of different titles, one that can be as complex or as simple as a fan's investment allows. See also n. 4 following.

2. While this essay acknowledges the ongoing debate over the authorship of Marvel characters, Lee, Kirby, and Ditko are presented as the three individuals most indicative of the unified vision of the architects of the Marvel Universe. Similarly, where excerpts from Stan Lee's biography are presented they should be viewed as being indicative of the structural choices made in each hero's creation, rather than as evidence of Lee being the sole creator or even greatest contributor to each hero.

3. For more on this, see Reynolds (1992) at 14–15, who notes, "Endless story possibilities can be designed around the theme of the superhero wrestling with his conscience over which order should be followed—moral or political, temporal or divine" (Reynolds 1992, 15). This relationship between the superhero and the law also seems to figure in Campbell's (1971 [1949]) model of what the hero must do in the modern world when he says: "It is not society that is to guide and save the hero, but precisely the reverse" (Campbell 1971, 391).

4. Given the serial nature of comics, there can only ever be "some sense" of narrative closure as readers are inevitably encouraged to follow the superheroes' further adventures in the next issue (often through an unresolved subplot). The serial form is therefore commercial because complete consumption of the commodity is indefinitely delayed, encouraging recurrent monthly purchases. Following Campbell (1975 [1949]), the serial form also serves to repeat the function of the hero in the monomyth structure by making it more intensively about the superhero, and the ritual of being a superhero, issue after issue.

5. In SHAZAM, each letter represents the mythic heroes Solomon, Hercules, Atlas, Zeus, Achilles, and Mercury from which Captain Marvel derives his wisdom, strength, stamina, power, courage, and speed.

6. Indeed, the only connections to the pulps are in Spider-Man's name (taken from the pulp hero The Spider) (Lee and Mair 2003, 130) and support character Ka-Zar, who predates the Marvel Universe as part of Martin Goodman's line of pulps.

7. Taking the 1961 "official" launch as our starting point with Fantastic Four 1. Unlike DC, with their Crisis on Infinite Earths, Marvel has never "rebooted" their universe, preferring instead to insert retroactive continuity, thus ensuring the appearance of a serial narrative. Retroactive continuity refers to "the adding of new information to 'historical' material, or deliberately changing previously established facts in a work of serial fiction. The change itself is referred to as a 'retcon,' and the act of writing and publishing a retcon is called 'retconning' " (*Wikipedia* at: http://en.wikipedia.org/wiki/Retroactive_continuity).

8. Melodramatic in the sense that soap operas are melodramatic, that is, notoriously serialized and interweaving the stories of characters and events. For more on the relationship between melodrama and popular media, see Cawelti (1976), who argues that all popular genres are gradations of melodrama.

9. Take, for example, the Fantastic Four's the Thing, who is an explicitly melodramatic character as "perhaps the first superhero who not only wasn't handsome,

he was downright grotesque . . . as a normal man who had become a monstrous freak, he provided a sense of pathos. Fate had dealt him a tragic hand when the superpowers were handed out" (Lee and Mair 117). The villain here would be Dr. Doom, head of the small European country of Latveria, and thus enjoying the privilege (power) of diplomatic immunity.

10. Mark Mullen (1998) extends Brooks's analysis by arguing that melodrama is characteristically concerned with the problem of expressing the radical interiority and communication of an individual's lived and felt experience. An important objective of melodrama therefore becomes the encouragement of the audience to feel sympathy towards the protagonist. Here, Mullen distinguishes between sympathy and empathy, the former including both a feeling of identification and the arousal to act on that feeling.

11. For more on this development of the genre, see Geoff Klock (2002).

12. Marvel's Squadron Supreme is included amongst these DC titles, as the Squadron Supreme were themselves thinly veiled versions of DC's Justice League. In this series writer Mark Gruenwald seems to be commenting on the power relations between individuals in that team. Squadron Supreme can also be viewed as a major influence on Brad Meltzer's later Identity Crisis series (see following).

13. Lee credits his decision to set many of the Marvel heroes' adventures in New York as being "the start of the Marvel Universe, a universe in which the Human Torch is apt to run into Spider-Man while chasing the Hulk down a busy street" (Lee and Mair 137).

14. Marvel also produced their own charity comics *Heroes* (December 2001) and *A Moment of Silence* (February 2002) with proceeds going to support those affected by 9/11, along with a short-lived *911*(2002) series focusing on policemen, hospital workers, and firemen.

15. There have been a number of crossovers between the DC and Marvel universes over the years, including the (unofficial) "Rutland Halloween parade" crossovers and a series of official crossovers commencing with 1976's *Superman vs. Spiderman*. None of these have been viewed as a legitimate part of either universe's continuity, though the later *DC vs. Marvel/Marvel vs. DC series* (1996) could be considered as such with the introduction of the character Access (co-owned by Marvel and DC). Whatever the case, *JLA/Avengers* does mark the premiere meeting of these teams and has been legitimated by the subsequent appearance of Krona's "chronal egg" in the pages of *JLA* and (arguably) Scarlet Witch's subsequent behavior in *The Avengers* (culminating in the *House of M* series [2005]).

16. In the *Avengers/JLA Compendium* (2004), Busiek makes it clear that he originally intended to deal with these differences in greater detail by having Krona's merging of universes create "a classic Marvel take on the DC heroes, full of violent emotion, and a classic DC take on the Marvel heroes, rife with fictional cities, Schwartzian SF ideas and more" (Busiek, "The JLA/Avengers you never saw," 45), again indicative of the fact that writers and artists in this medium are well aware of the different ideas of heroism being advanced here.

COMIC BOOKS

Busiek, Kurt, and George Perez. 2004. *JLA/Avengers: The Collector's Edition*. New York: DC Comics (individual issues originally appeared 2003–2004).
Gaiman, Neil, Stan Lee, Jill Thompson, Kieron Dwyer, et. al. 2001. *9–11—The World's Greatest Comic Book Writers and Artists Tell Stories to Remember*, Vol. 2. New York: DC Comics.

Gruenwald, Mark, Bob Hall, John Buscema, Paul Neary, and Paul Ryan. 1985–
1986. *Squadron Supreme*. 12-issue miniseries. September–August. New York:
Marvel Comics.
Loeb, Jeph, and Jim Lee. 2003. "Hush Chapter Ten: The Grave." *Batman* #617.
September. New York: DC Comics.
Meltzer, Brad, and Rags Morales. 2004. "House of Laws." *Identity Crisis* #2. July.
New York: DC Comics.
Moore, Alan, and Dave Gibbons. 1986–1987. *Watchmen*. 1- issue miniseries. Sep-
tember–October. New York: DC Comics.
Straczynski, J. Michael and John Romita Jr. 2001. "Stand Tall." *Amazing Spider-
Man* #36. New York: Marvel Comics.
Waid, Mark, and Alex Ross. 1996. *Kingdom Come*. Books 1–4. New York: DC
Comics.

BIBLIOGRAPHY

Beatty, Scott. 2002. *Superman: The Ultimate Guide to the Man of Steel*. London:
Dorling Kindersley.
Benton, Mike. 1989. *The Comic Book in America: An Illustrated History*. Dallas:
Taylor Publishing Company.
Brooker, Will. 2000. *Batman Unmasked: Analysing a Cultural Icon*. London:
Continuum.
Brooks, Peter. 1976. *The Melodramatic Imagination*. London: Yale University
Press.
Busiek, Kurt. 2004. "The JLA/Avengers You Never Saw." *Avengers/JLA Compen-
dium*. New York: DC Comics.
Campbell, Joseph. 1971 [1949]. *The Hero With a Thousand Faces*. Princeton, NJ:
Princeton University Press.
Cawelti, John. 1976. *Adventure, Mystery, and Romance: Formula Stories as Art
and Popular Culture*. Chicago and London: University of Chicago Press.
Daniels, Les. 1991. *Marvel: Five Fabulous Decades of the World's Greatest Com-
ics*. Harry N. Abrams: New York.
Eisner, Will. 1970. *Comics and Sequential Art*. New York: Kitchen Sink.
Feiffer, Jules. 2003 [1965]. *The Great Comic Book Heroes*. Washington: Fanta-
graphics Books.
Gerschick, T. J., and A. S. Miller, 1994. "Coming to Terms: Masculinity and Physi-
cal Disability." *Masculinities*, 2:349.
Goulart, Ron. 2000. *Comic Book Culture: An Illustrated History*. Portland, OR:
Collectors Press.
Harvey, Robert C. 1996. *The Art of the Comic Book: An Aesthetic History*. Jack-
son: University Press of Mississippi.
Heilman, R. B. 1968. *Tragedy and Melodrama: Versions of Experience*. London:
University of Washington Press.
Hyslop, Gabrielle. 1992. "Pixérécourt and the French Melodrama Debate: Instruct-
ing Boulevard Theatre Audiences." In *Melodrama*, James Redmond, ed. Cam-
bridge: Cambridge University Press.
Jacobs, L. 1993. "The Women's Picture and the Poetics of Melodrama." *Camera
Obscura*, 31:121–47.
Jones, Gerard. 2004. *Men of Tomorrow: Geeks, Gangsters, and the Birth of the
Comic Book*. New York: Basic Books.
Khoury, George. 2003. *The Extraordinary Works of Alan Moore*. Raleigh, NC:
TwoMorrows Publishing.

King, Stephen. 1986 [1981]. *Danse Macabre*. London: Futura.
Kill Bill: Volume Two. 2004. Quentin Tarantino, dir. Miramax Studios.
Klock, Geoff. 2002. *How to Read Superhero Comics and Why*. New York: Continuum.
Lee, Stan, and George Mair. 2003. *Excelsior! The Amazing Life of Stan Lee*. London: Pan Macmillan.
Lyotard, Jean-Francois. 1984. *The Postmodern Condition: A Report on Knowledge*. Manchester, UK: Manchester University Press.
McCloud, Scott. 1994. *Understanding Comics*. New York: Harper Perennial.
Millar, Mark. 2000. "O Brave New World!" *SFX Superhero Special*, 108–10.
Mullen, Mark. 1992. *Sympathetic Vibrations: The Politics of Antebellum Melodrama*. Los Angeles: University of California Press.
Murphy, R. 1990. *The Body Silent*. New York: Norton.
Nietzsche, Friedrich. 1968. *The Will to Power*. R. J. Hollingdale and Walter Kaufman, trans. New York: Vintage.
Pearson, Roberta E., and William Uricchio. 1991. *The Many Lives of the Batman: Critical Approaches to a Superhero and His Media*. New York: Routledge.
Pustz, Matthew. 1999. *Comic Book Culture Fanboys and True Believers*. Jackson: University Press of Mississippi.
Reitberger, Reinhold, and Wolfgang Fuchs. 1972. *Comics: Anatomy of a Mass Medium*. Nadia Fowler, trans. Boston: Little, Brown.
Reynolds, Richard. 1992. *Superheroes: A Modern Mythology*. London: B.T. Batsford Ltd.
Rogers, Mark Christiancy. 2003. *Beyond Bang! Pow! Zap!: Genre and the Evolution of the American Comic Book Industry*. Ann Arbor, MI: UMI.
Romita, John, Jr. 2004. "Sequential Thoughts." *Cinescape Comics*. November 11. http://www.cinescape.com/0/editorial.asp?aff_id=0&jump=back&obj_id=30299&this_cat=Comics (accessed: February 10 2005).
Ross, Alex. 2000. *Alex Ross Millennium Edition*. New York: Wizard Entertainment.
Singer, Ben. 2001. *Melodrama and Modernity: Early Sensational Cinema and Its Contexts*. New York: Columbia University Press.
Smith, Jerome. 1973. *Melodrama*. London: Methuen & Co. Ltd.
Steranko, James. 1970. *The Steranko History of Comics*. Reading, PA: Supergraphics.
Wright, Bradford W. 2001. *Comic Book Nation: The Transformation of Youth Culture in America*. Baltimore: Johns Hopkins University Press.

5 Baroque Mutants in the 21st Century?
Rethinking Genre Through the Superhero

Saige Walton

"It's not really a question of asserting that a cinematic genre is a vast single film, but rather seeing what one comes up with if one decides to treat it as such."

—Christian Metz.

Tucked into the pages of *Amazing Fantasy #15* (1962), Stan Lee and Steve Ditko's inaugural Spider-Man contains a panel in which teen dweeb Peter Parker feels his body changing at the molecular level. Having undergone that fateful radioactive spider bite and shifting towards the proportionate strength of a spider, he cries out: "What's happening to me? I feel—different! As though my entire body is charged with some sort of fantastic energy!" That panel got me thinking: about how energy defines all superhero bodies in their extraordinary capacity for undulating movement, flight, and exertion; about how energy, too, informs genre as a perpetually unfolding signification, loaded with unexpected possibility; and about how energy is a trait associated with the baroque and its illusionistic tensions between stasis and mutability. Indeed, Norman K. Klein's recent study of baroque special effects suggests that the desire to animate the immobile amounted to a kind of baroque-animated cinema of the seventeenth century (Klein 2004, 61).

And yet, alongside the baroque's illusionistic energy, in which perspectival tricks seemed to smash right through the ceiling, render flat surfaces curved, and reach achingly close to the divine, there was still time to pause, to catch your breath and take respite within the glow of an interior chapel. Instead of the exuberance of untethered movement, these chapels were spaces of enframed stasis relying on their "framing devices to hold you" (Klein 2004, 57). In the flux of the one against the many, the singular against the series, I began to think about how genre can work as a similar momentary pause within a larger, perhaps even ceaseless development. Like the pause offered by a chapel in a baroque church, the genre experience is a brief visitation; a peculiar type of stasis that draws upon its media 'framing' devices to hold you, encouraging the phenomenal precedence of this particular articulation before moving on, in pursuit of its own formation.

Unlike the more obvious seriality of comics and television, the notion of genre as cumulative or 'unending' is often overlooked, especially in terms of its baroque connotations. In his early semiotics of the cinema, Metz grafts cinematic genres to a vast, continuous system, hinting at their potentially infinite renewal. Genres exceed the materiality of each film, but each film exists as the smaller portion of a larger process, one that contributes to an ever-expanding "universe of meaning [that] includes a mass of signifying-units self-embedded *ad infinitum*" (Metz 1974, 124). What happens, though, when the snarls of generic signification unfurl across media, willfully traversing and absorbing the conventions of a range of genres, as the mobile signifier of the superhero does? Taking up the challenge that Metz issues and stretching genre into a *vast trans-media system*, this chapter argues for the 'baroque' basis of generic production. Rather than relegating the baroque to the parodic and/or degenerative end-state of a genre's development, I want to rethink or, in comic book terms, reboot the baroque's continuing relevance to genre theory. I argue that the baroque provides us with a means of accommodating the superhero's generic fluctuations and the capacity for alteration and cross-media renewal within all genres.

This essay concentrates on the moment of impact when superheroes and genre collide—FWAAM! SKRAKK! THOK!—as a serialized, baroque process cutting across comics and film, in particular. Today's media mutation of the superhero might be at an unprecedented level in its history, but the current filmic consolidation of the genre continues the baroque process of renewal. The *Spider-Man* series (Raimi 2002, 2004) suggests that, if anything, this renewal occurs at a technological level, by maintaining connections with its Marvel comics past while drawing attention to media reframings, through temporally heightened, filmic, and digital metamorphoses of the superhero. The cross-media dispersal of the superhero yields phenomenologically specific pleasures, though, which are experienced in fundamentally different terms in the exchange between comics and film.

RETHINKING THE BAROQUE

The idea that form—regardless of its medium—passes through a set of aesthetic stages before hitting the baroque stems from the French art critic Henri Focillon. In his *The Life of Forms in Art* (1934), Focillon proposed that forms are subject to constant, cyclical renewal; an idea that would considerably influence genre film theory. Style is the means by which forms are coordinated as they move through the ages of experimentation, classicism, refinement, and, finally, baroque. However, as ongoing processes of regeneration and renewal, styles defy the fixity of historical junctures because "form is inseparable from movement: forms are alive in that they are never immobile" (Molino in Focillon 1992, 10). Focillon, for instance, claims that the baroque "reveals identical traits existing as constants within the most diverse environments and periods of time" (Focillon 1992, 58). In this sense, he preempts a number of contemporary theorists of the baroque and neobaroque (Deleuze, Calabrese, Bal, Klein, Ndalianis) who view the 'baroque' as radiating beyond the historical confines of the seventeenth century, in which spectacular cultural production was harnessed to meet the ends of the church/absolutist state.[1] Like any good superhero, the baroque's origin story has given way to a divergent, unwieldy mass of signification; so entangled in multiple circulations of meaning that it is no longer reducible to a definitive point in history. To take up the words of art historian Mieke Bal, the baroque inhabits something of a "preposterous history" seeping into the contemporary through the reiteration of citation (Bal 1999, 1). Once approached along these transhistorical lines, the baroque, like Focillon's forms in art, yields potential "metamorphoses [that] endlessly begin anew" (Focillon, 1992, 44).

Focillon paves the way for engaging with the baroque in our own era and for its metamorphic reactivation in a range of media guises, especially through genre. As a formal concept, the 'baroque' infiltrated film studies through the domain of genre. During the fifties, French film theorist André Bazin was amongst the first to begin work on individual Hollywood genres, looking to the morphologies of art history (classical/baroque) to understand genre-as-form. In his essay on the 'evolution' of the Hollywood western, Bazin identified unexpected mutations in the fifties western or what he termed the "superwestern" (Bazin 1971, 150). The superwestern is a "western that would be ashamed to be just itself, [it] looks for additional interest to justify its existence—an aesthetic, social, moral, psychological, political or erotic interest, in short, some quality extrinsic to the genre . . ." (Bazin 1971, 150–51). Films like *Shane* (Stevens, 1953) and *High Noon* (Zimmerman, 1952) are the baroque embellishments of a classical ideal, typified for Bazin by *Stagecoach* (Ford, 1939). The superwestern had surpassed previous expectations of the genre, redirecting its energies towards social realism, overt stylization, and the amplification of preexisting conventions to ensure its postwar survival. Bazin might have viewed the superwestern somewhat damningly as the baroque's formal 'decadence' creeping into cinematic classicism, but he puts forth a dynamic conceptualization of genre hinging on open rather than closed approaches to form. Even more intriguing is how he stumbles onto the potentially 'super' operations of genre—its mobile capacity to exceed previous frames of reference and its willingness to embrace "some quality extrinsic to the genre," a fact that is nowhere more evident than in the consolidation of the superhero genre (Bazin 1971, 151).

Arguably, the superhero genre is one of the most historically hybrid of all, embracing and redeploying conventions derived from other genres as well as other media throughout its comic book development. The inception of the superhero was, in itself, a decidedly intergeneric and transmedia formation, with DC incorporating sensational content gleaned from thirties and forties pulp fiction (the Shadow, the Spider) while capital-izing on the ready-made distribution network of the pulps (Raphael and Spurgeon 2003, 11).[2] Despite the success enjoyed by early DC heavy-weights such as Superman and Batman, they were still forced to jostle and compete with the attention given to other genres: westerns, romance, crime, and, most significantly, horror titles.[3] If DC effectively assimilated the thrills and anxieties of the pulps, that was nothing on the Marvel onslaught of the sixties, which extended Stan Lee's earlier ventures like *Strange Tales, Worlds of Fantasy,* and *Journey Into Mystery* (drawn by Jack Kirby) as rampaging monster/alien/science-fiction titles to new and untold levels (Raphael and Spurgeon 2003, 62). At the helm of the Mar-vel superheroes revival, Lee would favor the overt blending of multiple genres (comedy, romance, melodrama, science-fiction, horror), stretching the superhero universe to accommodate a wide variety of tales and the visual dynamism of its artists, typified by Kirby's panel-bursting slugfests: its superhero teams (Fantastic Four, X-Men), freak accidents, and genetic mutations that, in themselves, bordered on horror (Hulk, Spider-Man) were set against largely pedestrian backdrops, playing on stylistic clashes between the fantastic and a 'real' urban environment.[45]

Little wonder, then, that Marvel would continue to invoke diverse con-ventions, gesturing towards the elastic possibilities and mutable realities that mark the superhero genre. Generic reinvention in Spider-Man alone saw the wall crawler meet up with the "Not Ready For Prime-Time Play-ers" in *Marvel Team-Ups* #74 (1978), otherwise known as the original cast of *Saturday Night Live.* During the nineties, Marvel launched its series of possible futures in their *2099* titles; the short-lived *Spider-Man 2009* focused on Miguel O'Hara, a genetic engineer studying the original Spider-Man, who's able to produce webbing from his own body after a mutation accident. A dramatic rehauling of continuity in the 'Ben Reilly' cloning saga saw nearly twenty years of comics' history ascribed to a Spider-Man clone. The new/old Spider-Man shift created *The Sensational Spider-Man* and a brief renaming of Marvel's lead title *The Amazing Scarlet Spider,* after Reilly's own costumed identity. Needless to say, fans rebelled at the impostor and the exiled Parker returned to the titles. The cloning debacle was ultimately blamed on the machinations of Norman Osborn, the origi-nal Green Goblin, rather than Marvel's misguided attempt at forging a new Spider-Man continuity. Introduced in 2000, *Ultimate Spider-Man* proved far more successful, completely rebooting decades of built-up Spider-Man continuity by returning to the origin story of the superhero all over again and appealing to a whole new generation of readers, while still maintaining its existing titles to satisfy long-term fans.

In a recent discussion of Alan Moore's *Watchmen* (1986), Sean Carney suggests that acts of comic book revisionism present the implicitly baroque thesis that "everything is happening simultaneously" (Carney, 2006).[6] Indeed, as I will argue, when it comes to genre, everything *is* happening simultaneously; hastening backwards and forwards to reiterate the past while moving in unforeseen directions through regulated variance and media renewal. Revisionism aside, though, *Watchmen* inherits a comic book history in which superheroes have *always* been prone to assimilating the conventions of other genres, inhabiting multiple (generic) realities at the same time—escaping the vibrant hues of the panel to spill out into other media and into our world.

In *Amazing Spider-Men* (Vol. 2) #36, Spider-Man has even narrated the September 11 attacks on the World Trade Center. A double splash page features him pausing on top of a New York building, stricken with horror, as he watches the towers collapse, dwarfed by the burning debris. "Where were you?! How could you let this happen?" fleeing New Yorkers ask their resident superhero. Depicted alongside 9/11 rescue and emergency workers, Spider-Man joins the muscle-bound Thing, Thor, Mr. Fantastic, and other Marvel superheroes and supervillains at the ground-zero site. Admittedly, Straczynski and Romita Jr. lost me with this one, around about the time that Doctor Doom started to cry in the rubble. Sometimes, the superhero genre just never knows when to stay put.

Rebooting Genre and the Energy Within

A number of theorists characterize the baroque as an investment in the infinite through movement, deferral, and the serialized drawing out of formation, often visualized as the spatialization of time. For Giancarlo Maiorino, the historical baroque revels in sequential representations—an episodic mentality that gives voice to the labor of its own media artistry. Poets like Lope de Vega write sonnets on the composition of sonnets; painter Diego Velázquez foregrounds different stages of completion in his paintings; the Spanish novelist Miguel Cervantes writes prologues about the act of writing prologues and has his Don Quixote encounter other fictional characters claiming to inhabit the same realm as the reader. Dutch artist Johannes Vermeer returns time and time again to the same fragmented portion of the same setting in the same room. In these quotidian "chambers of being," each painting unravels as an episodic sequence, and yet, the narrative recurrence of everyday acts and the return to the same setting allude to the ongoing consciousness of his characters (Maiorino 1990, 111).

An episodic unraveling of meaning has also come to inform baroque theory. Gilles Deleuze, in his philosophical study of Leibniz and the baroque, recognizes the baroque as a transhistorical experience—as present in mathematics and philosophy as it is within art, science, and costume design. For Deleuze, via Leibniz, the baroque refers to a recognizable operative function or trait, which is expressed in the visually resonant concept of the fold. According to Deleuze, the baroque fold strives to invent "the infinite work or process. The problem is not how to finish a fold but how to continue it, to have it go through the ceiling, how to bring it to infinity" (Deleuze

1993, 34–35). Like the baroque, genre, too, shares little interest in the narrative telos of fulfillment. Such an open, restlessly mobile appreciation of genre has been embraced more recently by genre critics like Steve Neale and Rick Altman, who argue for genre as the unfolding process of meaning rather than the stasis of a definitive conclusion. Their interpretation of genre complements a baroque "interest [which] concentrates not on being but on happening" (Wölfflin 1922, 10).

German literary historian and theorist Hans Robert Jauss reveals a strikingly 'baroque' sensibility, too, in his insistence on the nonteleological dimensions of generic production. For Jauss, genres are the episodic realization of a perpetually deferred series, which is precisely what makes for their somewhat 'tricky' refusal to adhere to a predetermined list of elements. But the expanding and unexpectedly mutable nature of generic signification only emerges if we are prepared to "destabilize the classical concept of genre" by resisting fixed, essential features in which form remains forever closed in on itself (Jauss 1982, 79).

The simultaneously open/closed workings of a genre are best embodied in Jauss's "horizon of expectation," which links generic production to its outside effect on the viewer (Jauss 1982, 88). In their continual founding and alteration of our horizon of expectation, genres reveal a process-like development that is entirely consistent with the baroque (see Ndalianis 2003). *Spider-Man 2*, for instance, draws us into a dense, multilayered frame of reference that encourages interpretation across a series of texts

Figure 5.1 Doctor Octopus in *Spiderman 2* (2004). © Columbia/Marvel/The Kobal Collection.

drawn from comics and film, held together by the genres that unite them. Retelling the comic book origin of one of Spider-Man's more famously dogged nemeses, Dr. Otto Octavius/Doc Ock, *Spider-Man 2* plays the horror underpinning the superhero genre to the hilt. After Octavius's "smart" mechanical arms are accidentally welded to his spine, he is rushed to the hospital and the generic framework of horror takes over. "Anybody here take shop-class?" a surgeon jokes, primed to slice through Ock's metal. Rearing up from behind, Ock's prostheses assume a life of their own by seeking out and catching hold of the hospital workers, crushing them to death and dragging them (fingernails and all) along the floor, screaming off into the darkness—Doc Ock is launched on the unsuspecting city in the blatant guise of horror.

A number of elements in this scene call up very specific horizons of expectation. Raimi, of course, had made his directorial name from the low-budget, cult-horror films of the *Evil Dead* series (1987, 1983, 1993). Ock's rampage in the hospital recalls the possessed cabin in the woods of the first two *Evil Dead* films, which had referred back to the stalker/slasher tradition of horror, involving gruesome murders in a contained space. The camera's hyperkinetic antics and high-speed tracking shots (a Raimi trademark) that herald the demon's arrival in the *Evil Dead* series are replayed as the viewpoint of Doc Ock's own mechanical (and demonic) arms. The sudden appearance of a chain saw (in an antiseptic operating room?) alludes to the wisecracking hero of the *Evil Dead* series, Ash, played by the fabulous Bruce Campbell. Ash later went on to adopt the chain saw as his very own prosthetic extension and a signature weapon of choice against demons. When the chain saw suddenly materializes in *Spider-Man 2*, its joking, highly intertextual resonance with the *Evil Dead* series implies a similar staging of events. But this is definitely not the same chain saw, nor is the poor, nameless schmo who wields it the "groovy" Ash. Instead, our last glimpse of him is the severed arm that drops to the hospital floor, a reprisal of Ash's own amputation in *Evil Dead 2*, laughingly staged beneath a copy of *A Farwell to Arms*.

As Jauss argues it, the continual founding/alteration of our subjective horizons occurs through "the relationship of the individual text to the succession of texts that forms the genre" (Jauss 1982, 88). In this scene, our own horizon of expectation encircles us in the production of generic meaning. As Ndalianis (2003) argues with regard to the *Evil Dead* films, the previous stylistic/thematic "rules of the game" that Raimi had established in these films are called upon once more in *Spider-Man 2*. However, this time, those rules do not exist to battle demons but to retell the origin of Doc Ock, by teasing out all the horrific elements of his supervillain transformation. In a porous and baroque fashion, we are deliberately enfolded into the generic process of formation, as it plays itself out as a game about genre, about intertextuality and the process of its own meaning production. *Spider-Man 2* offers yet another contribution to the polysemic assemblage of the superhero, where the preestablished rules of the (generic) game might be "varied, corrected, altered, or even just reproduced" in the shift from comics to film (Jauss 1982, 23). The recycling of horror, Raimi's stylistic practice, and the superhero's own cross-generic inclinations play a set of games with its audience that move beyond the self-contained, diegetic world of *Spider-Man 2*. As a simultaneously open/closed process, these games depend on our own subjective horizon of expectation: our level of familiarity with Raimi, with horror, with Lee's own enthusiasm for angry behemoths as it led to a litany of sixties Marvel characters, and with the first film.[7]

The *Spider-Man* films complicate the superhero's hybridity still further, in their allusions to the western and musical genres. As Scott Bukatman has argued, the performative and kinetic body of the superhero owes considerable debt to the Hollywood musical. Not only is the overt kinesis of the superhero's body a fixture of the genre; a costumed flair for the theatrical indicates just how much "superheroes all hide in plain sight" despite or more precisely because of their supposedly 'secret' identities (Bukatman 2003, 213).[8] I would add that the *Spider-Man* series tends to collapse the generic traditions of the musical *and* the western into its rendition of the superhero. The Hollywood western has always relied on the well-nigh supernatural powers that weapons could hold in the right hands; heroes displayed a startling sensitivity to their environment, being able to sense the slightest movement of those around in the lead up to the duel. *Spider-Man* inherits the duel structure of the western in which the contrasting values of civilization versus wilderness (order versus chaos) must be resolved through violent scenarios of action. However, that generic confrontation is reworked as a choreographed, public duel between the Green Goblin and Spider-Man, played out across the upper reaches of New York. Encountering each other in a burning building, the energetic display of the superhero's hyperkinetic body again takes center stage. Superheroes no longer require the external draw of the weapon that had dominated the western; the almost-superhuman properties of the weapon have been internalized and the body is the only vehicle needed for flight and fight. Dodging the Goblin's blows, Spider-Man spins in rhythmic slow motion against oncoming shards of metal, skirting the burning debris. Leaping backwards and forwards, twisting and turning, Spider-Man maneuvers the Goblin away only to pull him back with his web. This elaborate choreography of tension and release indicates the dynamism of the musical, as Bukatman has noted, at the same time as it is matched with the energy of the western.

According to Leo Braudy, both westerns and musicals are structured around the "private energy" of individual bodies. These bodies resolve narrative conflict in the larger community; a regeneration that occurs through acts of violence or the spontaneity of music and dance (Braudy 1977, 139–40). The musical hinges on "the assertion of personal force; in the western, by the assertion of personal morality" (Braudy 1977, 140). Analyzing the cross-generic resonance between these seemingly disparate genres, Braudy raises a shared convention that is also fundamental to the superhero—that of the hidden/secret self. He asserts that westerns and musicals reveal a strong fascination with the hidden self. In the western, that hidden self is not amenable to social integration because it is founded on antisocial acts of violence; in musicals, the hidden self rebels against the staid inhibitions of the social community through the potentially libratory movement of song and dance. This shared fascination with the hidden self is, significantly, expressed as a dual identity. In the Astaire and Rogers pairings of thirties musicals, for instance, Astaire's hidden self resides in a "musical-comedy exuberance beneath the fashionable dinner-jacketed cool of the social surface" (Braudy 1977, 139).

The *Spider-Man* series combines the morality of the western, outlaw hero with the freedom of movement offered by the musical—shifting from an everyday persona into the undulating energy of costumed-bodies-in-motion, played out in violent combat. In *Spider-Man*, Parker is taking photographs in one moment and running to unbutton his shirt the next, as his hidden costume (the energy within) signals the transition. In *Spider-Man 2*, he shifts into that hidden self whenever the occasion (and his conscience) demands: knocked off his scooter by a police car chase, he is next seen as Spider-Man, pirouetting through the narrow spaces of oncoming traffic only to shift back to Parker, once more, and the awkwardness of his everyday life. Just as the thirties musicals of Astaire worked as spontaneous eruptions of energy, as Astaire's body almost seemed to liquefy as walk became dance and speech became the lilting cadence of song, the superhero spontaneously shifts into the private energy of his or her hidden self on demand. If the secret identity of the superhero makes for an irresolvable narrative struggle, it also allows for the fluidity with which they move between their dual selves, not to mention the ease with which they readily adopt the conventions of other genres.

REWORKING ORIGINS, RETHINKING GENRE THEORY

Given the baroque's porous attitude towards visual/narrative framing devices, it is surprising that it was *ever* used to abet self-contained, teleological approaches to genre. Not only does this seem utterly un-baroque at a formal level; the evolutionary model assumes that a self-reflexivity towards generic conventions or even its own media occurs only during the latter stages of generic development. In his *Hollywood Genres*, Thomas Schatz draws upon Focillon and Metz's evolutionary discussion of the western (classic-parody-contestation-critique) to argue for the evolutionary model of cinematic genres. According to Schatz, genres undergo a series of stages, hastening towards patterns of increasing self-consciousness at the end of their life span. Saturation leads us into the final phase of a genre—its baroque stage—where conventions are parodied or subverted and "we no longer look through the form . . . rather we look at the form itself" (Schatz 1981, 37–38).

Superhero comics are already positioned according to a set of historical phases, so the 'evolution' argument seems ready-made and available in discrete plastic pockets. We could kick off with the Golden Age comics of DC and move onto the Silver Age consolidation of the genre, dominated by Marvel; and, having mapped out the evolution (and consequent bodily mutation of superheroes) up to this point, the works of Frank Miller, Alan Moore, Mark Waid, Grant Morrison in the eighties, nineties, and beyond could signal another point of rupture—as the formation of the so-called revisionary superhero narrative. If there is a baroque phase to the superhero, then surely it lies in the revisionism of superhero comics. Introducing Miller's *Dark Knight Returns*, Moore himself wrote that the radical restructuring of a superhero's most recognizable elements means that "everything is exactly the same, except for the fact that it's all totally different" (Moore in Miller, 1986). Morrison, in particular, is famous for his borderline-psychotic ensemble of characters, indebted to the mutant bodies/teen neuroses of Marvel's *X-Men* but who inhabit a dizzying array of metaphysical realms and are forced to battle constant slippages of reality rather than mundane, embodied villains in his *Doom Patrol* series.[9]

However, the superhero's longstanding intergeneric dialogue with noir, horror, comedy, fantasy, and science fiction (to name only a few) and its reconfigurations of the past frustrate enclosed, evolutionary approaches to genre. All genres thrive on repetition but this is especially the case for the serialized adventures of the superhero. Reinterpretation has become nothing short of a practical strategy of survival for the comics, where the revisiting of origins, retroactive changes, and outright narrative reversals predominate. Given the long-standing strategies of reinscription and reinvention that pervade superhero comics, I cannot agree with Geoff Klock that revisionist comics signal the "birth of self-consciousness in the superhero narrative" (Klock 2002, 3). Fixed distinctions between past and present incarnations of a genre seriously underestimate the flexibility of the generic process, as if cross-generic contagion or self-reflexivity hits at a particular moment in time in which it is assumed that *now* we produce, consume, and recognize this media reflexivity (read: baroque, postclassical, or postmodern periods). However, during the fifties, DC had relaunched a new 'improved' version of its popular forties series, *The Flash*; the success of the Flash's revival ushered in ongoing trends for adopting characters from past continuity and refashioning them for contemporary audiences— those readers who remembered the older comics could enjoy the reflexive pleasure of connecting emerging plotlines to their memory of earlier titles (Raphael and Spurgeon 2003, 76). Instead of positioning revisionist superhero comics as a later evolutionary stage in the genre in which meaning production now derives from their "relationship with other comics,"

I would suggest that revisionist comics point to the already mutable possibilities of the superhero; possibilities that were always present because of the ongoing renewal that a genre can undergo (Klock 2002, 25). Maintaining historical and theoretical divisions between the genres of earlier eras of production as opposed to revisionist/postclassical/postmodern periods (in which the former is virtually forced to assume qualities of closure, while the latter instigates formal traits of reflexivity, instability, and hybridity) results from 'fixed' interpretations of genre—a fixity obtained at the expense of the actual industrial practices of the comics/film industry and at the expense of a genre's own baroque process.[10]

In a similar manner, Schatz's interpretation of genre admits variation and change but within the predetermined terms of an internal evolution. Genres are deemed closed, continuous systems that invariably pursue their own internal dictates (Schatz 1981, 29). By way of Focillon, Schatz sets up a model of generic evolution that can be distilled down to yet another progression from the not-yet-classical towards the no-longer-classical. Genres effectively shift between the selfsame aesthetic binary that dates back to art historian Heinrich Wölfflin—that of classical and baroque, where freedom of form is gauged between the dual poles of stylistic clarity and formal self-reflexivity.[11] Reducing genres to self-enclosed histories, Schatz rarely acknowledges the possibility of generic hybrids, paying little attention to the many and varied interactions that go on between the histories of individual genres and admitting parody and critique only in their later stages. The evolutionary model of genre (teleological, self-contained, utterly predictable) has the unfortunate effect of belying its anthropomorphic basis, for, as Rick Altman reasons, biological evolution actually "depends heavily on unexpected mutation," whereas Schatz furthers homogeneity and "dwells on entirely predictable patterns" (Altman 1999, 22). By contrast, superheroes teach us never to underestimate the energetic power of mutation. For Schatz, genres hasten towards a penultimate, baroque state (and where do they go from there?), but the evolutionary model ignores what Bazin recognized in the fifties: the 'super' potential of all genres to, at any stage, start incorporating elements that had not as yet existed in their *always emergent framework*.

The more evocative connections between the baroque and genre have either been misinterpreted or ignored in genre theory, necessitating a return to Focillon. He suggests that all forms adopt the "system of the series" in which discontinuous elements are outlined, rhythmical and a stable, symmetrical space guards its borders from metamorphosis (Focillon 1992, 67). However, the system of the series spawns the "system of the labyrinth" where beginnings and endings are hidden, indeed, "perpetually sliding away to a secret objective of its own" (Focillon 1992, 67). I would argue that genres effectively unite the system of the series with the system of the labyrinth. The repetition of previous conventions is rhythmically matched with a baroque predilection for the infinite, as the energy of generic forms moves simultaneously outwards and inwards.

In *Quoting Caravaggio,* Mieke Bal claims a preposterous history for the baroque that is achieved through the innate 'stickiness' of semiotics and the reiteration of citation. Reveling in tensions between present expression and the power of the past, she links the baroque to the ongoing transformation of sign systems. In her terms, the "word does not forget where it has been . . . and neither does the image . . . [although] every use of pre-existing material changes it" (Bal 1999, 100). Bal's take on the baroque holds intriguing possibilities for a more mobile appreciation of generic form, one that resonates far more with Focillon than that of Schatz. As Focillon writes, all forms engage in dialogue with those of the past, but new forms "bear the trace, the multiple traces of the old forms among which they have taken place . . . the finished work is always only the provisionally definitive version of a series that is in theory infinite" (Focillon 1992, 27). In generic terms, then, past conventions cling to the baroque process of citation as each generic articulation 'sticks' to a preexisting framework, but that framework will be extended by adding new elements or altering the existing citations of the past (Neale 1990, 56).

Evolutionary interpretations of genre are limited in their premise that generic self-awareness, media reflexivity, or cross-generic contagion only comes about with a postclassical/baroque decadence. However, in his analysis of Batman, Jim Collins usefully identifies the superhero as an enduring cultural artifact or a "mobile signifier" that has been dispersed across media, in tandem with superhero comics (Collins 1991, 167). Subject to constant reactivation in comics, film, and television, multiple and even conflicting narratives of the same figure are available simultaneously. During the forties alone, the DC flagship filtered through syndicated newspaper strips, radio, animated cartoons, and live-action movie serials with Superman, Batman, Captain Marvel, and Spy-Smasher. The pronounced cultural dispersal of the superhero, as it has historically veered from comics into other cross-media productions, means that superheroes end up working more along the lines of a generic "encyclopedia rather than a dictionary, as an assemblage of intertextual [and transmedia] representations rather than a set definition" (Collins 1991, 180).

Superhero films are obviously indebted to comics but rework this inheritance through cinematic and digital renewal. As Ndalianis points out, the real success of current cross-media entertainment synergies lies in drawing on a pool of common images, characters, and narrative situations while differentiating each product as a virtuoso performance, one that asserts the precedence of its own articulation (Ndalianis 2004). As a mobile sign, historically dispersed across an array of media, the superhero continues to forge strong thematic links between comics and film, in particular. Each incarnation is 'framed' according to its specific media, pausing to offer interrelated but phenomenologically distinct articulations of the superhero assemblage.

DIGITIZING THE PANEL

The *Spider-Man* films are prefaced as a superhero assemblage—the cross-media collaboration between Columbia Pictures (a subsidiary of Sony Entertainment) and Marvel. Marvel's logo encapsulates the look and tactility of comics through its rapid presentation of brightly colored panels that collide with speech bubbles, text, captions, and images. *Spider-Man* showcases the visual signatures of Spider-Man and his filmic transition through the credits' rotating series of spider webs: DNA strands mesh with the spiderwebs, hinting at genetic rather than radioactive mutation; teasing flashes of red and blue appear before Spider-Man's costume is revealed; the Green Goblin's helmet emerges and the webs start to connect the chasms between skyscrapers. "Who am I?" a voice-over asks, soon to be identified as resident New York nerd Peter Parker. "You sure you want to know?" Fading into a small web spun into the corner of a building (a tiny portent of the massive visual shifts in scale to come), Parker's voice-over continues: "The story of my life is not for the faint of heart . . . if somebody told you I was just your average, ordinary guy . . . somebody lied." Parker's narration gestures towards the abiding fascination of the origin story in superhero comics as well as its subsequent retellings across media. In this version of Spider-Man, though, Parker is bitten by a genetically modified 'super' spider, attaining a set of arachnid powers that will, ultimately, be revealed to us in overtly digital terms: the ability to jump, to spin intricate webs of tensile strength, and a reflex system so fast it borders on precognition.

Like other filmic adaptations of superhero comics (X-Men, Hulk, Batman, again), the origin story of the superhero becomes a convenient means of consolidating multiple decades of comic book continuity—beginnings, powers, their visual transformation, enemies, and weaknesses. For the sixties Marvel set, the origin was the all-important moment in which ordinary bodies were severed from the everyday laws of physics through untimely acts of mutation. The metamorphic source was never simple and usually the result of scientific/technological alteration: a radioactive spider bite; a scientist irradiated by gamma radiation or the bombardment of cosmic rays, just outside Earth's atmosphere. In the Marvel universe, becoming a superhero was more the result of accidental collision than a birthright or choice, as it was for DC. *Spider-Man* looks to the much repeated origin story as the filmic inception of the superhero body and its visual transition into a costume/dual identity. Costume can, in turn, be intimately linked to the origin story: Superman's cape, for instance, is woven from the blanket that swaddled him on his journey to Earth from Krypton. The more enduring supervillains possess their own origin stories (even if they attain them retroactively) and costumes that reflect their own physical capabilities (Reynolds 1992, 49).

Both comics and film continue to look to the origin story as an effective means of rebranding the superhero, according to the interpretation of different creative teams (Reynolds 1992, 48). Each retelling might bring another facet of the character to light or, in superhero films, a different techno-presentation. In *Spider-Man 2*, the opening credits adopt the formal sensibility of comics but recapitulate the superhero's filmic origin: the same shifting series of webs appear as oscillating red, white, and blue panels synthesize the events of the first film. Ending on the final frame of *Spider-Man* with Parker walking away from MJ, newly committed to his superhero identity, a different narrative conflict can begin. Loosely based on the "Spider-Man No More" saga of Lee and Romita's *Amazing Spider-man* #50 (1967), the real struggle of *Spider-Man 2* is to maintain the body's integrity by reconciling the split between Parker/Spider-Man, seen in the two suits (one super!) hanging in the superhero's closet. Forging a nexus of repetition/variation with each other and the comics, the *Spider-Man* films point to the perpetually infinite renewal of genre. In adhering to the infinite seriality of the baroque rather than an evolutionary and discrete set of aesthetic stages, the superhero genre inhabits a vast, transmedia system where the "elements and conventions of a genre are always *in* play rather than being *re-played*" (Neale 1990, 56). Harking back to Focillon's perpetually mobile life of forms, genres can be seen as at once closed (the system of the series) and open (the system of the labyrinth), revealing an inherently open attitude towards intergeneric dialogue and their own construction. Recursively moving inwards through the repetition of preestablished conventions, genres also hasten outwards, tapping into variance through the hidden beginnings/endings of cross-media circulation.

Spider-Man draws attention to the varying spatiotemporal sensibilities of comics and film. Sitting down to sketch his superhero costume possibilities, Parker rules out a utility belt, concentrating on a symbol that will externalize his spider-derived strength, opting for more color than the black garb he initially designs (which, by no mere coincidence, resembles the black costume introduced in *Marvel Super Heroes Secret Wars* #84/85, worn by Spider-Man until it was found that it possessed strange, alien powers and became the supervillain, Venom). Parker sits drawing in the foreground while these costume sketches are displayed in the background; words appear, written across the image and a large drawn spider is superimposed over Parker; after dissolving into a close-up of MJ's eyes, a three-dimensional spider crawls across the screen. Tracking out of a hollow, spider-shaped symbol, the camera shows us Parker within, at his desk. The frame splits again, with Parker on one side and the inking of the costume in its telltale red and blue colors on the other. Eventually, Parker reveals his final sketch—the signature Spider-Man costume—positioned in a state of readiness, with his web behind him in an almost nostalgic recollection of

Ditko. *Spider-Man* evokes the sixties comic book origins of its superhero, yet it makes us aware of just how different the filmic retelling of superhero comics can be. That difference is not only registered in terms of narrative or continuity but through varying phenomenological modes of engagement: that is, the way a genre will *feel and move differently* in its cross-media dispersal.

To call up the multilayered, highly textured feel of comics necessitates montage or a splitting of the spatiotemporal coherence of the cinematic frame. In his formal analysis of comics, Scott McCloud points out how "space does for comics what time does for film" (McCloud 1994, 7). I am looking at the closing pages of *Amazing Spider-Man (Vol. 2)* #38 in which Aunt May confronts Parker about his superhero 'secret': it certainly *looks* like Spider-Man's filmic flight through the city, vaulting from streetscape to skyscraper. Previously seen in a smaller panel, Spider-Man's mournfully perched atop a fire escape, a darkened silhouette that flares white and blue around the edges ("our great power, and our responsibility, is to one another . . . I won't let her down. . . ."); the following splash page showcases Spider-Man in midflight, a storm of full color, as New York recedes behind him at the height of propulsion (" . . . ever"). And yet, despite their longstanding exchange, film and comics retain unique formal qualities that are not easily translatable. Film frames inhabit the same space of the screen whereas each panel occupies a series of spaces on the page that the reader can trace, visibly, through time and space: Parker takes his superhero costume out; Aunt May leaves his apartment; Spider-Man's poised at the edge of building in one panel and airborne across rooftops the next. As McCloud notes, the sequential organization of comic panels deliberately fractures time and space, whereas film (at least when it adheres to the demands of classical narrative continuity) coherently replaces one image with the next (McCloud 1994, 7).

Comics have often been designated 'cinematic' because of their alteration of image scale. Artists like Kirby or Eisner would incorporate bold filmic techniques to frame dramatic moments, employing staccato rhythms to explode and reassemble the panel, punching villains out beyond the panel's borders or toying with page layouts, rendering the comics page a storytelling unit in its own right (Raphael and Spurgeon 2003, 22). The idea of separating comics from their entrenched cross-media resonance seems not only naïve in a historical sense but increasingly redundant, especially in the face of someone like Morrison, who strives for a comic book 'feel' adopted from a slew of media experiences. As Morrison hyperbolically puts it, the "frantic glow of the image crazed hallucination of 21st century media culture" means that comics do not just look to filmic inspiration but to sources as varied as percussive rhythms and digital editing effects to cut the action (Morrison in Klock 2002, 174). If "perception is a cut-up" to adopt his words, the modality of perceptual experience is lost by the collapse of comics into film or vice versa (Morrison in Shaviro 2006). The disjunctive mix of words and flow of images, lines, color, and rhythmic panel alteration in comics does not have to work like film nor are comics a small-scale version of cinema, held at your fingertips.

For this reason, I hesitate to categorize comics as a "mono-sensory" medium, as McCloud has done (McCloud 1994, 89). According to McCloud, comics work as an exclusively visual presentation that relies upon sight to invoke our other bodily senses: written sound effects and speech bubbles create the effect of sonic atmosphere while panel-breaking and flowing lines represent continuous, dynamic movement. A heightened reliance on vision is certainly true of comics, but film theorists such as Linda Williams, Vivian Sobchack, and Laura Marks have all forcefully argued against the disjunctive isolation of vision from our other bodily senses in the cinema.[12] Vision can involve bodily experiences of tactility that are not metaphorically situated but felt, palpably, in the embodied and material contact that reverberates between screen and spectator, as if you were brushing up against the surface of another body. To quote Williams, touch can never be disassociated from sight because sight comes already laden with "carnal density and tactility" (Williams 1995, 15). Intersensory experience is no less the case for comics, which also involve tactility at the literal level of form.

Like Williams, I would suggest that comics yield inherently tactile plea-sures as much as they do visual/narrative ones. That tactility comes from a very real sense of their manual handling; the density of their material weight (glossy or newsprint, hardcover anthology, or mass-produced paper) as it is turned at your fingertips; not only as you pour back over titles to study panel details but also as comics are exchanged and passed around, between academics trying to make comics a critical field of study, between fans, between friends—or, perhaps, quite pointedly *not* passed around. Because there are certain comics owned by a friend of mine that will never be retrieved from their plastic pockets and I will not (and I *am* quoting here, believe me) be "getting [my] hands on them" (end quote). The very fact that I will never be getting my hands on certain titles speaks volumes about how comics can be enjoyed through touch as well as vision. In fact, the act of reading comics practically forces the embodied intertwining of our senses. Because comics are structured around the simultaneous copresence of mul-tiple panels, their juxtaposition of images/text/panels (not to mention their shifting configurations) forces the eye to scan and to kinesthetically follow the narrative trajectory. Suspended between the stasis of the panel and the spatiotemporal movement of the sequence, comics work according to tac-tile and fully embodied modes of vision (Collins 1991, 173). Optical scan-ning in tandem with manual handling helps enact the flow of comics, as an intersensory experience that is physically performed by their reader, rather than technologically externalized, as it is in the superhero film.

The transition from comic book panel to cinematic frame forges a differ-ent articulation of the superhero genre, which is experienced in phenomenologically distinct terms. Discussing the "gutter" as the structuring "heart" of comics, McCloud rightly points to the alchemy of the gutter as the catalyst for narrative motion; as the blank space existing between panels, the gutter is the primary "agent of change, time and motion" in comics, with the reader connecting even the most disparate of images and mentally mobilizing panel transitions (McCloud 1994, 65–66). By contrast, the *Spider-Man* films present the superhero as a heightened temporal experience made possible by digital effects. The odd duration of the gutter is externalized in unedited, explicitly visual terms—the haptics of handling and reading superhero comics is translated into the haptical excesses of the camera. This heightened temporal presentation of the superhero, rendering visible that which was once contained in the limbo space of the gutter, is a refashioning of the panel *and* the cinematic frame. Whereas *Hulk* (Lee, 2003) expresses spatiotemporal fracturing through recurring multiscreen montage and digitally animated transitions that elegantly choreograph the image, the *Spider-Man* films revel in a heightened temporality, allowed by digital imaging.

The Marvel comics often presented the tingling of Parker's spider-sense through wavy lines emanating from his skull or by the superimposition of Spidey's mask. However, for the superhero's filmic transition, effects teams sought the realization of his spider-sense as a digitally "expanded moment" (Fordham 2000, 34). In *Spider-Man*, the digitally expanded moment takes over during Parker's fight with high-school bully Flash Thompson; the camera inhabits an indeterminate temporality, seemingly stopping time in and around Parker. As the articulation of Spider-Man's sensory point of view, the camera hones in on random details (a spit-wad, a buzzing housefly, a

Figure 5.2 Spiderman performs his digital acrobatics in *Spiderman* (2002). © Columbia/Marvel/The Kobal Collection.

passing paper airplane) in its search for danger. The unanchored ability to traverse the scene and isolate objects while still staying in motion was achievable only by layering computer-generated imagery into real-time photography (Fordham 2000, 34). Digital close-ups endowed a strong sense of detail and texture to objects, allowing the camera to track into rather than circulate around them. Even as the scene reverts back to real time, the digital acceleration of Parker's body remains—now, only digital effects can register the sheer energy of the superhero's body and no mere human body's visible *enough* to function as a superhero in film. In *Spider-Man 2*, the digital articulation of the superhero extends to the Manhattan cityscape itself. As Doc Ock and Spider-Man battle it out on a hurtling train, the expanded moment begins with a close-up of Spider-Man (as a live blue-screen element) but hastens through space and time to a train buffer, overhanging the East River (Fordham 2004, 87–88). Roving through swaths of entirely virtual environments, *Spider-Man 2* gestures towards the increasingly digital world that our filmic superheroes now inhabit.

Heightening the temporality of the gutter through the possibilities of digital imaging assumes pride of place in Spider-Man's concluding flight that bookends each film. Once again, a different phenomenological feel to the genre is created by presenting the haptics of reading comics through the visual dynamism of externalized, digital movement. Continuous and unedited takes follow Spider-Man through the gridded troughs of New York, reworking the panel in digital terms, as if the superhero trailed his own agile cameraman in tow (Fordham 2000, 22). For both films, in fact, effects teams sifted through hundreds of Spider-Man comic books to select poses that properly reflected the comics' presentation and the sheer range of Spider-Man's movement (Fordham 2000, 2004). As Bukatman has established, such an explicit phenomenology of movement has always defined the superhero genre (2003). Although Spider-Man proper exists as an entirely computer-generated entity in these sequences, his swinging arcs from the pavement to fifty stories above street level were animated to hit a succession of existing comic book poses, reconfiguring the panel as an unbroken, temporal traversal of the city. The *Spider-Man* films effectively create a *new* phenomenology of movement—in "a way that none of us could move," as Raimi himself states—that only digital imaging can supply, even as it remains indebted to the history of Marvel for Spider-Man's digital performance (Raimi in Fordham 2000, 20).

AND NOW . . .

Superheroes know, better than most, the baroque potential that genres yield— their innate capacity for moving through the sticky citations of the past to forge difference and regulated variety, while gesturing outwards to include us in the production of meaning or to incorporate intergeneric dialogue. The cross-media circulation of the superhero assemblage continues the infinite process of the baroque, renewed across media and experienced in different phenomenological terms within the *Spider-Man* films. Indeed, as Christine Buci-Glucksmann once so elegantly wrote, in the baroque, "history becomes a representation . . . subject to dramatization or theatricalisation of the sensible world in a backward movement toward a missing centre" (Buci-Glucksmann 1994, 134). Still, even in its recursive movement back through the dense and accumulated significations of the past, the baroque knows no weight of sadness nor nostalgic longing for a singular origin story, as if a somehow more 'correct' version of its own formal history existed. In a baroque world, there really is "no centre, no site, no fixed point of reference . . . the centre is everywhere and the circumference nowhere . . . the fixed point has become [just] a point-of-view" (Buci-Glucksmann 1994, 134). Mutants to the core, superheroes embrace the unexpected fluctuations of their genre (as just one of many possible points of view) as well as the potentially infinite and baroque process of renewal that informs the generic production: a parallel world, a possible future, retroactive erasures, reconfigured continuity, a different media-framing device to hold you. . . . Move. Pause. Reboot. Everything is happening, simultaneously.

NOTES

1. See Deleuze (1993) on the baroque as philosophy; Mieke Bal (1999) on the baroque as embodied semiotics; Norman K. Klein (2004) on the ongoing history of baroque special effects; Omar Calabrese (1992) on the neobaroque logic of contemporary/postmodern culture; and Angela Ndalianis (2004) on the neobaroque organization of the entertainment industry. I retain the term *baroque* within the contemporary not only because of its historical resonance but to avoid the slippage of the neobaroque into the postmodern.
2. See Will Brooker (2000) and his detailed study of Batman, for instance, for the sheer range of generic and cross-media influences that led to Bob Kane's creation.
3. Entertaining Comics (EC) proved to be one of the industry's most popular, artistically influential competitors by the early fifties, publishing in multiple genres at a time in which superhero comics were experiencing a postwar lull. Known for its graphic output, EC specialized in crime, war, science fiction, and horror, until the Comics Code Authority was introduced to regulate content, leading to the demise of many EC titles. See Raphael and Spurgeon (2003).
4. Lee is also said to be responsible for creating an in-house Marvel style cutting across artists; he formulated the plot in conversation with Marvel artists, but it would be left to the artist to visualize the plot and break down the panel organization. See Raphael and Spurgeon (2003) for more on the Marvel working method.
5. Also see Geoff Klock (2002) for another in-depth discussion of Moore's revisionism and Watchmen.
6. Prior to the Marvel superheroes revival, Lee and Kirby were heavily involved in gigantic monster stories, featuring characters like the immense dragon Fin

Fang Foom and others with increasingly ridiculous names. See Gross (2002) and Raphael and Spurgeon (2003) for more on Lee's background.

7. See Scott Bukatman's essay, in this volume, which extends his previous work on the superhero as a performing and performative body.

8. See my Grant Morrison expert, Martyn Pedler, in this volume for more of Morrison's wacky antics.

9. Tag Gallagher's (1986) wonderful work on the "hyperconsciousness" of the pre-1910 western is a fine example of how generic reflexivity can and indeed should be historically and industrially situated in genre criticism.

10. Wölfflin (1922) was one of the earliest art historians to take the baroque 'seriously' by setting up the systematic comparison between baroque/classical form that still holds sway to this day.

11. For examples of a sensuous and fully embodied film criticism, refer to Sobchack (2004) and on visual tactility see Marks (2002) and Williams (1995).

12. Williams is, admittedly, discussing early forms of mass-produced pornography but her equally weighted attention to both the generic body-on-display as well as how our viewing bodies are engaged by varying media technologies remains significant to the superhero.

COMIC BOOKS

Lee, Stan. 1987. *Marvel Masterworks Presents Amazing Spider-Man.* New York: Marvel Comics (reprints *Amazing Spider-Man #1–10 & Amazing Fantasy, #15*).

Miller, Frank. 1986. *The Dark Knight Returns.* New York: DC Comics.

Moore, Alan. 1986–87. *Watchmen.* New York: DC Comics.

Straczynski, J. Michael. *The Amazing Spider-Man: Revelations.* New York: Marvel. (reprints *Amazing Spider-Man (Vol. 2) #36–39*).

BIBLIOGRAPHY

Altman, Rick. 1999. *Film/Genre.* London: BFI.

Bal, Mieke. 1999. *Quoting Caravaggio: Contemporary Art, Preposterous History.* Chicago and London: University of Chicago Press.

Bazin, André. 1971. "The Evolution of the Western." *What Is Cinema?* Vol. 2, 149–57. Berkeley, Los Angeles, and London: University of California Press.

Braudy, Leo. 1977. *The World in a Frame: What We See in Film.* New York: Anchor/Doubleday.

Brooker, Will. 2000. *Batman Unmasked: Analyzing a Cultural Icon.* London and New York: Continuum.

Buci-Glucksmann, Christine. 1994. *Baroque Reason: The Aesthetics of Modernity.* London: Sage.

Bukatman, Scott. 2003. "The Boys in the Hoods: A Song of the Urban Superhero (2000)." *Matters of Gravity: Special Effects and Supermen in the 20th Century*, 184–223. Durham, NC, and London: Duke University Press.

Calabrese, Omar. 1992. *Neo-Baroque: A Sign of the Times.* Princeton, NJ: Princeton University Press.

Carney, Sean. 2006. "The Tides of History: Alan Moore's Historiographic Vision." *ImageTexT*, 2(2): 1–59. http://www.english.ufl.edu/imagetext/archives/v2_2/carney/ (accessed May 11, 2006).

Collins, Jim. 1991. "Batman: The Movie, Narrative: The Hyperconscious." In *The Many Lives of the Batman: Critical Approaches to a Superhero and His Media*, ed. Roberta E. Pearson and William Uricchio, 64–181. New York: Routledge.

Deleuze, Gilles. 1993. *The Fold: Leibniz and the Baroque.* Minneapolis: University of Minnesota Press.

Focillon, Henri. 1992. *The Life of Forms in Art.* London: Zone Books. (Originally published 1934)

Fordham, Joe. 2000. "Spin City." *Cinefex*, 90: 15–54, 123–30.

Fordham, Joe. 2004. "Armed and Dangerous." *Cinefex*, 99: 69–89, 123–24.

Gallagher, Tag. 1986. "Shoot-out at the Genre Corral: Problems in the 'Evolution' of the Western." In *Film Genre Reader*, 202–16, ed. Barry Keith Grant. Austin: University of Texas Press.

Gross, Edward. 2002. *Spider-Man Confidential: From Comic Book Icon to Hollywood Hero.* New York: Hyperion.

Jauss, Hans Robert. 1982. *Toward an Aesthetic of Reception.* Minneapolis: University of Minnesota Press.

Klein, Norman K. 2004. *The Vatican to Vegas: A History of Special Effects.* New York and London: The New Press.

Klock, Geoff. 2002. *How to Read Superhero Comics and Why.* New York: Continuum.

Maiorino, Giancarlo. 1990. *The Cornucopian Mind and the Baroque Unity of the Arts.* University Park, PA, and London: Pennsylvania State University Press.

Marks, Laura U. 2002. *Touch: Sensuous Theory and Multisensory Media.* Minneapolis and London: University of Minnesota Press.

McCloud, Scott. 1994. *Understanding Comics: The Invisible Art.* New York: Harper.

Metz, Christian. 1974. *Language and Cinema.* The Hague: Mouton & Co. N.V.

Ndalianis, Angela. 2003. "The Rules of the Game: *Evil Dead II* . . . Meet Thy *Doom.*" In *Hop on Pop: The Politics and Pleasures of Popular Cultures,* eds. Henry Jenkins, Tara McPherson, and Jane Shattuc. Durham, NC: Duke University Press.

Ndalianis, Angela. 2004. *Neo-Baroque Aesthetics and Contemporary Entertainment.* Cambridge and London: MIT Press.

Neale, Steve. 1990. "Questions of Genre." *Screen,* 31(1): 45–66.

Raphael, Jordan, and Thomas Spurgeon. 2003. *Stan Lee and the Rise and Fall of the American Comic Book.* Chicago: Chicago Review Press.

Reynolds, Richard. 1992. *Superheroes: A Modern Mythology.* Jackson: University Press of Mississippi.

Schatz, Thomas. 1981. *Hollywood Genres: Formulas, Filmmaking and the Studio System.* New York: McGraw Hill.

Shaviro, Steven. 2006. *Doom Patrols, Chapter 1: Grant Morrison.* http://www.dhalgren.com/Doom/ch01.html (accessed May 11, 2006).

Sobchack, Vivian. 2004. *Carnal Thoughts: Embodiment and Moving Image Culture.* Berkeley, Los Angeles, and London: University of California Press.

Williams, Linda. 1995. "Corporealized Observers: Visual Pornographies and the Carnal Density of Vision." In *Fugitive Images: From Photography to Video*, 3–41, ed. Patrice Petro,. Bloomington: Indiana University Press.

Part II

"We Act Normal, Mom! I Want to Be Normal!"[1]

Superbodies, Identities, and Fans

6 Secret Identity Politics

Scott Bukatman

This essay begins with the once-fugitive pleasures of reading superhero comics, and then moves to consider the extrapolated pleasures of actually *being* a superhero. It is also, in many ways, part of the never-ending battle to find the right language to discuss the fragile niche that fantasy occupies within the waking experience of the real. In search of a rhetoric, I've recently been drawn to writings about popular music—pop music and superhero comics having much in common. For example, Sasha Frere-Jones wrote in a recent issue of *The New Yorker*, "Popular music is good at using speed, physical sensation, and unmediated language to articulate the experience of life" (Frere-Jones 2005). And this finds an echo in Geoffrey O'Brien's evocation of late 60s culture (including Jim Steranko's comics): "Wherever you looked there was the possibility of finding the aesthetic essentials—urgency, immensity of perspective, speed, depth, improvisational ecstasy, and unwobbling balance—if possible, all at the same time, packed into a single image or a single note" (O'Brien 2004a,120).

We'll get back to "improvisational ecstasy," but let's stick with speed for a moment. Speed is of course a fundament of comics, whose visual language has a number of ways of representing rapid motion. The medium itself scans quickly. And superheroes possess speed in abundance—the Flash is not alone. Vast speeds and scales, fundaments of the sublime, structure the superhero universe. In the words of Reed Richards (who ought to know), "Everything is moving faster now! The universe has become a vast kaleidoscope of light and sound!" *Speed and scale*. But right now I want to emphasize a different speed and scale; *not* the scale of Negative Zones and multiverses; *not* the speed of the Flash, Superman, or the Silver Surfer. Instead, the *speed* is 45 rpm, and the *scale* is the pop single of the 1960s.

Geoffrey O'Brien has written wonderfully about film, fiction, music, and comics. A strong autobiographical streak cuts through his writing, but not only is this not unusual in writing about comics, it's practically required. One of the best recent books to appear on comics, Sean Howe's anthology *Give Our Regards to the Atomsmashers!,* is at least as dedicated to the authors' encounters with comics as it is to the comics themselves. It's interesting to compare two of O'Brien's writings that only *seem* to be about different topics—his *Atomsmashers* piece on the insistent groovi-ness of Steranko's *Nick Fury: Agent of Shield*, and his earlier essay on the insistent grooviness of the songs of Burt Bacharach.

The essay on Bacharach is partly about the pop single itself. While long-form recordings had significantly reshaped the ambitions of composers and performers, O'Brien notes that the 45 returned to the aesthetic of an iso-lated song. With albums, "Listeners could go about their housework or their lovemaking for as long as half an hour without having to change the music," while the brevity of the 45 forced one's attention (O'Brien 2004c, 17). An appealing analogy can be drawn between the 45 and the single issue of a comic book. O'Brien discusses them in similar terms: the 45 represented "a fragile metaphysic" in which "the gossamer speculations of a stretched-out and mostly pleasurable afternoon—was sustained, perhaps provoked, by certain chord changes" (O'Brien 2004b, 232) while comics "came and went like those otherwise uneventful summer afternoons that the reading of them so thoroughly occupied" (O'Brien 2004a, 124). The similarity is not too surprising given that they belong to the same time—not just summer afternoons, but the mid-60s (or thereabouts), as well as *adolescence* (or thereabouts . . .). Like a couple of teenagers sprawled on the floor in their pastel capris, spinning platters on a portable player with a mass of black disks and garishly-colored sleeves arrayed about them, com-ics readers, too, are often pictured surrounded by the latest hits, pursuing their pleasures with a similarly alluring informality.

The 45—like the comic book, we might add—"could be held in the palm of the hand yet contained immeasurable depths and reaches, a per-fect mystical object made of cheap plastic"—or even cheaper paper. And, like a comic, the 45 "focused attention unwaveringly on a solitary object of desire . . . If the B side turned out to be worthy of attention that was merely a gratuitous extra fillip"—a welcome bonus that we might compare to discovering a surprisingly compelling backup feature about Asgard, the Elongated Man, or the Bizarro World. (O'Brien 2004c, 17)

(A question, though. Just when the heck did "the comic book" get demoted to the lowly "pamphlet" in the language of fans and collectors? The willful repression of the term *comic book* has been staggering—first we were reminded that it wasn't comical (OK? OK?); now it isn't even a *book*. But let's go with that for a moment. A Marvel comic of the 1960s rarely offered an entirely self-contained story—it would usually be one issue of a longer story arc, set in a universe populated with recurring characters in overlapping sagas. Despite the involuted, incomplete status of an individual comic, however, a single issue possessed its own charms and powers com-pelling enough to sustain repeated readings in every conceivable position.)

O'Brien returns repeatedly to the self-contained space carved out by the 45: "Listening to a 45 was a separate act, preceded by careful selection and attended by reverently close attention. Each was judged by how completely and unpredictably it mapped a reality in its allotted playing time. The best carved vast stretches out of that limited duration, while the worst felt interminable even at a minute and a half" (O'Brien 2004c, 17–18). I think that in this formulation of O'Brien's, *listening* constitutes something more totalizing than *reading*, but the compactness of the comic book—its brevity, pace, and punch—turn the reading experience into something akin to listening: more of a sensory engagement than a purely cognitive processing. Of course, listening to singles (or even albums) also contains aspects of looking and reading: liner notes, lyrics, photos, and other desiderata were fundamental to the experience (and distinguish it from today's iPod culture). Comics lacked the sonic dimension—for which they compensated with the bombast of lettered sound effects—but were as textural as they were textual. Nearly any issue of *Fantastic Four*, which I began reading somewhere around 1967 or 8, indeed "carved vast stretches" out of their "limited duration." I'm looking at the awesome cover of *FF* #77, with Psychoman wielding (or merged with) a Kirbyoid machine whose intricacies mark the architecture of the composition, within which we see glimpses of all the action somehow contained on the twenty pages within. Lo, even the mighty Galactus and the mercurial Silver Surfer are but small elements of the burgeoning whole! (Stan Lee's rhetoric really is the only language adequate to these images).

O'Brien evokes comics as "a dream that could be shared, passed around, that did not dissolve on waking" (2004a, 122–23). Comics and pop music need to be shared; to listen or read is to participate in a community of implied or actual like-minded connoisseurs, like the guys hanging out at the record shop in *High Fidelity*. Songs, perhaps, have a more intimate edge than comics, linked as they are to the heady dreams of pure love and love lost. "The song is the place where perfection stays," writes O'Brien, "a shared space"—shared between lovers this time rather than chums—"one degree removed from this world" (O'Brien 2004a, 202). But one should not entirely underestimate the intimacy of the superhero comic, and Marvel's in particular, which whispered and buzzed with uncontainable emotions and energies. Christopher Sorrentino, in his *Atomsmashers* essay, describes the private/public realm of superhero readers: "the satisfaction of identifying with the lone heroes of Marvel, of embracing their stark emotional seclusion, shoulder to shoulder with a group of fellow adherents" (Sorrentino 2004, 69). DC comics had recurring villains and occasional crossovers, but Marvel built a *universe* of superheroes and true believers. And washing over it all, the voice of Stan Lee, the Murray the K of the comics industry, the babbling disk jockey whose alliterative patter bound the whole *megillah* together and cajoled the willing reader into a sense of participation.

In a 2005 review/essay, John Updike discussed the child-centered novels of Stephen Millhauser, Jonathan Lethem, Jonathan Safran Foer, and others whom he notes "have devoted their most ambitious and energetic efforts to detailing the fervent hobbies and the intoxicating overdoses on popular culture, the estrangement and the dependence that characterize contemporary American childhood." He proposes that:

> Childhood's new viability as novelistic ground may signal a shift in the very nature of being a human being, considered anthropologically as a recipient and continuer of tribal myths, beliefs, and strictures. Older novelists . . . portrayed the pained shedding of this traditional baggage; the newer novelists, having inherited almost no set beliefs from their liberal, distracted middle-class parents, see childhood as the place where one invents the baggage—totems, rituals, lessons to live by—of a solitary one-person tribe. (Updike 2005)

We move to adulthood, passing among the signifiers of popular culture, choosing or being chosen by certain images that offer certain (or uncertain) possibilities, that resonate within the one-person tribes as well as larger communities of fanboys and friends.

What Updike identifies as the need to invent the baggage of one's later life also lies at the core of the comics themselves, especially through their obsession with *the origin story* ("origin"—a word learned from superhero comics). Origin stories are told and retold, often by the character himself (and often *to* himself). "If the *bildungsroman* is the passage from childhood to maturity," John Hodgman wrote, with characteristic dryness, in a *New York Times* article about comics, "then the origin story is a shorter trip, from childhood to a prolonged immaturity" (Hodgman 2005). This is a bit mean, but not wrong. Maturity is held in abeyance by the superhero comic, and perhaps nowhere more so than with the "adult" superheroes of the 1980s with their more emphatically traumatic "origins." Hodgman notes that all readers of superhero comics, which he refers to as "the still disreputable muscle that drives the medium," know "the seductions of the origin story. There are many strengths of serialized storytelling, but resolution is not one of them. Death, of course, is never final in a comic." Thus, "Beginnings are where it's at, where the story hums with the irony and compact power of the novel" (Hodgman is clearly a member of the superhero tribe, which, for me, tempers his sarcasm).

SUPERHERO AND/AS AUTOBIOGRAPHY

Perhaps it was Jules Feiffer's *The Great Comic Book Heroes* that began weaving the web which connected the actions on the page to the adventures of reading or creating them. The book recalls acts of reading within a savvy community. Jonathan Lethem has described a shift from a slightly older generation of writers' interest in the metamorphic possibilities of comic strips (writers such as Jay Cantor, Stephen Millhauser, and Tom de Haven) to the more recent fascination/obsession with comic books, superhero comic in particular, in novels by Chabon and Lethem himself (Lethem 2003). With this generation—somewhere between baby boomer and Gen X—the superhero comic becomes a fundament of childhood, a crucial scenography against which one's own origin took shape (or flight). Comics become a crucial site of escape to, rather than escape from, a protected terrain of self-definition (assuming one is a certain kind of adolescent boy), and this extends beyond literary figures and the essayists of *Atomsmashers!* to the "alternate universe" of academia. David Carrier's *Aesthetics of Comics* features a charming kid on the cover absorbed in a comic book; it's a picture of Carrier in earlier days. Will Brooker's dissertation on Batman is partly a saga about writing a dissertation on Batman. Henry Jenkins has discussed the death of his mother in the context of his world of comics reading. And my own writing on superheroes remains heavily invested (overinvested, they tell me) in an autobiographical questing—discovering new territory, taking flight, moving (if not moving on).

Meanwhile, autobiographical comics, which had arisen as a virulent rejection of the monomythical irreality of the superhero universe (for the tip of that iceberg, see work by Crumb, Pekar, Spiegelman, Doucet, or Brown), began to edge back towards the world of caped crusaders and supermen. (I am using the term *autobiography* loosely to incorporate naturalist comics sagas about people much like the authors themselves—low-rent twenty-somethings struggling to survive within a mundane world of first loves and dead-end day jobs.) Superman returns in Chris Ware's work as a despairing figure gone to seed and possibly suicide. By now this overlap constitutes its own subgenre, not only in independently published anthology titles like *Project Superior* but also in work published by Marvel and DC, such as Peter Bagge's *The Megalomaniacal Spider-Man*. In an afterword to a recent rerelease of *Batman: Year One*, the artist David Mazzuchelli appropriates images from Batman comics to articulate his own deep connection to the character ("It's an omen! I shall become a comic book artist!"). Steven Seagle's script for *It's a Bird . . .* tells the story of a reluctant Seagle being offered the chance to write Superman, which leads to a set of riffs on the character's definition and significance. Like *Maus, It's a Bird . . .* explores the author's relationship to his father, a Holocaust survivor in one, a man struck down by Huntington's chorea in the other. A recent essay by Jonathan Franzen in *The New Yorker* tried, perhaps a bit too hard, to interweave family history with an appreciation of Charles Schulz's Peanuts.

Much of this has already been brilliantly skewered by Patricia Storm's online comic strip "The Adventures of Lethem & Chabon." In response to a cry for help ("It's my boyfriend! He's lost all interest in reading fiction! Nothing inspires him. Nothing sparks his imagination, nothing connects to his masculine sensibilities!"), the "dynamic literary duo" swoop down to save the day: "With us on your shelves you'll have action, drama, intrigue, male-bonding and self-discovery, and, of course, that most important element in contemporary fiction for the modern male intellectual—comics, dude!" "Yeah, Yeah! I'm re-connecting to my über manly self! Life made total sense back when I read comics!!" (Franzen is presented as a desperate wannabe, still babbling about Peanuts).

O'Brien writes that "we appreciated the liberty that comics gave us: we were free to move in and out of what we could see was an illusion. We could allow it to be as real as we wanted it to be; we could dissolve it at will" (O'Brien 2004a, 123). The opulent fantasy realm of superhero comics was a realm of performance, of performance as liberation, of performance as a self-conscious exercise. Superheroes offered not just escape but a phenomenology of escape. "What they were supposed to be about dissolved if you thought about it too much: the mysteries of secret origins . . . the possibility of suddenly acquiring an alternate body or entering a parallel dimension" (O'Brien 2004a, 124). It is this phenomenon of the *alternate body* that I'd like to consider, by way of another detour through music; this time, the musical.

THE PHENOMENON OF THE ALTERNATE BODY

The superhero can be understood as visually, kinetically, and even verbally performative. The visual element is the most obvious; the iconography of superheroes depends upon costumes and masks. Batman's dark garb, which owes more than a little to such earlier pulp prototypes as the Shadow and the Spider, is atypical in that it is designed for hiding—in general, superhero costumes are a means of putting the body out there, on display. And even Batman's costume is designed, as the latest film reminds us, to control the theatrics of self-display, the quick-change art of surprise entrances and exits. But for the most part, superheroes hide in plain sight, and with the exception of Superman (and his semilibelous cousin Captain Marvel) and Wonder Woman (are masked women too direct a threat?), the classic heroes announce their "hidden" nature though the vehicle of the mask. (How does anyone even know that Superman *has* a secret identity?) The mask can be as large as a cowl or a mere hint of the harlequin's diamond pattern, but it was, for many years, a constant of the genre. Wendy Doniger has written that "Putting on a mask gets us closer to one self and farther from another, and so does taking off the mask" (Doniger 2005, 231), and we can therefore infer that superheroes have an innate *investment*—which means, after all, *to dress*—in "the infinite regress of self-discovery" (Doniger 2005, 232). I don't think it's overly generous to claim that the superhero can be seen to embody some fluidity of self, despite a strong countertendency towards reification and stasis (see my essay "X-Bodies: The Torment of the Mutant Superhero" [Bukatman 2003d]).

One effect of the mask is to hide the face, and thus the complex semiotics of facial expression has little place in superhero comics. I'm sure this has been a boon to fledgling artists of successive generations, but the implications are more far-reaching. The expressivity of the face is displaced onto an expressivity of body. Superheroes enact a full-bodied, kinetic performance, very comparable to bodily performance in musical films. Peter Wollen has argued that the virtuosity of the body in the musical preserved the visual expressiveness of the human body in the cinema, which Rudolf Arnheim feared would be repressed with the advent of talking pictures. Arnheim argued that the virtues of a given medium emerge from its limitations, including, in the case of cinema, the absence of depth, color, and sound. It is the absence of the *voice*, more than anything else, that underlies the term *silent film*, since these films included not just music, but often a battery of sound effects. A rhetoric of performative gesture had to arise to compensate for the missing voice; the body had to articulate what the verbal could not. In his analysis of *Singin' in the Rain* (Gene Kelly and Stanley Donen, 1952), Wollen argues that the musical, a genre that would seem most antithetical to silent cinema, inherited that expressive, gestural body, a body that must perform what it cannot say. Pantomime is elevated into dance (and what better example than *Singin' in the Rain*, which is about the moment when voice supplanted body in the cinematic imagination). Similarly, the superhero, denied the expressivity of the face, must rely on the boldness of bodily presentation. Posture, kinesis, and pose structure the theatrics of superheroic performance (while the grandiose posturing—and its verbal equivalent, *monologuing*—of a Lex Luthor or Dr. Doom further connects superhero comics to the traditions of nineteenth-century stage melodrama).

The soaring acrobatics of the increasingly popular genre of superhero films inherit the musical's emphasis on virtuoso bodily performance. And yet, ironically (a word I learned from *Batman* comics), in superhero films, the expressive body is increasingly a *digital* body. The cinematic superhero is a function of special effects, effects of programming (perhaps by some of the very boys that grew up dreaming of having a superhero body of their own). Science-fiction film has long been associated with new cinematic technologies (optical and mechanical effects, color, sound, widescreen, 3D). The cinematic apparatus, I've argued, mediates the alienation produced by unsettling new technologies (Bukatman 1993). The superhero film is surely a variant of the science-fiction film (it's almost a hybrid of science-fiction film and film musical). But the special effects of this wave of science-fiction films do not describe an environment and vehicular movement, as they did in the 1980s and early 90s, environments that translated electronic technologies to the terms of human vision (Bukatman 2003a, 2003c). Now the terrain of special effects is a human body that will become uncontainable, a body that not only expresses emotion and physical power (not to mention emotion and physical *trauma*), but also the more-human-than-human capabilities of digital imaging. (Something that has roots in earlier films—the liquid Terminator, for example.) The cinematic superhero is becoming the incarnation (ironic word!) of electronic technology;

Figure 6.1 Helen, a.k.a. Elastigirl from *The Incredibles* (2004), reveals the flexible potential of her body. © Disney/Pixar/The Kobal Collection.

digital beings that embody the fact of being digital. So after Tobey Maguire pulls Spider-Man's mask over his face the figure onscreen literally ceases to be Tobey Maguire, which has the unfortunate effect of fundamentally severing the connection between the inexpressive body and the liberated, expressive one. This might be one reason why *The Incredibles* (Brad Bird, 2004) succeeds so well as a superhero film: because the entire film is digital, everything belongs to a shared level of reality. And rather than disguise the digital by overemphasizing the simulacrum of the real, the design of the characters and decor depends upon exaggeration and caricature (Cane-maker 2004).

The Incredibles is the first film to tap into the subgenre of the 'banned superhero' narrative. In *Watchmen* (1986–87), *The Dark Knight Returns* (1986), *Astro City: The Dark Age* (2005), other titles too numerous to mention, and *The Incredibles*, superheroes have been literally legislated out of existence, or at least out of public view.[2] But circumstances will lead to their return, first as a clandestine force, and finally as public heroes. The saga of the banned superhero can be understood as a riff on the history of superhero comics themselves, which were effectively legislated out of exis-tence following the Wertham hearings in the 1950s,[3] but they also resonate on a further psychological level. Given that *Watchmen* and *Dark Knight* ushered in the 1980s shift to dark and gritty "adult" superheroes, banned superheroes are clear metaphors for the repression of superheroes in the cultural imaginations of adolescent comics fans, most of whom had to put superheroes aside and cathect onto more appropriate objects. The return of the banned superhero to a position of public adulation is thus easily under-stood as a heroic return of the repressed for the aging superhero reader yearning for past days of fantasized glory.

Within my own understanding of superheroes as flamboyant, perfor-mative figures, the saga of the banned superhero represents still another narrative of repression—what is being repressed is precisely *the expressive body*. An early scene of *The Incredibles* finds the superheroed family gathered around the dinner table. Helen Parr, aka the former Elastigirl (Figure 6.1), tries to feed the baby while mediating the bickering between the two older kids, Dash and Violet. Mr. Incredible, aka "Bob," who now works as a claims adjuster, is tuned out, by turns distracted and disinterested. As tensions mount, everyone's "repressed" abilities come into play: Bob absentmindedly carves through a plate and Dash and Violet fight with superspeed, invisibility, and force fields until Helen intervenes by elongating her arms to forcibly separate them (Helen is clearly stretched too thin). The characters are defined by the unique expressivity of their bodies. They are, in this scene, uncontained, *which is what the plot of the film is about*. In *Singin' in the Rain,* Kelly splashes around the puddles with abandon until, noticing the policeman, he freezes in midturn, eyes widened with the realization that he's busted. Similarly, when Bob lifts the family car over his head in frustrated rage, he is also brought up short by a witness: a little kid on a tricycle who watches in stunned awe. Just as Gene Kelly before him, Bob momentarily freezes before curbing his physical excess, relaxing back into the anonymity of the normal. The expressive body exists at the limits of the law, its virtuosity here constrained by socially ascribed limitations. The movement of the dancer frequently distinguishes him (and even in the musical, it usually is a him) from mortal men. In the "Singin' in the Rain" number Kelly exists on an entirely different plane from the rest of us all. He flouts convention (failing to come in out of the rain), his movements are sustainedly and increasingly outsized, and he reconfigures objects in the world as vehicles of his own euphoria (lamppost, umbrella, puddles). The appropriation of everyday objects (as in silent comedy) both anchors and dislocates the performer—while the familiar object connects the performer to reality— our reality—that reality is demonstrably, if temporarily, transformed by the action of the dance.

We might even see the end of Kelly's dance as a bit like a superhero's slipping back into the mundane world of his secret identity, melting back into the crowd, and in the context of superhero narratives, it's interesting to note that the dance is halted by the entry of a stone-faced and decidedly noneuphoric cop (Figure 6.2). Leo Braudy has written that "The cop who stops Kelly's exuberant dance in *Singin' in the Rain* asserts the reality of the streets and the rain and the lamppost Kelly is holding on to—a reality that is in opposition to what dance would like to make of the world" (Braudy 1976, 157). So there is some opposition here between the liberatory euphoria that marks the city as one's personal territory and the realm of law, which enforces the colder reality of social norms. Extend this to superheroes: It's no accident that urban superheroes become the outlaw vigilante—their performative display is fundamentally egotistical and antisocial (*and I don't mean either word pejoratively*).

Figure 6.2 Gene Kelly's character in *Singin' in the Rain* (1952) comes back down to Earth. *Singin' in the Rain* (dir. Donen/Kelly, 1952). © MGM/The Kobal Collection.

Philip Fisher has written about a shift in American urban fiction in the early part of the twentieth century that manifested itself narratively and linguistically. The "victim narratives" of the nineteenth century yielded to "narratives of bohemian freedom" as urban fiction moved "from accounts of suffering to catalogues of pleasure, from a picture of the city as a single-minded machine of indifference and destruction to a picture of the city as a small-scale field of daily opportunities for adventure, for experience, for excitement" (Fisher 1999, 239). It's not difficult to locate superhero comics within that shift—I have written about the fundamental connection between superheroes and cities elsewhere. Fisher's history takes him to 1940, two years after the appearance of Superman, when the superhero craze was in full flower. Superhero narratives retained some of the "victim narrative"—victims are, after all, the superhero's *raison d'etre*. But the emphasis isn't on the victims; it's on the daily adventures of the brash young heroes. Lois Lane does become something of a perpetual victim, but she's actually a very modern woman: a risk-taker, independent, a Hildy Johnson for the funny papers. For the most part, the victims are props, part of the metropolitan landscape, something to be rescued and forgotten. If Fisher isn't quite describing the superhero city, which must fundamentally remain a city of potential victims, it does open onto some aspects of superhero experience: the sensual pleasures of mobility, the daily encounter with adventure, the city as an exhilarating site of self-invention.

Fisher contends that "the city novel after 1920 places at the center figures determined to live, hungry for experience, amoral in their individualism and in their egotistic relation to the possibilities around them" (Fisher 1999, 243).[4] The superhero is fixated on pleasure: every day (or, for Batman, every night) offers more exhilaration, more opportunity for masquerade, street theater, performance pieces that contain the merest hint of risk. "The city as we see it reflected in the novel became, by 1920, a world rich in novelties of personality and fate" (Fisher 1999, 239). Superheroes are singular figures who often seem fated to become what they are ("It's an omen—I shall become *a bat!*"). If the comics are not exactly great American literature, they do belong to the *history* of literature, which was learning a lot from the bold, ephemeral realms of daily newspapers, popular song, radio, and the comics.

IMPROVISATIONAL ECSTASY

Leo Braudy writes that "The essence of the musical is the potential of the individual to free himself from inhibition at the same time that he retains a sense of limit and propriety in the very form of the liberating dance" (Braudy 1976, 140). I'm pretty sure that Braudy wasn't thinking of the Batusi (the dance invented by Arthur Murray for the *Batman* TV series of the 1960s), but superheroes also participate in a dance balancing liberation and constraint. A formal example of "limit and propriety" is provided by the panel borders themselves, which frame, delimit, and measure action, struggling to contain a body whose uncontainable presence forces its way past the frame lines. The law, together with moral codes (superheroes don't kill, for example), suggests voluntary limits to superheroic excess within which the character is free to trespass and do his super-thing. Superheroes are often defined by only a single power or two and have further levels of explicit constraint: Dr. Mid-Nite, who can see in the dark, works better at night; Green Lantern's power ring can only be charged for twenty-four hours and is useless against yellow stuff; and poor Hourman's limitations are pretty evident from his name (Hourman would probably *kill* for a twenty-four-hour charge, yellow b.s. or no yellow b.s.). Whenever a character like Superman becomes too powerful, new constraints must be engineered, through new plot elements (hence Kryptonite or, as Kevin Spacey would say, *Krrrrrrryptonite!*) or even complete reboots of the characters themselves (in titles like *Batman: Year One,* or *Ultimate Spider-Man*).

But limits, as Arnheim observed, can also be understood as opportunities. Because of these constraints, good superheroes need to be as adaptable as Gene Kelly, always alert to new ways of manifesting their talents. The agile superhero is something of a *bricoleur,* making something new out of the mundane objects of daily life. Elastigirl uses a lamppost to anchor herself for an inventive slingshot maneuver, and the tensile flexibility of a flagpole allows Spider-Man to break his fall and abet his next leap. Sometimes the body itself does the unexpected: Fred Astaire dances up a wall, while Spider-Man is referred to as "Wall-Crawler."

It's more than just performance that binds superheroic adventure and the musical—it's the nature of the performance. Superheroes and dancers turn in spontaneous, *improvisational* performances that reveal the dormant magic underlying the ordinary; a new urban physicality often coupled with an urbane wit, a mental dexterity equal to the physical dexterity. Few heroes simply rampage—the Hulk is a powerful but telling exception—they strategize and improvise. Even the Hulk manages to use the materials close to hand (his big green hand) in his battles: a tank, a building, a mountain, whatever's convenient. The genius of superhero improvisation is surely Plastic Man, created by Jack Cole, whose infinitely malleable corporeality fairly proclaims his ability to adapt. Plas snakes around an array of flying daggers, stretches upward to allow a hurtling car to pass beneath, and coils like a spring to absorb the impact of a falling safe. He makes suction cups of his feet, molds his face into anyone's likeness, oozes through the narrowest gaps—all the while keeping up a level of patter that makes the whole thing seem easy if not effortless. Plastic Man thematized what David Kunzle refers to as the *machined body* in late-nineteenth-century comics. "In its more industrially conscious phase, the comic strip imagines the human body violently flattened, stretched, twisted, kinked or wrapped around a spinning drum," Kunzle writes, noting that "both fear and fascination reside in the artist's rendering of the body as machined almost beyond recognition" (Kunzle 1990, 357). Plastic Man, like the comedic bodies of silent comedy two decades earlier, riffed off cultural anxieties about technology.

MONOLOGUIN' IN THE CITY OF TALK

Patter is fundamental to urban identity, and superheroes are nothing if not urban denizens (see Bukatman 2003b). Superman was a bit of a wiseacre in the early days, and Robin was strangely given to making puns while throwing punches. Plastic Man and the Spirit were wittier figures whose comical sidekicks emphasized the absurdism of the whole superhero thing. If, like the body in musical films, the body of Plastic Man was indebted to the pantomimic body of an earlier moment, his constant line of patter connected to still another performance tradition—vaudeville. Wisecracks during fight scenes also emphasized the nonchalance of the heroes, who always had enough surplus energy to summon up the appropriate *bon mot*. Spider-Man lifted wisecracking to a whole new level: "What do you try next, masked man?" asks one linguistically challenged foe. "Search me!" Spidey answers. "Maybe we could have a tiddly-wink contest!" (*Amazing Spider-Man* # 28, p. 12).

In *The Incredibles*, ex-superhero Frozone recounts, apparently not for the first time, one of his earlier adventures. Captured by Baron von Ruthless, Frozone's doom was assured. But, he asks rhetorically, "What does Baron von Ruthless do?" Mr. Incredible knows where this is going: "He starts monologuing." "He starts *monologuing*! . . . He starts monologuing! He starts like, this prepared speech about how *feeble* I am compared to him, how *inevitable* my defeat is, how the world will soon be his, yadda yadda yadda . . . I mean the guy has me on a silver platter and he won't *shut up*!"[5] Philip Fisher argues that the urban novels of the twentieth century produce what he calls a "city of talk." He notes the emergence of a "colloquial urban style." With characters created by later writers such as Miller, Salinger, and Bellow, "the tirade, the rant, and the spiel produce an overall style of self-performance" (Fisher 1999, 246). In other words, they start *mologuin'!*

Monologuing is only one instance of verbal performance in the world of superheroes, a world in which talk is surprisingly ubiquitous. The function of talk in superhero comics is manifold: in early comics, description could convey what amateurish drawing often could not—atmosphere and emotion—and a little talk could compress a lot of narrative information ("Lucky I heard this subway train coming, and could hold out till it got below me! Now that I'm riding out of range of the *Kryptonite rays*, I'll watch those crooks with my telescopic vision and have the police get them and their *Kryptonite*" [*Superman* #127, 8]). Talk also helped regulate the pace of the fight scenes, preventing them from scanning too quickly; the reader had to pause, briefly, to decode the words ("What th—?!") before moving on to the next panel. And talk, conveyed in solid speech balloons, let us in on the interior thoughts of the characters without the overly ruminative, existential connotations of the cloudy thought balloon. On the 1940 radio program, Bud Collyer signaled the switching of identities from Clark

Kent to Superman by dropping an octave midsentence: *This looks like a job—for SUPERMAN!*

An interesting book about urban language and subculture, David Maurer's *The Big Con*, appeared in 1940 (just when the superhero craze had really taken off). Maurer, a linguist, explores the rich insiders' language used by those economic tricksters known as confidence men. "Con men, as contrasted to other professional criminals, have creative imagination. Their proclivity for coining and using argot extends much beyond the necessary technical vocabulary" (Maurer 1995, 282). I would argue that another professional criminal class, supervillains, also have a proclivity for coining and using argot—they, too, have creative imagination.[6] Ominously named machines abound, and DC villains had a proclivity for choosing crimes based around elaborate puns.

Maurer notes the con man's emphasis on *monickers*, those "vastly connotative" names that become "even more suggestive when one knows the circumstances which lead to its acquisition" (Maurer 1995, 283)—names are thus connected to origin stories, as surely as Batman's. Some monickers referred to the crook's place of origin: *The Indiana Wonder, The Kenosha Kid*, or, perhaps, *Goom, the Thing From Planet X.* "Sometimes it reflects some striking physical characteristic of the bearer, as for instance, the Bow Legged Lip who had the misfortune to be both bow-legged and hare-lipped" (Maurer 283). The Sandman was a villain made of sand, and the Vulture not only had wings, but kind of an unfortunate nose. But superheroes also indulge in this same linguistic play: many of the X-Men have names commemorating their physical aberrations: the visored Cyclops, the winged Angel, the increasingly bestial Beast. Superhero and supervillain names are often based on resemblance: Spider-Man (who does whatever a spider can), Wolverine, the Joker. "By whatever manner the monicker is acquired," Maurer writes, "it fits the personality of the bearer well; . . . once it is applied and accepted, it becomes one of his few permanent possessions. It is tagged to him for life" (Maurer 284). He adds that it "is often the only permanent home a grifter has."[7] Supervillains come with one name, while superheroes, permitted the refuge of a secret identity, often have two, a duality that might hint that superheroes lack that "permanent possession" shared by even the lowliest grifters. It's interesting, then, that the more recent trend has been away from the assimilationist fantasy of secret identities and has moved toward purple- or green-skinned heroes contentedly hanging out together at their official headquarters, Bat Caves, Baxter Buildings, orbiting satellites, or schools for gifted mutants.[8]

Superheroes and villains were also gifted at argot formation: Batarangs, Fantasticars, Negative Zones, Phantom Zones, and image duplicator rays only begin to hint at the neologisms at work. Spider-Man was pretty good at argot formation: "I wish you had the courtesy to say ouch when I *klonk* you!" (*Amazing Spider-Man* 43, p. 11). "Klonk" has a nice ring to it; a comic book sound effect recontextualized as dialogue. Verbal performance, an improvisational mastery of language, is part of being a superhero.

Maurer writes that con men:

> Like to express all life-situations in argot, to give their sense of humor free play, to revolt against conventional language. Thus they have a large stock of words and idioms for expressing ideas . . . In fact, if con men find it necessary or convenient to discuss any topic for long, they will soon have an argot vocabulary pertaining to that particular subject. And one may rest assured that they will use good rich, roistering, ribald words which will radiate connotations for the initiate. (Maurer 1995, 282)

I'm struck by the way this applies to comic book *fans* as much as comic book *characters*.

LOOK AT ME

Philip Fisher writes that the outsider continued to be the central figure in urban fiction but is "no longer beaten down and destroyed, but free-spirited, improvisational, even joyfully marginal in the style of bohemian life" (Fisher 1999, 240). Given this, it becomes possible to read the eternally kvetching Spider-Man as perhaps the Holden Caulfield of superheroes, and certainly the Alexander Portnoy of superheroes.[9]

Philip Roth has written of the protagonist of Saul Bellow's 1953 novel *The Adventures of Augie March* that "Augie's is an ego triumphantly buoyed up and swept along by the strong current of life . . . The ego roar amplified by *Augie March's* prose exuberance Augie joyously articulates on the book's final page: 'Look at me, going everywhere!'" (Roth 2000). *Look at me*—the vigorous child's demand for attention, the cry of exhibitionistic confidence (Roth adds that in this novel, Bellow was "hipped on super-abundance"—a felicitous phrase in this context). Despite the Freudian baggage with which they are increasingly saddled, I think that superheroes actually constitute an ego roar of their own. Improvisational and alert, visually, verbally, kinetically performative, possessed of an ability to assert the fact of alternate ways of being in the world, the superhero exists as an exuberant means of writing the self onto the world; an exuberance shared by the seemingly solitary reader of comic books and the occasional academic. *Look at me, going everywhere!*

NOTES

1. Helen in *The Incredibles*.
2. It could be argued that this honor might actually fall to *X-2* (Bryan Singer 2003), although there mutants, more than superheroes, are the issue.

3. Henry Jenkins in conversation, June 2005.
4. He cites work by John Dos Passos, Henry Miller, and F. Scott Fitzgerald.
5. Note that "yadda yadda yadda" is a catch-phrase popularized on Seinfeld, a show about a stand-up comedian (or monologist) and his unabashedly urban friends, masters of the domains of tirades, rants, and spiels. . . .
6. For some reason they also surround themselves with low-grade morons for sidekicks (Snidely Whiplash: "Ah, Dudley Do-Right will certainly fall for my nefarious plan." Moron Sidekick: "I don't even know what nefarious means, boss!"). Gene Hackman's Lex Luthor (*Superman*, Richard Donner 1978) relished a good turn of phrase, while Marvel Comics provided an array of preening monologists: Dr. Doom, Loki, The Kingpin, and who knows how many others (a remarkably chatty bunch).
7. One con man, Yellow Kid Weil, derived his monicker from his favorite comic strip, and there's a Wildstorm superhero out there named Grifter.
8. I find it disconcerting that Superman and Batman call each other "Clark" and "Bruce" while in costume (I once complained about this online, to which someone replied, "And how about when they called each other 'Honey'— what was up with that?").
9. I like thinking about superheroes as bohemians, so associated have they become with nerds and squares. . . .

COMIC BOOKS

Miller, Frank, and David Mazzucchelli. 2005. *Batman: Year One Deluxe Edition.* New York: DC Comics.
Seagle, Steven T., and Teddy Christiansen. 2005. *It's a Bird . . .* New York: Vertigo.
Storms, Patricia. 2006. *The Amazing Adventures of Lethem & Chabon.* Available at: http://www.stormsillustration.com/L&C-1.html.

BIBLIOGRAPHY

Braudy, Leo. 1976. *The World in a Frame: What We See in Films.* Garden City, NJ: Anchor Press.
Brooker, Will. 2001. *Batman Unmasked: Analyzing a Cultural Icon.* New York: Continuum.
Bukatman, Scott. 1993. *Terminal Identity: The Virtual Subject in Postmodern Science Fiction.* Durham, NC: Duke University Press.
Bukatman, Scott. 2003a. "The Artificial Infinite: On Special Effects and the Sublime." In *Matters of Gravity: Special Effects and Supermen in the 20th Century.* Durham, NC: Duke University Press.
Bukatman, Scott. 2003b. "The Boys in the Hoods: A Song of the Urban Superhero." In *Matters of Gravity: Special Effects and Supermen in the 20th Century.* Durham, NC: Duke University Press.
Bukatman, Scott. 2003c. "The Ultimate Trip: Special Effects and Kaleidoscopic Perception." In *Matters of Gravity: Special Effects and Supermen in the 20th Century.* Durham, NC: Duke University Press.
Bukatman, Scott. 2003d. "X-Bodies: The Torment of the Mutant Superhero." In *Matters of Gravity: Special Effects and Supermen in the 20th Century.* Durham, NC: Duke University Press.

Canemaker, John. 2004. "A Part Human, Part Cartoon Species." *The New York Times*, October 3, Sections 2, 13.

Chabon, Michael. 2000. *The Amazing Adventures of Kavalier & Clay*. New York: Random House.

Doniger, Wendy. 2005. *The Woman Who Pretended to Be Who She Was: Myths of Self-Imitation*. New York: Oxford University Press.

Feiffer, Jules. 1965. *The Great Comic Book Heroes*. New York: The Dial Press.

Fisher, Philip. 1999. *Still the New World: American Literature in a Culture of Creative Destruction*. Cambridge, MA, and London: Harvard University Press.

Franzen, Jonathan. 2004. "The Comfort Zone." *The New Yorker,* November 29. http://www.newyorker.com/printables/fact/041129fa_fact.

Frere-Jones, Sasha. "Drablands." *The New Yorker,* May 9. http://www.newyorker.com/goingson/recordings/articles/050509gore_GOAT_recordings.

Hodgman, John. 2005. "Righteousness in Tights." *New York Times*, April 24. http://query.nytimes.com/gst/fullpage.html?res=9503E4DD103EF937A15757C0A9639C8B63.

Jenkins, Henry. Forthcoming. "Death-Defying Comics." In *Evocative Objects*, ed. Sherry Turkle.

Kunzle, David. 1990. *The History of the Comic Strip: The Nineteenth Century*, Vol. 2. Berkeley, Los Angeles, and Oxford: University of California Press.

Lethem, Jonathan. 2003. *Who's Afraid of Doctor Strange*. http://www.randomhouse.com/features/fortress/essay2.html.

Lethem, Jonathan. 2006. *The Fortress of Solitude: A Novel*. New York: Doubleday.

Maurer, David W. 1995. *The Big Con: The Story of the Confidence Man and the Confidence Game*. New York: Anchor Books. (Originally published 1940)

O'Brien, Geoffrey. 2004a. "Nick Fury's Dream." In *Give Our Regards to the Atomsmashers!: Writers on Comics*, ed. Sean Howe. New York: Pantheon.

O'Brien, Geoffrey. 2004b. "The Lonely Sea." In *Sonata for Jukebox: Pop Music, Memory, and the Imagined Life*. New York: Counterpoint.

O'Brien, Geoffrey. 2004c. "The Return of Burt Bacharach." In *Sonata for Jukebox: Pop Music, Memory, and the Imagined Life*. New York: Counterpoint.

Roth, Philip. "Rereading Saul Bellow." *The New Yorker,* October 9. http://www.newyorker.com/archive/content/?050411fr_archive02.

Sorrentino, Christopher. 2004. "The Ger Sheker." In *Give Our Regards to the Atomsmashers!: Writers on Comics*, ed. Sean Howe. New York: Pantheon.

Updike, John. 2005. "Mixed Messages." *The New Yorker,* March 14. http://www.newyorker.com/critics/books/index.ssf?050314crbo_books1

Wollen, Peter. 1993. *Singin' in the Rain*. London: British Film Institute.

7   The Superhero as Labor
The Corporate Secret Identity

Greg M. Smith

The secret identity is one of the most persistent tropes in superhero comics, beginning with the very first appearance of Superman and continuing unabated today.[1] Although the practice has its roots in literature (the double life of Dumas's *The Man in the Iron Mask* [1845] and *The Count of Monte Cristo* [*Ten Years Later, or The Vicomte Bragelonne,* 1847] or the Baroness Orczy's *Scarlet Pimpernel* series [1905–1940]) and in pulp novels (*The Mark of Zorro* [1919], an explicit precursor to Batman, or Philip Wylie's *The Gladiator* [1930], which Jim Steranko [1970, 37] has argued establishes the primary elements for Superman),[2] fiction seems to have largely abandoned the practice to comics. An ordinary protagonist may be thrown into extraordinary circumstances (causing him or her to inhabit a new identity for the course of the fiction), unlike superhero comics, where the double identity necessarily continues because of the serial nature of its narratives. Spy series foreground the use of masquerade by their protagonists, but here the duplicitous identity is fluid (based on the espionage situation), not consistent as in the classic superhero binary.

Comics scholars have posited a wide range of explanations for this continuing presence of the secret identity. It allows the reader the fantasy of being extraordinary on the inside while continuing to seem ordinary on the outside. Danny Fingeroth voices this combination of power and pitifulness well: "IF ONLY THEY (whoever your 'they' may be) KNEW THE TRUTH (whatever that truth may be) ABOUT ME (whoever you believe yourself to be), THEY'D BE SORRY FOR THE WAY THEY TREAT ME" (2004).[3] Certainly the secret identity acknowledges the schizophrenic splitting of identity into divided subjectivities in modern society. In particular, the secret identity typically allocates the self into a more stereotypically "feminized" (passive, weak, inept) version and a more "masculinized" (active, powerful, capable) side.[4] The superhero/secret identity pairing flatters comics readers, allowing us to feel superior to those dupes who can't see that Clark Kent is indeed Superman, thus forming an insider alliance between us and the superhero (Gordon 2001, 184). The secret identity also embodies the American immigrant experience of assimilation,[5] in which the alien Other must put on a mainstream costume in order to "pass" within society, a masquerade that is always in jeopardy of being exposed.[6]

No single reason can fully explain such a long-term, widespread phenomenon, and all these explanations seem to have a kernel of truth. In this chapter I wish to add a neglected factor to the set of explanations for the secret identity by pointing out a connecting trend in those alter egos: the importance of the corporate professional. Note the kind of jobs that superheroes tend to have: Clark Kent (Superman) is a journalist; Matt Murdock (Daredevil) is a lawyer; Tony Starks (Iron Man) is an industrialist; Barry Allen (Flash) and Ray Palmer (the Atom) are scientists working in large labs. They are professionals who fit within their corporate, institutional worlds. There are no day laborers and almost no small-business people among the classic secret identities. The rare entrepreneur is also a professional ensconced within a larger institution, such as Matt Murdock's small law practice. Characters who initially are disinclined to participate in the corporate world (Bruce Wayne's playboy, for instance) seem to feel the pull toward the corporate self (summoning Batman's alter ego into Waynecorp and Waynetech).

What we have neglected to notice is the portrait of the Organization Man that is consistently articulated in the superhero secret identity. This article articulates this portrait of the secret identity both as cog in the social machine and as critique[7] of the limits of this role, giving us a popular version of the social assessment given by David Riesman (1953) and William H. Whyte (1956). This chapter first examines the role of the corporation in the "classic" superhero secret-identity configuration, which clearly maintains a public separation of the super persona and the mundane one in the comics' world. Individual comic stories may encourage us to muse about how Batman's heartless obsession with justice truly differs from Bruce Wayne's emotionally limited public self, but there is little doubt raised about the narrative necessity for maintaining both roles. The latter portion of this chapter turns to look at superheroes whose private identities are not so secret, where the distinction between public and private has collapsed not only thematically but also in terms of the actual plot. There is a historical slant to this distinction between the classic and the modern superhero secret identity, although I do not draw a hard line between two periods in time. The classic secret identity has its roots in the comics' Golden Age characters (Superman, Batman, Wonder Woman), though many characters emerging in the Silver Age and later also function similarly in their secret identity construction (the Silver Age Flash, Daredevil). The characters who blur the difference between super and secret identities tend to come from later periods when comics creators are questioning or tinkering with the classic configuration of superhero secret identities, and so they necessarily appear more modern comics, although not all modern comics use public/private identities in this way. The norms established early in comics history continue to have power in later eras, just as earlier attitudes about work and the corporation do not entirely disappear in a period of high capitalism. In examining the rough historical trend from classic to modern superhero

Figure 7.1 As is typical of many superheroes, issue 296 of *Superman* (1976) shows Superman's double, the young professional Clark Kent. © DC Comics.

secret identities, I sketch the evolution of the corporate secret identity in comics, which mirrors changes in the nature of the corporation itself.

The overt narrative justification for superheroes choosing a professional/ corporate career for their secret identities is that the hero needs to be at a hub of information so that they will know immediately about various crises. Thus Clark Kent is a journalist, and Jim Corrigan (the Spectre) is a police detective. Without access to such a nexus, there must be an alternate mechanism for the superhero to receive information (the Batsignal, for instance). But narrative expedience does not fully justify the professional choices of secret identities. There is also an aspect of career aspiration within the youthful fantasy of the work world that superhero comics depict. Because the superhero is so much more glamorous than his or her secret identity, this leads us to forget that the business careers chosen by superheroes are quite prestigious. The young reader dreaming of being superpowered realizes that he or she will undoubtedly grow up to be something significantly lesser, someone more like Clark, but as fallback fantasies go, being a metropolitan journalist is not a bad one. One of the beauties of the corporate secret identity is that it sneakily disguises an upscale career choice as being within the grasp of a hardworking Kansas farm boy. It seems a small step from the Smallville paper to a job on the leading newspaper in Metropolis. Young readers for whom the work sphere is a mysteriously fantastic future world can feel "realistic" about their aspirations ("I know I'll never be able to fly") while simultaneously "settling" for what is a dream job (rich industrialist, television news anchor).

The connections between the superhero and the professional secret identity are richer and broader than can be explained through narrative expedience or reader wish fulfillment. This fictional binary occurs within and plays with the real life context of the rising visibility of the corporate man. The most influential portraits of this type emerge in the 1950s in two widely read and discussed social analyses: David Riesman's *The Lonely Crowd* (1953) and William H. Whyte's (1956) *The Organization Man*, although both books note that this figure has its origins in earlier decades.[8] Riesman describes a shift in the "social character" of the American man from an "inner-directed" emphasis to an "other-directed" character. The inner-directed man has his values implanted early in his life, and he holds firm to those values throughout adulthood without needing to be further monitored by rigid external forces (figures of church or state). Exemplars of this type range from Benjamin Franklin to Superman, whose early socialization to Midwestern farm virtues forms the core of his heroic impetus. Riesman argues that the American focus is increasingly on producing the other-directed character, a bureaucratic middle-class figure whose main source of direction comes from closely monitoring signals from the world around him. Whyte calls his closely related type the Organization Man, recognizing that the corporation man is its most visible instance but also arguing that this figure has a broader ideological reach that extends to virtually all professional work. Whyte argues that a Social Ethic is beginning to supplant the Protestant Ethic as a guiding principle for conduct in work and elsewhere, an ideology that demands that people should subsume their individuality for the good of the whole. The primary need of this figure is "belongingness," and without sublimating their individuality and autonomy to the organization, the individual is without meaning. The Organization Man does not simply work for a corporation, but he *belongs* to it, recognizing its superior claims on his loyalty and his conduct. Whyte depicts the Organization Man as an ideal, but he traces the importance of this figure through corporate training practices, child rearing, and fiction.[9]

Note that both of these influential works posit a binary (inner- vs. other-directed, Protestant Ethic vs. Social Ethic) that has strong parallels with the professional secret identity. Both books pit an individual who listens to his own drummer against the more malleable soul who receives pleasure not only by following the dominant beat around him but also by ensuring that the beat goes on uninterrupted. Riesman and Whyte's analyses try to find a balance between the two forces, acknowledging the pull of both belongingness and autonomy but arguing that the dominant force of the Organization Man needs to be counteracted with more emphasis on individuals changing the organization from within. What neither author suggests is an alternation between the two roles, the notion of that one can possess both the pleasures of individuality and conformity in succession. It is this fantasy that the classic superhero secret identity presents.

The classic secret identity is oriented around a series of role switches in time and space. Which persona is better equipped to handle the crisis at a particular moment? Is it the figure of the Organization Man working within the social network, or is it the superheroic individual who bypasses the rules? In fact, the sticking point is often the difficulty of switching from one to the other without getting caught. This dynamic creates numerous opportunities for narrative suspense: will Lois catch Clark changing into Superman (or, perhaps more accurately, how will Clark/Superman evade getting caught between roles once again)? In this alternating manner, the classic superhero secret identity reduplicates the plot device that links doppelgangers in Robert Louis Stevenson's *The Strange Case of Dr. Jekyll and Mr. Hyde* (1886, another literary precursor to the comics secret identity) or in werewolf stories/films. It is this switching between selves (one human, one superhuman) that makes the Wolf Man and Jekyll/Hyde monstrous, and the classic secret identity can be seen as an equally inhuman alternation. A figure like Clark/Superman fits the definition of the monster that Noël Carroll (1990) proposes in his articulation of "art-horror": a being that combines inconsistent categories in ways that, according to current scientific beliefs, cannot coexist (living/dead, animal/human, human/alien). Clark/Superman is, by this definition, a "monster," but not a horrifying monster. Like fantasy creatures such as mermaids, Clark/Superman combines categories in ways that technically make him a "monster" without inspiring the kind of fear/disgust that would make him the centerpiece of horror (except, perhaps, to villains).

The classic corporate secret identity exposes the seemingly monstrous nature of the Organization Man's task. One is expected to participate within the corporation for the greater good of all, and yet one recognizes the need to bypass the organization's structure to exert one's individual will. The classic secret identity holds out the fantasy that we can switch between the two, like Jekyll and Hyde, potentially making monsters of us all. In its particular use of the identity-switching plot mechanism, however, the classic corporate secret identity points out what Stevenson emphasizes and Riesman and Whyte do not: that there is *not* such a radical disjunction between the two personas as it might appear on the surface, that Hyde's animalism and Jekyll's rationalism are linked, and so are the corporate and individualist realms. The two worlds, so seemingly different, demand similar tasks from their participants. In many instances the lessons made salient by the superhero are exactly the same skills needed by the secret identity to survive in the corporate world.[10] For example, Richard Reynolds has noted that classic superheroes are reactive. They do not instigate the action; instead, they wait for the supervillain to act, and only then do they go to work. They are not reluctant heroes, but they are passive. Without some other person or external crisis to precipitate the drama, the superhero would remain on call indefinitely[11] (Reynolds 1992, 50–51). The superhero models for the corporate worker how to wait for the next work assignment and then quickly performs the assigned mission. Unlike the entrepreneur, who seeks out and structures work, the corporate worker accepts the given task (whatever it is) without question and marshals his or her skills to dispatch the problem.

One reason that the superhero is so closely linked to the professional secret identity is that the rhythm of superhero exertion mimics the interruptibilty of professional life. Since superheroes respond to unscheduled crises, the secret identity must be put on hold while the fire is put out. The secret identity, therefore, must be a form of labor that is not so directly supervised that the worker cannot escape. It's hard to respond to the Batsignal if you have a working-class job. If Superman worked on a factory assembly line, how would he punch out his time card to save the world? The advantage of a professional job is the amount of freedom given to well-trained workers who are entrusted to account for their time as they see fit. The flip side of this freedom is the constant interruptions experienced by the corporate executive, who would recognize the panic of a Clark Kent being jerked from one work task to another. The classic superhero/secret identity pair models the handling of interruptions that is at the heart of corporate survival.

The job of the Organization Man is to subsume the individual needs to those of the larger whole. While examining the importance of domination and submission within William Marston's Wonder Woman narratives, G. C.

Bunn (1997) does not limit his discussion to the imagery of bondage that is obviously a part of the character's imagery of lassoing and subduing men. Bunn argues that a larger form of submission plays across Wonder Woman's narratives: that the character must become a servant of the greater good. What Bunn argues is true for Wonder Woman also applies to other classic superheroes: in spite of their extraordinary individuality, superheroes must subsume themselves for the service of the collective. Individual glory is an inevitable by-product of such labor, but it is not the classic superhero's goal. The work itself is the important thing, not the worker. The superhero and the Organization Man must assert themselves within the circumscribed sphere of their task, but their larger aims are predefined.

Once the superhero has been given a task, the comic book story does not unfold by having the superhero deploy their powers in a routine manner. Part of the challenge of constructing an interesting superhero conflict is that the superhero has so many advantages that it is hard to create an antagonist who could not be easily dispatched with a brief exertion of force. A good supervillain is one who stymies and traps the superhero, in spite of his remarkable powers. As Reynolds points out, instead of thinking of Superman tales as simple power fantasies, one can usefully consider them as stories detailing the experience of powerlessness: "Time and again, Superman's great physical powers are useless when set against the trickery, deceit, and immorality of his enemies" (1992, 66). For instance, Superman's powers are helpless against magic, and so his victories over mischievous interdimensional imp Mr. Mxyztplk depend entirely on his ability to outsmart the supervillain into saying a magic word. Kryptonite in its various forms serves the narratively useful purpose of robbing Superman of his powers, and other stories make use of similar mechanisms. The dramatic tension depends as much on drawing out these instances of inability as it does on depicting the moments of triumph.

Superhero narratives are obviously a daydream of effectivity, of having the ability to overcome whatever obstacles lie ahead. Although it is now familiar to discuss these stories as fantasies fed by the frustrations of youth, they may also be productively read from the vantage point of the older Organization Man. His quiet desperation comes from the experience of powerlessness, lost in the minute role one plays within the large coordinated effort. These superhero stories of utter potency must necessarily first create moments of impotence that are recognizable in spirit to anyone dealing with the frustrations of corporate bureaucracy. That even superheroes feel powerless at times is heartening to the mere mortal. If we do not face a Braniac or a Galactus, we at least face unreasonable tirades from our own version of Perry White or J. Jonah Jameson (which would certainly be recognizable by any writer or artist being paid a page rate for their labor in the Marvel or DC bullpen). These superhero stories evoke and depend on the frustrations of powerlessness in the ordinary world, providing a fantasy of having the supernatural capability to overcome those barriers.

And yet the "normal" exertion of superpowers is not enough to triumph in these stories. Rarely is a good punch the solution to a classic superhero's dilemma. To overcome a particular trap, the superhero must put forth what Reynolds calls "extra effort" (1992, 41), a phrase that sounds much like corporate-speak. This extra effort not only provides much needed drama (given the power capabilities of the superhero), but it also demonstrates the superhero's moral superiority of will. The superhero must problem solve in innovative ways to overcome the current menace. Clearly the superheroes here model the ideal professional: they must be able to adapt their skills, using the "extra effort" that distinguishes the professional from the day laborer. For example, in Alan Moore's famous "Must There Be a Super-man?" story (*Superman Annual* 11, 1985), Superman spends much of the narrative immobilized by an alien life-form that presents him with a compelling fantasy of an unexploded Krypton. Superman is released from paralysis when he realizes that the "reality" is merely an illusion. He imme-diately snaps into action against Mongul, who prepared the hallucinatory trap. When Superman hesitates to kill Mongul, he begins to lose the fist fight, only to be saved by Robin's quick thinking, placing Mongul's own hallucination-generating life-form on the supervillain, ensnaring him in his own dreams. Here we see the superhero/Organization Man epitomizing the trends I have mentioned thus far: reacting to an unexpected crisis in spite of one's prolonged feeling of powerlessness, putting forth the extra effort to solve the dilemma with quick improvisational thinking.

After the superhero dispenses with the crisis of the moment, the classic superhero universe returns to status quo with little mention of the impact of the superhero's recent effort. As Umberto Eco notes, the combination of Superman's mythological status (his godlike invulnerability) and the com-mercial structure of regular serial publication necessitates this narrative structure. In the individual comic book, the classic superhero overcomes the obstacle, adding to the accomplishments, but to acknowledge that the hero has changed in the aftermath of such action would violate his invio-lably steadfast nature. The classic Superman story takes place in what Eco calls an "immobile present" where the seemingly powerful superhero can only make "infinitesimal modifications of the immediately visible" (2004, 156, 164).[12] Superman can only stop bank robbers or prevent alien inva-sions; he cannot make wholesale changes in his world. In making connec-tions between the comic's narrative structure and its mythic underpinnings, Eco comes close to discussing the portrait of the corporate man within the Superman narrative, arguing that "[i]n an industrial society . . . where man becomes a number in the realm of the organization which has usurped his decision-making role" (2004, 146), the lesson to be learned from the nar-rative time scheme of superhero narratives is one of immobility. Planning and action by individuals are insignificant since even superhuman efforts result in no lasting change in the world around you. The Organization Man would recognize the corporate celebration of achieving one's momentary goal, only to return to the sense of Sisyphean futility of having to confront a remarkably similar obstacle the next day.

After engaging in a series of such ineffectual endeavors, the professional runs the danger of evacuating his or her private identity in service of the corporate aims. The danger is in becoming the Organization Man, in being reduced to his function within the system. The health of the functionary's other life is of little concern if the job is well done. The reward of professional effectiveness can be indifference to the soul of the worker. Why should anyone care about the person trapped inside either a metal suit or a gray flannel suit, each one of which is built by a corporate industrial complex to serve its own purposes, as long as either the corporate professional or the superhero risks his or her humanity to bring peace of mind to their world? Classic superhero comics require us to acknowledge the complex linkages among the restricted corporate self, the fantasy image of effectivity, and the private soul that can be found somewhere in between.

The superhero and the professional secret identity, then, are not simply depictions of binary opposites of power. Superheroes and professional secret identities are different modes of heroism requiring similar kinds of effort (subsuming individual needs for the corporate good, handling assigned tasks, confronting powerlessness) in very different realms. Film theorist Robert Ray has defined these two separate forms of heroism, arguing that these two basic heroic forms structure the classic American cinema.[13] Ray says that Hollywood over and over offers audiences the "official hero" and/or the "outlaw hero." The official hero works entirely within the system. Although the official hero has conflicts, he or she has confidence that these may be settled by working within the parameters laid down by the existing institutions. Atticus Finch in *To Kill a Mockingbird* is an official hero, as are the protagonists of *C.S.I.* and *Law and Order*. The outlaw heroes may overtly work for the institution, but they have lost their faith in the institutional order, working outside the system according to their own individual set of rules. Dirty Harry is an outlaw hero, and so is Andy Sipowicz of *NYPD Blue*. Although most Hollywood films center around one or the other, some films depict both. Ray's classic example is *Casablanca*: Ilsa must choose between official hero Victor, the hope of the free French, and outlaw hero Rick, a mercenary turned disaffected saloonkeeper. Although Ilsa chooses the official hero, the movie makes certain that our sympathies lie with the outlaw, which the American cinema tends to favor.

One of the primary distinctions of the conventions of superheroism developed in comics is that superhero comics combine the official hero and the outlaw hero into a single entity. Superheroes are not paid police officers who must follow legal procedures; they are by definition vigilantes (even those who are deeply complicit with institutional power, such as many moments in Superman's history). The classic corporate secret identity works within the system of law, industry, science, or the press, all standard occupations of the official hero.[14] Although the comic book's sympathies (like those of the American cinema in general) are with the outlaw/superhero, we do not have to choose between the two, as we must do in *Casablanca*; they are the same person.[15] They are not irreconcilable options; they coexist (at times complementarily, at other times, uneasily) as irreversibly linked aspects of the same pursuit. Matt Murdock may put on the Daredevil costume because he has encountered a limit to what he can do as a lawyer, but that does not prevent him from continuing his efforts on the legal front. It is not, as Thomas Andrae argues, that the secret identity is solely a "sham" that "exposes the powerlessness of the individual in modern society and simultaneously effaces it by affirming an escape into a realm of fantastic adventure beyond the repressions of daily life." Yes, the classic secret identity voices the frustration of the individual trying to live up to the ideal of the Organization Man, but it also points out the continuities between that figure and the outlaw hero. Both are subject to moments of powerlessness, of losing their own selves for the collective good. Both are creatures who react more than they act, who improvise deftly in the face of unpredictable circumstances. Their combination is not necessarily a monstrous amalgamation or a simple fantasy split or an irreconcilable difference between two orientations: instead, the classic secret identity acknowledges the interconnection between two necessary modes of heroism.

The radical fantasy aspect of combining the classic superhero with institutional secret identity is that one is an extension of the other. It is not simply that one turns into the other over time, in the way that we watch a good cop go bad as he or she becomes frustrated with the impossibility of justice within the justice system. Instead, this figure is placed within a serial narrative and so transforms over and over from official to outlaw and back again. This interrelationship acknowledges the limitations of each mode of heroism and the necessity of both. As the 60s bring about a widespread questioning of an unproblematic faith in the wisdom of institutions and an open rebellion against the strictures of the corporate mind, it becomes more difficult to maintain the more straightforward, classic linkage between the professional secret identity and the superhero. As certain superhero comics tinker with this relationship, they provide a vantage point that allows us to see the unproblematized assumptions of their predecessors. In particular, certain Marvel comics of the 60s and 70s bring to the forefront the economics kept hidden by the professional occupations we have just discussed.

Slowly the "secret" part of the secret identity began to slip away, becoming more a dual identity with less need for concealment. Minor characters such as the Wasp (a superhero who frequently changed costume) seemed not so far away from their professional identities (Janet Van Dyne, a professional clothing designer). Major characters such as Reed Richards began their superhero careers already having a measure of celebrity (as an astronaut), and having all the major characters in the Fantastic Four's "family unit" being superpowered meant that there was little need to protect Mr. Fantastic's alter ego so that his loved ones could be safeguarded.

But the major change in the institutional dual identity came with a new acknowledgment of economic pressures in the superhero universe. Although the Marvel revolution of the 60s is frequently seen as a turn toward more complexly "alienated" and internally troubled characters (Jones and Jacobs 1997), I want to emphasize their foregrounding of the external monetary troubles associated being a superhero. Peter Parker spends a great deal of time worrying about money; after all, the chemicals to make web fluid are expensive. Here we get a superhero who worries about where the money will come from to pay the mortgage. Although Parker initially tries to market his newfound powers for profit, Spider-Man's origin story emphasizes that this is not a viable option for the hero. In fact, Spider-Man's origin story is a double story: one about Parker gaining superpowers (through a radioactive spider bite) and a second, more economically based story about his assuming the role of hero. Having failed in his attempt to parlay Spider-Man's powers into financial gain, he eschews financial gain, learning that the role of the hero is to accept responsibility without expecting monetary consideration. By classical superhero standards, heroism and financial hardship do not mix.

These barriers (of economics and secrecy) are broken down further with the logical emergence of a superhero who works for money: Luke Cage, hero for hire. It is significant that when we have a hero who cannot afford the luxury of selfless labor, we also have a hero who makes no attempt to split his superhero identity from his professional one. After it becomes clear that Cage will be more popular than most other attempts at intermingling blaxploitation and superheroes, he is given a more "superheroey" moniker (Power Man), but still he does not duplicate the well-established dynamics of identity concealment. Of course, it is obviously important that when such a figure emerges in comics, he is a black character, but here I wish to emphasize class over race (though obviously they are not separate).[16] Luke Cage helps us better see the class assumptions that underlie the professional secret identity of the classic superhero. There is no discussion of bill paying in Clark Kent's or Tony Stark's world, and thus the importance of their secret identities as *professionals*. Journalists and industrialists are professions who assume a certain basic standard of living above the economic fray. In order for the economically selfless understanding of superheroism to function, it needs the invisible support provided by the professional secret identity. The classic superhero cannot accept money for his or her labor both because it sullies the nobility of their heroism and because a paycheck would place the superhero more squarely within the world of the official hero. Luke Cage, lacking both a secret identity and the economic class associated with such identities, must do what previous superheroes avoided: selling their labor on the open market.

The assumption of a certain measure of economic class is built into the very origins of the secret-identity trope. It is important that Sir Percy in the Scarlet Pimpernel novels is a flighty fop because the seeming distance between the secret identity and the hero identity keeps people from suspecting Sir Percy of heroism (just as Bruce Wayne's playboy image helps preserve his secret identity as Batman). But in our emphasis on how weak Sir Percy is, we forget to notice how important it is that he is an aristocrat. His good breeding (like that of *The Man in the Iron Mask* and *The Count of Monte Cristo*) gives rise to his derring-do and to his ability to maneuver among various worlds, and his deep pockets underwrite the expense of his masquerade and his large underground organization (just as the unlimited Wayne fortune makes it possible for Batman to afford all those wonderful toys).

Luke Cage, then, exposes the unacknowledged class bias built into the secret-identity concept. He also makes clear one of the economic ramifications of superhero labor: that superheroism is a crappy business model. There ain't no margin in saving the world. It is ignoble to stop and ask a person dangling from a skyscraper ledge if he or she is willing to pay for rescue, and neither can one ask for payment after the services have already been delivered. Crisis, the basic dramatic structure of the superhero narrative, is a poor basis for business; it is too intermittent and too unpredictable. To put superheroes on salary is either to make them overtly answerable to a particular political institution or to position them more as "ordinary heroes" such as firemen.[17]

Superhero parodies are useful to point out the inconsistent economic assumptions of our classic mode of superheroism. Bob Rozakis's and Stephen DeStephano's *Hero Hotline* (1989) posits a bureau of heroes whose services are only a phone call away. *Hero Hotline* depicts a superhero team operating not from a centralized seemingly nonprofit and rent-free headquarters (like the Avengers mansion or the Legion of Super Heroes' clubhouse) but within a corporate call center, complete with a mechanized dispatcher and a corrupt manager. Rather than answering summons to avert major global crises, the heroes must deal with stereotypical problems that face ordinary beat cops and firemen. On the Hero Hotline team, heroes are called to break up domestic disputes, and the seemingly ever-present stretchable hero (for instance, Plastic Man, Elongated Man, Mr. Fantastic) bemoans his fate of being dispensed to deal with an unending series of cats stuck in trees. Robert Kirkman's *Capes* (2003) explicitly foregrounds the discord that comes from placing superhero labor within modern labor practices. Teams of superheroes operate in shifts (only dealing with emergencies when they are on call); they get overtime pay and have disability insurance (much needed in the superhero business).

The intermingling of various understandings of labor that we see in overt superhero parodies has now become part of more mainstream superhero narratives. The introduction of certain real-world economic concerns in Spider-Man and Luke Cage gave rise to the imbedding of superhero narratives within the everyday fictional world of Marvels. This person-on-the-street perspective on superhero action seems to have opened up myriad possibilities for comic writers and artists to consider worlds where superheroism and ordinary work commingle (such as Kurt Busiek's *Astro City* [1995–], Moore's *Top 10* [1999–2006], Brian Michael Bendis's *Powers* [2001–]).[18] Geoff Klock has examined how such modern "revisionist" comics have dealt in various ways with the "anxiety of influence" caused by having to function within the confines of a superhero universe. Situating the fantasy element of the superhero within a variety of more "realistic" contexts, Klock argues, has become a dominant mode of re-enlivening the superhero narrative in the 1980s and beyond. By placing the superhero within work paradigms other than the Organization Man context of the classic professional secret identity, the modern revisionist comics not only encourage us to interrogate our assumptions about superheroes but also foreground the changing nature of work in high capitalism.

In current comics we see the breaking down of classic lines separating secret identities, corporate/institutional roles, official and outlaw heroes. We have characters who have abandoned their superhero identity to occupy full-time roles as what would once have been their professional secret identity: Jessica Jones as the detective/reporter of *Alias* (2001–2004) and *The Pulse* (2004–2006), Detective Walker in *Powers*. The recent reincarnation of *She-Hulk* (2004–) centers on the conflict seemingly caused by a lawyer trying to determine if she has been hired because of her not-so-secret super identity or for her own all-too-human legal abilities. The question in these series is which set of labor skills is salable in which particular environments, and the answer in each case is that both superhero and ordinary talents become equally useful in resolving the narrative quandary.

For the postmodern corporation, image creation is as much a part of the business as manufacturing is. The actual product cannot be separated from its place in the marketplace of ideas, and so the process of image construction of the commodity is foregrounded in public discourse. Superheroes from their early days have been real-world commodities (as Ian Gordon [2001] details), but in early superhero stories the forces of commodification existed as villains. For instance, in a 1941 story in *Action Comics* that gave voice to Siegel and Schuster's anger over the trademarking of their character Superman, the villain is an unscrupulous businessman who sells the commercial rights to Superman's name, marketing his image on everything from cereal to comic strips. By contrast, in Jonathan and Joshua Luna's *Ultra* (2004–2005) the superheroes work for a corporation that both serves as a central dispatch to send superheroes to crises (as in *Hero Hotline*) and as a public relations agency that fields offers for the heroes to do product endorsements. The superheroes' agent concerns himself with how the heroes' actions will affect the marketability of their image, and so he monitors both their battles against supervillains and against the paparazzi looking for tabloid fodder about the superheroes' love lives. In a playful story entitled "Sweeps Week!" *Noble Causes* creator Jay Faerber presents the reader with the reflexive possibility that the comic that they are reading (a parody of soap-opera form using superheroes) may be an actual soap opera, a fictionalized version of the "actual" super Noble family's life created under the supervision of matriarch and spin doctor Gaia (*Noble Causes* Extended Family 2). In *Noble Causes* (2003–) Gaia chastises her

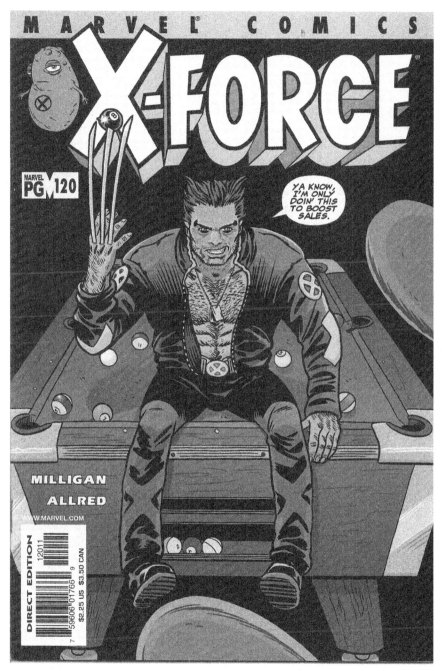

Figure 7.2 One cover from one of Peter Milligan's and Mike Allred's *X-Force* series (2001–2004) where the heroes have not so secret secret identities and engage reflexively on their place within a corporate world. © Marvel Entertainment.

children when their actions hurt the family's public image, thus interfering with the commodification of their celebrity.

Perhaps the most distinctive reconfiguration of these elements is Peter Milligan's and Mike Allred's *X-Force/X-Statix* (2001–2004, Figure 7.2). The comic combines the shifting composition of a frontline military unit undergoing frequent casualties, the overt marketing of boy bands, the public relations manipulation of celebrity tabloid journalism, and the instant popular polling of reality television, all within the familiar structure of the bickering comic superhero team. If there is no profit margin in saving the world, there certainly is profit in merchandising, and the heroes of *X-Statix* muse aloud about how their actions will affect their Q-ratings and the prospective sales of their action figures. In *X-Statix* the cross-marketing of merchandise is the payoff that drives the superhero enterprise, making the characters consider the bottom line before choosing which missions to accept. Here we see the superhero fully within the postmodern corporation: one that is actually *more* concerned with royalties gained from marketing its image than gaining money as a direct result of its actions. Far from being the villainous opposite of heroic action, image marketing in this world is the accepted practice of the postmodern corporation and therefore can be the guiding concern of a contemporary superhero.

Members of *X-Statix* (like those in *Ultra*) have dual identities, but they are not secret ones. In fact, their open dual identities become part of their public personas, part of what is being sold to the public. In *Noble Causes* there is no dual identity; the public knows the characters by their given names (Gaia, Race, Rusty Noble). The fact that their proper names also describe their superpowers (Gaia commands the natural elements; Race is superfast; Rusty's consciousness is placed in a robot) shows that there is no longer a need for secret identities in this universe. What becomes marketed in this case is the balance between public and private that constitutes the celebrity industry. The superhero *is* the corporate product, and the hero participates in his or her own packaging.

With *X-Statix*, *Ultra*, and *Noble Causes*, we come to the current state-of-the-art integration of the corporate identity and the superhero. In its initial configuration in classic superhero imagery, the secret identity depended on an unacknowledged assumption of economic class and professionalism. Instead of considering the superhero and the secret identity as opposites, I find it more useful to examine the continuities in their activities, how the superhero models the appropriate behavior for the corporate worker. As the nature of the corporation changed, so did the relationship between the corporate identity and the superhero. From the professional Organization Man to the worker for hire to the postmodern, image-conscious public relations officer, the superhero's handling of a dual identity provides a fantasy vista for evoking and critiquing the place of the individual within the corporate institution.

BIBLIOGRAPHY

Andrae, Thomas. 1980. "From Menace to Messiah: The Prehistory of the Super-man in Science Fiction Literature." *Discourse*, 2: 84–111.

Axelrod, Alan. 2004. *Office Superman: Make Yourself Indispensable in the Work-place*. Philadelphia: Running Press.

Braudy, Leo. 1986. *The Frenzy of Renown: Fame and Its History*. Oxford: Oxford University Press.

Brown, Jeffrey A. 2001. *Black Superheroes, Milestone Comics, and their Fans*. Jackson: University Press of Mississippi.

Bukatman, Scott. 2003. "X-bodies: The Torment of the Mutant Superhero." In *Matters of Gravity: Special Effects and Supermen in the 20th Century*, 48–80. Durham, NC: Duke University Press.

Bunn, G. C. 1997. "The Lie Detector, Wonder Woman, and Liberty: The Life and Work of William Moulton Marston." *History of the Human Sciences*, 10(1): 91–119.

Carroll, Noël. 1990. *The Philosophy of Horror, or Paradoxes of the Heart*. Rout-ledge: New York.

Eco, Umberto. 2004. "The Myth of Superman." In *Arguing Comics: Literary Mas-ters on a Popular Medium*, ed. Jeet Heer and Kent Worcester, 146–64. Jackson: University Press of Mississippi.

Engle, Gary. 1987. "What makes Superman so Darned American?" In *Superman at 50: The Persistence of a Legend*, 79–87, ed. Dennis Dooley and Gary Engle. Cleveland, OH: Octavia Press.

Feiffer, Jules. 1965. *The Great Comic Book Heroes*. New York: Dial Press.

Fingeroth, Danny. 2004. *Superman on the Couch: What Superheroes Really Tell Us About Ourselves and Our Society*. New York: Continuum.

Gordon, Ian. 2001. "Nostalgia, Myth, and Ideology: Visions of Superman at the End of the American Century." In *Comics and Ideology*, ed. Matthew P. McAl-lister, Edward H. Sewell, Jr., and Ian Gordon. New York: Peter Lang.

Jones, Gerard, and Will Jacobs. 1997. *The Great Comic Book Heroes*. Rocklin, CA: Prima Publishing.

Klock, Geoff. 2002. *How To Read Superhero Comics and Why*. New York: Continuum.

Ray, Robert. 1985. *A Certain Tendency of the Hollywood Cinema, 1930–1980*. Princeton, NJ: Princeton University Press.

Reynolds, Richard. 1992. *Super Heroes: A Modern Mythology*. Jackson: Univer-sity Press of Mississippi.

Riesman, David, with Nathan Glazer and Reuel Denney. 1953. *The Lonely Crowd: A Study of the Changing American Character*. New York: Doubleday.

Steranko, Jim. 1970. *The Steranko History of Comics*, Vol. 1. Reading, PA: Super-graphics.

Whyte, William H. 1956. *The Organization Man*. New York: Simon & Schuster.

NOTES

1. Richard Reynolds notes that "The first-ever Superman story establishes the [secret identity] convention by using it as if it already existed" (1992, 15).
2. For more on the prehistory of Superman, see Andrae (1980).
3. See also Reynolds: "Individual stories explore this contrast between cos-tume as a source of power and costume as a means of hiding identity" (1992).

4. "Superhero comics clearly split masculinity into two distinct camps, stressing the superhero side as the ideal to be aspired to; but unlike the fascist ideology of phallic masculinity as mutually exclusive of the softer, feminized other, comic book masculinity is ultimately premised on the inclusion of the devalued side. Even if Clark Kent and Peter Parker exist primarily to reinforce the reader's fantasy of self-transformation and to emphasize the masculine ideal of Superman and Spider-Man, they are still portrayed as a part of the character that is essential to their identities as a whole" (Brown 2001, 175).

5. For example, Gary Engle argues: "Though a disguise, Kent is necessary for the myth to work. This uniquely American hero has two identities, one based on where he comes from in life's journey, one on where he's going. One is real, one an illusion, and both are necessary for the myth of balance in the assimilation process to be complete. Superman's powers make the hero capable of saving humanity; Kent's total immersion in the American heartland makes him want to do it. The result is an improvement on the Western: an optimistic myth of assimilation but with an urban, technocratic setting" (1987, 85).

6. "Identity is the obsessional center of superhero comics, as revealed by endless processes of self-transformation and the problematic perceptions of others—Batman hunted by police, Lois hunting for Superman's secret identity" (Bukatman, 54).

7. Jules Feiffer considers the secret identity as a social critique of a broader sort than I do here. Feiffer inverts the normal assumption that Superman is Clark Kent's secret identity, asserting that Superman is the "true identity" and Clark Kent merely a "put-on . . . He is Superman's opinion of the rest of us, a pointed caricature of what we, the noncriminal element, were really like" (1965, 18–19). This argument was made more popular when restated by Bill (David Carradine) in a climactic scene in *Kill Bill, Part 2.*

8. For example, Thomas Andrae (1980) situates a Depression-era shift from comics' early socially progressive narrative tendencies toward a more corporate stance that fits better with the New Deal's emphasis on the collective.

9. Leo Braudy also notes that the twentieth-century corporate world no longer needs the qualities required to pioneer America. In fact, those qualities of innovation and self-reliance actually destabilize the lower levels of the corporate enterprise, and so Braudy argues that these values are more relegated to fiction (513–14).

10. This article is eerily anticipated by a self-help book entitled (unsurprisingly) *Office Superman That Peppily Encourages People to Follow the Example of the Man of Steel in Becoming the "Perfect Employee"*: "The Office Superman transforms himself into a compulsively useful being, like the Superman of Siegel and Shuster, a savior, even. He makes sure that everyone sees him at the go-to guy in just about any situation that matters, any situation that calls for strength, intelligence, integrity, and character" (Axelrod, 11).

11. This tendency fits awkwardly when superhero comics are translated into the conventions of Hollywood film, where the superhero is neither an active pursuer of a single-minded goal nor an ordinary person responding to unusual circumstances.

12. In Eco's words, Superman cannot "consume himself." His mythic static status does not allow events in his present to impinge on his future because to do so would acknowledge that the godlike superhero "has taken a step toward death" (2004, 150). Eco is writing about the classic superhero narrative structure, where each individual comic book issues almost always presented a complete story with a beginning, middle, and end. Arranging those

comics in a particular order (designated by issue numbers) creates comic book "continuity" (the overarching serial narrative unfolding in a particular comic book universe), but in classic superhero storytelling the serial nature of this larger story rarely impinges on the narrative demands of the individual tale. In more recent times, superhero narratives have participated in more strongly serial storytelling.

13. Although Ray's discussion centers on a particular medium (film) in a particular era (America from 1930 to 1980), I extend his concept here to other popular media (comics, television) in a broader time frame. I do so because his argument is based largely on the ideological underpinnings of the outlaw/official hero dichotomy. If Ray's argument holds true that popular film reveals these deep undercurrents in American mythology, those same currents are likely to continue to appeal in other mainstream media.

14. Other descendants of the classic superhero (one not discussed in this paper) are the antiheroes who emerge later in comic book history. Some of these maintain the classic relationship between the secret identity and the superhero (Selina Kyle/Catwoman, for instance). Others are so alienated from society that they have no narrative justification for a secret identity. The Punisher (Frank Castle) takes up his antiheroic, murderous quest after his family was killed, and so he has no loved ones who might be jeopardized by a villain seeking revenge on him (unlike Batman, who maintains familial relations with Alfred, Robin, or other key figures in his life). These figures (cat burglars and killers) pose a different challenge to the norms of the classic superhero than the ones I present later in this chapter.

15. This convention provides another structural difficulty for a mainstream film trying to adapt a superhero comic. Classical Hollywood films tend to present a dual plotline in which the protagonist (either an official or outlaw hero) pursues both an action-oriented and a romance-oriented goal. The classic superhero comic is organized as a different split between the official and outlaw hero combined into one figure. Hollywood has not developed narrative patterns for telling such stories, and thus the tendency to begin superhero films with the character's origin story, which emphasizes that the hero began as a person without the dual identity, thus making the identity split, is a result of a cataclysmic event that happens to a unified character. This is a story that Hollywood is much more equipped to tell, instead of a story about a character that begins divided. Mainstream filmmaking often compounds the difficulty by emphasizing the romance plotlines in superhero films, which makes sense given its narrative norms but which can complicate the storytelling of a superhero adaptation even more.

16. Also it is significant that the first major superhero character to relinquish her secret identity is a woman (Wonder Woman), and she does so at the moment when she explicitly puts herself in an institutional context. The revamping of the Wonder Woman character in 1987 placed Diana Prince as ambassador from Amazonia to the United Nations in a role that acknowledged her identities.

17. In the wake of the events of September 11, several comics explicitly pointed to the different models of heroism represented by superheroes and by firemen. See, for example, DC Comics' *9–11: The World's Finest Comic Book Artists and Writers Tell Stories to Remember* (2002).

18. "Like *Marvels*, *Astro City* attempts to avoid anxiety [of influence] by shifting perspective. It often acts as a negative of traditional superhero stories, reversing big and little moments, showing in one panel something that traditionally would take a whole issue, like major battles, and spending time on small moments, like waking up and putting on a costume one leg at a time" (Klock 2002, 88).

8   When Fangirls Perform
The Gendered Fan Identity in Superhero Comics Fandom

Karen Healey

So I'm doing this Batman essay for a book, right? My editor just sent me the proofer's comments, and he refers to the author (me) as 'he' throughout it. Despite my name being RIGHT THERE.

—Mary Borsellino

"Comics," Scott Bukatman declares in his essay in this anthology, "become a crucial site of escape to, rather than escape from, a protected terrain of self-definition (assuming one is a certain kind of adolescent boy)." But what if one isn't? For those comics fans who are not any kind of boy, adolescent or otherwise, the terrain of comics and comics fan culture can pose significant hazards to self-definition. Bukatman's expressive, kinetic world is unabashedly masculine. His "alternative universe" of academics using autobiographical comment to illustrate their comics writing is populated entirely by men; the origin stories of characters are "told and retold, often by the character himself (and often *to* himself)"; with the exception of the female members of the Incredible family, the expressive bodies enabling the kinetically exuberant self-definition Bukatman celebrates all belong to men. True, Bukatman concludes that this exuberance is shared by the admirably gender-neutral "seemingly solitary reader of comic books and the occasional academic," but by then the damage is done. I am irresistibly compelled to demand, as Jessica Alba's Invisible Girl does, "Look at me!" in the face of a fandom that so often replies, "I can't" (Tim Story 2005).

I don't mean to especially pick on Bukatman, whose essay I otherwise admire. "Secret Identity Politics" is the example closest to hand, but in truth, I'm wearily accustomed to being an invisible woman, my fan presence ignored by the academy and industry alike. It doesn't help that there is no easy way to determine how many women are currently reading superhero comics; Marvel and DC periodically perform market research surveys but do not reveal the results.[1] Estimates that women make up 5 to 10 percent of superhero comics fans are frequently cited in fan discussion, but the research I could find to support those numbers is no more recent than the late 90s, where Jeffrey A. Brown writes:

The most easily recognizable fact about the comic book audience in the 1990s is that it is overwhelmingly male. Bierbaum's 1987 study of comic book stores indicated that with even the most generous of estimates only 6–10 percent of customers are female. Likewise, none of the over thirty retail store managers I spoke with estimated their clientele to consist of more than 10 percent women. (Brown 2001, 62)

In *Comic Book Culture: Fanboys and True Believers*, Matthew Pustz is more vague, but equally assured in describing the mid-90s regular customers of comic book store Daydreams as mostly male—"even though Daydreams is more female friendly than most comic book shops" (Pustz 1999, 5). Why do women keep away? Pustz has some theories:

[W]omen are turned off by comic shops' atmosphere. Female visitors commonly become uncomfortable or feel unwelcome as a result of the gazes of male patrons who are surprised to see women in that setting or by posters that frequently objectify women and/or glorify violence. Other women are simply turned off by the fact that there do not seem to be any comics interesting to female readers. (Pustz 1999, 8)

Pustz's comments here reveal more than his assessment of comics fandom's gender bias. They suggest, perhaps unconsciously, that superhero comics are inherently uninteresting to the female reader. It is entirely possible that a woman might especially object to a poster objectifying women but somewhat less clear why one glorifying violence would automatically make her uncomfortable. Glorified violence, however, is central to the power fantasies of the superhero comic, and Pustz's reference to a lack of comics "interesting to female readers" refers also to the predominantly superheroic content of most comic book stores. It is not, he implies, merely the objectification of women that is a turnoff for potential female readers; the glorified violence of mainstream comics, and perhaps their very existence, are off-putting to women, who are (possibly inherently) uninterested in them.

The perception that superhero comics are not only not written for women, but that there is nothing in them that women could find interesting, is also articulated from within the industry. *Inside the World of Comic Books*, a collection of essays and interviews, edited by Jeffery Klaehn and published in 2007, features an interview with renowned superhero comics artist Bob Layton:

JK: The American superhero has endured for almost a century, sustaining both commercial and cultural relevance. Why do you feel this has been the case?

BL: . . . The struggle of "gods and mortals" in comics is a theme as old as storytelling itself. Comics are the modern mythology that we, as a society, template our fears and dreams onto. It's the

> universal power fantasy we all dream of—to have the abil-
> ity to soar above our problems—or pummel them into dust.
> (Klaehn 2007, 45–46)

Layton, describing superhero comics as a modern mythology for a universal
"we," is perhaps overly optimistic in linking the popular modern mythology of the superhero to the format of the superhero comic, but the "universal power fantasy" is promisingly nongender-biased. Later, however:

> *JK:* Why don't more women read comic books in North America, in
>   your view?
> *BL:* Because—they're not written for women. Why don't you read
>   Harlequin romance novels? I would speculate that they sim-
>   ply don't appeal to you. I tried very hard to create products
>   for female readers while at Valiant [the comics company he
>   cofounded]. *The Second Life of Dr. Mirage* was specifically
>   created for women readers. Although the title was popular,
>   it never succeeded in bringing in significantly more female
>   readers. (Klaehn 2007, 50)

Layton's assertion that superhero comics—even those he specifically creates to cater to women—"simply don't appeal" to women is not only a
disingenuous reinforcement of assumed gender norms[2] but jarring when
compared to his earlier claims of a "universal power fantasy" directed at
an ungendered "we," members of "our" society. Instead, we discover that
this unmarked "we" is neither ungendered nor universal, but assumed
to be male. In Layton's conception of superhero comics fandom, the
unmarked, natural, universal state is masculine. According to Layton,
women don't read superhero comics because they "simply don't appeal"
to them; female fans of superhero comics are therefore violating the natural order of what fantasies they—not "we"—ought to have and of what
media is "for women."

Clearly, when it comes to comics, "fan" isn't a gender-neutral term. In
Textual Poachers Henry Jenkins describes "media fandom" as "largely
female," but in superhero comics fandom, the industry and the academy,
the "fan" is male (Jenkins 1992, 1). The female comics fan is discursively
erased from fandom, both by mainstream media and by those performing
comics fandom, the scholar fan and the producer fan not excepted. In the
quote from Mary Borsellino that begins this essay, the proofer who refers
to her as "he" not only ignores the evidence of the writer's femininity—her
name, which is "RIGHT THERE"—but eschews gender-neutral reference
to the author in favor of identifying the fan-scholar as masculine. "He" is,
after all, writing about Batman.

In the superhero comics themselves, the activity of reading comics is diegetically situated as a largely masculine activity. In *Sensational She-Hulk*,

She-Hulk's would-be ally Gopher is a male teenage intern at the "Marvel Comics" which exists within the Marvel Universe to create retellings of the adventures of that universe's "real" heroes (Bryne 1993, #51). In *She-Hulk*, Stu Cicero works at the law firm at which She-Hulk's civilian identity, Jennifer Walters, works as an attorney. He is a comics fan, along with his friends Lewis and Chas (Slott and Templeton 2007, #21). (Jennifer Walters herself uses the comics of "Marvel Comics" as resources when relevant evidence for her cases but does not read them for pleasure or exhibit other fan behaviors.) The comics fan of superpowered sibling team *Power Pack* is ten-year-old Jack, whose scorn of his sisters' enthusiasm for going to the library is based on his view of reading as an activity for "nerds and losers"—unlike comic books, which are "totally different" (Sumerak 2006, 2, 14). Nor is the character-as-comic-fan restricted to a role as a comic-relief side character or as part of an ensemble team. Virgil Ovid Hawkins/Static of Milestone's *Static*, Bart Allen/Impulse of DC's *Young Justice* and *Impulse*, and Wildstorm's *Ex Machina*'s Mitchell Hundred were or are all title-carrying main characters, comics fans, and male (McDuffie 1993–1997; David 1998–2003; Vaughan 2004–present). One notable female exception is *The Authority*'s Dr. Angela Spica, a brilliant scientist and DC Comics fan who deliberately made herself a superhero (Millar 2000). Overwhelmingly, however, superhero comics themselves support "male" as the default gender for their readers.

So what's an invisible woman to do? I do not dispute that most superhero comics fans are male. Nor do I disagree with Brown, who argues that the study of the way male fans (particularly straight male fans) use texts that "are commonly defined as 'men's genres' " is a vital and relatively neglected facet of fan culture studies (Brown 2001, 96–102). It's the widespread assumption that superhero comics are inherently uninteresting to all female readers that makes me want to break out the force shields; as a quick perusal of the contents page of this very collection will reveal, it's an assumption that's demonstrably untrue. The oft-quoted 5–10 percent may or may not be based in fact, but even as this statistic demonstrates that male superhero fans greatly outnumber their female counterparts, it ignores that 5–10 percent of all superhero comic readers does not represent, *en masse*, an insignificant number of people.

My intentions for this essay are neither to prove that sexist elements of superhero comics culture can alienate female comics fans nor that, despite these metaphorical "NO GURLS" signs on the comics clubhouse door, superhero comics culture contains many female participants. Rather, these points hopefully being made, I want to go on to consider the gendered performativity of the female fan in response to what is not, in the end, their invisibility but the blindness of others. Especially in cyberspace, female superhero comics fans have established clubhouses of their own, and there they vigorously perform and articulate feminine comics fandom as they explore the rocky terrain of self-definition.

THE PERFORMANCE OF NORMATIVE
FEMININITY IN FEMALE FANDOM

Comics fan culture, like most fan cultures, has greatly benefited from the technologies of the Internet, and female fans have taken advantage of this shift to online comics culture. In cyberspace, geographical distance from one another is much less of a barrier to female fans than it might have been in the mid to late 90s. One fan might be one of only a few female regulars at the local comics store, but online she can communicate with other fans and discover that she is not alone. The virtual geography of the Internet can be much less intimidating than the comic stores with the intrusively gazing patrons that Pustz describes.[3] Nevertheless, even online, gender matters. As Rhiannon Bury puts it in *Cyberspaces of Their Own: Female Fandoms Online*, "bodies, and body-based identities matter a great deal in cyberspace" (Bury 2005, 4).

Judith Butler's theory of gender performance asserts that "[t]here is no gender identity behind the expressions of gender; . . . identity is performatively constituted by the very 'expressions' that are said to be its results" (Butler 1990, 25). Fan studies scholar Matt Hills provocatively argues that, rather than being a "thing," "fandom is . . . also always performative . . . an identity which is (dis-)claimed, and which performs cultural work" (Hills 2002, xi). The intersection of these performances of gender and fannishness, with regard to the expressions of female comics fans online, is of interest precisely because the physical body in the physical community is less important in this setting; it is the imagined female body in the imagined comics community that female fans refer to when defining their cyberspaces and selves. Bury remarks that online, "the body continues to signify gender intelligibility *linguistically*" (Bury 2005, 8, author's italics). I want to therefore examine the most immediately obvious linguistic markers of female online fanspaces; the names given to those cyber clubhouses.

Figure 8.1 Banner from the 'When Fangirls Attack' Web site. Banner mixed by Chris Sims of http://the-isb.com for use by Lisa Fortuner and Melissa Krause of http://womenincomics.blogspot.com. © Lisa Fortuner and Melissa Krause.

What follows is a biased and partial list of some of the more popular Web spaces that identify as primarily for or by women. In addition to collectives like the Web site for the long-established *Friends of Lulu* (an organization focused more on alternative comics than on mainstream, and on female creators than fans) and the monthly magazine *Sequential Tart* ("a Web Zine about the comics industry published by an eclectic band of women"), there are the more recent establishments *Girl-Wonder.org* (a feminist collective with blogs, comics, fan campaigns, and a thriving forum, concentrating on superhero comics—Figure 8.2, left), *When Fangirls Attack* (a blog that links without commentary to items deemed relevant to its topic of women in comics—Figure 8.1), *The Ormes Society* (a site for "supporting black female comic creators and promoting the inclusion of black women in the comics industry as creators, characters and consumers," named after cartoonist Jackie Ormes), and *Girl-A-Matic* (Web comics aimed at an audience of "either young adult or adult women") (Sequential Tart 2008; The Ormes Society 2008; Jonte 2008). General female-centered pop culture sites like *Pink Raygun, Feminist SF: The Blog!* and *The Hathor Legacy* include comics content, and there are also a diverse and plentiful range of individual blogs by creators who identify as women dedicated to or inclusive of superhero comics fare, such as: *Occasional Superheroine; Brainfreeze: Comic Love; Pretty, Fizzy Paradise; Written World; Seeking Avalon; Digital Femme; Comics Fairplay; Heroine Content; Ami Angelwings' Heavenly Comics Reviews, and Ami Angelwings' Supercute Rants of DOOOM XD* [sic].

The title of my own blog, *Girls Read Comics (And They're Pissed)*, not excluded, many of these names linguistically perform femininity. They refer to female creations or creators (Lulu, Jackie Ormes), female deities (Hathor), female spaces (Avalon), or contain words that expressly refer to the female (girl, femme, heroine, tart). Many of them, regardless of the creator's age, also contain markers that signify *girlishness*—either the word itself or references to prettiness, pinkness, or cuteness. These references to girlishness might not be devoid of irony (*Girls Read Comics (And They're Pissed)* was a sarcastic response to the often breathlessly astonished approach of mainstream media—Amazing! Girls read comics!), but these names nevertheless suggest not only femininity but the stereotypical, normative feminine.

It is possible to read this performative femininity as a preemptive defense against accusations of a transgresssive and undesirable masculinity—we may read comics, but we're still girls! However, Bury writes that "[p]erformance and articulation are critical to understanding an online media fan culture that defines itself and is defined by others through the female body" (Bury 2005, 10). In reference to female-only or female-centric cyberspaces in *X-Files* fandom, she argues that names that refer to the normative feminine "both recognize and refuse that which Dale Spencer (1995) calls the *plus male/minus male* dichotomy, whereby those practices

Figure 8.2 Left, the media publicity image for Girl-Wonder.org (http://girl-wonder. org/index.php), a blog dedicated to female characters and creators in mainstream comics. Why? "Because capes aren't just for boys." Created by Jempuu. *Right,* "Karen Healey: Bad-Arse Interwebs Superheroine," from the Web site *Girls Read Comics (And They're Pissed)* blog (http://girl-wonder.org/girlsreadcomics/). Illustration by Matt Powell. © Girl-Wonder.org.

associated with femininity are measured against masculinity and found to be lacking" (10). By invoking the normative feminine in their linguistic performance of online gender, these linguistically feminine comics blogs and Web sites are thereby not only laying claim to a female fan identity in a male-dominated fandom but are rejecting the notion that their fan identity lacks legitimacy *because* of its femininity.

The frequent performance of femininity in the names of female-identified cyberspaces becomes particularly interesting when viewed in contrast with the names of some of the better-known blogs by men. *I Against Comics* and *Fortress of Fortitude* are gender-neutral names. *Mike Sterling's Progressive Ruin, Scott (the Mad Thinker)'s Blog, Beaucoup Kevin, Dave's Longbox,* and *Chris's Invincible Super-Blog* contain masculine names, but rather than referring to male comics creations, creators, or deities, they are the names of the blogs' authors. These are not hard and fast distinctions: the female-written *Written World, Comics Fairplay,* and *Brainfreeze: Comic Love* all have gender-neutral names; *Ami Angelwings' Heavenly Comic Reviews* and *Ami Angelwings' Supercute Rants of DOOOM XD* refer to their female author; *2 Guys Buying Comics* is a male-written comic blog whose title refers to a more general masculinity. However, the general trend appears to be that while male-written blog titles are more likely to make a statement of masculine ownership specific to the writer, the normative femininity linguistically performed by female-written blog titles makes a claim to a more general female fan identity.

I do not wish to suggest that this articulation of normative femininity among online female comics fans is unproblematic or unquestioned. Indeed, female fans often consider and debate the terminology of female comics fandom, including what words should be used to describe female fans. I have in this essay consciously employed "female fan" as a suitably academic descriptive term, uncomfortably aware that in claiming a place for "female fans" among unmarked male "fans" I am also presenting women reading superhero comics as Other. Other female fans articulate similar difficulties with gendered fan terminology, and I want to examine first the history and then the debate that surround two terms that clearly indicate gender: "fanboy" and "fangirl."

THE SECRET ORIGINS OF FANBOY AND FANGIRL

The fanboy is well-established. According to Francesca Coppa's "A Brief History of Media Fandom," the term originated from science-fiction fandom and antedates 1919, before migrating into other media fandoms and online (Coppa 2006, 43). *Comic Book Culture* claims that the term "fanboy" became popular in superhero comics culture in the speculation boom of the mid-80s to mid-90s. Pustz writes that "fanboy" was derisively aimed at adolescent speculators who were popularly supposed to buy comics purely for their value as an investment property (Pustz 1999, xii). Unlike legitimate "fans," who bought comics primarily for the pleasure afforded in reading and interacting with other fans, "fanboys" might not even read the titles they acquired, much less evince a fannish involvement in their contents. However, this term later became applied to readers with an intense fannish involvement; Pustz later argues that "[s]ometimes . . . this intensity backfires, thereby helping to create fanboys, comic book readers who take what they read much too seriously" (Pustz 1999, 71). Leaving aside the difficulty implicit in determining what comprises taking comics "much too seriously," Pustz notes: "In fact, the term fanboy is used almost exclusively among comic book fans to refer to practices with which they disagree, titles they do not like, or people with whom they simply do not want to be associated" (Pustz 1999, 72).

As Pustz points out, within comics culture, "[t]he concept of fanboys very closely corresponds to the typical depiction of fans in popular culture" (Pustz 1999, 71). He compares the construction of the "fanboy" to the "Trekkie" stereotype portrayed in the famous *Saturday Night Live* skit and dissected by Henry Jenkins in *Textual Poachers* (Pustz 1999, 71–72). Jenkins writes that the skit "distills many popular stereotypes about fans," including that they are "brainless consumers" devoted to "the cultivation of worthless knowledge," who "place inappropriate importance on devalued cultural material"; "social misfits"; "feminized and/or desexualized"; "infantile, emotionally and intellectually immature"; and "unable to separate fantasy from reality" (Jenkins 1992, 10). "Fanboy" in its original context did not primarily identify male fans—since all fans were male—but boyish ones; petulant, obsessive, desexualized adolescents (regardless of their actual age). Little wonder, then, that "normal" comic fans wish to disassociate themselves from such stereotypes.

The fangirl has a much more recent critical history. Pustz does not mention her at all in *Comic Book Culture* (which is subtitled *Fanboys and True Believers*); nor does she appear in *Textual Poachers*, which refers solely to "fans," who are in that context understood to be primarily female. In the context of media fandom, Bury identifies the fangirl as "a powerful heteronormative minus-male subject position offered to those of us with female bodies who express admiration for a male celebrity" (Bury 2005, 37). She recognizes "the specter of the fangirl whose desires control her and not vice versa" and finds that members of the *X-Files* fanfic communities she studies are quick to reject "the fangirl discourse of desire as delusion" (Bury 2005, 38, 39). In 2006, the glossary section of the introduction to *Fan Fiction and Fan Communities in the Age of the Internet* defines "fangirl" as less derogatory: "*BNFs* [Big Name Fans] are surrounded by worshipping *fangirls*, although this term is also used in a nonpejorative sense for fans of the media source. *Fangirl* has also become a verb, as when one *fangirls* another writer or an actor, perhaps by squeeing (a squeal of uncontained appreciation or excitement)" (Hellekson and Busse 2006, 11). Later in this essay collection, during "Cunning Linguists: The Bisexual Erotics of *Words/Silence Flesh*," Eden Lackner, Barbara Lynn Lucas, and Robin Anne Reid write specifically of slash fangirls, arguing: "Few would debate the notion that slash fangirls define themselves in sexual terms in relation to the objects of adoration, which can include the source text and actors as well as favourite fan fiction writers" (Lackner et al. 2006, 202).

Within media fandom, then, a "fangirl" can be a derogatory term but is also used neutrally, as a synonym for "fan," or affectionately, to describe oneself or one's fellow fans in the pursuit of pleasurable activity. In this context, the most obvious traits of the fangirl are that she is appreciative, enthusiastic, and even worshipful towards her fannish objects of interest. Perhaps most striking, she is defined in terms of her sexual desires related to persons, fictional or living, situated within her fandoms.

However, in general online culture, this fangirlish performance of sexual desire is often presented as frightening or unnatural. Open-submission online dictionary *Urban Dictionary*'s most popular definitions of the "fangirl" also emphasize her sexual desires but characterize them very differently:

1. fangirl. A rabid breed of human female who is obesessed [sic] with either a fictional character or an actor. Similar to the breed of fanboy. Fangirls congregate at anime conventions and livejournal. Have been known to glomp, grope, and tackle when encountering said obsessions [sic].

> *Hugh Jackman: 'ello.*
> *Fangirl: SQUEEEEEE! *immediately attaches to Jackman's leg**
> *Jackman: Security!* (2007, 1)

2. A female who has overstepped the line between healthy fandom and indecent obsession.

> *Fan: Hakkai from Saiyuki is really cool, he's smart and nice and hey, he's pretty cute.*
> *Fangirl: Lyke OMG!!!11!one! Hakkai iz so lke totly my huzbend!*
> *Fan: You DO realize he is a two dimensional image on your television screen right?*
> *Fangirl: NOOO!! He'z reel and he iz al myne!* (2007, 1)

3. fangirl, n.

   1. (derogatory) a female fan, obsessed with something (or someone) to a frightening or sickening degree. Often considered ditzy, annoying and shallow.
   2. (playful, good-natured) less extreme, a female fan who can laugh at their own passion for their particular interest (or even obsession). (2007, 1)

These definitions characterize the fangirl's expressions of desire not as fun or affectionate but as delusional, verbally aggressive, and/or physically invasive ("glomp" refers to an enthusiastic and clinging hug/squeeze from a jump start). Here, the fangirl is "obsessed" and "rabid," not merely appreciative or worshipful, and her obsession is not playful but "indecent." Definition 2 makes a telling differentiation between the "fan" and the "fangirl" similar to that made in comics fandom between the fan and the fanboy, and the fangirl is linguistically defined as employing the abbreviations and misspellings of Standard English that denote the often-derided netspeak. Definition 4 makes allowances for a female fan who can laugh at—and thereby downplay or deprecate—her passion. She may merit the term being used in a "good-natured" fashion, but a female fan who is too serious about her interest becomes "frightening" or "sickening." Her open expression of sexual desire is socially inappropriate to the point of repulsion.

Definition 1 defines the fangirl as "similar to the breed of fanboy," but in their most derogatory uses, there is a striking contrast between the "fanboy" and the "fangirl." The pejorative use of "fanboy" characterizes him as a desexualized, trivia-collecting loner "fanboy" obsessed with the acquisition and dispensation of obscure knowledge. The pejorative use of "fangirl" characterizes her as a hypersexual, mindless obsessive whose desire is inappropriate and excessive. Though both are understood to take the object of their affection too seriously, they express their obsession very differently. These derogatory definitions support a strict gender binary of male/female, mind/body, logic/emotion, and fact/fantasy. The fanboy is negatively asexual, so caught up in his collection of trivia that he neglects his body. The fangirl is too emotional, indulging in sexual fantasy and lusting inappropriately for the bodies of others, and her own body-based identity is threateningly sexual.

In practice, in superhero comics fandom, neither "fanboy" nor "fangirl" is necessarily abusive. "Fangirl" can be used in superhero comics fandom as a neutral equivalent for "fanboy," used as a means of differentiating fans by gender. Nevertheless, I argue that such negative associations color less-derogatory uses of either term. This is particularly true of the "fangirl," who is associated with traits and behaviors devalued in the superhero comics fandom; romance, whether hetero or queer, and the sexual desire for male heroes. Moreover, if the epithet "fanboy" is leveled at a male fan, he can reject it by claiming to be instead a rational, legitimate "fan." The superhero comics "fangirl" cannot so easily deny the negative-gendered stereotype, since the legitimate "fan" is male. Women interested in reading superhero comics are already displaying gender-inappropriate socially transgresssive behavior; they are engaging with what are commonly understood to be masculine texts indulging male fantasies.

"FAN-WHAT?": REJECTION, RECLAMATION, AND PERFORMANCE OF THE FANGIRL

"Fanboy" and "fangirl" suggest a performative gender specific to fannishness, supported by a strict gender binary and dependent on behaviors and traits performed rather than any essential nature of the person so defined or self-defined. In her blog *Written World*, superhero comics fan Ragnell's 2006 entry "Fan-What?" explores her own response to the term "fangirl," which is neither as simple as an outright rejection nor a positive reclamation. She reports that following a conversation with another female fan, she began thinking about the vocabulary of identity in superhero comics fandom: "It's a linguistic issue, mainly. In theory, Fanboy and Fangirl are simply gendered terms to differentiate a male fan and a female fan. In practical use, they have not only a different gender but an entirely different meaning" (Ragnell 2007). She goes on to identify some of the familiar identifying characteristics of the pejorative fangirl: a fan fiction writer, particularly of slash; a manga reader; wearing a Sailor Moon costume;[4] interested primarily in romance and "The Angst" and "excited by the idea of two gay men not because it affords the opportunity to appreciate the male form, but instead because it showcases two males in a loving, caring relationship" (Ragnell 2007). She then compares the identifying traits of the fanboy (comic book store and Dungeons and Dragons enthusiast; "dark blue/black T-shirts with superhero logos/smartass phrases"; "an argument about whether the Hulk or Superman would win in a fight") and argues that: "Gay or Straight, he wants to cut the Angst and get on with the Action, he feels the best reason for cheesecake and sexually explicit scenes is the titillating view it offers, and he just giggled at the first syllable in the word 'titillating' " (Ragnell 2007). Ragnell's definitions are the stereotypical negative ones: both fanboy and fangirl are immature but express their immaturity in gendered fashion.

However, Ragnell articulated the fangirl and fanboy as defined by possessions and behaviors as well as by apparently intrinsic traits. She goes on to identify the "moods" associated with each term:

> Fanboy is a "Blue" term, as in "Blue is for Boys." Whereas, Fangirl is a "Pink" term, as in "Pink is for Girls." There is nothing inherently wrong with blue or pink. Both are fine colors, moods, acceptable lifestyles. But these colors represent traditional gender roles. The pink term of Fangirl embraces traditionally feminine traits like emotional/romantic thinking, pastel colors, cutesy things, and an audible high-pitched squeal associated with hearing about an opportunity to meet David Cassidy. The blue term of Fanboy embraces traditionally masculine traits like logical/statistical thinking, primary colors, blood and gore, and manly grunting/deep voiced "oh yeah"s. (Ragnell 2007)

Ragnell is clearly unimpressed with the traditional gender roles implicit in the "fangirl" descriptor. She writes: "I'm becoming increasingly uncomfortable with the term 'Fangirl'—mainly because I'm not fitting the stereotyped role very well" and identifies herself as, by behavior, more of a "fanboy": "Basically, I, and most of the fans I associate with (of either gender) are a mixture of both types, but leaning towards the 'Fanboy' " (Ragnell 2007). This revelation came about as she discussed which of two Green Lanterns would win a fight with her friend and colleague Kalinara,[5] which she describes as "cross[ing] the line":

> We . . . proceeded to . . . hammer out a chart which stated who would win under what conditions, after discussing the planning and combat abilities of each characters [sic].

> During the entire conversation, we never once discussed whether they would kiss, or feel bad about the battle afterwards, or even if their clothes would be torn off. Once we'd ironed out the winner in each

circumstance, Kalinara remarked that we'd given up female status on this one. I laughed then.

She concludes: "Unfortunately, it's not so funny when you think about it" (Ragnell 2007).

Ragnell argues that if one judges by behaviors performed rather than by biological sex or identified gender, she is more—but not completely—a fanboy than a fangirl. However, her ambivalent response to giving up "female status" is in keeping with the problematic claim of being "one of the boys." Women rejecting feminine descriptors can endorse the minus-male subject position and reinforce the "natural" desirability of behaving in stereotypical masculine fashion. Rejecting fangirlishness can also mean denigrating behaviors marked as feminine in superhero comics fandom; netspeak, emotional enthusiasm, an interest in romance and angst, and the writing of fan fiction, particularly slash. Women claiming to be "fanboys" (either as rejection of negative female stereotyping or as a description of their own traits and behaviors) are not uncommon in superhero comics fandom, but the reverse is rare.

Since Ragnell identifies as female, she may never be able to escape the label "fangirl"; others, discerning a self-identified female fan, are likely to use the term to describe her, regardless of her lack of involvement in stereotypical "fangirl" practices. By claiming to be more fanboy than fangirl, Ragnell is "crossing the line": fan gender identity online is linguistically performative, but boundaries still exist, confining Bury's "body-based identity."

Brainfreeze, on the blog *Brainfreeze: Comics Love*, also rejects the "fangirl" descriptor for herself, but without laying claim to "fanboy" in response. She also asserts that "fangirl" is an age-inappropriate definition for her fan self. In "What is a fangirl, anyway?" she reiterates the familiar romance-obsessed stereotype and writes:

> I'll grant that it's been a few years since anyone would have called me a fangirl (and "fanwoman" just doesn't have the same ring), but is this [the stereotype] really true? I like my comics with plenty of character moments (though a plot or some punching is also important), and relationships are part of that, but honestly, I don't look for them outside of what's in the books. "Shipping" just isn't something I do. (I gather that "shipping" refers to pairing up characters that aren't actually paired up in the books?) I also don't read fan fiction. (Brainfreeze 2007)

She continues: "It may be that most of this material is generated by female fans. (I don't know this for sure, as I don't gender-check the blogs I read.) But even if that's so, that's not the same thing as it being characteristic of female fans in general, right? Basic logic, right?" (Brainfreeze 2007). Her conclusion, "[i]t just strikes me that if there *is* a defining characteristic, this isn't it," denies the gender-essentialism of the fangirl stereotype (Brainfreeze 2007, author's italics).

Brainfreeze does not expressly propose an alternative to "fangirl," but her rejection of "fanwoman" and unconscious use of "female fan" is significant. Commenting on the post, Shelly posits that "[m]aybe there's a difference between being a female fan and a fangirl. ;)" (Brainfreeze 2007). She writes that she did write fan fiction "but not the relationship stuff" for TV shows, and that she "did write a couple of short fan fic stories for [DC superhero] Roy Harper years ago, to fill in some gaps, as I saw them" but concludes "same as you, I prefer my comics stories to be in the books. And it's been decades since I was a girl. :)" (Brainfreeze 2007). SallyP agrees that "fangirl" is an inappropriate descriptor for all superhero comics fans who are female, opining: "And the moral of the story is, you just can't make huge generalizations for any group of people" (Brainfreeze 2007).

However, also in comments on "What is a fangirl, anyway?" the Discriminating Fangirl disagrees with the wholesale rejection of "fangirl" as a descriptor:

> I consider myself a fangirl because . . . well, I'm a fan and I am, in fact, female. (And like you said, "fanwoman" just doesn't have the same ring to it.) I do like shipping and romantic relationships, but I also study comics academically. I wrote my thesis as a feminist reading of the Dark Phoenix Saga. So . . . am I somehow less of a fan because I choose to label myself a fangirl for kicks and giggles? (Brainfreeze 2007).

She agrees that "[i]t's impossible to paint an entire group of people with the same brush," arguing that "there are lots of female fans who focus exclusively on relationships and fanfic, but there are also male fans who do the same thing. Same goes for fans who'd much rather debate canon" (Brainfreeze 2007). The Discriminating Fangirl's claim to legitimacy as an academic can be read as an elitist defense of her fangirl self, with her academic credentials legitimizing the "fangirl" performances of liking fan fiction and romance (class identity, of course, is also performative). However, she identifies making a distinction between "fangirl" and "female fan" as elitist discrimination: "The whole fangirl/female fan distinction rankles me because it comes off as more of a way for some fans to feel more important or like better fans than others" (Brainfreeze 2007).

Comments in response to Ragnell's "Fan-What?" also included arguments for a conscious reclamation of the term. Redlib argues that calling oneself a fangirl can remove the power of the term to insult when used by others: "Fangirl—I embrace it like I do geek, nerd, and other terms that could be used in a deragatory [sic] way, but if you call yourself them first . . . you own it" (Ragnell 2007). Megs is even more positive, arguing that applying "fangirl" to those female fans who don't fit the stereotype will encourage a more sympathetic understanding of what constitutes a fangirl within the fandom: "I'm taking back 'fangirl'! Fangirl 4 Life! I dunno, this is one of those things where I encourage people who'd dub themselves 'equalist' to just go ahead and use 'feminist' and let their opinions speak for themselves. Go ahead and use 'fangirl' and let people sort you out" (Ragnell 2007).

"Fan-What?" and "What is a fangirl, anyway?" both recognize that "fangirl" and "fanboy" are performative identities, forcibly rather than inherently gendered. Brainfreeze's dismissive rejection of "fangirl" as age-inappropriate and unsuited to her practices is distinct from Ragnell's more consciously problematic claim to be a "fanboy," with her implicit reluctance to devalue "female status" and so employ the discourse of the "minus-male" female fan. In contrast, Discriminating Fangirl reclaims "fangirl" as a fan identity, and notes her participation in typical fangirl behaviors. In her comments, however, she does not linguistically perform the stereotypical fangirl with netspeak or the squees of "uncontained appreciation or excitement" found in media fandom (Lackner et al. 2006, 202).

Comics fan Ami Angelwings does regularly employ the linguistic markers of the "fangirl," including the frequent use of emoticons like XD (angry face) :D (happy face) and :((sad face) and netspeak, such as "dun" ("don't"), "rly" ("really"), or "ppl" ("people"). The following excerpt is linguistically typical:

> *Neways* : (This whole thing got me rly upset b/c all my dream jobs are in heavily male entertainment industries (comics, video games, etc) and it just scares me that ppl will care more about my looks than nething else. That just b/c I'm an attractive woman in an environment where these fanboys didn't expect to find one, I'm going to be put on that pedestal and then knocked down and called a slut and a whore and stuff b/c they're going thru their "cheerleader wun date me, she's clearly a slut" sour grapes highschool flashback phase. (Ami Angelwings 2007b)

Ami encounters occasionally heated resistance to the linguistic performance of her fan identity. Marionette, commenting on Ami's blog post "Alexandra Dewitt meet Tasha Yar," complains that she cannot easily parse Ami's writing: "It's a shame, because I was enjoying the essay, but after a couple of paragraphs it gets like fingernails on a blackboard to me" (Ami Angelwings 2007c). Later, in response to a guest column by Ami on another blog, Marionette calls Ami's use of netspeak an "affectation," while again explaining that she finds it a "barrier to communication" (Marionette 2007). Comics creator Lea Hernandez, responds to a comment Ami left in multiauthored Livejournal Manstreamcomics thusly:

> Ami, I am begging you to STOP USING CHATSPEAK, at least when you comment in other people's blogs. At LEAST in mine and Manstream. It undermines your points ENTIRELY.

> I want to read what you have to say, you're intelligent. But the chatspeak makes you sound uncommonly idiotic, not cute, not funny, not gamine. STOP IT. (Hernandez 2007)

Ami, however, maintains that her use of typically fangirlish markers is not affectation, but a genuine expression of self, and resists all pleas and commands to desist. In response to a post by Kevin Church, who wonders if a post by Ami on the VA Tech murders is satirical, she replies:

> I know a lot of ppl dun like the way I write, or the way I talk, or the way I think. That's fine :3
>
> . . .
>
> I dun mind that ppl are turned off by it.
> I just wanted to state definitively that I'm not somebody trying to be satirical or mocking feminists (as some ppl apparently believe) or nething else like that :D
> I'm just a girl who reads comics and likes to write :D
> (Ami Angelwings 2007d)

Ami links the way she writes to both the way she talks and the way she thinks; a self-described performance of fan identity as genuine as any linguistic performance of the self online. Rather than an attempt to foment discord by satirizing the fangirl stereotype, or an affective attempt to be "cute," "funny," or "gamine," Ami's use of normative fangirl signifiers linguistically perform a gendered fan subject which she asserts is the "real" cyberher: just a girl who reads comics. That her linguistic performance of fangirlishness appears fake or affected to several of her detractors[6] is an indictment not only of Ami's comprehensibility (which I would argue is considerably less opaque to nonusers than, for example, the language of a typical academic essay) but of her perceived attempts to be "cute"—that is, girlish. Female superhero comics fandom is able to consciously articulate the performative aspects of the gendered fan self, but some members are, it appears, uncomfortable not with the female but with the *too* feminine.

CONCLUSIONS

Gender matters: online; in comics fandom; in the performance of the fan identity. Female superhero comics fans are aware of their apparent invisibility, and their linguistic performances of gender reveal a complex relationship with the normative feminine. The claim to femininity through cyberspace names that invoke the feminine may be ironic or sarcastic, but the gender of the creator's online fan self is thus emphasized, in what may be a simultaneous recognition and rejection of plus male/minus male logic.

The term "fangirl" as an articulation and performance of the self receives particular attention from female comics fans. Fans like Ragnell and Brainfreeze wrestle with the history of "fangirl" and "fanboy," arguing that they are terms linked to behaviors, not essentials. Some female fans resent and reject the term "fangirl," arguing that the stereotypes do not apply to them. Other female fans attempt to positively reclaim the term as a more neutral expression denoting only the body-based gender identity of the fan, while still others engage in more complex negotiations, aware that rejecting the "fangirl" stereotype can also be read as a problematic rejection of the feminine in favor of more patriarchy-approved methods of reading and responding to superhero comics. Moreover, rejecting the fangirl stereotype can also mean rejecting fellow female fans: fans like Ami Angelwings employ the linguistic markers of stereotypical fangirlishness to perform their own fan selves. If this is uneasily perceived as *too* girlish, *too* feminine, then a backlash may be engendered against this transgression against the "real" female fan, provoking questions about whether the normative fangirl can (or should) be embraced or erased within superhero comics culture.

Whether they articulate and perform the female fan self as "fan," "female fan," "fanboy," or "fangirl," the online presence of female comics fans, the gendered terms that they employ and debate, and the boundaries they place around the feminine fan identity are of obvious value when considering the performance of the fan identity. Perhaps most personally satisfying is the gusto with which such women refuse to be invisible. "Look at us," they proclaim. "We're RIGHT HERE."

NOTES

1. One possible exception: *Comics Worth Reading*, a blog written by former DC Comics employee Johanna Draper Carlson, published the results of a reader survey commissioned by DC in 1995. The study "was all based on under 1000 answered questionnaires out of 3200 inserted in comics" with a signed copy of *Zero Hour* #0 as an incentive to reply. According to Carlson, "92% of DC readers were male" and "80% of them were ages 18–39, with a median age of almost 29" (Draper Carlson 2007). To my knowledge, DC has neither confirmed nor denied the accuracy of the statistics cited.
2. Layton's assumptions regarding the audience of romance novels are also inaccurate. Setting aside the question of categorization and genre within the fiction industry, where romantic literature written by authors identified as female is often shelved and sold as "chick-lit," where romantic literature written by authors identified as male is often shelved and sold as "literary fiction," the Romance Writers of America report that of the 64.6 million Americans who read at least one romance novel in 2005, 22 percent were male. This is "a significant increase from the 2002 survey that showed only 7% of readers were male" (Romance Writers of America 2008).
3. In 2008, it is still possible for superhero romance novel author Jennifer Estep to describe the following conversation at a used-book store where she bought several (superhero-focused) graphic novels: "Something funny that happened was the checkout guy said something about the graphic novels belonging to my significant other. I corrected him. No, dude, those are mine. Chicks read comics, too" (Estep 2008).

4. *Bishoujo Senshi* [Pretty Soldier] *Sailor Moon*: a popular manga, then anime about an ordinary girl who discovers she is the reincarnation of a moon princess. With her friends, she fights various monsters in a colorful sailor-suit costume. Both the manga and anime have been translated as *Sailor Moon*, to an appreciative English-speaking audience. Despite the presence of costumes, secret identities, superpowers, and a life-or-death struggle between the powers of good and evil, *Sailor Moon* is not widely regarded as a superhero title, probably because of its non-Western origin.

5. Ragnell's approach to "fangirl" as a problematic identity is interesting in light of the fact that she and colleague Kalinara together founded and run the linkblog *When Fangirls Attack*. Ragnell does not explore this potential irony in "Fan-What."

6. The debate is not one-sided: Ami also has supporters within general comics fandom and the feminist fan movement who defend her linguistic markers of girlishness as a form of (fan) self-expression.

BIBLIOGRAPHY

2 Guys Buying Comics. http://2guysbuyingcomics.blogspot.com/.

Ami Angelwings. 2007a. *Ami Angelwings' Heavenly Comics Reviews*. http://ami-angelwings.blogspot.com/.

Ami Angelwings. 24 Nov. 2007b. "Me and My Genes Do Not Exist for You." In *Ami Angelwings' Supercute Rants of DOOOM XD*. http://ami-rants.blogspot.com/2007/11/me-and-my-genes-do-not-exist-for-you.html.

Ami Angelwings. 14 Jul. 2007c. "Alexandra Dewitt Meet Tasha Yar." In *Ami Angelwings' Supercute Rants of DOOOM XD*. http://ami-rants.blogspot.com/2007/07/alexandra-dewitt-meet-tasha-yar.html.

Ami Angelwings. 18 Apr. 2007d. Comment in *Beaucoup Kevin*. Archived: http://www.haloscan.com/comments/beaucoupkevin/1510293529170834311/.

Beaucoup Kevin. http://www.beaucoupkevin.com/.

Borsellino, Mary. 31 Aug. 2007. "Random Fact You Might Have Use For." E-mail to Karen Healey.

Brainfreeze. 24 Sep. 2007. "What Is a Fangirl, Anyway?" In *Brainfreeze: Comics Love*. http://-brainfreeze-.blogspot.com/2007/09/what-is-fangirl-anyway.html.

Brown, Jeffrey A. 2001. *Black Superheroes, Milestone Comics, and Their Fans*. Jackson: University Press of Mississippi.

Bryne, John. May 1993. *Sensational She-Hulk* #52. New York: Marvel Publishing.

Bukatman, Scott. 2008. "Secret Identity Politics." In this volume.

Bury, Rhiannon. 2005. *Cyberspaces of Their Own: Female Fandoms Online*. New York: Peter Lang Publishing.

Butler, Judith. 1990. *Gender Trouble: Feminism and the Subversion of Identity*. New York: Routledge.

Draper Carlson, Johanna. 10 May 2007. "Superhero Comic Reader Stats." In *Comics Worth Reading*. http://comicsworthreading.com/2007/05/10/super-hero-comic-reader-stats/.

Chris's Invincible Super-Blog. http://the-isb.blogspot.com/.

Comics Fairplay. http://comicsfairplay.blogspot.com/.

Coppa, Francesca. 2006. "A Brief History of Media Fandom." In *Fan Fiction and Fan Communities in the Age of the Internet*, 41–61. Eds. Karen Hellekson and Kristina Busse. Jefferson: McFarland and Company.

Dave's Longbox. http://daveslongbox.blogspot.com/.

David, Peter, et al. 1998–2003. *Young Justice*. New York: DC Comics. Digital Femme. http://www.digitalfemme.com/journal/.

Estep, Jennifer. 21 Jan. 2008. "I've Been a Bad, Bad Girl . . ." In *Jennifer Estep's Blog*. http://www.jenniferestep.com/blog/?p=380.

Feminist SF: The Blog! http://blogs.feministsf.net/.

Fortress of Fortitude. http://fortressoffortitude.wordpress.com/.

Friends of Lulu. http://www.friends-lulu.org/faq.php.

Girls Read Comics (And They're Pissed). At Girl-Wonder.org: http://girl-wonder.org/girlsreadcomics/.

Girl-Wonder.org. http://girl-wonder.org/index.php.

Hellekson, Karen, and Kristina Busse, eds. 2006. *Fan Fiction and Fan Communities in the Age of the Internet*. Jefferson, Ohio: McFarland and Company.

Hernandez, Lea. 3 Jun. 2007. Comment on "Nymphet Na-Na-na-na-Naaaaaaaaaah" in *Manstream Comics*. http://manstreamcomics.livejournal.com/4619.html?thread=35083.

Heroine Content. http://www.heroinecontent.net/.

Hills, Matt. 2002. *Fan Cultures*. New York: Routledge.

I Against Comics. http://iagainstcomics.blogspot.com/.

Jenkins, Henry. 1992. *Textual Poachers: Television Fans and Participatory Culture*. New York: Routledge.

Jonte, Lisa. "Editorial." Girlamatic.com. http://www.girlamatic.com/comics/gam-edit.php.

Klaehn, Jeffery, ed. 2007. *Inside the World of Comic Books*. Montreal: Black Rose Books.

Lackner, Eden, Barbara Lynn Lucas, and Robin Anne Reid. 2006. "Cunning Linguists: The Bisexual Erotics of *Words/Silence/Flesh*." *Fan Fiction and Fan Communities in the Age of the Internet*. Eds. Karen Hellekson and Kristina Busse. Jefferson, Ohio: McFarland and Company.

Layton, Bob. 2007. "'Some Real Shit Winds up Selling Like Hot Cakes': Bob Layton." In *Inside the World of Comic Books*. Ed. Jeffery Klaehn. Montreal: Black Rose Books.

Marionette. 15 Oct. 2007. "Re: [Comment Thread] Guest Column: Fantasy Land." On Girl-Wonder.org forums. http://girl-wonder.org/forums/viewtopic.php?p=56470#p56470.

McDuffie, Dwayne, et al. 1993–1997. *Static*. New York: Milestone/DC Comics.

Mike Sterling's Progressive Ruin. http://www.progressiveruin.com/.

Occasional Superheroine. occasionalsuperheroine.blogspot.com/.

Pink Raygun. http://www.pinkraygun.com/.

Pretty, Fizzy Paradise. http://kalinara.blogspot.com/.

Pustz, Matthew. 1999. *Comic Book Culture: Fanboys and True Believers*. Jackson: University Press of Mississippi.

Ragnell. 3 Apr. 2006. "Fan-What?" In *Written World*. http://ragnell.blogspot.com/2006/04/fan-what.html.

Romance Writers of America. "Romance Literature Statistics: Readership Statistics." http://www.rwanational.org/cs/the_romance_genre/romance_literature_statistics/readership_statistics.

Scott (The Mad Thinker)'s Blog. http://scottthemadthinker.vox.com/.

Seeking Avalon. http://seeking-avalon.blogspot.com/.

Sequential Tart. "A1B1C1.gif." http://www.sequentialtart.com/.

Slott, Dan, et al. Oct. 2007. *She-Hulk* #21. New York: Marvel Publishing.

Story, Tim, dir. 2005. *Fantastic Four*. DVD. Australia: Twentieth-Century Fox Film Productions.

Sumerak, Mark, and Gurihiru. 2006. *Avengers and Power Pack Assemble!* New York: Marvel Publishing.

The Hathor Legacy. http://thehathorlegacy.info/.

The Ormes Society. http://theormessociety.com/.

Urban Dictionary. "Fangirl." http://www.urbandictionary.com/define.php?term=fangirl&page=1.

Vaughan, Brian K., and Tony Harris. 2004–present. *Ex Machina.* New York: Wildstorm/DC Comics.

When Fangirls Attack. http://womenincomics.blogspot.com.

9 Recruiting an Amazon
The Collision of Old World Ideology and New World Identity in *Wonder Woman*

Clare Pitkethly

Amazons must be opposed and overcome as a fresh contest in every age.

—Kleinbaum 1983, 2

Wonder Woman wings her winning way from Paradise Isle,
secret home of the Amazons, where gorgeous girls rule supreme,
to the hearts of millions of Americans,
fighting ever fearlessly to conquer evil and create permanent
peace and happiness in the world!

—Marston 1943 March, 1

Condemned to the far reaches of the known world, the mythological Amazon owes her existence to the antagonism of same and other, of hero and villain. Amazon encounters serve to define, through negation, the cultural identity of those who encounter her. She necessitates structures of dominance and submission and, as female barbarian, compels conquest through marriage and war. Originating in classical mythology, the defeat of an Amazon served to uphold the *kleos,* or renown, of the victorious Greek hero, and the dominance of the culture from which he emerged. Revived in the Renaissance, Amazon encounters allowed European explorers to view a strange New World through the familiar classical framework of dominance and submission. This mythological opponent personified America, and thus conquistadors' conquests were reframed as the victories of mythic heroes. This colonial discourse is also played out in Renaissance literature, as the untamed Amazon submits to domestication within marriage. In both war and marriage, her submission asserts the hierarchical relationship between the Old and New Worlds, Europe and America. As America developed into a Western power, the significance of the Amazon shifted. In 1942, when America stood up on the global stage of World War II, an Amazon emerged as a figure of victory, and of American dominance. Wonder Woman, the Amazon Princess, inverted the hierarchy of dominance and submission that had condemned her mythic predecessors. Victorious in war, Wonder Woman defeated America's WW II enemies and became a national icon. Refusing to submit to domestication through marriage, Wonder Woman motivated women's entry into the workforce and emerged as a prominent feminist icon. The Amazon Princess' victories, however, were achieved by joining the 'man's world' that the mythic Amazons had opposed, and thus the hierarchical framework structuring war and marriage remained intact. Clad in a scant American flag, Wonder Woman represents an ally rather than an opponent. Viewing the Amazon through a framework of cultural imperialism, I will illustrate her journey from colonized to colonizer. Utilizing both Old World and New World Amazon symbolism, I will ascertain the challenge posed by Wonder Woman to this enduring mythological opponent.

Fuelled by the fifth-century BC Greek victories in the Persian wars, Athenian art and literature boasted of previous Greek victories in mythological battles. Along with Trojans and Centaurs, Amazons emerged as one of the most prominent symbols of hostile otherness in fifth-century art (Stewart 1997, 191). Representations of her submission to Achilles, Bellerophon, Heracles, and Theseus served as visual analogies for Greek dominance. At the conclusion of the Persian wars, the Amazon emerged as a fluid representation of otherness, acquiring the attire and weaponry of the Persian enemy. Integrating contemporary fears into reconstructed mythological battles, both Amazons and Persians were reduced to barbarian other, while Greek soldiers acquired the *kleos* of the great Greek heroes. The classical distinction between same and other, an ideology fundamental to Western thought, is examined by Page DuBois in *Centaurs and Amazons*. DuBois observes the Greek transition from artistic and literary discourse to philosophical discourse in the fifth and fourth centuries. The mythological defeat of an Amazon evolved into the philosophical structuring of difference and hierarchy, and thus the conflict between Greek and Amazon affirmed a hierarchy within the dichotomies Greek/barbarian and male/female. Falling into the categories barbarian and female, the mythological Amazon must submit to the Greek hero. Her defeat confirms the privileged position attributed to the Greek male in Athenian society and stands as a warning to any who would attempt to invert the established hierarchy. Lysias's fifth-century Athenian funeral oration clearly positions the Amazon within these hierarchical structures. Drawing on Homer's sixth-century characterization of Amazons as "the equal of men" (Homer 1951, Book III v. 89), Lysias declares: "for their courage Amazons used to be considered men rather than women" (Lysias 1997, v. 4). Continuing his tale, however, Lysias affirms the hierarchical structures which Amazons invert:

> Then, hearing of the great renown spoken of this land, [the Amazons] gathered their most warlike nations and marched against the city in pursuit of a glorious reputation and high expectations. But here they met brave men and came to possess spirit alike to their physical nature. Gaining a reputation that was the opposite of the one they had, they proved to be women. . . . (Lysias 1997, vv. 4–5)

The fate of Lysias's Amazons appears inevitable, and indeed it is inevitable, for the same fate is repeated in each classical Amazon encounter. In *Amazons: A study in Athenian Mythmaking*, William Tyrell argues that the Amazons of Athenian myth existed only to die: "the myth emphasizes the death of Amazons in individual combat, rape, and mass slaughter" (Tyrrell 1984, 128). Allaying the fear of social upheaval, the defeat of an Amazon was a means of restoring order to the world and reestablishing Greek male control. As Greek philosophy and literature spread throughout Europe, the Amazon persisted in Western culture, embraced for her validation of Western dominance.

Asserting a geographic distinction between same and other, classical Amazons were located at the boundaries of the known world (Diodorus 1935, Book III v. 53); and as the known world expanded following 1492, Amazons appeared at these new uncharted boundaries. Columbus's belief that he would reach the Far East by sailing west shaped his expectations for the exploratory voyage. Fifteenth-century European cosmology located mythical monsters and strange beasts at the eastern ends of the earth, and Columbus's arrival in the Indies would, therefore, be verified by the presence of these marvelous inhabitants. Initially, Columbus's presumption proved incorrect: "In these islands I have so far found no human monstrosities, as many expected" (Columbus in Hulme 1986, 14). After questioning the native inhabitants, however, Columbus found his mythical monster. Familiar with the thirteenth- and fourteenth-century Asian expeditions of Marco Polo and Sir John Mandeville, Columbus confirmed their discovery of an island of Amazonian women in the Indies, an island Columbus named Matinino. Although he excludes the name Amazon, Columbus's account of women who "engage in no feminine occupation, but use bows and arrows of cane" (Columbus in Hulme 1986, 14–15) recalls the Amazons of Herodotus, the fifth-century BC father of history: "Our business is with the bow and the spear, and we know nothing of women's work" (Herodotus 1954, 4.114). While classical sources shaped Columbus's initial account, it was medieval Amazon mythology that inspired the relentless European search for New World Amazons. Rich in yellow metal, Columbus's Amazonian island confirmed the medieval geographers' association of Amazons with gold. Although absent in classical mythology, the idea of Amazonian wealth grew as the promise of exotic Asian riches lured European explorers further east. The wealth of the new territories merged with existing Amazon mythology and became a prominent feature of medieval Amazon encounters. The conquest of an Amazon not only affirmed the victorious Christian knight's valor, a remnant of their classical origins, but also yielded wealth to share throughout his Christian homeland. The search for, and conquest of, Amazons thus became a Christian duty, a notion Father Christoval de Acuña confirms in his seventeenth-century New World travel narrative: "if these are the Amazons made famous by historians, there are treasures shut up in their territory, which would enrich the whole world" (Acuña 1963, 123).

To sixteenth- and seventeenth-century explorers, the widespread popularity of the search for Amazons was a confirmation of an Amazonian presence in the New World: "it is not credible that a lie could have been spread throughout so many languages, and so many nations, with such an appearance of truth" (Acuña 1963, 122). Although New World travel narrative abounds with rumors and missed encounters, only one first-hand Amazon encounter appears. Francisco de Orellana's 1541 journey in search of El Dorado and the Land of Cinnamon uncovered, instead, a tribe of Indians who were "the subjects of, and tributaries to, the Amazons." The Indians summoned their "women captains," and Orellana's scribe, the Dominican monk Gaspar de Caravajal, recorded the ensuing battle:

> These women are very white and tall . . . and they are very robust and go about naked, [but] with their privy parts covered, with their bows and arrows in their hands, doing as much fighting as ten Indian men . . . Our Lord was pleased to give strength and courage to our companions, who killed seven or eight (for there we actually saw) of the Amazons, whereupon the Indians lost heart, and they were defeated. (Caravajal 1934, 214)

Orellana's battle is unique within New World travel writing, replicating the classical structure of hero against Amazon. This vision of Christian conquistador against Amazon resonated throughout Europe, and the 'River of the Amazons' became a defining feature of the New World. Old World myths about Amazons had found a home in the New World, and European perceptions of New World inversion were thus confirmed.

When Amazon mythology is understood as a narrative of dominance and submission, her resurgence during a period of conflict between the Old and New Worlds seems appropriate. The very existence of the New World created tension in Europe, as conventional wisdom about the nature of the world crumbled. The Catholic Church was destabilized, as the Bible proved an inadequate and incomplete source of knowledge. Classical cosmological authorities were also undermined. Reminiscent of her role in classical mythology, the defeat of an Amazon allayed fears of social inversion, and thus, her resurgence during the philosophical upheaval of the Renaissance served to reestablish order. Applying Amazon imagery to America established a framework of European comprehension and control. Theodore Galle's 1600 graphic representation of America as an Amazon clarifies this association. Holding a spear and the severed head of a conquistador, the nude Amazon embodies the danger and desire of the New World. Emerging from the Western imagination, she reveals the Western desire for conquest, at the same time as her savagery justifies this conquest. Viewed in the context of classical

Figure 9.1 Allegorical sculpture of America as Amazonian warrior, from a series on parts of the world, design by Charles Lebrun for the gardens of the Château de Versailles, Paris, c. 1680–85. © The Art Archive/Gianni Dagli Orti.

Amazon mythology, her personification of the New World asserts an inevitable submission to Western culture. A similar depiction of America as a warrior determined in her conquest appeared later in the century in the allegorical sculpture designed by Charles Lebrun for the gardens of Versailles (Figure 9.1). Armed with sword, bows and arrows, and an alligator as companion, in this example, America's nether regions are covered rather than revealed—nevertheless, her bosom is exposed shamelessly to the world.

As America grew into a twentieth-century Western power, an Amazon emerged as the embodiment of American dominance, rather than of American submission. Her Amazonian origins reflect America's disparate colonial history, but her passionate loyalty to America during WW II reflects a consolidated America, one united by ideology. The patriotic times of WW II coincided with a boom in superhero comic sales, and American psychologist William Moulton Marston was keen to capture this growing young audience. Working as an educational consultant for DC Comics, Marston proposed the creation of a new kind of superhero, one previously unseen within the "blood-curdling masculinity" of the medium, a female superhero. The suggestion was met with "a storm of mingled protests and guffaws," Marston recalls, but publisher M. C. Gaines eventually conceded: "I'll take a chance on your Wonder Woman! But you'll have to write the strip yourself. After six months' publication we'll submit your woman hero to a vote of our comic readers. If they don't like her I can't do any more about it" (in Marston 1944, 43).

Marston published the first Wonder Woman comic book story in *All Star Comics* #8, December 1941, the same month as the Japanese attack on Pearl Harbor. The strip was a runaway best seller, and the results of Gaines's promised poll showed that Wonder Woman had secured more than 80 percent of the vote (Marston 1944, 43). Having captured the imagination of young Americans, Wonder Woman received a comic book of her own in 1942. Relevant in times of war, Marston utilized the mythic Amazonian themes of strength and courage. His interpretation of Amazon mythology, however, was otherwise very liberal. Reflecting her classical origins, Wonder Woman comes from an isolated Amazonian civilization, renamed Paradise Island in the comic book series. An undiscovered utopia concealed within the Bermuda triangle, Paradise Island evokes the location, but not the disposition, of Columbus's Matinino. Remaining outside the boundaries of the known world, Marston's Amazons are isolated from 'man's world' and safe from male domination. Their isolation is threatened in the comic book's debut, when 'man's world' brings WW II to the skies over Paradise Island. Marston's Amazon Queen, Hippolyte, is counseled by her Greek gods:

Aphrodite: The gods have decreed that the American Army Officer crash on Paradise Island. You must deliver him back to America—to help fight the forces of hate and oppression.

Athena: Yes, Hippolyte, American liberty and freedom must be preserved! You must send with him your strongest and wisest Amazon—the finest of your wonder women!—For America, the last citadel of democracy, and of equal rights for women, needs your help! (Marston 1941 December, 5)

In Marston's narrative, the Amazon Princess, renamed Wonder Woman by the American army officer who crashed on Paradise Island, is sent by the gods to help America. This divine intervention legitimizes the comic book character by placing her in a league of mythic heroes and ancient gods, whilst also providing divine justification for both America's entry into WW II and American patriotism.

The Amazon is a convenient motif to draw upon in times of war, while her ideological malleability has ensured her enduring presence in wartime propaganda. Reflecting her pervasiveness, shortly before America recruited an Amazon Princess, the Nazi enemy also utilized the Amazon in propaganda. In Christian Weber's "famous Nazi glamour show" *Nacht der Amazonen*, the night of the Amazons, Amazon warriors participated in a sexualized spectacle, providing one observer with what he imagined as an insight into what "the war of the sexes must have been like before clothing had been invented" (Pope 1942, 41). Ludwig Lutz Ehrenberger's 1938 advertising bill reflects the amalgamation of militarism and sexuality in *Nacht der Amazonen*. Comprised of a lone Aryan archer, the single combat she offers provokes expectations of pleasure, rather than anguish. Combining danger and desire, the threat of her poised bow and arrow is offset by the statuesque beauty of her nude figure. The image recalls romanticized notions of classical warfare, while the grace and splendor of Ehrenberger's Amazon offers a vision of warfare to counteract that which the Germans had observed and endured two decades earlier, during WW I. Weber's theatrical performance of warfare, enacted by the dancers and actresses posing as Amazons, is positioned in gendered contrast to the reality of warfare, as executed by the Secret Service soldiers participating in *Nacht der Amazonen*. The polarization of female dancers and male soldiers stressed the same gender division voiced by Hitler: "Neither sex should try to do that which belongs to the sphere of the other" (in Steinem 1982, 147). Hitler's warning, declared in a speech given to the National Socialist Women's Organization in September 1934, recalls the inevitable fate of the classical Amazons, subjugated for their transgression. In the same speech, Hitler offers German women an alternative source of martial empowerment: "Every child that a woman brings into the world is a battle, a battle waged for the existence of her people" (in Steinem 1982, 147). To ensure reproductive capacity, the cultivation of the female body was embraced by Nazi Germany. An American visitor, Ruth Woodsmall, remarked on her 1935 visit to a German Women's Labor Service Camp: "a generation of young Amazons is being trained for the physically fit future motherhood of Germany" (Woodsmall 1935, 301). In Marston's comic book, American girls were also encouraged to adopt 'Amazon training,' a practice referred to regularly throughout the narrative, but one which was never entirely elucidated. Nonetheless, Marston's 'Amazon training' was the source of his Amazons' physical superiority, and when adopted by 'man's world' girls, could make "*any* girl powerful" (Marston 1943 #6, 3). Despite their similar training methods, Germany and America utilized their armies of young Amazons in different ways. While Hitler's gender ideology focused on reproduction, America embraced the robust woman's ability to adopt the physically demanding jobs left vacant by outbound soldiers.

America and Germany both suffered labor shortages during WW II and sought female labor to fill the gap, although America's more "intensive and pervasive" propaganda campaign resulted in greater female employment, with a rise of 32 percent (Rupp 1978, 174, 75). In the spirit of the times, Marston encouraged female military employment in his comic book, with the promise of female independence:

> *Mars' Slave-Secretary:* Here is the report you asked for—There are eight
>   million American women in war activities—by 1944 there
>   will be eighteen million! Women are warriors—WAACS,
>   Waves, Secret Agents!
> *Mars:* Silence—enough! If women gain power in war they'll escape
>   man's domination completely! They will achieve a horrible
>   independence! (Marston 1943 #5, 1)

Unique within the glut of "get a war job" propaganda, Marston inverted the male-centered structure of the official government slogans: "Longing won't bring him back sooner . . . GET A WAR JOB!," "Every idle machine may mean a dead soldier," "I'm proud . . . my husband *wants* me to do my part" (in Rupp 1978, 156, 96, 153). The women warriors envisioned by Marston remained absent in the official party line, and instead, the U.S. Office of War Information recommended that women's fear of becoming "half-male, half-female hybrids" be countered with material such as the following: "Many service women say they receive more masculine attention—have more dates, a better time—than they ever had in civilian life" (in Rupp 1978, 98). The fickleness of propaganda became apparent after the war, as women who were recruited into the workforce with promises of patriotism and glamour were discharged, accused of being "emotionally unstable feminists," their lost femininity lamented (in Rupp 1978, 163). The 'Rosie the Riveter' of wartime propaganda was only a transient identity, a temporary worker ready to step aside as the soldiers returned. In contrast to popular postwar representation, Wonder Woman and her alter ego Diana Prince would not step aside, and remained in Military service after the conclusion of the war, for without their 'war jobs' there would be no heroic adventures.

Despite America's victory in WW II, the threat of war and injustice continued in the comic book's narrative to provide an ongoing role for Wonder Woman. She remained in America to fight costumed supervillains as well as political enemies, but her opposition to Nazi Germany was such a significant part of her identity that the original television version of *Wonder Woman*, produced in 1976, featured the Wonder Woman of the WW II era fighting Nazi agents. To coincide with the television series, the comic book's narrative also returned to the early 1940s. *Wonder Woman*'s publisher, DC, eager to reclaim the boom in sales that came during the patriotic times of WW II, continues to feature Nazi villains, as it relives *Wonder Woman*'s Golden Age with reprints and the occasional new WW II–era story. While critics have highlighted the "Nazi-bashing" of Golden Age superhero comics (Bongco 2000, 97), the fight against America's past and present political enemies continues within the pages of Wonder Woman's comic book. Joining the war against America's most recent foreign threat, the graphic novel *Wonder Woman: Spirit of Truth* portrays Wonder Woman defeating Middle Eastern terrorists, in a cause motivated by "justice, not punishment" (Ross 2001, 10). The two justifications offered in the text conceal a third motivation for American intervention in the Middle East. Recalling America's colonial history, just as the sixteenth-century conquistadors veiled their desire for New World gold behind the notion of God's will, the American desire for Middle Eastern 'black gold' is veiled by an idealized notion of justice. Justice, constructed as an absolute ideal, is affirmed by the representation of Wonder Woman as an "impartial advocate of peace" (Ross 2001, 29). Wonder Woman preaches peace and justice, while defeating foreign forces of evil. Merging war with justice not only validates her opposition to America's political enemies, both past and present, but also places this opposition beyond dispute.

Amazon mythology is a narrative of conquest, and Wonder Woman maintains, although inverts, the Amazons' position within allegorical cultural imperialism. The Amazon Princess' role as a cultural missionary has remained a defining feature of her Amazonian identity: "The outside world could benefit from our knowledge, but any ambassador would surely face distrust. It would be a mission that would tax the stamina of the greatest Amazon" (Ross 2001, 1). This idealized representation of cultural imperialism in *Spirit of Truth* continues throughout the text, and recalls the opening lines of Rudyard Kipling's *The White Man's Burden*:

> Take up the white man's burden—
> Send forth the best ye breed—
> Go, bind your sons to exile
> To serve your captives' need. (Kipling 1899)

The British poet's 1899 response to the United States' colonization of the Philippine Islands has been read alternatively as a justification for colonization and as a satirical warning. Irrespective of ironic inferences, Kipling's term 'White man's burden' emerged as a colonial catchphrase, justifying U.S. foreign intervention and cultural imperialism. It is this moral duty that Wonder Woman adopts, bringing "Amazon courage and knowledge" to "all people in need" (Ross 2001, 2). Wonder Woman's cultural colonization of 'man's world,' specifically America, emerges analogous to her more prominent role in the text, that of American missionary in the wider world. Representing 'truth, justice and the American way,' elucidated by her allegiance with Superman in the text, Wonder Woman's missions take her to territories in conflict with an idealized 'American way.' Wonder Woman follows her defeat of Middle Eastern terrorists with an attempt to halt the Brazilian destruction of the Amazon rainforest and the salvation of peaceful protesters in Communist China's Tiananmen Square massacre. As Wonder Woman reflects on an idealized Paradise Island and ponders, "I do wish the outside world could be more like my home" (Ross 2001, 18), the contrast between the text's unjust global setting, and Wonder Woman's other home, America, supports U.S. foreign intervention and cultural imperialism. Wonder Woman's utopian homeland appears analogous to an idealized 'American way' and thus her global campaign for truth and justice enacts and necessitates American cultural expansion.

Affirming her role as an advocate of 'the American way,' Wonder Woman joined the first American army of superheroes, the Justice Society of America, shortly after her comic book debut. Uniting DC superheroes, the Justice Society of America faced adversaries too great for the individual superheroes to overcome. Wonder Woman first appeared with the group in *All-Star Comics* #11, joining them in the defeat of Japanese soldiers (Fox 1942, June). This issue appeared after the Japanese attack on Pearl Harbor, a "national emergency" which inspired Wonder Woman's allegiance to the group. Reflecting the gender ideology of the 1940s, in the subsequent issue *All-Star Comics* #12, Wonder Woman volunteered for the role of secretary, while the male members of the group went off to war. By the 1960s, however, Wonder Woman was a fully fledged member of the Justice Society of America's successor, the Justice League of America, emphasizing her iconic status and distinguishing her as a prominent symbol of American justice. Wonder Woman's unwavering allegiance to patriarchal 'man's world,' however, infers an opposition to her matriarchal homeland. This contradiction is realized on the cover of *Justice League Adventures* #4 (Slott 2002). Under the caption "Battle of the Sexes" (Figure 8.2), Wonder Woman stands in battle formation with the male members of the Justice League of America, while menacing Amazons surround the group of superheroes from 'man's world.' When the Amazons are temporarily transformed into a threat, Wonder Woman's allegiance is to America, rather than to her Amazon sisters. Within the comic book's narrative, Wonder Woman is forced to choose a side, thus asserting an incompatible and irreconcilable difference between matriarchal and patriarchal rule.

Despite the parallels between the two social structures, the conflict between matriarchy and patriarchy is a familiar theme within Amazon mythology. Matriarchy, like patriarchy, is based on a model of social organization defined by division and hierarchy. Privileging women rather than men, a matriarchal model reaffirms rather than questions the division of society based on gender; thus, male anxieties about female power are

Figure 9.2 Wonder Woman stands in battle with the male members of the Justice League of America against Amazons. Cover of *Justice League Adventures* #4, April 2002. © DC Comics.

placed in a familiar model of gender domination. Despite being organized by identical, although inverted, divisions and structures to patriarchal cultures, matriarchies, and in turn Amazons, are seen as strange deviations to the 'natural' order. In *Kinship and Marriage*, Robin Fox reasons that without patriarchal social control, an Amazonian solution would emerge. In an Amazonian model, Fox speculates, "the women would hold the property, and the power, and men would be of no account and would be used for breeding purposes only. Such a sinister practice exists only in the imagination" (Fox 1967, 113). From the imagination of Marston evolved a different vision of matriarchy, idyllic rather than "sinister." A well-published and versatile author, Marston's enthusiasm for female dominance is apparent in several of his popular and psychological texts. Women emerge as potential instigators for positive social reform, a theory developed in *Emotions of Normal People*, a psychological study of dominance, submission, compliance, and inducement, first published in 1928. Marston's formula for positive social reform relies on the submission of individuals with appetitive dominance to "love leaders," or individuals with love supremacy and appetitive subservience (Marston 1989, 393). Determining that "male love leadership is virtually impossible," Marston singles out women as the only potential "love leaders" (Marston 1989, 393). When it is considered that women lack "sufficient dominance" for the role, and men "dislike intensely the idea of submitting to women," the need for "emotional re-education" emerges (Marston 1989, 395, 396). *Wonder Woman* popularizes this psychological theory. Amazons appear as idealized "love leaders" and thus female dominance is reframed and glamorized for a reluctant audience. Despite Marston's transgressive politics, his social ideal maintains the antagonism of male and female. Indeed, Marston's idealized matriarchy seizes power through force, following a "sex battle for supremacy" (Marston in Valcour 1999, 22). Despite this apparent replication of patriarchal social dominance, Marston envisions matriarchy as a more "enlightened" stage of social development (Marston 1942 #1, 1), a stage destined to follow patriarchal dominance in America. In an interview appearing in the *New York Times*, November 11 1937, Marston predicted: "the next one hundred years will see the beginning of an American matriarchy—a nation of Amazons in the psychological rather than the physical sense" (Marston in Daniels 2000, 19). Marston's vision of a matriarchal future for America is reminiscent of his utopian matriarchal creation Paradise Island, and Wonder Woman's presence in America brings his vision of American utopianism one step closer. Indeed, Wonder Woman's rejection of her idyllic island paradise, and adoption of America as her homeland, affirms American utopianism.

Consistent throughout *Wonder Woman*'s 60-year comic book run is the construction of her matriarchal island home as a paradise "free from the violence and the tyranny of men" (Messner-Loebs 1994 #0, 18). This freedom from men, and the violence they represent, is constructed as a response to necessity rather than desire. Indeed, the threat posed by men remains ever present on Paradise Island. As decreed by Aphrodite's law, which governs the Amazons, if any man sets foot on Paradise Island, the Amazons lose their powers, their immortality, and ultimately their lives. Although men are excluded from the matriarchal island, through their imposing threat, the ultimate power of the patriarchy is affirmed: "what the daughters of Aphrodite have always dreaded *most* is finally *happening*—an *army* of marauding *men* is about to set foot on Paradise Island!" (Pasko 1976 #223, 1).

Affirming their sexuality, the term "daughters of Aphrodite" reframes Paradise Island as an alluring and exposed target, while the threat posed by the approaching army of "marauding *men*" is implicitly sexual rather than martial. This threat of sexual defeat recalls a significant theme within classical Amazon mythology, as the defeat of an Amazon was not confined to her submission in warfare. Preceding Theseus' marriage to Antiope was the rape and abduction of this Amazon Queen. Antiope's sexual defeat inspired Amazon retaliation: the invasion of Attica, and the seizure of the Acropolis. As Theseus's sexual misdemeanor allocated responsibility for the Amazon invasion of Athens to the Athenian hero, this aspect of the myth was discarded in the fourth century BC, and the Amazon attack on Athens was reframed as a desire for cultural expansion (Tyrrell 1984, 15). Contrasting the explicit, although short-lived, sexual defeat of Antiope by Theseus is Heracles's implicit, and enduring, sexual defeat of Hippolyte. Heracles's ninth labor required the possession of the Amazon Queen's girdle. Identified as the girdle of Ares in Apollodorus's *The Library*, this token symbolized the Amazon Queen's martial superiority (Apollodorus 1921, 203). Hippolyte failed to relinquish her girdle promptly, Heracles seized the prize, and thus the symbolism compounded. The removal of a girdle served as a classical euphemism for sexual intercourse, and thus the seizure of Hippolyte's girdle implies the use of force (Tyrrell 1984, 91). As an assertion of male dominance, the rape of an Amazon functions as a punishment for her rejection of male control. Hippolyte was stripped of her martial (male) dominance through an affirmation of her sexual (female) vulnerability. With warfare the maturation process for boys in classical Greece, and marriage, specifically sexual defloration, the maturation process for girls, Hippolyte is forced to assume the role of a woman. The unconquered Amazon embodied the threat that the unmarried woman posed to patriarchal rule in classical Greece. Existing outside male governance, both the unmarried woman and the Amazon must be subject to male domination and defeat. The meaning of classical Amazon mythology, Tyrrell argues, can only be completely understood within the context of marriage: "the Amazon myth explains why it is necessary for daughters to marry by creating a scenario of the dangers inherent in her not marrying" (Tyrrell 1984, xix).

While marriage remained an implicit theme in classical mythology, it became an explicit and monopolizing theme in Renaissance literature. In

Tough Love: Amazon Encounters and the English Renaissance, Kathryn Schwarz argues that sixteenth- and seventeenth-century stories about Amazons are interested less in the Amazons' resistance to patriarchy than in their participation in it (Schwarz 2000, 3). Shakespeare's *A Midsummer Night's Dream*, written in the late sixteenth century, exemplifies literature from this era. Based on the classical account of the marriage of Theseus and Antiope, Shakespeare's successful domestication of an Amazon queen affirms the legitimacy of patriarchal domestic structures. Rewriting Theseus's abduction of Antiope as Theseus's victory over Hippolyta in battle, the Amazon Queen's submission in war becomes analogous to her submission in marriage:

> *Theseus:* Hippolyta, I woo'd thee with my sword,
> And I won thy love doing thee injuries;
> But I will wed thee in another key,
> With pomp, and triumph, and with reveling.
> (Shakespeare 1992, Act 1, Scene 1, vv. 16–19)

Shakespeare's grand wedding of Theseus and Hippolyta is symbolic of both Theseus's "triumph" and the "triumph" of patriarchal culture over that of the matriarchal Amazons. When Amazon appearances in Renaissance literature are considered in conjunction with Galle's 1600 representation of America as an Amazon, Amazon submission acquires additional significance. The literary defeat of an Amazon emerges as an enactment of the hierarchical structuring of the Old World over the New. The taming of a matriarchal Amazon Queen through patriarchal domestication in *A Midsummer Night's Dream* serves as a metaphor for the taming of an inverted New World through Western colonization. Written in the mid 1590s, Shakespeare's *A Midsummer Night's Dream* coincides with the emergence of England's colonization of the New World in the 1580s.

In classical and Renaissance Amazon mythology, it was the dominant culture that was imposed on the Amazons; in contrast, the *Wonder Woman* comic book series inverts this structure. Wonder Woman preaches a utopian and enlightened Amazonian culture to those in 'man's world.' In Marston's text, the comparative cultural inferiority of 'man's world' is attributed to one factor alone, that of patriarchal dominance. He creates a clear link between the dichotomous categories of good and evil and those of feminine and masculine. This association was maintained after Marston ceased writing the comic book in 1948, and the belief that "males may be convulsed with conflict, poisoned with hatred, but women are only looking for a better way . . ." (Messner-Loebs 1998 #4, 7) is characteristic of the portrayal of gender in the comic book's later years. Although female villains feature prominently in *Wonder Woman*, these women are portrayed as victims of their culture. They are women who have fallen prey to malicious males, adopting male psychology as their own:

> *Wonder Woman:* You stupid girls! When you let your men bind you—
> you let yourselves be bound by war, hate, greed, and lust for power!
> Think! And free yourselves! Control those who would oppress others!
> You can do it! (Marston 1948 #32, 8)

In Marston's comic books, women who have been corrupted by 'man's
world' are treated on Transformation Island, an Amazon reformatory
located on an islet neighboring Paradise Island. Villains are cured when
they can submit to the "loving authority" of the Amazons, rather than
to the war, hate, and greed of male domination. It is only submission or
weakness in the face of male forces of power that results in the slavery or
bondage of women. This threat of male domination is symbolically represented in the comic book series by Wonder Woman's moment of greatest
weakness, which occurs when a man binds her bracelets.

Emerging as a backlash, the critical focus on bondage and submission in *Wonder Woman* came to prominence after perceptions of Wonder
Woman's "militant feminism" provoked "contempt and alarm" from male
critics (Daniels 1971, 13). While *Wonder Woman* did not find favor with
male critics, young female readers embraced the empowerment offered in
Marston's text:

> *Wonder Woman:* Look girls! I'm just an ordinary Amazon—but I *feel*
>   that I can do things, so I *can* do them!
> *Girls:* Oh, Princess, you're superb—you're magnificent—you're a won-
>   der Amazon!
> *Wonder Woman:* Ha Ha! Don't be silly, girls—you can do the same
>   thing! (Marston 1945 #13, 4)

Heeding Marston's message, young female readers were inspired to emu-
late Wonder Woman's heroics. Judy Collins, a childhood reader of *Wonder Woman*, recalls: "If she could . . . create love and beauty and fight
crime and prejudice, other women could do the same. I could do the same.
Wonder Woman taught us we could fly" (Collins in Marston 1998, 7).
Along with the inspiration Wonder Woman provided came a desire and
an expectation to achieve similar empowerment. Living up to Amazonian
standards within a 'man's world,' however, proved to be more challenging that it appeared in the comic books. Collins reveals that she was in
therapy for twenty years, "trying to learn to be as fearless as Wonder
Woman" (Collins in Marston 1998, 7). The relevance of the mythical
Amazon as a figure of female empowerment was questioned by Jungian
analyst Toni Wolff, in her 1956 paper "Structural Forms of the Feminine
Psyche." Wolff adopts the figure of the Amazon as a feminine archetype,
although she suggests that this form of femininity "may not be totally
consistent with a woman's natural structure" (Wolff 1995, 85). Marston,
it should be noted, based his creation, Wonder Woman, on a male model,

intending that she should embody "all the strength of a Superman plus all the allure of a good and beautiful woman" (Marston 1944, 42–43). Suggesting that his comic book heroine was intended to enthuse a male, rather than a female, audience, Marston refers to his creation as "the alluring Amazon," and in an article appearing in the *American Scholar*, reveals he blended beauty with dominance to manipulate his predominantly male audience: "Give them an alluring woman stronger than themselves to submit to and they'll be *proud* to become her willing slaves!" (Marston 1944, 43).

Marston's Amazon reverses the gendered hierarchy of dominance and submission structuring classical and Renaissance Amazon mythology, and Wonder Woman's rejection of marital submission emerges as a significant theme within the text. Through the comic book's narrative, Marston warns girls about the dangers inherent in the institution of marriage:

> *Wonder Woman:* If I married you, Steve, I'd have to pretend I'm *weaker* than you are to make you happy—and that, *no* woman should do! (Marston 1945 #13, 16)

Marston's message of female emancipation was not lost on the comic's young female readers, who eagerly embraced Wonder Woman's transgressive gender ideology: "Wonder Woman was a female mentor who showed girls like me that they could break out of their bondage and cast aside their traditional roles" (Collins in Marston 1998, 3). While domesticity and marriage may have been rejected by Wonder Woman and her young female readers, romance was embraced. Preceding the popular genre of romance comics that emerged in 1947, love and romance were driving forces within *Wonder Woman*'s Golden Age narrative. With love and romance between men and women encouraged, but marriage ill advised, Marston's *Wonder Woman* concludes that it is the institution of marriage itself that fosters relationships of dominance and submission between men and women. Male domination appears as a consequence of marriage, rather than a reflection of patriarchal dominance in 'man's world.'

With the institution of marriage appearing as the scapegoat in Marston's critique of male dominance, love functions as the ideal, providing an opportunity for male and female equality. Indeed, it was love that encouraged the Amazon Princess' journey to 'man's world.' In her comic book debut, the Amazon Princess fell in love with Steve Trevor, the first man she had ever laid eyes on, while she nursed him back to health on Paradise Island. After following him to the United States, she adopts the secret identity of Diana Prince from an army nurse of the same name, allowing her to stay close to the hospitalized Steve Trevor. Diana Prince is the bespectacled and demure alter ego of Wonder Woman, a disguise which allows her to blend in with American women. While Wonder

Woman's alter ego, Diana Prince, represents 'normative' femininity within America, her Amazonian identity, Wonder Woman, represents an alien or foreign form of femininity. Introduced by Marston, and maintained throughout the first series of the comic, is the notion that if she married, Wonder Woman would become as powerless as any other woman in 'man's world' and would be forced to remain as her assimilated identity, Diana Prince. This is so, because Aphrodite's law, which governs the Amazons, decrees that any Amazon who marries will forfeit her Amazon birthright, powers, and paraphernalia. Wonder Woman is, therefore, unable to marry and remain an Amazon:

> *Hippolyte:* I know that Steve loves *Wonder Woman,* the *glamorous* Amazon Princess. But if you marry, you will no longer be an Amazon. You will be *plain* Lt. Diana Prince forever. Do you think Steve will love you then, in *that* identity? (Kanigher 1950 #96, 5)

Recalling the Amazons of sixteenth- and seventeenth-century literature, marriage is symbolic of her submission and defeat. Wonder Woman defies domestication for over forty years; however, in the final issue of the original comic book series, Wonder Woman laments her resistance: "Steve . . . We've been fools for too long. Playing at love like children . . ." (Conway 1986 February, 15). The issue concludes as the Amazon Princess forfeits her Amazonian superhero identity and marries her long-suffering admirer Steve Trevor. Assuming the role of a woman, Wonder Woman's ultimate domestication affirms Kleinbaum's assertion that in Amazon mythology, "the traditional gender system will always prevail in the end" (Kleinbaum 1983, 202). Although the marriage is not maintained in the subsequent comic book series, it is a significant deviation from Marston's Wonder Woman, who dismissed marriage: "there's too much to be done without my trying to keep house in a man's world!!" (Marston 1944 #9, 11). But marriage, it seems, is the inevitable fate for the Amazon who escapes death, and Wonder Woman joins her classical and Renaissance sisters in her eventual submission to 'man's world.' Wonder Woman's fate may be an unfortunate one for a superhero, but it is the only 'happy ending' available to an Amazon.

Within the context of Amazon mythology, Wonder Woman does appear to pose a challenge. While her mythic predecessors were bound by the rigidly defined dichotomies of Greek/barbarian and male/female, Wonder Woman asserts a fluid interpretation of these categories. As the product of a postcolonial nation, she reflects the complex and conflicted notion of identity in a population of assimilated immigrants. As the product of a postmodern pop psychologist, she reflects the changing role, and growing consumer power, of women in America. A manifestation of her era, Wonder Woman questions the existing boundaries of national and gender identity to become a postcolonial and postmodern Amazon. Although Wonder Woman may push these boundaries, the boundaries between same and other do remain ingrained and intact. Amazon representations are unique reflections of their era, but despite any differences, ideologies of difference and hierarchy endure. Amazon encounters in classical mythology served to affirm the privileged position of the Greek male, while Renaissance encounters asserted a hierarchy between the Old World and the New. Amazon mythology can be read as a narrative of conquest, her characterization compelling and justifying Western expansion. Wonder Woman continues this narrative, her cultural dominance emerging analogous to that of her new homeland, America. An enlightened missionary, Wonder Woman's characterization validates American cultural imperialism, while the characterization of her comic book foes necessitates this intervention. Remaining bound by the antagonism of hero and villain, Wonder Woman has simply switched sides. Her very allegiance to the 'man's world' that her mythic predecessors had opposed is symbolic of yet another Amazon's defeat. When America recruited an Amazon Princess to its cause, America joined those great enough to tame an Amazon.

COMIC BOOKS

Fox, Gardner. 1942. "The JSA Joins the War on Japan." *All Star Comics* June #11. New York: DC Comics.

Kanigher, Robert. 1950. "Wonder Woman's Romantic Rival." *Sensation Comics* March #96. New York: DC Comics.

Marston, William Moulton. 1941. "Introducing Wonder Woman." *All Star Comics*. December #8. New York: DC Comics.

Marston, William Moulton. 1942. "Wonder Woman Comes to America." *Sensation Comics* January #1. New York: DC Comics.

Marston, William Moulton. 1942. "Dr. Poison." *Sensation Comics* February #2. New York: DC Comics.

Marston, William Moulton. 1943. "Victory at Sea." *Sensation Comics* March #15. New York: DC.

Marston, William Moulton. 1943. "The Rescue of Gerta Von Gunther." *Wonder Woman*. March #3. New York: DC Comics.

Marston, William Moulton. 1943. "Battle for Womanhood." *Wonder Woman* June #5. New York: DC Comics.

Marston, William Moulton. 1943. "The Conquest of Paradise." *Wonder Woman* Fall #6. New York: DC Comics.

Marston, William Moulton. 1944. "Wonder Woman vs. Achilles—Part 3." *Wonder Woman* Summer #9. New York: DC Comics.

Marston, William Moulton. 1945. "Slaves in the Electric Gardens." *Wonder Woman* Summer #13. New York: DC Comics.

Marston, William Moulton. 1945. "The Icebound Maidens—Part 1." *Wonder Woman* Summer #13. New York: DC Comics.

Marston, William Moulton. 1948. "Uvo of Uranus—Part 2: Thunder in Space." *Wonder Woman* November #32. New York: DC Comics.

Marston, William Moulton, and H. G. Peter. 1998. *Wonder Woman Archives: Volume 1*. New York: DC Comics.

Messner-Loebs, William. 1994. "The Blind Eyes of Times." *Wonder Woman* October #0. New York: DC Comics.

Messner-Loebs, William. 1998. "*Legends of the DCU* Moments—Part 1." May #4. New York: DC Comics.

Pasko, Martin. 1976. "Welcome Back To Life . . . Steve Trevor." *Wonder Woman* April #223. New York: DC Comics.

Ross, Alex, and Paul Dini. 2001. *Wonder Woman: Spirit of Truth*. November. New York: DC Comics.

Slott, Dan. 2002. "World War of the Sexes." *Justice League Adventures* April #4. New York: DC Comics.

Wagner, Matt. 2003. *Batman/Superman/Wonder Woman: Trinity* #2. New York: DC Comics.

BIBLIOGRAPHY

Acuña, Christoval de. 1963. "New Discovery of the Great River of the Amazons." In *Expeditions into the Valley of the Amazons, 1539, 1540, 1639*. New York: Burt Franklin.

Apollodorus. 1921. *The Library*. Translated by J. G. Frazer. Vol. 1. London: William Heinemann Ltd.

Bachofen, Johann. 1967. *Myth, Religion and Mother Rite*. Princeton, NJ: Princeton University Press.

Bongco, Mila. 2000. *Reading Comics: Language, Culture, and the Concept of the Superhero in Comic Books*. New York: Garland Publishing, Inc.

Caravajal, Gaspar de. 1934. *The Discovery of the Amazon According to the Account of Friar Gaspar de Caravajal*. New York: American Geological Society.

Daniels, Les. 1971. *Comix: The History of Comic Books in America*. London: Wildwood House Ltd.

Daniels, Les. 1995. *DC Comics: Sixty Years of the World's Favorite Comic Book Heroes*. Canada: Little, Brown and Company.

Daniels, Les. 2000. *Wonder Woman: The Complete History*. San Francisco: Chronicle Books.

Diodorus, Sicculus. 1935. *Diodorus of Sicily*. Translated by C. H. Oldfather. Vol. 2. London: W. Heinemann Ltd.

DuBois, Page. 1982. *Centaurs and Amazons: Women and the Pre-history of the Great Chain of Being*. Ann Arbor: University of Michigan Press.

Fox, Robin. 1967. *Kinship and Marriage*. Baltimore: Pelican Books.

Hale, Edward Everett. 1864. "The Queen of California." *Atlantic Monthly: A Magazine of Literature, Art and Politics*, 13(77): 265–78.

Herodotus. 1954. *Herodotus: The Histories*. Baltimore: Penguin Books.

Homer. 1951. *The Iliad of Homer*. Translated by R. Lattimore. Chicago: University of Chicago Press.

Honour, H. 1975. *The New Golden Land: European Images of America From the Discoveries to the Present Time*. New York: Pantheon Books.

Hulme, P. 1986. *Colonial Encounters: Europe and the Native Caribbean, 1492–1797*. London: Methuen.

Kipling, R. 1899. "The White Man's Burden." *McClure's Magazine*.

Kleinbaum, Abby Wettan. 1983. *The War Against the Amazons*. New York: New Press.

Leonard, Irving. 1964. *Books of the Brave, Being an Account of Books and Men in the Spanish Conquest and the Settlement of the Sixteenth-Century New World.* New York: Golden Press.

Lysias. 2005. *Funeral Oration of Lysias.* Wm. Blake Tyrrell, Michigan State University 1997 [cited 2005]. Available from http://www.msu.edu/~tyrrell/LYSIAS.htm.

Marston, William Moulton. 1944. "Why 100,000,000 Americans Read Comics." *The American Scholar,* 13(1): 35–44.

Pope, Ernest R. 1942. *Munich Playground.* Sydney: Angus & Robertson.

Powell, Barry B. 1998. *Classical Myth,* 2nd ed. New Jersey: Prentice-Hall, Inc. (Original edition published 1995)

Reynolds, Richard. 1992. *Super Heroes: A Modern Mythology.* London: B. T. Batsford Ltd.

Rupp, L. J. 1978. *Mobilizing Women for War: German and American Propaganda, 1939–1945.* Princeton, NJ: Princeton University Press.

Schwarz, Kathryn. 2000. *Tough Love: Amazon Encounters in the English Renaissance.* Durham, NC: Duke University Press.

Shakespeare, William. 1992. *A Midsummer Night's Dream.* Cambridge: Cambridge University Press.

Smith, Matthew. 2001. "The Tyranny of the Melting Pot Metaphor: Wonder Woman and the Americanized Immigrant." In *Comics and Ideology,* eds. Matthew McAllister, Edward Sewell, and Ian Gordon. New York: Peter Lang.

Steinem, G. 1982. *The Nazi Connection. Speak Out Against the New Right.* H. F. Vetter. Boston: Beacon Press.

Steinem, Gloria, and Phyllis Chesler. 1972. *Wonder Woman.* New York: Bonanza Books.

Stewart, Andrew. 1997. *Art, Desire, and the Body in Ancient Greece.* Cambridge: Cambridge University Press.

Tyrrell, William Blake. 1984. *Amazons: A Study in Athenian Mythmaking.* Baltimore: Johns Hopkins University Press.

Wolff, Toni. 1995. "Structural Forms of the Feminine Psyche." *Psychological Perspectives* (31): 77–90.

Woodsmall, R. F. 1935. "Women in the New Germany." *Forum,* (93): 299–303.

10 'Oy Gevalt!'

A Peek at the Development of Jewish Superheroines[1]

Jennifer Dowling

> Hardly underrepresented in the New York–based comic book indus-
> try, Jewish tradition was nevertheless completely invisible to comic
> book readers for many years.
>
> —McCloud 2000, 132

Since the inception of the 'superhero' genre of comic books, women have
had a continuous presence. With the exception of Wonder Woman, however, it took a long time until female superheroes came to the fore. When
they did, they were generally representatives of mainstream white American culture, and subordinate to the more dominant, ubiquitous superheroes
and their sidekicks. The 1970s, the same decade that saw the rise of *The
Black Panther*—the first African-American superhero to receive his own
series despite the fact that he had been in *The Fantastic Four* since 1966
(Daniels 1991, 158)—witnessed the arrival of a number of ethnic superheroes in the Marvel universe, including Luke Cage (African-American), Red
Wolf (Native American) and Shang-Chi (Asian) (Baron 2003, 49). The core
membership of the X-Men, Marvel's most successful series, grew to include
Storm, an African-American who believed that she was the reincarnation
of a goddess. Easily quantifiable, that is, 'racial,' qualities were the dominant way in which ethnicity was signaled to the reader. During the 'ethnic
revival' of the 1960s and 1970s, superheroes began to display other, more
subtle signals of difference. Seventeen years after the X-Men's first appearance, John Bryne and Terry Austin drew female superheroes marked not by
physical difference but rather by the reliance on signs and iconic imagery
that carried symbolic and, often, stereotypical signification (Robbins 1996,
131). Interestingly, the first of these was Jewish; the Southerner appeared
the following year.

It follows that the first openly Jewish superhero would be a part of
the Marvel universe: rather than reiterating the superhero qualities of the
Superman model (Bongco 2000, 101–2), it was *The Fantastic Four* that
introduced readers to superheroes with faults and idiosyncrasies (Pustz
1999, 52–53, 135) and later Spiderman, the anxiety-ridden, reluctant hero.
In addition, the history/story of the X-Men is overtly tied to the Holocaust: the persecution of mutants; the antimutant laws; Xavier's nemesis,

Magneto. Magneto is Jewish, torn from his parents and interned in Auschwitz when he was but a child, the object of Nazi fascination and terror. His goal is to protect—at all costs—persecuted minorities such as mutants from suffering the same fate. Yet readers only know this because Magneto's personal history has been disclosed over the course of his encounters with the X-Men. That he is portrayed without the physical and linguistic markers an audience might expect from a Jewish character led to confusion about his ethnicity, as evidenced in the discussion in the *Racxmfaq* (Hah 2000–3, n.p.). More often than not, male comic book Jews are without the phenotypic attributes that American audiences would expect. Bobby Drake, a.k.a. Iceman, is the epitome of 'Aryan' appearance: blond hair, blue eyes, athletic build. However, according to Jewish precepts, which require matrilineal descent (or conversion) for inclusion in the Jewish community, Iceman is Jewish: his mother is Jewish (his father is not). Later, other comic universes incorporated Jewish heroes, or recharacterized existing members of their stable to include Jews, for example, the Atom of *The Justice League of America* (DC), Marvel Boy 1 and 3 (Marvel), the Thing from *The Fantastic Four* (Marvel). However, like Magneto, no physical characteristics were provided to visually or linguistically support these characters' ethnicity; readers had to rely on information provided by the characters themselves. Lack of a defining attribute, be it symbolic or semiotic, compels the audience to read the character as homogenous, sharing the same nondescript (although often white, middle-class American) traits as the other superheroes.

Once ethnicity is established, however, and if continuity maintains this attribute, readers will expect, retrogressively if need be, characters to look, act, and react according to cultural stereotype. While the ideology of stereotype is inherent with flaws and dangers (Barker 1989, 196–210), it is, however, a valuable tool for the analysis of comic books. The danger of an arbitrary reading of the texts always remains, but since the "stereotype is an essential tool in the language of storytelling" (Eisner 2003, 4), it is the employment of the shared experience of the audience and the creators which will permit the narratives' messages to come across. Stereotypes, whether employed negatively or with sensitivity, are a shortcut for culturally shared expectations behaviors; once this shorthand is employed audiences generate a series of likely behaviors from the characters.

The incorporation of Jewish characters in comic books is a sign of the acceptance of the plurality of American culture (Gilman, *Jewish Self-Hatred* 1986, 189). The perception of Jews, both from within and without, is intimately tied not only to modern politics but also the political tensions which evolved within Jewish communities since the end of the nineteenth century in general, and the foundation of the state of Israel in 1948 in particular. For centuries, Jewish men had been acculturated to believe in acquiescence as a solution to conflict and persecution; aggression does not sit well with the Jewish cultural ideal of a scholar. Furthermore, 'history' had demonstrated that the Jews were particularly vulnerable to persecution, expulsion, and genocide; better they remain submissive if they were to live peacefully in the Diaspora. According to convention, male superheroes—another 'alien' group marginalized because of apprehension, fear, and ignorance—are expected to be aggressive vigilantes, their quest for justice falling just short of murder. Through these heroes, young Jews could vicariously defend themselves, fight for justice without reprimand or cultural censor, then return to their studies, their cultural and familial obligations.

Why limit the present analysis to women? Much has been written about female characters in superhero comics in general (see, for example, Robbins 1996; M. J. Smith 2001). Yet Jewish women get little mention, except in works dealing specifically with Marvel comics (*The Official Handbook of the Marvel Universe* 1986; Fries 2001), since Kitty Pryde has continued to be an integral part of the X-Men universe. The most pragmatic answer, however, would be that with the exception of a group of Orthodox superheroes—namely the members of the Jewish Hero Corps[2]—the number of Jewish women with superpowers (and who didn't dally with villains, as did Harley Quinn of *Batman*) is very limited and yields itself to close scrutiny. It is within this group of characters that the stereotypes of Jews, and in particular Jewish women, come to the fore. These shared judgments, that Jews are perpetual outsiders, intellectuals, either passive or overly aggressive, always fearing victimization, are prominent in American culture. Woodbury (1996, 47–54) briefly outlines the stereotypes of Jews in the American television and film media, some of which (the Jewish American Princess, the Jewish mother, alienated Jews) also arise in comic book culture. More importantly, the characterization of Jewish women as manifested in the superheroine are used both positively, as an agreement that not only middle/upper-class, white, Christian males are capable of overpowering the forces of evil, but also negatively as a reinforcement of acculturated images of the Jewish woman. Interestingly enough, as powerful as our superheroes are, they cannot escape the valorization of the stereotype. The sociopolitical tensions that rage around Jews in general in popular culture become manifest in the Jewish superheroine.

THE CHARACTERS

Katherine Pryde (Figure 10.1), a.k.a. Kitty, Sprite, Ariel, Shadowcat, and Kate, is thirteen years old when we first meet her in 1980 (*Uncanny X-Men* #129), and when she herself is just discovering her mutant ability. She became the youngest member of the original X-Men team and remained with them even when a secondary group of mutants closer to her age was formed. In 1988, whilst recuperating from wounds received unsuccessfully defending the Morlocks, she joined Excalibur, a nascent international group based in Britain. She also became a temporary member of S.H.I.E.L.D., receiving her own three-part series in 1997–98. At the same time, she featured in a miniseries, together with her partner, Peter Wisdom (*Pryde & Wisdom*). Excalibur disbanded in 1999, allowing Kitty the chance to rejoin the X-Men. However, following Peter Rasputin's (Colossus) self-sacrifice to cure the Legacy virus, she left the X-Men to attend university and attempt to find her own path to mutant-human peace. Recently, under the scribal efforts of Joss Whedon in *Astonishing X-Men* (2004), Kitty has rejoined the X-Men.

Ruth bat-Seraph, a.k.a. Sabra (Figure 10.2), is Israeli and also a Marvel character. Her powers were discovered in preadolescence and were nurtured by the Israeli government until such time as she could be trained in the Mossad. Although she had a minor cameo in *Hulk* #250 (1980), she emerged fully on the scene six issues later, when the Hulk appeared in the Middle East; shortly thereafter, she participated in the famous *Contest of Champions* miniseries of 1982. She has been seen fighting both with and against other groups of mutant heroes (New Warriors, X-Men, S.H.I.E.L.D.) and was recruited by Charles Xavier to join another of his organizations, the PARIS X-Corporation. Despite still fighting alongside the X-Men, Sabra has never received her own (mini-)series or comic. At present, there is an online petition to Marvel to remedy this lack in her career (*Asifa* http://asifa.net/israel/sabra.html).

Daughter of a prominent lawyer, nineteen-year-old Rebecca Golden was a socialite and adventurer, enjoying a wealthy lifestyle and its relative normalcy when she drowned in a car accident in *Justice Machine Annual* #1 (Texas Comics, 1984). Fathom, as she became known after her death, was one of four recently deceased humans chosen and resurrected by the elements (the spirit embodiments of air, water, fire, and earth). Once resurrected by an element, these superhuman incarnations were sent out to combat the evil Lord Saker and the machine (Shadowspear) he created to control the powers of the elements. Fathom was the water elemental, able to control both water and weather. The series was picked up by Comico and printed, albeit sporadically, until the company's demise in 1997. Fathom herself was the focus of two miniseries and shared the spotlight in the swimsuit, lingerie, and sex issues (all special issues of the comic book, featuring the superheroines scantily clad, were published in 1996 and 1997 with the *Elementals Sex Special* being the last *Elementals*).

Deborah Konigsberg, whose superhero alias is Masada, is the Israeli member of Image Comics' international team, Youngblood. She first appeared in 1993 with the inaugural series and was still fighting in 2001. Masada was the focus of the August 1994 issue of *Youngblood*, where she saves an anti-Semitic leader from assassination by a rogue Mossad agent. Other than that issue, she has only appeared in conjunction with the team.

1967–1982: EVENTS PAVING THE WAY

Why were there no openly Jewish comic book superheroes before Kitty's appearance? In 1967, the Jewish world was shocked by the vehement threats of both the newly organized PLO (Palestinian Liberation Organization) and of President Gamal Abdel-Nasser before the Egyptian National Assembly to throw "the Jews into the sea," as well as the general lack of ecumenical response to such menaces (Zeitz 2000, 259, 269–70). When Israel defeated Egypt in six short days, the American Jewish community felt that it could, finally, be proud to be Jewish (Breines 1990, 58). The sense of security was short-lived, as a backlash of public condemnation over Israel's 'imperialist moves' was expressed at the New Politics Convention and by the 'New Left' (Zeitz 2000, 261). In 1967–1968, growing tensions between minority groups in the United States, coinciding with riots and trouble within impoverished, predominantly African-American neighborhoods, were exploited by the media, increasing the apprehension and, in Jewish communities, the fear of escalating anti-Semitism (Zeitz 2000, 264–66). These events fostered a need for the Jewish community to take action. In 1968, Rabbi Meir Kahane founded the Jewish Defense League, a militant group of Orthodox Jews, to provide the New York City Jewish community with an armed response to threats and violence.

In October 1973, Israel was once again forced to defend itself from an incursion, this time on both the Egyptian and Syrian fronts. The war ended in less than a month, with the Soviet Union threatening to intervene if it was not halted. While Israeli confidence was shaken (in contrast to the 1967 war, this attack was a surprise), the myth of Israel's strength grew in America. That a Jew was safe, whether s/he was residing in Israel or the Diaspora, was further bolstered in 1976 when hijackers, among them members of the PFLP (Popular Front for the Liberation of Palestine), took passengers of an Air France jet hostage in Entebbe. Reminiscent of Nazi tactics, the hostages were separated into two groups: non-Jews and Jews. An elite team of the IDF (Israel Defense Force) was enlisted to rescue the hostages. In less than an hour, and with only two fatalities (one hostage in hospital was killed, as was Lt. Col. Yoni Netanyahu), the hostages were freed. In 1977, the rescue mission was 'immortalized' on film and shown on American television. Jews, wherever they were, had military might watching their backs (Breines 1990, 5).

In 1982, during 'Operation Peace for Galilee,' Lebanese Phalangist troops went into the Sabra and Shatila refugee camps, located in the southern portion of Lebanon then held by Israel, to search out members of the PLO. When the IDF later entered into the camps, they found hundreds dead, among them women and children. In Israel, demonstrations and protests against the killings led to an official inquiry into the matter. The commission found the IDF responsible for the decision to allow the Christian militia into the camp, but declared that they could not be held responsible for the brutal murders. The commission also called for the resignation of the chief of staff and the minister of defense. Around the world's Jewish communities, the unwavering, unequivocal support for Israel's power had begun to show cracks.

PHENOTYPES, MARKERS, AND SIGNALS

Ask an American reader—Jewish or Gentile—to visualize a Jewish character, and they will conjure a mental image based on their experiences. For those who had never encountered a Jew personally, the source of choice for their image would be limited and more reliant, therefore, on the media. For the average American comic book reader in the 1980s, it is safe to say that their imagined Jew was more likely to look like Perchik, played by Paul Michael Glaser, in *Fiddler on the Roof* (Jewison 1971) rather than Ari Ben Canaan in *Exodus* (Preminger 1960), played by Paul Newman, or Inga Weiss in the television miniseries *Holocaust* (Chomsky 1978), played by Meryl Streep. For exactly those reasons, these casting choices worked. Had Ari Ben Canaan been dark-haired with an olive complexion, he would not have been successful in his covert operations among the fair-complexioned British; had Inga not had Aryan features, it is likely that the audience's shock and sympathies would not have been as strongly evoked when her family was ripped from her home and transported to the concentration camps.

Along similar lines, the four heroines here rely on the American stereotype of Jews (dark-haired, wealthy, either passive or overtly aggressive) to avoid surprises, to evoke a sense of familiarity, and, as a result, enable readers to predict behavior and support or contest the underlying messages. In 1980, Marvel's readers were introduced to Kitty Pryde, a thirteen-year-old Illinois resident wanted by both the X-Men and their adversaries, the Hellfire Club. With Kitty bursting across the cover, the reader's gaze is drawn to the Star of David pendant displayed prominently around her neck. Behind her we can see the X-Men, in flight in their mutant forms/uniforms but in the open—in a white background and visible to all. By contrast, the Hellfire Club is in shadow, with only the group's leader, Emma Frost, recognizable. The others are masked and virtually indistinguishable. Before readers are formally introduced, they know this new character is Jewish, marginalized from even peripheral groups and, with that knowledge, classified as a victim.

According to American preconceptions, Jews have a 'typical' appearance. Kitty shares at least one physical characteristic with the stereotype, and this distinguishes her from the contemporary females in the X-Men: Ms. Marvel has blonde, wavy hair; Jean Grey/Phoenix has long, red hair; Storm has *incredibly* long, straight, white hair; a year later, the newcomer Rogue with long, red hair and her trademark white stripes is introduced. Kitty, on the other hand, has a 'Jewfro' (Z. Smith 2000, 247; Bookstaver

2003), which she retains during her teenage years, although the latest renditions of *Ultimate X-Men*, from 2003–2004, depict Kitty with straighter, light-brown hair. Even when she wears her early superhero costumes, her bushy, curly hair is clearly visible, as it is on the cover of the Christmas issue, *X-Men Classic* #47.[3]

Sabra too begins her career with long, extremely curly black hair, although in her latest appearances, her hair is very short. While both Fathom and Masada also have long black hair (although at times Fathom's hair is green), they lack the 'Jewfro' that Kitty and Sabra sport. There are, however, moments when the bouffant styles reach astonishing heights, usually with Masada. Yet, even with the inclusion of dark eyes, nothing marks these four as *unmistakably* Jewish. Although the characters are all 'phenotypically Jewish'—none have porcelain skin tones, nor are they blondes or redheads, for example—they could be virtually indistinguishable from any other Caucasian character.

Perhaps the lack of distinctive physiognomy is one of the reasons Kitty is usually drawn wearing a Star of David (Figure 10.1). Kitty's necklace is visible when she is not fighting for justice: it does not appear when she is in one of her X-Men outfits, nor does it in *Pryde & Wisdom*. Her allegiance at those times is to the smaller group, those like-minded and similarly marginalized people who support her fight for justice. When, however, she cannot be identified as a member of the X-Men, her necklace once more becomes visible. Clearly, the two groups are equally important to her and demand purposeful, focused loyalty. Nonetheless, they cannot both command her allegiance at the same time. One cannot be simultaneously Shadowcat and

Figure 10.1 The *Ultimate X-Men* version of Kitty Pryde/Shadowcat from *Ultimate Spider-Man* issue #44. (Reprinted in the compilation hardcover of *Ultimate Spider-Man*, 2004.) © Marvel Entertainment.

Kitty Pryde. Thus, it is her Judaism that makes Kitty Pryde unique among mutants; likewise, it is the part of her persona that is open, something anyone can substantiate. Shadowcat, on the other hand, is a member of the X-Men. Unlike other superheroes (where the superhero identity is the one recognized and the 'normal' persona the secret alter ego), the Jewishness of Ariel/Sprite/Shadowcat remains a secret.

Figure 10.2 Sabra, the heroine of Israel, who first appeared in *Incredible Hulk* #256 (1981). Her costume is based on the Israeli flag. © Marvel Entertainment.

In contrast, Sabra's identity is inextricably tied into her nationality/ ethnicity (Figure 10.2). Like the Israeli flag, which is reminiscent of the *talit* (prayer shawl) that men drape over their shoulders during prayers, Sabra's costume bears blue stripes amid a sea of white. The Israeli flag demonstrates the nation's ties to Jewish sociopolitical history by its central Star of David. The centrality of the historical icon emphasizes that while Israel may not constitutionally be a religious state, it is an inherently Jewish one. Similarly, the repetitious display of the symbol on Sabra's outfit reiterates that while she clearly identifies with and serves to protect Israel, by extension she works to defend all Jews. Like the average superhero, as a Mossad agent, her 'true' identity is always in question, always hidden; yet as a superhero there is no doubt for whom she fights.

Neither Fathom nor Masada wear ethno-religious markers. Fathom's usual swimming costume is blue and white, but then again, so is Vortex's outfit (the Air Elemental, in life he was a Vietnam veteran). One could argue that their costumes are more likely to correlate to the elements under their control than ethnic affiliation. Masada, curiously, appears in a typical 'Good Girl Art'[4] costume, but the bits of costume that do exist are a military green. Of the other female members of Team Youngblood, hers is the only one of this color. Unlike Sabra earlier, whose costume is nationalistic, Masada's outfit is militaristic, reminding readers that all Israelis are obligated to serve in the country's armed forces. Hers is, however, void of the religious/national symbols found on Israeli Defense Force uniforms (such as the Star of David on Sabra's costume), forcing readers to rely on other signals. There is, on the other hand, one marker that applies to all four characters, regardless of their age, nationality, or religious affiliation: "the intentional display or indication of one's ethnic identification vis-à-vis specific others as part of the course of social interaction" (Plotnicov and Silverman 1990, 91). Ethnic signaling, in the case of our superheroines the use of Yiddish, is a way to tell a select few that you, too, understand the coded message.

The 'students' who attend Xavier's School for Gifted Youngsters are from all over the world: Germany, the Soviet Union, Canada, Egypt. Yet, strangely enough, with few exceptions, their 'speech patterns' are 'standardized,' middle American. Unlike Rogue, whose speech is written in a pseudo-southern dialect, as a Chicagoan, Kitty's dialect is a generalized, nondescript American accent. Her 'hometown' of Deerfield is actually a small, affluent village, located on the shore of Lake Michigan, less than thirty miles north of Chicago. Deerfield's ethnic makeup in the post–World War II period, the time in which Kitty's parents would have married and settled there, was predominantly Irish and German, although Deerfield could boast of a Humanist synagogue,[5] Congregation Beth-Or (*Congregation Beth Or*), and another non-Orthodox synagogue, Congregation Bnai Tikvah. Religious and ultrareligious Jews, those most likely to engage in ethnic signaling, or to integrate Yiddish into their English, would likely not have settled in Deerfield, as religious principles would prevent them from traveling to a synagogue on the Sabbath or holidays. Jews in Illinois were few in number at that time and keenly felt the stigma of their minority status until after the 1967 war (Gilman 1996, 183). Yet, Kitty does occasionally interject Yiddish into her everyday speech, thus utilizing ethnical signaling.

Like Kitty, Fathom was also from a religiously progressive background, yet she too uses linguistic ethnic signals. As a matter of fact, she demonstrates a more thorough integration of ethnic signposting than any of the four superheroines, relying on invectives as well as interjections. Marginal Jews, such as Fathom and Kitty, engage in linguistic signaling because those they signal perceive such tools as positive, convenient, and expressive (Plotnicov and Silverman 1990, 107–8). For example, in *X-Men Classic* #47 (1990, 5) when Kitty is told by Professor Xavier that he'll only be satisfied when she can put their stealth jet, the Blackbird, together out of spare parts and with her eyes closed, Kitty retorts with an "oy!" Readers familiar with this exclamation will understand her friendly banter in response to Professor Xavier's teasing. Thus, Kitty, and the other Jewish superheroines communicate to the reader a satisfaction in their heritage, while encouraging those others who can decode the signals to share their views. Nevertheless, it also functions as an othering device, erecting a wall to separate them from those readers not of a sufficiently multicultural background to have been exposed to the Jewish subculture. In other words, while Kitty's exclamations of "oy!" may have signaled to New Yorkers that she could be one of them despite her Midwest upbringing, it also tells the reader in Norman, Oklahoma, that she cannot possibly be one of them. Likewise, it takes a certain degree of familiarity with Jewish culture, or at least sufficient literacy to translate what Fathom meant when she called Vortex a 'schmuck' and why she chose that term as opposed to another. Although the context will provide enough detail for a reader to ascertain that Fathom is not happy, only exposure to Jewish culture is going to inform them how insulted she is, how much of an outsider she perceives herself to be.

An American audience would expect Israelis to also engage in ethnic signaling. What is interesting is that the characters do not utilize signals from Hebrew, but rather Yiddish, the usage of which would separate them from contemporary Israelis. Yiddish was, and to a large extent still is, seen as the language of the Diaspora Jew, and more importantly, as the language of victims. This imagery is one that dates back to the 'language wars' of the late nineteenth century, when language loyalty became a publicly contested—often heated and at times violent—nationalist issue. As a result of the devastation of the Holocaust, and the subsequent demographic elimination of Yiddish as the main competition against Hebrew as the national language of Israel/the Jews, Yiddish became the symbol of not only the Diaspora Jews, but more tragically the Holocaust. Yiddish was alleged to be the language spoken by those passive Jews who went into the ghettos, the work camps, and to the gas chambers; the propagandists chose to ignore the partisans, Free Unit soldiers, leaders of the ghetto uprisings. With such pejorative imagery attached to Yiddish, as well as the continuous stigmatization and government suppression of the minority Jewish languages in Israel, the interjection of Yiddish in everyday speech with other native-born Israelis was uncommon.[6] Thus the dialogues in which they make use of ethnic signaling are addressed to the reader. The use of "oy gevalt" marks the character, for the American reader, as Jewish first and foremost. In doing so it also reaffirms the misconception of the uniformity of Jews around the world. In short, the linguistic markers Americanize the Israelis.

PERSONALITIES AND POWERS

Jewish women have not had the tough role models that men have had—few as they might have been—even in literature. Traditionally, they were relegated to the role of matriarch and commander of the domestic sphere: it was the wife's/mother's obligation to ensure the kitchen was kosher, the house efficiently run, a haven for its members and a bastion of morality and observance. Defiance of convention, of the roles assigned them whether by religious precepts or community decree, was met with ridicule, punishment, or ostracism (in Jewish communities, a fate often worse than public punishment). Women were often major contributors to a family's income, ideally working to give the husband time to study. Yet, it was the men who quickly achieved social mobility. With few exceptions, women who attained similar progress were dismissed or forced to recede into the background. If they were acknowledged, their success was seen as a result of their husband's status, or their own rejection of the community and its ideals (Hyman 2002, 154). Thus, it was the women's demeanor which served as the public measure of the Jews' ability to adapt to the surrounding culture, of the men's ability to provide for their family. The labels attached to Jewish women, it follows, expressed the anxieties of the men to fulfill social expectations: onto their mothers and daughters they projected responsibility for their assimilation, for the maintenance of the religion and cultural values (Hyman 2002, 157). As Jews moved away from the 'Old Country' toward the opportunities that the Enlightenment and especially America afforded them, they began to spread their wings.

The Jewish American feminist movement, which had begun in 1922 with the first *bat mitzvah*, took fifty years to reach fruition when the first woman rabbi was ordained. In 1980, not only had Jewish women's history only just entered public discourse; there were few strong, historical Jewish—American or Israeli—women with whom readers could or can identify. American Jewish women, those who would have made it into the history books, were mainly social activists (Rose Schneiderman, Henrietta

Szold, and Emma Goldman, for example), advice columnists (Dear Abby, Anne Landers, Dr. Joyce Brothers), actresses, and a few politicians (including former Miss America, Bess Myerson). Likewise, ask for a famous Israeli woman and the answer is most likely Hannah Senesh, Golda Meier, or Ofra Haza, possibly Shulamit Aloni or Ora Namir. Four of those are politicians; most of those vocations are extensions of the social roles already afforded Jewish women.

Despite these notables, three stereotypes of Jewish women dominated American culture: the self-sacrificing, often domineering Jewish mother; the smart, successful Jewish woman; and the spoiled Jewish (American) Princess. These were adopted by the surrounding non-Jewish community, supported and disseminated by the media and persist even today, their ilk filling the ranks of organizations such as Hadassah, National Council of Jewish Women, the Women's Zionist Organization. The two American characters closely adhere to all three of the preceding stereotypes. In her premier issue, Kitty herself announces on page 12, quite immodestly, that she's intelligent; as a matter of fact, in high school and later at Xavier's School, she excelled in physics and was considered a genius in computer science. Throughout her career (the stages of which mirror the roller coaster fluctuations in her age), she remains the epitome of a smart, successful woman, using her knowledge to assist her various teams/agencies to solve crimes, defeat powerful enemies, send emissaries back from the future, and work to end the discrimination against mutants. During her brief departure from the X-Men, she enrolled in a Chicago university in order to pursue a major that would allow her to combine her scientific knowledge and expertise toward a peaceful solution to the mutant problem. When asked, she returned to the group to assist the newly re-formed X-Men and counsel/ teach the youngest recruits.

Kitty's superpower is phasing: the ability to pass through solid objects. With it, she is able to defend and protect others, but cannot utilize it for offensive maneuvers. While it is not uncommon for heroines to possess telepathic abilities (Jean Grey, for example) or less aggressive powers than their male counterparts, Kitty is the only one whose power is delineated as "a non-aggressive, protective power" (*Astonishing X-Men* #1, 16–17). In addition to being passive, Kitty is viewed as the most maternal of the original X-Men, and when convinced to rejoin the group, in addition to lecturing in advanced computational theory, she becomes counselor to students not much younger than herself.

While Kitty represents the 'smart Jew'—the highly successful young woman—Rebecca was the antithesis of this. Although she had attended an elite boarding school, she was more intent on socializing and spending her father's money, and in her afterlife as Fathom, she is the least intellectual of the Elementals. Rebecca's death, in a sailboating accident, is in spirit with the imagined lifestyle of a wealthy and exclusive group. Thus, she falls into the stereotype of the JAP (Jewish American Princess):

wealthy; self-involved; a social butterfly; possibly well educated but rarely concerned with intellectual pursuits. Life for a JAP revolves around family and social circles. Yet, Fathom too demonstrates a maternal side, as her superpower is the control of water and weather, the sources of life. While at times she can be aggressive (normally as a response to a threat rather than as a preemptive move), she is the embodiment of the ultimate mother. On the other hand, neither of the Israelis is seen as maternal despite the knowledge we gain from *New Warriors* (#58, April 1995) that Sabra had a young son who was killed by terrorists. The two of them are aggressive, displaying traits of both stages of the "mythological Sabra"[7] (Zerubavel 2002): Sabra representing the earlier and Masada the latter.

Ruth bat-Seraph, or Sabra, is known to be fiercely loyal, often jingoistic, harboring grudges and holding nothing back in her outspoken opinion of those around her. As such, she is the archetypical model of the Sabra, of the "new Jew":[8] "young and robust, daring and resourceful, direct and down-to-earth, honest and loyal, ideologically committed and ready to defend his [sic] people to the bitter end" (Zerubavel 2002, 116). Everything about her characterization is representative of this ideological 'new' Jew. Even her name represents a schism from the past of the exile (Zerubavel 2002, 117): Ruth was the Biblical character who broke with her own family and past by converting to Judaism and following her mother-in-law back to Israel. While it is traditional that female converts adopt a Hebrew name, to which 'bat Avraham-ve-Sarah' (daughter of Abraham and Sarah) is appended, it is not common for family names to bear the prefix 'bat' but rather 'ben' (son of) or a variation thereof. Therefore, 'bat-Seraph' is atypical in that it is not patronymic, but rather means 'daughter of a seraph,' a class of serpentine/hominoid servant of God. Sabra's name disassociates her from the patriarchy, from women's traditional roles, from her family's past. At the same time it upholds the archetype which the label 'Sabra' casts: the early Sabras, much like superheroes, were "orphans" (Zerubavel 2002, 122), yet from a family whose origins are alien (Witek 1989, 101–2), or in Ruth bat-Seraph's case, possibly heavenly, much like Superman's otherwordly beginnings.

Like the myth surrounding the Israeli army, Sabra is known for her superhuman strength, speed, endurance, and healing abilities. She is called upon to assist whenever world peace is threatened, and will go to extraordinary lengths to defend her people. Interestingly, the uncertainty of both the American and Israeli public regarding the Middle East peace process, particularly following the 1982 massacres in southern Lebanon, is reflected in issues 58 and 59 of the *New Warriors*. In those issues, Sabra has been assigned to protect the then Prime Minister Yitzhak Rabin as he attends a special Israeli-Palestinian meeting at the UN. She and the prime minister discuss the possibilities of peace, with Rabin taking the more dovish side as opposed to Sabra's hard-line hawkish approach. As with Israel, Sabra must often give her support to a stand that is contrary to what her allies uphold as the best course.

Unlike Sabra, who works alone or against various teams of superheroes or villains, Masada is a part of an international team, reflecting the cooperation between Israel, the United States, and its political partners. Masada appears to be much younger than Sabra, although, as we are reminded by her costume, she has already served her requisite service in the Israeli military. She has a buoyant but rather conservative nature, again what one might expect from a young adult with a military background. Like the post-1967, 1973 opinion of the Israeli army, she is able to grow to gigantic proportions, with the corresponding strength and speed, and crush her enemies whenever the situation necessitates. She's able to do so by channeling the memory of past Jewish martyrs and victims.

Masada's nonsuperhero name, Deborah Konigsberg, is European in origin and, unlike Ruth bat-Seraph, does not force a break with the past, but rather an acceptance. Furthermore, the name choice of 'Masada' inextricably links her to the present as well as the past. Excavated by Yigael Yadin in the early 1960s, the fortress Masada, located in the Judean desert near the Dead Sea, has been turned into a national symbol. The myth of the Herodian stronghold states that in 73 CE, after a two-year struggle against the Roman occupation of Jerusalem, a group of zealots—men, women, and children—committed mass suicide rather than surrender to the legions encircling the base of the complex. This act of martyrdom was seen as the ultimate resistance and turned Masada into not only a popular tourist spot but, for many years, the induction site for new soldiers. The 'Masada complex' was later adopted into English parlance to express the preference of martyrdom over capitulation; the 'Masada syndrome' became the term for the Israeli national paranoia that the neighboring countries and the world in general harbored negative intentions toward the country (Bar-Tal 1986, 34).

After the shock of the 1973 war, a decisive shift in the approach to the Israeli national myth began to emerge. A fractured narrative of the past was no longer acceptable by the youth and the earlier generations' dichotomies were challenged. A growing interest in the histories of the Diaspora, and especially in the Holocaust, materialized (Zerubavel 2002, 29, 119). Once survivors and their children were able to discuss what had transpired, once they felt the world was ready to hear their stories, the belief that remembrance is a collective victory over enemies (Zerubavel 2002, 132) began to shape the literature of not only American Jewish writers but Israeli writers as well. Characters began to display the psychological manifestations of the internal struggle between remembering and repression, the symptoms of an intergenerational posttraumatic stress. The backlash of Masada's power, the uncontrollable auditory hallucinations urging her to defend her people, exemplify the symptoms of a national repressed memory, continued trauma, as well as national paranoia.

CONCLUSION

If, as Bukatman maintains (1994, 94), superheroes embody social anxieties, then these four women might just be more anxious than the average
superhero, for they personify not only the apprehensions of the general
reading public—teenaged as well as adult—but those of the Jewish audience as well. By the 1980s, the images of the Jew in American culture
were already firmly entrenched (Gilman, *Jewish Frontiers* 2003, 189),
deriving their impetus from history, recurrences in the various media, and
contemporary world politics. Yet, for the openly Jewish comic book character, identity does not recede to the background (Bukatman 1994, 101); it
becomes central: both the Jewish stereotypes and the modifications to these
preconceptions that arose as a result of events of the latter half of the twentieth century are crucial to each of our female superheroes, inherent in her
personality and her powers. In particular, these identities are central not
only to American anxieties about Jews and Israelis, but to Jewish anxieties
about world politics and anti-Semitism.

The physical markers and linguistic signals unify the characters under the
rubric 'Jew,' force them into a collective group: homogenous despite their
differing nationalities. These markers and signals conform to the American
perception that all Jews look alike, understand the same code, this despite
the number—in America as well—who are blond or redhead, who do not
share the same Ashkenazic cultural heritage as our models here. Yet the
homogeneity encountered in the discussion earlier breaks down once one
looks at personalities and powers. Here, the schism pulls the nationalistic
characters away from a generalized, engendered stereotype.

The argument that Zionism gave rise to the 'tough Jew' has been shown
to be false (Breines 1990, 25). In the constant presence of anti-Semitism,
Jews needed the categories of tough and weak Jews. This division was
incorporated into politics, enforcing a fissure from historical reality. Thus,
with the advent of Jewish nationalism at the end of the nineteenth century, Jews were divided into two groups: Jews of the Diaspora, who were
derided as passive victims under the rule of antagonist non-Jewish regimes,
physically weak, overly concerned with either material or intellectual gains;
and the 'new' Jews—men (and women, eventually) depicted as ideologically determined, young and vibrant, able to re-create the strengths and
determination that Jews had demonstrated historically, before they were
dispersed (Zerubavel 2002, 116). This demarcation, while an outgrowth of
internal Jewish conflicts, was adopted into the discourse of the surrounding Gentiles, who in turn used it to bolster their stereotypes.

In this typology, Jews like Kitty and Fathom are *expected* to be weak,
either wealthy or intellectual, and submissive. As Jewish women (and young
adults), both are construed as a possible challenge to the governing social
structure, in their case, the male-dominated, Christian hierarchy (Bukatman 1994, 121). Kitty, especially, embodies the teenage and Jewish desire

to disappear when chaos erupts, to be able to fade into the woodwork and transport herself and others out of harm's way. While assimilation is one way to withdraw into safety, the Jewish reader knows it is not always a solution. Likewise, Kitty personifies the notion first set forth by Rabbi Hillel in the Mishnaic tractate *Pirkei Avot* (1:12): "If I am not for myself, then who will be for me? And if I am only for myself, then what am I?" Her superpower enables her to act out this injunction, fulfilling an acculturated sense of social justice through nonaggressive means.

Fathom, who typified the materialistic Diaspora Jew in life, becomes much stronger in death. Although she begins her Elemental career as a quiet superhero, she learns to control her element and develops a power as great as the other three. As a Jew, she joins them (a Vietnam vet, a police officer, and an exceptionally bright teenager) as a member of a group marginalized in the eye of the American public in the 1980s. Yet all four take on mythological stature in their afterlives. All four save the world (repeatedly) from the clutches of Lord Saker, (a.k.a. Lazarus), who disrupted the natural order by cheating death to promote evil. The Elementals were brought about to balance this evil. Thus, the world needs Jews, as well as peacekeepers and teenaged prodigies, to maintain the natural/social order. Yet, both of these female superheroes act in a manner that still qualifies them as Diaspora Jews: they are gentler than their Israeli counterparts, and they are driven to save the entire universe, not just a select few. While Masada does work as a part of a U.S.-backed team, she is the one called upon to increase her strength to pound her enemies into smithereens. Driven by the memories of past victims throughout, by the perpetual fear that the enemies surrounding her are plotting her demise, she is not able to discern which victims are crying out for defense (and retribution), nor is she able to hear, as far as we know, the voices of those victims who valiantly fought against persecution. Masada epitomizes both the Masada syndrome as well as the belief that Israel will use all her strength to come to defend both the world's Jews and the allies of the United States. Masada is always on the United States' side: she will even bring her own countryman down in the name of justice (*Youngblood Strikefile* #6).

At the same time, reevaluation of the 'smart Jew' into the aggressive, powerful Israeli becomes problematic (Gilman 1996, 188). Sabra, although credited with the valiant defense of her country from invasion, is often unable to discern ally from foe. She, like the reader, is easily misled in *New Warriors* #58 when the Syrian superhero, Batal, appears at the UN-sponsored peace conference. It is not that his costume looks coincidentally like the uniforms of the terrorists who attacked Prime Minster Rabin's motorcade that blinds Sabra: the fact that he is Syrian is enough, in her eyes, to condemn him as a cohort of the terrorist group. Her adamantly jingoistic response is excused by the fact that she is under the mind control of an unknown assailant. She is brought out of this programmed state by Marvel Boy 3, who recites the Kaddish (the Mourner's

Prayer), and all ends reasonably well. For the reader, this solves every-thing except who was controlling Sabra: the peace talks resume, Batal is still alive (albeit wounded by Sabra's attack), and the superheroes return to their appointed tasks.

That this storyline parallels America's interpretation of the Middle East conflict since 1978 (the signing of the Camp David Accord between Israel and Egypt) and especially 1982 is unambiguous. Israel's hard-lin-ers are blinded by powers beyond their control and under such influ-ence they cannot see the truth. Who is the true enemy if all Arabs look alike? Who really is out to destroy the Jewish state? Could it be that the person(s) with control are doing so from within? Suspicions and ques-tions remain, as does the antagonism (the similarity in costuming is not directly addressed). In Sabra's case, it is not the Israeli—the 'tough,' 'new' Jew—who saves the peace process and the Jewish people from the resultant backlash. Rather, she and her unyielding politics are malleable to brainwashing, and it is the American who must come to the rescue.

This mirroring of America's attitude toward Jews continues, at least for those characters still in press. Kitty is once again a member of the team, chosen for her intelligence as well as her protective nature. She even puts up with the insults and taunts of the only other female in the re-formed group. Masada still grows to an enormous size and pounds the enemy into submission, but only when necessity calls for it. Sabra has tempered her militant responses somewhat, like Israel herself, and having joined X-Corporation has become more of an international and cooperative player, working on behalf of the mutant universe, not just Israel, and at times without her government's knowledge. The tough Jew has had to learn to soften her edges and work with the Kitty Prydes to make their universe a—hopefully—safer place.

NOTES

1. Appreciation goes out to Kelly Foulstone of King's Comics, Sydney, who was a fount of knowledge, support, and illuminating discussions during the writ-ing of this paper. Plus, she didn't blink an eyelid at any of my bizarre choices/ questions. Also, thanks to those friends who edited, asked, and commented, and to Sean Sidky, who corrected my knowledge of the X-Men universe.
2. The Jewish Hero Corps consists of: Menorah Man (founder), Magen David, Minyan Man, Shabbas Queen, Dreidel Maidel, Kipa Kid/Yarmulkah Youth, and Hypergirl/Matza Woman.
3. All of the female X-Men have variable features, depending on not only fash-ion but the technical problems of inking and color separation. Sometimes, Storm's eyes are green, sometimes brown. Likewise, Kitty's eyes are occa-sionally blue. Nevertheless, it seems to me that Kitty's hairstyle has changed frequently over the years, more so than most of the X-Men of either gender.
4. "Good Girl Art" is the depiction of attractive women, often in provocative clothing and postures, drawn thusly to provoke an erotic reaction from the often young male audience.

5. The Jewish Humanist movement was a distinctly American movement, established in the late 1950s.
6. This is despite the fact that Modern Israeli Hebrew is peppered with Yiddish: calques, lexical items, and intonation. Most of it is so buried in the semantic structure of Hebrew grammar that Israelis know when a word is of foreign origin but not necessarily that it comes from Yiddish.
7. A Sabra is a native-born Israeli. 'Mythological' here has two significances: first, it refers to the anthropological definition of 'myth' as an event in the creation of the universe or of a nation/people. Secondly, 'mythological' also implies a connection to the historical Jews who fought for the preservation of their nation. Zerubavel discussed not only the creation of a new 'myth' but also the historical fallacy of the 'direct lineage.'
8. The "new Jew" is a concept born out of the early Zionist propaganda for the building of a homeland filled with robust, youthful Jews. As such, a "new Jew." According to the portrait painted by the nascent nationalist movement, the "new Jew" is the antithesis of the "old Jew," the Jews of Eastern Europe, stereotyped (by the early Zionist movement) as elderly, religious, passive, submissively yielding to the often abusive power of the majority culture in which they lived.

BIBLIOGRAPHY

Barker, Martin. 1989. *Comics: Ideology, Power and the Critics*. Manchester, UK: Manchester University Press.

Baron, Lawrence. 2003. "*X-Men* as J-Men: The Jewish Subtext of a Comic Book Movie." *Shofar: An Interdisciplinary Journal of Jewish Studies*, 22(1): 44–52.

Bar-Tal, Daniel. 1986. *Stress and Coping in Time of War*. New York: Brunnel/Mazel.

Bongco, Mila. 2000. *Reading Comics: Language, Culture, and the Concept of the Superhero in Comic Books*. New York & London: Garland Publishing.

Breines, Paul. 1990. *Tough Jews: Political Fantasies and the Moral Dilemma of American Jewry*. Basic Books.

Bukatman, Scott. 1994. "X-Bodies (the Torment of the Mutant Superhero)." In *Uncontrollable Bodies: Testimonies of Identity and Culture*. Edited by Rodney Sappington and Tyler Stallings. Seattle: Bay Press.

Congregation Beth Or. 2005. http:/www.bethor.com (accessed 6 April 2005).

Daniels, Les. 1991. *Five Fabulous Decades of the World's Greatest Comics*. New York: Harry N. Abrams.

Eisner, Will. 2003. *Faigan the Jew*. New York: Doubleday.

"The Escape." 2003. *The O.C.*, episode number 7, first broadcast 16 September by FOX. Written by Josh Schwartz and directed by Sanford Bookstaver.

Exodus. 1960. 208 mins. Written by Leon Uris and Dalton Trumbo and directed by Otto Preminger. USA.

Fiddler on the Roof. 1971. 181 mins. Directed by Norman Jewison. USA.

Fries, Bill. *Marvel Directory*. 2001. http://www.marveldirectory.com/ (accessed 6 April 2005).

Gilman, Sander L. 1986. *Jewish Self-Hatred: Anti-Semitism and the Hidden Language of the Jews*. Baltimore: Johns Hopkins University Press.

Gilman, Sander L. 1996. *Smart Jews: The Construction of the Image of Jewish Superior Intelligence*. Lincoln: University of Nebraska Press.

Gilman, Sander L. 2003. *Jewish Frontiers: Essays on Bodies, Histories, and Identities*. New York: Palgrave Macmillan.

Hah, Katharine E. 2000–2003. Racmxfaq. http://www.cs.uu.nl/wais/html/na-dir/comics/xbooks/main-faq/part6.html (accessed 30 April 2005).

Holocaust. 1978. First broadcast 16 April by NBC. Written by Gerald Green and directed by Marvin J. Chomsky.

Hyman, Paula E. 2002. "Gender and the Shaping of Modern Jewish Identities." *Jewish Social Studies,* 8(2/3), Winter/Spring (New Series): 153–61.

McCloud, Scott. 2000. *Reinventing Comics.* New York: Paradox Press

The Official Handbook of the Marvel Universe. Deluxe Edition #11. 1986. New York: Marvel.

Orich, Alan. The Jewish Hero Corps—A Jewish Adventure. http://www.jewishsuperhero.com/index.htm (accessed June 10, 2006).

Plotnicov, Leonard, and Myrna Silverman. 1990. "Jewish Ethnic Signalling: Social Bonding in Contemporary American Society." In *American Culture: Essays on the Familiar and Unfamiliar.* Edited by Leonard Plotnicov. Pittsburgh: University of Pittsburgh.

Polygon Animation Studio. "Give the Female Comic Character Sabra a Series of Her Own." In *Asifa Israel.* http://asifa.net/israel/sabra.html (accessed 22 March 2005).

Pustz, Matthew J. 1999. *Comic Book Culture: Fanboys and True Believers.* Jackson: University Press of Mississippi.

Robbins, Trina. 1996. *The Great Women Superheroes.* Northampton, MA: Kitchen Sink Press.

Smith, Matthew J. 2001. "The Tyranny of the Melting Pot Metaphor: Wonder Woman as the Americanized Immigrant." In *Comics and Ideology.* Edited by Edward H. Sewell, Matthew P. McAllister, Jr., and Ian Gordon. New York: Peter Lang.

Smith, Zadie. 2000. *White Teeth.* New York: Random House.

Witek, Joseph. 1989. *Comic Books as History: The Narrative Art of Jack Jackson, Art Spiegelman, and Harvey Pekar.* Jackson: University Press of Mississippi.

Woodbury, Marsha. 1996. "Jewish Images That Injure." In *Images That Injure: Pictorial Stereotypes in the Media.* Edited by Paul Martin Lester. Westport, CT: Praeger Publishers.

Zerubavel, Yael. 2002 . "The 'Mythological Sabra' and Jewish Past: Trauma, Memory, and Contested Identities." *Israel Studies,* 7(2): 115–44.

Zeitz, Joshua Michael. 2000. " 'If I Am Not for Myself . . . ': The American Jewish Establishment in the Aftermath of the Six Day War." *American Jewish History,* 88(2): 253–86.

Part III

"I'm Just a Puppet Who Can See the Strings"[1]

Revisions, Retellings, and Auteurs

11 Entering the Green
Imaginal Space in *Black Orchid*

Sallye Sheppeard

Myth emerges from the depths of what we usually associate with the human imagination, arising *de profundis* in word and image embodied as ritual, which is to say that myth is verbal, visual, and visceral. Whatever other names, epithets, and actions we attribute to them, heroes, superheroes, and their tales always contain verbal, visual, and visceral elements. As mythic manifestation, the superhero exists not *in* transition but *as* transition. As transition or liminality, then, the superhero beckons us to that region Henri Corbin calls the *mundus imaginalis,* the very real imaginal world that is neither intellect nor imagination but both: the region of 'and.' Yet to conceive of this world, to participate in it, one need not dwell solely in ephemeral theory, nor solely in reality as we know it. One must enter both worlds simultaneously. Myth does not speak about transformation within that region; myth is transformation within that region of 'and.' Born of the future and memory, Neil Gaiman (writer) and Dave McKean's (artist) *Black Orchid* (DC Comics 1991) operates as vision and re-vision within this imaginal space.

The title character of Gaiman and McKean's work originates as a human being but becomes a plant, a hybrid character named for a hybrid flower. She exists as human/plant, plant/human; she comes from the region of 'and.' In its way, *Black Orchid* is a *tour de force* of superhero/adventure comic book genre transition, juxtaposing conventional bullying and violence with unconventional finesse and beauty, a modern tale of déjà vu and DNA. Regarded generally as a milestone in the development of adventure comics, *Black Orchid* takes the conventions of the genre and turns them inside out or, more accurately, turns them on themselves. At the mythic level, the work accomplishes a similar inversion. Black Orchid herself experiences the hero's journey more in the ancient tradition of Perseus than his successors, carrying forward major elements of two disparate cultures, one violent, one nurturing. Yet one can argue that Black Orchid's experience suggests something of a reversal of Perseus's journey. Her quest for self-identity leads her through Gotham City, Arkham Asylum, the Louisiana swamps, and the Amazon rainforest. Along the way, she encounters Batman, Poison Ivy, and Swamp Thing, familiar genre gods who serve as her *psychopomps* as she descends from the world of heroic crime fighter to a nadir of violent madness and ascends to the world of "green" and, ultimately, to a new vision for herself. It is this vision that makes Black Orchid's return to the world unique among her peers and Gaiman and McKean's work unique within its genre.

Black Orchid opens with the murder of its superhero protagonist: Black Orchid is bound, doused with gasoline, and set afire (Figure 11.1). She struggles to free herself, but just as she appears to have done so, just as she seems primed to escape the conflagration, she dies when the building is destroyed with a remote control detonator. As Mikal Gilmore notes in his introduction to *Black Orchid*, the violent death of the superhero "in a brutal and unflinching manner" at the beginning of the story is "a startling moment" because "the killer tells Black Orchid that he understands how the rules of the super-hero genre work," that he intends to kill her rather than simply threaten her and give her an opportunity to escape and capture him as superheroes always do; in short, that he intends to break the very rules of the genre. Becoming "a stand-in voice for the writer," the killer declares that "all those rules that insure the hard-earned triumph and inevitability of justice" to which readers are accustomed no longer inhere. As Gilmore says, not only does such a beginning suspend "all the accepted customs of the genre's mythology" and instigate "a new *way* of telling such a story" but it also destroys "the ethos of the super-hero genre," the death of which, in Gilmore's view, is "long overdue" (Gaiman and McKean 1991, 4–5).

This brings the discussion back to Henri Corbin's *mundus imaginalis,* which draws its analogy from Sufism, that strain of Islamic mysticism that speaks, as Annemarie Schimmel explains, of "the consciousness of the One Reality," an ineffable reality "that cannot be understood or explained by any normal mode of perception" (1975, 4); it suggests "polishing the mirror of the heart" (171) through intuitive pursuit of the inner light. Sufism[2] often images the relationship between man and God as that of slave to Lord, lover to Beloved, or creature to Creator. Although all are analogous of the same principle, the latter instance, that is, the instance of creature to Creator, relates more directly to the present discussion. Sufism speaks through paradoxes that reveal truth by coordinating contraries, thus teaches of the region of 'and' alluded to previously as the region that Corbin calls the *mundus imaginalis*—the imaginal world.

Both Sufism and Corbin figure this realm of actuality in many ways, one of which is as the world not of the mirror, not of the thing before the mirror, but of the image reflected in the space between the mirror and the thing before it, what we perceive as the image in the mirror. The Sufi journey inward leads through arduous steps and stages that demand not merely the setting aside of diminution of the ego but its total annihilation: imaged as a drop of water disappearing into the ocean or a grain of sand into shifting sand dunes, thereby signifying that one exists only when one does not exist. Sufism suggests the transformative power in the borderland of the rational *and* intuitive. The *mundus imaginalis* of Sufi paradox resonates deep within the human psyche: the mind can hold the tension between the mirror and the thing before it just long enough, not to *see* the image on the surface (for that in itself is easy), but to entertain, if only for a moment, the notion that this image exists in its own world, an actual world, between the mirror and the thing before it.

Black Orchid belongs to this realm of reality: she is neither the conventional superhero that stands before that traditional mirror nor the traditional comic book mirror on the surface of which her image appears as she is held before it. Black Orchid belongs to the imaginal space, the paradoxical region of 'and' leading to an unpredictable redemptive conclusion, in Gilmore's words, "that uses violence as a critique of the uses of

Figure 11.1 Death and Rebirth of a Superhero. *Black Orchid*, 1991, p. 21. © DC Comics.

violence—that is, as a critique of not only how violence figures into our actions and our psychology, but also how it figures into our myths and our art" (Gaiman and McKean 1991, 6).

That Joseph Campbell's concept of myth and its relation to the mythic imagination lies at the core of Black Orchid's journey, her quest for identity mirroring that of the hero as articulated in particular in Campbell's *The Hero With a Thousand Faces*, becomes obvious at the outset. In the initial chapter of this work, Campbell asserts not only that "the prime function of myth and rite [is] to supply the symbols that carry the human spirit forward" (1973, 11) but also that "[t]hroughout the inhabited world, in all times and under every circumstance . . . and they have been the living inspiration of whatever else may have appeared out of the activities of the human body and mind." In fact, Campbell says, "[I]t would not be too much to say that myth is the secret opening through which the inexhaustible energies of the cosmos pour into human cultural manifestation" (1973, 3). In short, in Campbell's view, all belief systems, political and social institutions, scientific and technological discoveries, aesthetic expressions, and dreams—all of these expressions of the human unconscious brought to conscious fruition—"boil up from the basic, magic of myth" (1973, 3) and reveal themselves in metaphor.

To state Campbell's idea in another way, culture proceeds from myth and myth, in turn, proceeds from psyche. For this reason, Campbell argues that "the symbols of mythology are not manufactured; they cannot be ordered, invented, or permanently suppressed. They are," he continues, "spontaneous productions of the psyche, and each bears within it, undamaged, the germ power of its source" (4). This statement stands among the most important, perhaps as *the* most important, of Campbell's articulations of myth theory and is central to his discussion in *The Hero With a Thousand Faces*. Campbell shares Carl Jung's understanding that just as the psyche is fundamental to the human organism so too are the experiences of the psyche shared commonly among all members of the species. Though it may subsequently speak in tongues and symbols specific to diverse cultures at one level, at the level of the unconscious, the psyche projects these diverse expressions onto underlying patterns of experience that belong to the unconscious material of all humanity and that are then inflated locally. For this reason, then, all the stories of all the heroes from their primal narrative spark down to the present moment are, as far as Campbell is concerned, the same story with various inflections. Although initially one might mistake such a view as simplistic, redundant, or reductive, nothing could be further from the truth. Campbell's view is expansive and inclusive, as well as local and particular, because it is universal. It envisions for heroic adventure an essential narrative skeleton providing both cohesion and flexibility for its narrative body, that body, in turn, breathing and pulsing within its particular cultural *milieu* and clad in raiment at once exotic and familiar.

As Campbell notes early in *The Hero With a Thousand Faces*, this skeleton, in its generalized conception, parallels the tripartite *separation-initiation-return* pattern of the rites of passage (30), and the fleshing out of this pattern in terms of the hero provides the substance of Campbell's book. Even to novice students of myth the *separation-initiation-return* pattern of ritual is familiar and to those who have confronted Campbell's work previously, the stages of the heroic journey perhaps even more so. Notwithstanding the pitfalls into which one may be led by familiarity, assumed or otherwise, one must note the impossibility of rehearsing Campbell's theory in so short a space. Certain ideas, however, suggest themselves as particularly pertinent to the journey of Black Orchid previously mentioned and thus to the eventual discussion of that work of popular culture.

In his discussion of the separation phase, Campbell emphasizes that the hero not only is called away from the world of the familiar but also must answer that call or risk a psychological introversion not only potentially destructive but also tantamount to spiritual death (59). Answering the call, whatever form it takes, moves one from the familiar into the unknown: aided by "the personification of his destiny to guide and aid him, the hero goes forward in his adventure until he comes to the 'threshold guardian' at the entrance to the zone of magnified power." In short, Campbell continues, the hero finds himself in a liminal space of "darkness, the unknown, and danger" (77) and, one might add, of potential illumination, discovery, and regeneration. Such a space, as Campbell notes much later in *The Hero With a Thousand Faces*, is important not only to the hero's journey, to his descent, but also to his return. The initiation within the liminal space, of course, constitutes the so-called testing phase of the hero's journey, during which he encounters and survives the several aspects of the aggressive chthonic forces that seek to annihilate him or, worse, tempt him to stay.

Campbell argues that the journey necessitates the return: "[t]he two worlds, the divine and the human, can be pictured only as distinct from one another—different as life and death, as day and night" (217), that is, the familiar land from which the hero separates and that into which he descends and fulfills his adventure, "the two kingdoms are actually one." Significantly, "[t]he realm of the gods is a forgotten dimension of the world we know. And the exploration of that dimension, either willingly or unwillingly, is the whole sense of the deed of the hero." The discovery that these two kingdoms are one, Campbell continues, "is a great key to the understanding of myth and symbol (217).

So who is Black Orchid and why does her death mark the beginning rather than the end of the work that bears her name? Learning the answer to this question, of course, lies at the core of the 140-page comic book and its complex plot, which moves freely among conscious and partially conscious moments in the present and the past. Those unfamiliar with *Black*

Orchid may find a brief synopsis helpful. Phil Sylvian and Susan Linden had been childhood neighbors and close friends, Phil being older by four years. An abusive father prompted Susan's flight from home, after which time she traveled the world, worked at some unsavory jobs, and eventually fell in love with and married Carl Thorne, a petty criminal and weapons dealer. When he proved to be as abusive as Susan's father, she left Thorne, went to stay with Phil, and testified against Thorne, who, in turn, spent seven years in prison. Prior to going to prison, however, Thorne killed Susan Linden. Meanwhile, Phil Sylvian became a botanist whose dream was to create a species of plant people who could live in the Amazon rain forests and, by "breathing in carbon dioxide . . . breathing out oxygen . . . feeding on water and soil and air . . ." could "create a new world" and "save an old world from dying" (Gaiman and McKean 1991, 112). When Carl Thorne murdered Susan Linden, Phil Sylvian collected samples of her genetic material and realized his dream. Black Orchid, the first of Linden's plant people to come to fruition, became the famous, successful crime fighter and superhero whose death occurs at the beginning of the story.

After Black Orchid's death, violence begets violence throughout the narrative until few if any of the original cast of characters remain. In addition to Phil Sylvian and Carl Thorne, these characters include Lex Luthor, mastermind of all sinister plots to exploit or destroy Black Orchid and her descendents; Mr. Sterling, Luthor's front man; and a few henchmen who execute Luthor's orders at Sterling's command. An angry and intoxicated Carl Thorne brutally murders Phil Sylvian, destroys his laboratory greenhouse, and destroys all but two of Sylvian's maturing plant women. Sometime later, Thorne follows Sterling and Lex Luthor's henchmen to the Amazon Rainforest, kills several of them, and is, in turn, killed by one of them.

At the time Black Orchid dies, her consciousness infuses another hybrid orchid-woman who comes to flower, carrying the genetic material and some of Susan Linden's memories but as yet having no clear idea of either who she is or why or how she has come into existence. She is neither Susan Linden nor Black Orchid yet she is strangely both as well as something/someone else. On the same night she comes into being, a younger hybrid plant-child, called Suzy, comes forth, manages to escape Carl Thorne's destruction of Phil Sylvian's greenhouse lab, and discovers her older "sister" hiding in the upper branches of a tree outside Sylvian's house. Quickly understanding that Sylvian is dead, the plant sisters begin together to learn the truth about themselves and to discover Sylvian's purpose in creating them. Their journey, as mentioned previously, takes them to Arkham Asylum, to the Louisiana swamp country, and finally to the Amazon rainforest, where they find peace but not necessarily contentment after planting seeds for future generations of plant-women.

From the foregoing synopsis, one may readily recognize in bold strokes Purple Orchid's challenge to several superhero conventions as succinctly set forth by Richard Reynolds (1992, 16). Black Orchid's death at the outset

Figure 11.2 After Carl Thorne dies in the Amazon forest, Black Orchid refuses to return to Lex Luthor. *Black Orchid*, 1991, p. 149. © DC Comics.

attests to one such breach of convention. Additionally, Susan Linden, who would have been her alter ego, not only died much earlier but also supplied the plant-woman/superhero with human consciousness via Linden's DNA. This infusion of human DNA into a plant also means that the superhero is not, strictly speaking, costumed as a Black Orchid but *is* a Black Orchid. She has human consciousness, intelligence, conscience, and sensitivity to the futility of violence as a vehicle for positive and lasting change. So the new Black Orchid chooses to save Susan Linden's former husband and murderer Carl Thorne from a nearly successful gangland execution, for which he remains ungrateful.

Already strained to the breaking point, the conventions of superhero comics are shattered when the new Black Orchid rejects the role of crime fighter as merely another way of perpetuating violence in the world. Rather than triumphing over them in the conventional superhero manner, she allows her would-be captors and Carl Thorne to eliminate one another, as mentioned previously. The new Black Orchid refuses to return with Sterling and challenges him to do what he must (Figure11. 2). With no little irony, one of the henchmen, a young man named Brad, who had helped Sterling kill the original Black Orchid, loves the rain forests, understands the significance of their fate given humankind's destructive regress into the future, and refuses to help capture or kill the two orchid-women. Sterling is left to face the wrath of Lex Luthor, who will surely kill him for failing to fulfill his assignment.

Other clichés of crime fighter comics are inverted as well. The new Black Orchid realizes that refusing to allow violence to occur is not enough, that though the Amazon is for her and Suzy the long sought-after paradise, it can be and is despoiled by the likes of Luthor, Sterling, and Thorne, who know and live only by violence. Moreover, she realizes that she cannot stay there permanently because she, too, knows violence and carries its memories with her wherever she goes. Hope for genuine transformation inheres in the future generations of plant people who will come to fruition knowing only the potential for nonviolent life, understanding again the interdependence of life-forms still alive in the Amazon. The new Black Orchid and Suzy may travel between their two worlds but neither can be permanent occupants of either world. The Amazon now functions as the creative space of green that contains components not simply of Black Orchid or of Suzy but of both. The merger of these components must be nurtured on its own terms in order to be transformed into the paradoxical 'and' of something new. That is, the Amazon functions as a *mundus imaginalis*, where hope, already conceived, presently germinates.

"The dilettante—Italian *dilettante* (present participle of the verb *dilettare*, 'to take delight in')—is one who takes delight (*diletto*) in something," Joseph Campbell reminds us in "The Dilettante Among Symbols" (Zimmer 1975, 2). In this brief little essay prefacing his edition of Heinrich Zimmer's *The King and the Corpse,* Campbell urges the importance of remaining open to symbol and image rather than mastering them, that is, rather than becoming experts at limiting their interpretation within fixed theories and methodologies of interpretation and so-called definitive statements. In Campbell's view, delight "sets free in us the creative intuition, permits it to be stirred to life by contact" once again with older narratives and images, and helps us "give vent to whatever series of creative reactions happens to be suggested to our imaginative understanding. We can never," he continues, "exhaust the depths—of that we may be certain; but then neither can anyone else. And a cupped handful of the fresh waters of life is sweeter than a whole reservoir of dogma, piped and guaranteed" (in Zimmer 1975, 5). In other words, true symbols, images, myths do not point to "meaning," thus do not ask for interpretation, and certainly do not point to moral teaching. They speak of human experience in the universe, past, present, and potential. In Campbell's words, symbols, images, myths refer to "the idea that the fullness of our universe . . . proceeds from a superabundant source of transcendent substance and potential energy" that "cannot be diminished, no matter how great the donation it pours forth." Thus "[t]he true *dilettante* will be always ready to begin anew. And it will be in him that the wonderful seeds from the past will strike their roots and marvelously grow" (Zimmer 1975, 6).

In *The Inner Reaches of Outer Space*, Campbell makes a similar point. "The life of a mythology," he writes, "derives from the vitality of its symbols as metaphors delivering, not simply the idea, but a sense of actual participation in such a realization of transcendence, infinity, and abundance" (Campbell 1986, xx). Here, as on other occasions, Campbell argues that we are in a transition stage between an outmoded mythology that no longer reflects our experience of the universe and the creation of a new mythology that does. Because "mythology is not an ideology" it cannot be predicted. Rather, "[i]t is not something projected from the brain, but something experienced from the heart, from recognition of identities behind or within the appearances of nature, perceiving with love a 'thou' where there would have been otherwise only an 'it' " (1986, xix–xx).

Such a fundamental understanding of the realm inclusive of the gods and mortals also may teach us something about the realms of myth and imagination. Campbell's concept of the liminal space of the hero's journey, for all its implied oppositions, speaks not so much of irony as of paradox. That is, to recognize that the realms of the gods and mortals are identical is to approach the *mundus imaginalis,* the realm of both/'and' rather than of either/or. Although one may encounter this essentially Sufi concept of paradox initially in the works of Henry Corbin or James Hillman, on whose works Corbin's thought has been influential, Campbell's articulation of the hero's return seems particularly resonant of it. As Campbell asserts near the conclusion of his discussion of the return, "[t]he hero is the champion of things becoming, not of things become, because he *is*" (1973, 243). To see this one may backtrack a moment, recalling from the opening pages of

The Hero With a Thousand Faces Campbell's statement that the hero "is the man or woman who has been able to battle past his personal and local historical limitations to the generally valid, normally human forms. Such a one's visions, ideas, and inspirations," Campbell says, "come pristine from the primary springs of human life and thought. Hence they are eloquent, not of the present, disintegrating society and psyche, but of the realm of archetypes, the unquenched source through which society is reborn. The hero," Campbell continues, "has died as a modern man; but as eternal manperfected, unspecified, universal—he has been reborn" (Campbell 1973, 20). In the paradox—the both/'and'—of his rebirth, the hero *is*.

Ultimately, Black Orchid both demonstrates and undermines our usual perception of Campbell's monomyth of the hero and the heroic journey just as she does the conventions of superhero adventure comics. Whether the conventions themselves inhere seems not so much the issue as how they inhere; that is, whatever else one may think of Campbell's theories of the hero and heroic journey, he recognizes that mythic patterns underlie genre conventions and that even though conventions change, the underlying pattern does not. Black Orchid, like Campbell's hero, "is the champion of things becoming, not of things become" (1973, 243). To acknowledge this similarity is to underscore rather than to contradict her heroic nature and journey. She is separated out from her old superhero nature, behavior, and environment (the world of superhero conventions). She is literally sent on a quest that, although intended to destroy her, only severely damages her memory and necessitates her search for identity. She returns to her world with a new vision for its future. That she does so constitutes the Sufi sense of paradox rather than mere irony, for the vision of the new world is one not of either/or choices but of both /'and' transformation.

This sense of paradox carries forward into Campbell's *The Masks of God: Creative Mythology*, in which he asserts that the most important function of myth is "to foster the centering and unfolding of the individual in integrity," according him with "himself," "culture," "the universe," and "that awesome ultimate mystery which is both beyond and within himself and all things" (1976, 6). Creative mythology recognizes, on the one hand, that "the shaping force of a civilization is *lived experience*" (1976, 137) and, on the other, that in the contemporary world, no such shaping force inheres for larger communities of humankind but only for individuals. Thus for modern man, the hero pattern is personal rather than communal. As Campbell explains, "[r]enewing the act of experience itself, [creative mythology] restores to existence the quality of adventure, at once shattering and reintegrating the fixed, already known, in the sacrificial creative fire of the becoming thing that is no thing at all but life, not as it *will be* or as it *should be,* as it *was* or as it *never will be*, but as it *is*, in depth, in process, *here and now*, inside and out" (1976, 8).

In very real terms, acts of mythology, acts of the imagination, springing from the individual's experiences of life as it *is*, neither of the past nor of the future, yet of both/*and,* situate us in an ongoing initiation phase. That modern life itself is liminal, that we live in the *mundus imaginalis,* seems precisely the point of such a popular culture phenomenon as Neil Gaiman and Dave McKean's Black Orchid, her role as traditional superhero literally having been blasted away and her new one still germinating in the deep recesses of the "green."

NOTES

1. Doctor Manhattan in *Watchmen.*
2. The many fine additional sources on Sufism include Henri Corbin, *Creative Imagination in the Sufism of Ibn Arabi.* Trans. Ralph Manheim. Princeton, NJ: Princeton University Press, 1969; Carl W. Ernst, *The Shambhala Guide to Sufism.* London: Shambhala,1997; and James Fadiman and Robert Frager, eds., *Essential Sufism.* San Francisco: Harper San Francisco, 1997.

COMIC BOOKS

Gaiman, Neil, and Dave McKean. 1991. *Black Orchid.* New York: DC Comics.

BIBLIOGRAPHY

Campbell, Joseph. 1973. *The Hero With a Thousand Faces.* Princeton, NJ: Princeton University Press.
Campbell, Joseph. 1976. *The Masks of God: Creative Mythology.* New York: Penguin Compass.
Campbell, Joseph. 1986. *The Inner Reaches of Outer Space: Metaphor as Myth and as Religion.* Novato, CA: New World Library.
Corbin, Henri. 1995. *Swedenborg and Esoteric Islam.* Trans. Leonard Fox. West Chester, PA: Swedenborg Foundation.
Reynolds, Richard. 1992. *Super Heroes: A Modern Mythology.* Jackson: University Press of Mississippi.
Schimmel, Annemarie. 1975. *Mystical Dimensions of Islam.* Chapel Hill: University of North Carolina Press.
Zimmer, Heinrich. 1975. *The King and the Corpse.* Ed. Joseph Campbell. Princeton, NJ: Princeton University Press.

12 The Mild-Mannered Reporter
How Clark Kent Surpassed Superman

Vanessa Russell

Traditionally within comic book narratives, Superman's alter ego, Clark Kent, is depicted as "the mild-mannered reporter," the persistently denigrated butt of jokes.[1] The figure of the reporter is a dialectical construct, a dry, dull, mild persona who exists in opposition to Superman, the supercharged champion of the underdog and vigilante seeker of justice. There is no Hegelian synthesis in Superman:[2] Kent does not take on heroic characteristics without first changing into a cape and tights, and Superman does not take on Kent's "fear-struck" or "meek"[3] characteristics without first donning the clothes of the working journalist. Yet, reportage and comic books mutually inform one another, for Kent, like Peter Parker as a newspaper photographer, reports 'sensationally' on Superman, and Superman provides the sensational stories that continues Kent's journalistic career.

Kent is a performance that exists so that Superman may have a societally acceptable persona that can gather sensational news for his justice seeking. As a result, for nearly fifty years—from the introduction of Superman in 1938 to the publication of the first volume of Art Spiegelman's *Maus* in 1986—comic books have privileged fantasy over depictions of reportage. As such, Kent works as a symbol of the colorful superhero fantasy that keeps comic books in a state of arrested development.

Comic books have long struggled with the perception that they are a child's medium, and this perception is influenced by the form's origin in Britain at the end of the nineteenth century. Roger Sabin, historian of comic books, writes that the first 'funnies' were told in picture form that were cheaply produced for the adult working classes. These were typically satirical and slapstick in tone and earned the title of 'comics' in 1892. From 1914, production costs meant that while adult's comics were all but wiped out, the largest-selling comics—that is, children's comics—were expanded (Sabin 1993, 13–22). By the time Superman was introduced, comic books were directly aimed at the youth readership, despite a substantial adult readership. Shortly after DC Comics' introduction of Superman in March 1938, written and drawn by two Jewish teenagers, Jerry Siegel and Joe Shuster, superhero comics came to dominate the market with their depictions of heightened fantasy.

Yet these 'fantasy' figures lost popularity after the war ended. In the United States, the postwar years saw a growth in lurid 'real-life' crime and horror comics from EC Comics, whose full name is ironically Education Comics. These comics showed graphic depictions of crime and horror in an exploration of the actions and motivations of criminals. Although the tastes of comic book readers were evolving, a societal fear of juvenile delinquency grew and crime and horror comic books were scapegoated, leading to the introduction of the Comics Code Authority of America in 1954. The code chartered a self-regulating standard of morality that indicated the idealism of the time. For example, the code decreed that authority figures must always be depicted as being right; nudity, divorce, swearing, sex, and rape were to be excluded; and all crimes of violence must end with the criminal being brought to justice. In effect, the code banned realism from comics because comics could not overcome the perception that they were aimed at a readership of children.[4]

In the late 1960s, underground comic book artists such as R. Crumb, S. Clay Wilson, and Kim Deitch worked to reappropriate comics from the restrictive, codified genre of children's entertainment. They drew explicitly sexual, political, sadomasochistic, and scatological comics that directly flaunted the code's repressive restrictions. By its very nature, the underground comics scene was not popular enough to pull comic books from the margins and make them a respectable adult art form, but its influence resonated. Unease about U.S. participation in the Vietnam War and the growing gulf between comic book representations of 'social reality' meant that by February 1971 the code was revised (Nyberg 1998, 139). The preamble to the revised code acknowledged comic books' role as a tool of social critique: "Comic books have also made their contribution in the field of social commentary and criticism of contemporary life" (Nyberg 1998, 170). The revised code allowed depictions of drug use, as long as it was depicted as a 'vicious habit,' and vampires, ghouls, and werewolves were allowed if they followed in the literary footsteps of Edgar Allan Poe, Saki, and Conan Doyle (Nyberg 1998, 172). As a result, mainstream newspapers such as the *New York Times* ran articles about the maturation and 'relevance' of comic books (Wright 2001, 233).

Because of these innovations, the figure of the reporter in comic books was given the space to transform. In the work of two contemporary comic book artists, the reporter is no longer mild-mannered. Art Spiegelman's landmark depiction of the Holocaust in *Maus I* and *II* (2003) and Joe Sacco's compelling portrayal of Palestinian life under occupation in *Palestine* (2003)[5] move the reporter into the central, mediating role that attempts to silence and repress the fantastical role of the superhero. Like all repressions, it is not entirely successful. Both Spiegelman and Sacco use journalistic techniques to record their interview subjects' rekindling of trauma, contradictory narratives, agendas, sufferings, and misrememberings. Neither make any claims of objectivity, and both wrestle with the weight of depicting such serious subjects in the delegitimized form of comic books. In a sense, both have their own superhuman tasks to achieve: *Maus* simultaneously fights to gain legitimacy for the comic book while at the same time questioning it, while *Palestine* works to draw the reader through the comic book world into a representation of reality. The works of Spiegelman and Sacco use fictionalized personas of themselves-as-reporters to self-reflexively question the legitimacy of exploring adult content in what is perceived as a child's medium. By eschewing fantasy for a mediated realism, they explore the world that the code attempted to shut out. In doing so, they participate in the rise of the reporter and the displacement of the superhero to reveal what is actually the transformation of the comic book medium itself.

THE MILD-MANNERED REPORTER

As a reporter—no matter how mild-mannered—Clark Kent was required to chase the news. At his workplace, the newspaper the *Daily Planet*, Kent was at the epicenter of news collection where fellow journalists gathered, then disseminated, news by means of interviews, firsthand reporting, tip-offs, and hunches. Kent subverted this journalistic process by working not to get scoops but to be on the breaking wave of news so he could transform himself into Superman and sensationally intervene. There are conflicting motives at work here. Kent's job as a reporter was to objectively report on the newsworthy events around him, while as an alias for Superman, Kent's job was to intervene into the news story and, in doing so, disregard the journalistic code of objective integrity.

Journalistic objectivity is arguably a contested concept in contemporary journalism. Although for many years objectivity or lack of bias was considered the first principle of journalism,[6] objectivity is now a concept that is regarded more by those outside the journalistic profession than those in it.[7] Media analyst Denise Leith interviewed nineteen war correspondents and photojournalists from around the world and concluded: "Although journalists and photographers often profess professional objectivity, what they show us must first pass through the filter of their own experiences, prejudices and value systems, making claims of objectivity impossible" (Leith 2004, xv–xvi).

Problems with journalistic objectivity occur most acutely when a journalist has to decide whether or not to intervene in a news scenario. For example, Leith recalls the story of photojournalist Kevin Carter, who in 1993 photographed a starving child in Sudan who had a vulture hovering behind her. Carter took the photograph and left the child despite there being a feeding station one hundred meters away. In a true sense, Carter was objective and did not intervene, but his ethical choice weighed heavily upon him, and months later he committed suicide (Leith 2004, xii).

Such journalistic objectivity does not occur in 'Superman.' The comic book reader knows that Kent's reporting is opportunistic: Kent has no crises of conscience, no dilemmas about the justification of his lack of objectivity, and no struggles with journalistic integrity. A Superman in Sudan may have not only saved the child but the country as well as he meted out justice to the "evil dictator" Omar Hassan Ahmad al-Bashir, who had used starvation as a political weapon. This is part of the appeal of superhero comic books: the simplified visual and written nature of the medium heightens the good/evil dyad and enables easy categorization of nations and its leaders. However, a superhero who performs the impossible and cleans up decades-long conflicts within a few comic book pages risks losing credibility and making explicit the fact that the comic book superhero is a fantasy. Take, for example, Superman's single direct intervention into World War II.

In February 1940, Superman entered World War II in a separately commissioned two-page stand-alone strip published in *Look* magazine. In the strip, titled "How Superman Would End the War," Superman plucks Adolf Hitler and Joseph Stalin from their separate bunkers and flies them by the scruffs of their necks to an assembly of the League of Nations. The chairman pronounces them "guilty of modern history's greatest crime—unprovoked aggression against defenseless countries" (Daniels 2003, 65), and the comic ends, war solved.

The real test for Superman came twenty-two months after the *Look* magazine strip, in December 1941, when Pearl Harbor was bombed. After the United States entered the war, Superman's publisher, DC Comics, came under increasing pressure to enlist their star superhero. DC Comics was reluctant because it was feared that an instant Superman victory would undermine the nation, its troops, and its political leaders, not to mention sales (Wright 2001, 43). Superman's creators, Jerry Siegel and Joe Shuster, struggled before finding the solution: Clark Kent would take the blame. During a recruitment eye test, Kent accidentally turned on his x-ray vision and read the eye chart in the next room. The military doctor rejected him for active service, and Kent, and so too Superman, was declared 4-F, unfit for service (Wright 2001, 43). For the rest of the war, Superman ran a domestic campaign that concentrated on boosting troop morale.

Because of Kent's error in the eye test, Superman's superpowers were not exposed as being super-useless in the face of actual war. If Superman had fought in the war, and had visited the battlegrounds and participated in battles, the bringing together of escapism and realism would have revealed him as being nothing more than wish fulfillment. At that time, hundreds of thousands of Superman's readers were members of the armed forces, and his exploits provided short bursts of escapism (Harvey 1996, 14). Such a move would have been disastrous. The *Look* magazine piece had already come close to puncturing Superman's credibility when it depicted Superman acting as a cipher for the understandable, but nevertheless idealistic, justice fantasies of his two Jewish creators. But *Look* magazine was

Figure 12.1 Superhero-style justice in "How Superman Would End the War," *Look* magazine (1940) and reprinted in *Superman: The Sunday Classics*, 1999. © DC Comics.

a respectable magazine for adults, and the impact was lessened because it did not reach into Superman's monthly adventures in *Action Comics* or *Superman*. Siegel and Shuster's foray into political relations stands as one of the first comic book interventions into World War II.[8] Although this was a one-off, it demonstrated the potential for the overt politicization of comics. The postwar introduction of the code stifled this experimentation, and it was not until well after the code's passing that artists such as Spiegelman and Sacco could challenge the good/evil dyad to produce self-reflexive and deeply thoughtful meditations on the effects and conflicting narratives of reporting world events.

THE MOUSE-REPORTER

Art Spiegelman's *Maus* self-reflexively addresses the difficulties of credibly reporting the Holocaust in comic book form. In the opening pages of *Maus II*, which was published six years after *Maus I* received widespread critical acclaim, Spiegelman's version of himself-as-reporter, Artie, struggles with his project. Artie and his wife, Françoise (a version of Spiegelman's wife and fellow cartoonist, Françoise Mouly), are holidaying in Vermont when they receive a phone call from Artie's survivor father, Vladek. Vladek fakes a heart attack so that Artie and Françoise will visit. As Artie and Françoise travel to Vladek's holiday home in the Catskills, New York, Artie considers the enormity of his project. He sighs and says:

> I feel so inadequate trying to reconstruct a reality that was worse than my darkest dreams. And trying to do it as a *comic strip*! I guess I bit off more than I can chew. Maybe I ought to forget the whole thing. There's so much I'll never be able to understand or visualize. I mean reality is too *complex* for comics . . . so much has to be left out or distorted. (Spiegelman 2003, 176)[9]

Artie's worries reflect the perception that comic books lack maturity, complexity, and validity within literary culture. In 1986, three serious comic books, or 'graphic novels,' were released that changed the way comic books were perceived. Known as the 'big three,' these included Spiegelman's *Maus*; Alan Moore and Dave Gibbons's *Watchmen*, a work about a band of bitter, aging superheroes; and Frank Miller and Klaus Janson's *The Dark Knight Returns*, a work where Batman struggles with issues of morality and justice.[10] The challenge to the dyad was introduced with *Dark Knight Returns* and *Watchmen*. The greatest contribution of these comic books to the comics genre is that the 'big three' opened up the wider public's perceptions and showed that comics can be more than child-orientated, funny, lightweight entertainment.

This did not occur easily or quickly. A recurrent concern in critical literature about *Maus* is that the Holocaust should not be "trivialized" by being put in comic book form.[11] Many critics take on the persona of a shocked survivor and imagine outraged responses that actual survivors may not have.[12] According to Spiegelman, survivors who have read *Maus* universally praise the book (Berman 1993, 64). Confusion increased in 1992 when *Maus* won a Pulitzer Prize.[13] It was the first time a comic book had been awarded prestigious establishment recognition, and seemed to be the beginning of the legitimization of comic books. Usually the Pulitzer prizes have twenty-one categories: fourteen for journalism and seven for letters with the subcategories of fiction, drama, history, poetry, biography or autobiography, music, and general nonfiction (*The Pulitzer Prizes* 2004). *Maus* was not awarded a prize under any of these categories. Instead, a new category was created: Special Awards and Citations—Letters (*The Pulitzer Prizes* 2004). It seems that the 1992 Pulitzer Prize committee could not place *Maus* within the existing categories, because its comic book nature was troubling.[14] A special award, although an outstanding achievement, stands separate from other awards and reinforces the perception that a comic book with serious, adult content is an anomaly.

Literary critics had difficulties in defining a comic book that dealt with the Holocaust. Critics, in large, shied away from using the term 'comic book' and instead used terms which they believed to be more scholarly. Lawrence L. Langer tried "a serious form of pictorial literature" (*New York Times Book Review*, November 3, 1991), the *Village Voice* coined "cartoon novel" (Seligman 1991, 66), Elizabeth Pochoda used "comic art" (*The Nation*, April 27, 1992), *Tikkun* attempted "comic novel" (Buhle 1992, 9), until, finally, the term "graphic novel" was applied.

The term "graphic novel" had been in circulation since at least 1978 when Will Eisner, comic artist and one of the first comics theorists, subtitled his full-length book, *A Contract With God and Other Tenement Stories: A Graphic Novel*. The term "graphic novel" had a twofold aura of acceptability that tried to ameliorate the unacceptable (comic and cartoon) with the acceptable (novel, literature, art). Spiegelman later commented:

> *Maus* was exempted from being a 'comic' and the 'graphic novel' category was created—*graphics* being respectable, *novels* being respectable. Booksellers probably decided that a double whammy of respectability would help make the stunted hunchback dwarf look better by dressing it up in evening clothes. (Spiegelman 1997, 25)

Spiegelman does not claim that the term "graphic novel" was created in his honor, but that the category was for booksellers who could place *Maus* in their newly created "graphic novel" sections instead of vacillating over which section to place it in.[15]

To relabel a comic book as a graphic novel can be seen as an attempt to distance comic book history and relaunch the text in the 'higher' category of literature. This cannot be achieved. A comic book, regardless of content, remains a comic book as long as its creator uses the stylistic devices that differentiate comics from any other expression of art. These devices include sequential drawings with frames, captions, dialogue, and thought balloons, and the use of these devices echoes the history of its medium. Eisner defines comics as "the printed arrangement of art and balloons in sequence. . . ." (Eisner 1995, 6) while comic book artist and theorist Scott McCloud somewhat convolutedly defines comics as "juxtaposed pictorial and other images in deliberate sequence, intended to convey information and/or to produce an aesthetic response in the viewer" (McCloud 1993, 9). The initial critical reception to *Maus* indicated a resistance to the inclusion of comic books in the higher category of literature, but, after Spiegelman's Pulitzer win, an increasing number of academic articles appeared that were instrumental in legitimizing *Maus* as worthy of serious academic attention.

Maus's post-Pulitzer critical reception reflected the recurring motif of speechlessness in the work itself. The centrality of speechlessness in *Maus* expresses the struggle of pushing the comic book genre into the terrifyingly adult world. Although Superman occasionally grappled with Hitler, he did not enter the death camps, and it is here, in Auschwitz, that Spiegelman articulates his struggle. Comic books are compressed narratives: a handful of words can convey a speech, or a facial expression can stand in for a whole moment in history. In *Maus*, Spiegelman compresses the inexpressible horror of the Holocaust into "the printed arrangement of art and balloons in sequence." The task continually threatens to overwhelm Artie. Moments of speechlessness mark the points where Artie reaches the limits of the comic book form, where the pen and ink are exposed as representations next to the stark experience of a survivor. Spiegelman's inclusions of these moments are his attempt to show how he, as the reporter, struggles with the horror of his father's experience. In the face of such horror, there is not titillation, such as in the early EC horror comics, but a recognition of the burden of doing his father's experience of justice.

Maus's use of speechlessness is best highlighted in the second chapter of *Maus II*. There is a temporal shift forwards from the scene where Artie and Françoise visit Vladek in the Catskills. It is six and a half years later, and during that time Vladek has died and *Maus I* has been published to critical acclaim. Up until this point, the central conceit of the comic book is that all of the characters are depicted as animals according to nationalist groupings. For example, Jews are drawn as mice, Germans as cats, Americans as dogs, Polish as pigs, and so on. As a Jew, Artie is a mouse, but in this scene, Artie sits at his drawing desk and wears a mouse mask over his disheveled human head. The symbolic ontology of identity becomes unsteady as Artie agonizes about the authenticity of reporting Vladek's story of the Holocaust. Reporters trample over a pile of Holocaust victims to interview Artie as he sits at his drawing desk. The reporters ask: "could you tell our audience if drawing Maus was cathartic? Do you feel better now?" (Spiegelman 2003, 202). At each barrage of questions, Artie shrinks until he is a tiny, bawling child. Spiegelman then cleverly segues into the next scene where the shrunken Artie visits his shrink, Holocaust survivor Pavel.

Pavel also wears a mouse mask, but his mask depicts the face of Vladek. In effect, Artie speaks to an idealized father who, instead of stealing napkins from restrooms and picking up discarded wire (Spiegelman 2003, 118, 134), has Pavel's mild wisdom. Fittingly for such a Freudian scene, critic Alison Landsberg describes the space between Vladek and Artie as "transferential" (Landsberg 1997, 72). In general, the "talking out" of Vladek's memories enables him to transmit his memories to Artie in an affective, visceral way that enables him to take on the memories of the Holocaust through which he did not live (Landsberg 1997, 72–73). As Vladek's story unravels while Artie listens, both Vladek's and Artie's present-day lives become tangled within the narrative and develop into the story.

Artie's reporting is therapeutic: it is a way for him to work through the trauma of growing up as a second-generation survivor. Literary critic Dominick LaCapra also applies interpretive Freudian models of 'working through' and 'acting out' to explain the therapeutic relationship between Artie and Vladek. LaCapra writes that the problem of transference is everywhere in *Maus*, but is not confronted. Artie is insistently preoccupied with reporting the story of his father's life, which LaCapra writes is "dangerously close to becoming the master narrative of his own life." Although Artie is very self-reflexive, at no time does he question his own motivations like he questions his father's (LaCapra 1998, 177). As an example, in the therapy scene, Pavel says:

> I'm not talking about *your* book now, but look at how many books have already been written about the Holocaust. What's the point? People haven't changed . . . Maybe they need a newer, bigger Holocaust. Anyway, the victims who died can never tell *their* side of the story, so maybe it's better not to have any more stories.

Artie replies:

> Uh-huh. Samuel Beckett once said, 'Every word is like an unnecessary stain on silence and nothingness.'

Pavel replies with a "yes." Then Artie and Pavel sit in silence, smoking, meditating on speechlessness in a wordless frame. Artie breaks the silence with a home truth: "On the other hand, he *said* it" (Spiegelman 2003, 205).

Perhaps LaCapra's reservations hinge on the fact that oral history as a therapeutic exercise is influenced by psychoanalysis, but it cannot be as extensive; it cannot provide the intensive psychological support in helping to reconcile the traumas of the past. By the end of *Maus II*, Vladek seems to have received little benefit from Artie's oral history project. In fact, he seems more traumatized than before. Vladek tells Artie: "All such things of the war, I tried to put out from my mind once for all . . . until you *rebuild* me all this from your questions" (Spiegelman 2003, 258). At this, Artie is drawn as being speechless, with a raised mouse eyebrow his only response. Themes of speechlessness recur throughout *Maus* as an issue that Spiegelman never fully resolves. How can comic books, or any other writings, represent a reality so horrific that words, let alone pen and ink, cannot convey? If Superman explores the outer reaches of fantasy, so too *Maus* explores the outer limits of representations of reality in comic books. Similarly, in *Palestine*, Sacco faces moments of speechlessness when confronted with the sufferings of the Palestinian people. Such silences are untranslatable in regular newsprint, which highlights the unique medium of the comic book as place for such speechlessness to resonate.

THE COMICS JOURNALIST

In *Palestine*, Joe Sacco draws himself as the self-effacing journalist known as 'Joe.' In late 1991 and early 1992, Sacco spent two months in the Gaza Strip and the West Bank, interviewing Palestinians about their experiences under Israeli occupation. A qualified journalist, Sacco then returned home and transcribed his interviews into comic book form. A new term, "comics journalism," was coined to express his melding of comics and journalism (Bennett 1995). Joe is no Kent, and he is certainly no Superman. Sometimes he is the hard-nosed journalist gathering interviews, interpreters, and ticking off his wish list of misery (Sacco 2003, 59), and sometimes he is a knee-trembling weakling, whooshing great sighs of relief when he can jump into a taxi and be driven away when trouble begins. Sacco draws himself as a comic book character caught in the act of interviewing, ensuring that his style is highly subjective. By placing himself firmly within his work, he breaks down the semblance of objectivity and follows the lead of opinion writers such as Hunter S. Thompson and Noam Chomsky.

In an interview with Sacco (*Financial Times*, June 27, 2003), Peter Aspden describes how Sacco studied journalism at the University of Oregon and began to reject the objective model of reporting when he got to Palestine: "It is almost preposterous to think that a western reporter could be objective in a situation like [Palestine]." Sacco explains to Aspden why he was unable to remain journalistically objective:

> You meet such good people in these circumstances, who have the grace to invite you in and share with you the little they have. It is very moving. And that is why it is important to write in the first person. It would be very difficult to get that feeling across if you were pretending you were not even there, as traditional US journalism does. I wanted the reader to feel for the people, to be introduced to them as if it were real life.

However, journalistically, this creates problems for Sacco's credibility as a journalist. Darren Garnick, in an article on Sacco (*Jerusalem Report*,

December 1, 1994), persistently undermines the journalism aspect of Sacco's work. He instead terms *Palestine* an "illustrated intifada," and Sacco as a "cartoonist," that most scorching of insults by a fellow journalist.

Interestingly, Garnick brings in Spiegelman to critique Sacco's journalism. Spiegelman comments: "He's obviously got the calling. His stuff is very well wrought, with dizzying pages and good rhythm. What I don't know is how good the journalism is." Casting doubts on Sacco's journalistic objectivity could be politically motivated as a technique to disregard the findings of his work: Garnick reads *Palestine* as a pro-Palestinian provocation but cannot entirely dismiss it because Sacco is open, in both interview and comic book, about his intentions and political biases. "I had no intention to be balanced," [Sacco] admits in an interview. "I'm trying to bring Palestinian stories out."

Sacco brings journalistic techniques to his work, interviewing Palestinians and recording his own experiences of the situation. Yet, in the text, Joe shows an anxiety about the comic book's small readership and the effectiveness of his endeavors.[16] After conducting his first informal interviews on the West Bank streets, an interview subject clasps Joe's hand and says: "You write something about us? I showed you, you saw! You tell about us?" Joe smiles ingratiatingly, but reports his thoughts back to the reader: "Of course of course! I'm off to fill my notebook! I will alert the world to your suffering! Watch your local comic-book store!" (Sacco 2003, 10).

Palestine mirrors similar concerns with witnessing and listening as *Maus*. Of the two texts, *Maus* is based on oral history, while *Palestine* is more explicitly journalistic in intention. Both texts delve deeply into the gap between witnessing and listening where the listener, despite the best efforts of the witness, can never fully enter the witness's experience.[17] Joe repeatedly faces questions from his interview subjects about the benefits of witnessing. In a refugee camp in Rafeh, Joe interviews a woman who recounts how her sons died by Israeli soldiers. As Joe makes to leave, his translator tells him the woman says, "She asks, what good is it to talk to you?" Flabbergasted, Joe says "Huh?" The translator continues: "She says she's been interviewed before, even Israeli TV interviewed her. She's used to it. She wants to know how talking to you is going to help her. We don't want money, she says, we want our land, our humanity." Joe responds with windy statements that the woman rebuts as "just words." Finally, he stands there, arms limp, and turns away. Eventually he says, "Well . . . tell her I don't know what to say to her" (Sacco 2003, 242–3). The gap between the witnesses' experience and the listener's experience is ultimately speechlessness (Figure 12.1). However, the further into Joe's journey the reader gets, the more the readers feel that Joe is corporeally 'feeling' the lives of the Palestinians.

Demonstrating Nietzsche's concept of "burning in" where, if something is to be retained in the memory, it needs to be burned in by a bodily

Figure 12.2 Joe's speechlessness. Joe Sacco. *Palestine*. London: Random House–Jonathan Cape, 2003, p. 243.

experience,[18] Joe tells the reader that he too has read the journalistic documents, but that it is not until he has personal experiences of being with and listening to the Palestinians' testimony that their memories get "burnt in" and become lived to him. At the beginning of the text, before he arrives in Palestine, Joe says: "And if Palestinians have been sinking for decades, expelled, bombed and kicked black and blue, even when it's made the evening news I never caught a name or recall a face, to say nothing about their cornflakes" (Sacco 2003, 8). After Joe begins to talk to Palestinians he becomes journalistically excited: "Palestinian victims all right! The real-life adaptation of all those affidavits I've been reading!" (Sacco 2003, 10). Joe's empathy (and tactfulness) evolves through the trajectory of *Palestine*, but it is by expanding on his burning in: the more Palestinian pain he shakes hands with, the more the comic book reflects his increasing identification to their situation.

But personal identification and objective reporting are two different things. Journalist Duncan Campbell writes that the detailed immediacy of Sacco's work—and the comic medium—means that the reader is inserted into the situation and travels with Joe the narrator: "What makes Sacco's work so powerful is its self-awareness, its lack of self-righteousness, its attention to odd, humanising detail . . . so that readers feel they are discovering things at the same speed as Sacco" (*Guardian*, October 23, 2003).

The absorbing nature of the comic book can trick readers into believing that they have reached the depths of memory, and that the book is reflecting reality. In the critical reception to *Palestine,* this reaction is endemic. For example, in a review of *Palestine* (*New York Times Book Review*, September 1, 2002) journalist Margo Jefferson writes that she had examined the journalistic documents about Palestine (and Bosnia), but did not "feel the facts" until she read Sacco's work: "I thought I had read diligently about the Serbian war on Bosnia and about the Palestinians in camps in the occupied territories of Gaza and the West Bank. But I had not felt the facts as I did this time around" [in *Palestine* and Sacco's text about Bosnia, *Safe Area Goražde*]. How does someone "feel the facts"? Jefferson explains that she became emotionally affected when reading *Palestine* because of the sensations produced by the words and images of Sacco's comic book. She writes that she felt herself *entering the text* about halfway through *Palestine* when Sacco draws an ant's-eye view of Joe sludging across mud and, in the next frame, shows him stepping into a doorway. Inside a text box are the words "You come to someone's house, you enter through the door, you expect a hallway or front room . . . But none of that here, no roof, no floor even, just sand" (Sacco 2003, 151). Jefferson comments: "At that moment, what else would one experience but the physical shock of walking into such a space?"

That Sacco can draw his readers into the situation of his text is testament to his skills, but critics who have physically experienced Palestinian life have notably different reactions. Palestinian-born literary critic Edward Said writes that Sacco's work is not "real" but "graphic" (Said 2003, iii). This suggests that Said's firsthand experiences of Palestine keep his descriptions of *Palestine* anchored in representation. Said writes that it is the comic book techniques that Sacco uses that produce jolts of recognition by those who know the places and with those who do not:

> Without losing the comics' unique capacity for delivering a kind of surreal world as animated and in its own way as arrestingly violent as a poet's vision of things, Joe Sacco can also unostentatiously transmit a great deal of information, the human context and historical events that have reduced Palestinians to their present sense of stagnating powerlessness. (Said 2003, iv)

For Said, comics are surreal distortions of reality and create a hyperworld where incidents are heightened and emphasized, whether in a high or low key. It is the very medium of comics that produce such responses: the immediacy of the words and images work together to create what seems to the reader to be a new reality.[19]

This is the point at which the possibilities of comic book representations of reality seem limitless. It is the point when a comic book can affect readers and so effect change. The reporter has more power than the superhero in this respect, for the comic book reporter can effect change without the use of fantastical superpowers. When a comic book reporter can take readers beyond the surface of the comic book and into the world of his or her subjects, then barriers of speechlessness are breached and empathy and understanding are created.

With the rise of a comic book reporter such as Sacco, together with the work of Spiegelman, the unrecognized work of Clark Kent as a journalist has been revealed to be as worthy of the spotlight as Superman's antics. Both Spiegelman and Sacco, in very different ways, use the reporter figure in a replacement capacity for the superhero. The superhero is superfluous because the reporter, through extensive research, interviews, physical trips to the conflict site, photographs, oral history, and memory work can reproduce a coherent authenticity that mimics a superhero's vision of omniscience. There is no need for journalistic objectivity, for the power of the works resides in a didactic subjectivity that invites the reader to enter the text and so the politics. Like Superman, Spiegleman and Sacco fight for truth and justice; however, instead of resorting to superpowers they use reporter's techniques, which result in works that are anything but mildmannered. As the reporter steps forward into the comic book spotlight, his or her position becomes more visible, and the need for the superhero lessens. Thus, in the works of Spiegelman and Sacco, the reversal of comic book authority from Superman to Clark Kent is complete.

NOTES

1. This study particularly focuses on Superman during the 'golden years' of 1938 to 1958 where Superman was not involved in imaginary fantasy storylines. In 1958, Mort Weisinger took over the editorship of the *Superman* comic where his background in science fiction broadened the storylines into fantasy sequences, the merit of which is still hotly debated. See Bradford W. Wright. 2001. *Comic Book Nation: The Transformation of Youth Culture in America*, 61. Baltimore: John Hopkins University Press.
2. A Hegelian dialectic is the existence of two opposing points of view that find a meeting ground in the middle. These are known as the thesis and the antithesis, and the meeting ground is the synthesis.
3. See *Superman* #1, p. 71, and *Superman* #3, p. 180, in Jerry Siegel and Joe Shuster. 1989. *The Superman Archives: 1939–1940*, Vol. 1. New York: DC Comics.
4. See Joseph Witek. 1989. *Comic Books as History: The Narrative Art of Jack Jackson, Art Spiegelman, and Harvey Pekar*, 49–50. Jackson: University Press of Mississippi.
5. I use the dates of each text's publication in collected form. *Maus* was first published from 1980 to 1991 in serial form in *Raw*, Spiegelman's and Françoise Mouly's 'graphix magazine.' For a fuller history of *Raw* see Art Spiegelman. 1999. *Art Spiegelman: Comix, Graphics, Essays and Scraps (from Maus to Now to Maus to Now)*, 10. New York: Raw Books and Graphics. In 1986, the *Maus* serials were collected in the first volume of *Maus* and published as *Maus I: A Survivor's Tale; My Father Bleeds History*. The second

volume, *Maus II: And Here My Troubles Began,* was published in 1991. A compilation of both volumes was published as *The Complete Maus* in 2003. Similarly, *Palestine* was first published in nine issues from 1993 to 2001 through Fantagraphics Books. In 2003, these issues were collected into book form and published as *Palestine*.

6. In particular see Jeffrey Olen. 1988. *Ethics in Journalism.* Englewood Cliffs, NJ: Prentice-Hall; Andrew Belsey and Ruth F. Chadwick. 1992. *Ethical Issues in Journalism and the Media.* London: Routledge; Bruce Wayne McKinzie. 1994. *Objectivity, Communication, and the Foundation of Understanding.* Lanham, MD: University Press of America.

7. An interview with Eddie Adams, a photojournalist most famous for his photograph of the execution of a Vietcong prisoner in 1968, concurs: 'I believe that there is no such thing as what people say is objective reporting or pictures. So they can lie all they want about the great journalistic guy who goes right down the middle. That is bullshit.' Denise Leith. 2004. *Bearing Witness: The Lives of War Correspondents and Photojournalists*, 14. Milsons Point, NSW, Australia: Random House. See also Karen S. Johnson-Cartee. 2004. *News Narratives and News Framing: Constructing Political Reality.* Lanham, MD: Rowman & Littlefield Publishers; Eytan Gilboa. 2002. *Media and Conflict: Framing Issues, Making Policy, Shaping Opinions.* Ardsley, NY: Transnational Publishers; Stephen D. Reese, Oscar H. Gandy, and August E. Grant. 2001. *Framing Public Life: Perspectives on Media and Our Understanding of the Social World.* Mahwah, NJ: Lawrence Erlbaum Associates.

8. During the same month as the *Look* magazine strip, DC Comics' main rival, Marvel Comics, mobilized their superheroes in a war against the Nazis. On the front cover of February 1940s *Marvel Mystery Comics*, the Sub-Mariner ripped a gun turret off a Nazi U-boat and proceeded to wage his own 'deep-sea blitzkrieg.' See Ron Goulart. 2000. *Comic Book Culture: An Illustrated History.* Portland, OR: Collectors Press.

9. Spiegelman writes dialogue in capital letters with emphasis shown in bold. For ease of reading, in my transcriptions I have changed from capital letters to lower case and indicate Spiegelman's emphases in italics. The ellipses that appear in the transcriptions reproduce the original where an ellipsis indicates a pause or shift in thought rather than an omission of material.

10. For more on the history of this period see Chapter 6 of Roger Sabin. (1993). *Adult Comics: An Introduction.* London: Routledge.

11. For discussion about concerns of Maus 'trivialising' the Holocaust, see Andrea Liss. (1998). Between *Trauma and Nostalgia: Christian Boltanski's Memorials* and Art Spiegelman's Maus *Trespassing Through Shadows: Memory, Photography, and the Holocaust*, 55–7. Minneapolis: University of Minnesota Press and Joseph Witek. 1989. *Comic Books as History: The Narrative Art of Jack Jackson, Art Spiegelman, and Harvey Pekar.* Jackson: University Press of Mississippi.

12. In particular see Witek; Michael Rothberg. 1994. 'We Were Talking Jewish': Art Spiegelman's *Maus* as 'Holocaust' Production. *Contemporary Literature*, 35; Alice Yaeger Kaplan. 1989. *Theweleit and Spiegelman: Of Mice and Men. Remaking History.* Seattle: Bay Press; Dominick LaCapra. 1998. " 'Twas the Night before Christmas: Art Spiegelman's Maus." *History and Memory After Auschwitz.* New York: Cornell University Press.

13. The Pulitzer was awarded to both volumes of *Maus*.

14. It can be argued that *Maus* fits the criteria of three of the letters categories: history; biography or autobiography; and general nonfiction. For more on the subject of Maus and its genre-defying Pulitzer win, see Thomas Doherty.

1996. "Art Spiegelman's Maus: Graphic Art and the Holocaust. *American Literature*, 68.
15. For a more complete history of the development of the graphic novel, see Sabin, 93–6.
16. Garnick consoles himself with the fact that the comic (which was then sold by the issue) was selling on average only 2,300 per issue; 20,000 sales per issue was the usual threshold for alternative comic success.
17. See Shoshana Felman and Dori Laub, eds. 1992. *Testimony: Crises of Witnessing in Literature, Psychoanalysis, and History*. New York: Routledge.
18. For more on Nietzsche's concept of burning in, see Alison Landsberg. 1997. "America, the Holocaust, and the Mass Culture of Memory: Toward a Radical Politics of Empathy." *New German Critique*, 71. Landsberg formulates an impressive metaphor called 'prosthetic memory' where the living memory of an event that has not actually been lived through is experienced through cultural technologies. Together with Nietzsche's concept of 'burning in,' Landsberg then asks 'is it possible for the Holocaust to become a bodily memory for those who have not lived through it?' Landsberg, "America, the Holocaust, and the Mass Culture of Memory: Toward a Radical Politics of Empathy," 66.
19. See also Dick Doherty, who has spent time in the Gaza Strip. Like Said, Doherty does not make statements about the realism of Palestine, but rather emphasizes the graphicness of the book: '[Sacco's] distorted, occasionally grotesque faces and fisheye-lens point of view convey the sheer madness of life under occupation: Sacco captures the soul of the experience with all its mud, sweat, ignoble fears, four-letter words, and lasting damages' (99).

COMIC BOOKS

Sacco, Joe. 2003. *Palestine*. London: Random House-Jonathan Cape.
Siegel, Jerry, and Joe Shuster. 1989. *The Superman Archives: 1939–1940*. Vol. 1. New York: DC Comics.
Siegel, Jerry, and Joe Shuster. 1999. *Superman: The Sunday Classics*. New York: DC Comics.
Spiegelman, Art. 2003. *The Complete Maus*. London: Penguin.

BIBLIOGRAPHY

Belsey, Andrew, and Ruth F. Chadwick. 1992. *Ethical Issues in Journalism and the Media*. London: Routledge.
Bennett, K. 1995. "Joe Sacco's *Palestine*: Where Comics Meets Journalism." *Subliminal Tattoos*, 5: 12–9.
Berman, A. 1993. "The Maus That Roared." *Art News*, 63–4.
Buhle, P. 1992. "Of Mice and Menschen: Jewish Comics Come of Age." *Tikkun*, 7: 9–16.
Daniels, Les. 2003. *DC Comics: A Celebration of the World's Favorite Comic Book Heroes*. New York: Watson-Guptill.
Doherty, T. 1996. "Art Spiegelman's *Maus*: Graphic Art and the Holocaust." *American Literature*, 68: 69–84.
Eisner, Will. 1995. *Graphic Storytelling*. Tamarac, FL: Poorhouse.
Felman, Shoshana, and Dori Laub, eds. 1992. *Testimony: Crises of Witnessing in Literature, Psychoanalysis, and History*. New York: Routledge.

Gilboa, Eytan. 2002. *Media and Conflict: Framing Issues, Making Policy, Shaping Opinions*. Ardsley, NY: Transnational Publishers.

Goulart, Ron. 2000. *Comic Book Culture: An Illustrated History*. Portland, OR: Collectors Press.

Harvey, Robert C. 1996. *The Art of the Comic Book: An Aesthetic History*. Jackson: University Press of Mississippi.

Johnson-Cartee, Karen S. 2004. *News Narratives and News Framing: Constructing Political Reality*. Lanham, MD: Rowman & Littlefield Publishers.

Kaplan, A. Y. 1989. "Theweleit and Spiegelman: Of Mice and Men." *Remaking History*, 151–72. Eds. Barbara Kruger and Phil Mariani. Seattle: Bay Press.

LaCapra, D. 1998. " 'Twas the Night Before Christmas: Art Spiegelman's *Maus*." *History and Memory after Auschwitz*, 139–79. New York: Cornell University Press.

Landsberg, A. 1997. "America, the Holocaust, and the Mass Culture of Memory: Toward a Radical Politics of Empathy." *New German Critique,* 71: 63–86.

Leith, Denise. 2004. *Bearing Witness: The Lives of War Correspondents and Photojournalists*. Milsons Point, NSW, Australia: Random House.

Liss, A. 1998. "Between Trauma and Nostalgia: Christian Boltanski's *Memorials* and Art Spiegelman's *Maus*." *Trespassing Through Shadows: Memory, Photography, and the Holocaust*, 52–68. Minneapolis: University of Minnesota Press.

McCloud, Scott. 1993. *Understanding Comics: The Invisible Art*. Northampton, MA: Tundra.

McKinzie, Bruce Wayne. 1994. *Objectivity, Communication, and the Foundation of Understanding*. Lanham, MD: University Press of America.

Nyberg, Amy Kiste. 1998. *Seal of Approval: The History of the Comics Code*. Jackson: University Press of Mississippi.

Olen, Jeffrey. 1988. *Ethics in Journalism*. Englewood Cliffs, NJ: Prentice-Hall.

The Pulitzer Prizes. 2004. http://www.pulitzer.org (accessed 12 January 2005).

Reese, Stephen D., Oscar H. Gandy, and August E. Grant. 2001. *Framing Public Life: Perspectives on Media and Our Understanding of the Social World*. Mahwah, NJ: Lawrence Erlbaum Associates.

Rothberg, M. 1994. " 'We Were Talking Jewish': Art Spiegelman's *Maus* as 'Holocaust' Production." *Contemporary Literature,* 35: 661–87.

Sabin, Roger. 1993. *Adult Comics: An Introduction*. London: Routledge.

Said, Edward. 2003. "Homage to Joe Sacco." *Palestine*, i–v. London: Random House-Jonathan Cape.

Seligman, C. 1991. "Maus Redux." *Village Voice,* 65–6.

Spiegelman, Art. 1999. *Art Spiegelman: Comix, Graphics, Essays and Scraps (From Maus to Now to Maus to Now)*. New York: Raw Books and Graphics.

Spiegelman, Art. 1997. "Interview." *Dangerous Drawings: Interviews with Comix and Graphix Artists*, 6–27. New York: Juno Books.

Witek, Joseph. 1989. *Comic Books as History: The Narrative Art of Jack Jackson, Art Spiegelman, and Harvey Pekar*. Jackson: University Press of Mississippi.

Wright, Bradford W. 2001. *Comic Book Nation: The Transformation of Youth Culture in America*. Baltimore: Johns Hopkins University Press.

13 It's a Jungle in Here
Animal Man, Continuity Issues, and the Authorial Death Drive

Steven Zani

REINTRODUCING ANIMAL MAN

Grant Morrison was one of a number of authors who participated in the revisionist trend of the 1980s comic medium by reviving, both literally and figuratively, a hero created in 1965 from the DC archives, "Animal Man," who absorbs the abilities of nearby animals as his superpower. The character had been used only sporadically in the DC Universe until 1988, when he was given his own title, and the character became a springboard for discussions of identity construction and textual continuity, with author Morrison interjecting himself into the work and eventually revealing the intent of his own brushstrokes. However, despite any innovation that Morrison's particular run on the series (1988–1990) may have shown, *Animal Man* remains relatively unnoticed and uninfluential in critical treatments of comic books in the 1980s, or in general. One reason for this is the company that the series keeps. Morrison's work on *Animal Man* took place when writers Alan Moore, Neil Gaiman, and Frank Miller were establishing themselves as the big guns of the comic industry, destroying stereotypes and radically revising the future of the genre[1] with works that are frequently cited, such as *Watchmen* (1986–87), the *Sandman* series (1988–96), or *Batman: The Dark Knight Returns* (1985–86). In comparison to such works, *Animal Man* languishes in obscurity. Morrison himself has referred to the text in a diminutive fashion as "trippy metatextual stuff,"[2] and much of what the comic has to offer is not new. Comics with overt political messages have been a part of the superhero genre since its World War II propagandistic origins, which continues well into the contemporary era (the obvious standout is the acclaimed revelation of the heroin addiction of sidekick "Speedy" in the 1970s *Green Lantern & Green Arrow*). Nor is there much new in having characters plagued with self-doubt and ethical dilemmas. Spider-Man's introspective anxieties, his constant wavering between following his own desires and serving the community, are enduring elements of his popularity, and the "reluctant hero" has easily become a structurally consistent element of many comics of the last several decades. What aspects, if any, of Morrison's *Animal Man* make it worth retrospective attention?

To begin, the metatextual approach of the series distinguishes it from its predecessors. At the very least, Morrison's sometimes capricious inclusion of himself as a protagonist eventually turns *Animal Man* into a comic book version of *Tristram Shandy*, revealing that what is at stake in comic books is nothing less than what is at stake in all artistic representation. More importantly, though there were a number of extraordinary, genre-breaking comics in the 1980s, there is an element in *Animal Man* not present in those other, oft-cited works. *Animal Man* uses its metatextual focus to confront directly the recent revision that DC Comics had done to its own textual universe. *Animal Man* takes place within the DC Universe after the *Crisis on Infinite Earths* (1985), an attempt to focus DC texts and eliminate contradiction by radical revision of the catalog of available worlds and themes. In the *Crisis*, several heroes were killed, and entire fantasy universes and populations were destroyed. In short, the multitude of universes and settings (Earth-1, Earth-2, etc.) that had been the milieu of the DC catalog of heroes was abolished and a new, singular universe was created for DC characters to inhabit.[3] Ostensibly, the purpose for the shift was that both readers and authors would be more comfortable in a single realm, where contradictions could be resolved, and where no one had to worry about "continuity" issue—how the events of one world fit, or did not fit, into alternate worlds and timelines in the DC collective.

What makes *Animal Man* interesting in relation to its 1980s contemporaries is that the work specifically addresses its own place in the superhero comic book genre. In doing so, the comic does more than just reveal its own metatextual themes and structures (as the works of Gaiman, etc., did at the time), but also reveals authorial intent and authorial construction. In the process, the apparently polemic messages of this particular series—its own obvious vegetarian and left-wing political themes—were called into question, but larger structural concerns were also addressed. In situating *Animal Man* in relation to authorial intent and the *Crisis*, Morrison's work asks fundamental questions about texts themselves, questions that hadn't been addressed previously by the comic book superhero genre. Why re-create a comic book hero? What is served in "death" and "rebirth" on the textual level? How does a project like the *Crisis* reveal the structures of desire that underlie the reading and writing we perform when we open a book? *Animal Man* offers an oblique criticism of the desire for completion and satisfaction that comic books offer their audience, and reveals the loose ends and plot complications that occupy the empty spaces of all texts, despite our attempts to narrate them out of existence. For Morrison and *Animal Man*, texts only make sense because we force our structures upon them, and the lesson of the book is to remind us that those structures are our own.

TRIPPY METATEXTUAL STUFF

Issue number one of *Animal Man* begins with B'wana Beast, another obscure superhero with animal-related powers, walking along an interstate towards San Diego. Narration describes his headache, and the fourth panel shows blood dripping from his nose. A narrative box, which may or may not be expressing the thoughts of B'wana Beast, proclaims, "Why did we ever come down? Why did we come down out of the trees?" Obviously this can be read as a gesture towards recognizing animal suffering and animal rights—a theme to be carried out in many explicit gestures in Morrison's run on the comic (for example, when Animal Man turns vegetarian in issue number five). However, the words are given paradigmatic meaning once readers turn the page, to discover Animal Man, in his civilian identity as Buddy Baker, up in a tree, attempting to retrieve his neighbor's kitten. Admittedly, the connection is fairly trivial; the more profound, Caliban-esque complaint that B'wana Beast makes about the burdens of embracing civilization has been reduced to a visual gag of a man awkwardly saving a kitten.[4] But the connection between words and images reveals a gesture towards irony that Morrison will repeat constantly in the series, just as he does later even in the same book, when a hunter proclaims that he feels "Free as a damn bird!" (21) in the same panel showing the carcass of the bird that has just been shot.

This irony is the technique by which much of *Animal Man* enacts its effects upon the reader. Written text and art are juxtaposed in a specific order to reveal a meaning that would be otherwise cumbersome or impossible, in a different artistic medium, to reveal in the same space or to the same effect.[5] Issue number two ends with a rat creature tearing Animal Man's arm from his body. Readers can only realize that the arm is severed, however, after more than one panel has shown Animal Man's human fist, as he attempts to strike the rat. As readers proceed sequentially on the page, only in the third panel surrounding the clenched fist has enough of the foreground been revealed to show that the fist is disconnected from its arm. The picture, then, takes on an ironic meaning, as readers are forced to understand that the initial sight of the fist, indicating rage and aggression, is now revelatory of castration and loss.

The technique of unveiling multiple meanings for a single image is not particularly new for sequential art, or any other form of art, and surely few comic book readers escaped the influence of such a technique after being bombarded with the multiplicity of meanings in Alan Moore's blood-ied *Watchmen* smiley face, coming only a few scant years before the publication of *Animal Man*. Morrison borrows other ideas from Moore, as well, for example, when Animal Man refuses to do anything to B'wana Beast after subduing him in issue number four. "What was I supposed to do? Take him to jail like a good superhero?" (18). These words, with their revelation about typical superhero behavior, have an obvious parallel to a phrase Moore employs in the final issue of *Watchmen* as the character Ozymandias similarly reveals the mechanics of the comic book format, "I'm not a Republic serial villain. Do you seriously think I'd explain my masterstroke if there remained the slightest chance of you affecting the outcome?" These moments where the text underscores its own existence as comic are supplemented a number of times throughout the *Animal Man* series, such as in issue number seven, where the "Red Mask" laments the fact that a meteor, which gave him super powers, gave him only a death touch instead of the ability to fly.

> *Red Mask:* I mean, look at you—you can fly. I'll bet that was an accident . . .
> *Animal Man:* Yeah. Spaceship blew up in my face, gave me animal powers.
> *Red Mask:* There you go. That's exactly what I'm saying. You get your animal powers, I get a death touch. Fickle finger of fate . . . So, in the end, what else could I do with a death touch? I became a bad guy. (12)

The functional message is to reveal to the readers that traditional comic elements are in place in this text, and yet their shortcomings are being exposed. Ultimately, it is this gesture of dissatisfaction and exposure that will be the capstone of Morrison's run on the series.

THE TEASER PARAGRAPH

There are any number of other moments where Animal Man is revealed as a nontraditional hero, such as the time that he vomits in issue number nine, has a five o'clock shadow at the end of issue nineteen, or the multiple times throughout the series that he bleeds, cries, or appears in costume while simultaneously wearing civilian clothing (he regularly wears a jacket over his superhero outfit). In short, just as characters such as the Red Mask are revealed as people who are not necessarily comfortable with their given comic book roles, Animal Man is demythologized in the book by being humanized into "Buddy Baker," a person with human emotions and physical states.[6] As the series continues, however, Morrison takes another direction as he begins to dehumanize Animal Man altogether, not revealing him as "animal" (a tactic taken by subsequent series writer Peter Milligan, who has Animal Man leaping upon a horse and tearing its throat out in issue number twenty-seven), but rather revealing that Animal Man is a constructed character—neither human nor animal but rather text.

The first obvious gesture in this direction is taken in issue number five. Morrison had originally intended to write only a four-issue miniseries with the character, and the arc of the initial storyline ends with the fourth issue.

However, when the proposal was given to DC Comics they approved the creation of an entire new title. Morrison himself explains the development in a two-page letter to his readers, printed the end of issue number two, which elaborates the directions the book would take.

> From #5 onward I hope I can try some more interesting and experimental stuff, all of which is going to lead to a major reworking of Animal Man's origin and abilities and an assault on the fundamental reality of the DC Universe. (That, by the way, was the "teaser" paragraph, which is supposed to be so mysterious and tantalizing that you just won't be able to stop yourself buying every issue of this book.) (25–26)

It would be a mistake to think of this Morrison quote as a "secondary source." It's true that the material, like an interview piece, is the author's own commentary on his work, but keep in mind that these are comments that appear *in the book itself.* If the comic is to be taken as a coherent unit, it must be taken "warts and all," with the advertisements, editor's remarks, and fan writings from the letter column included—because all of those elements taken together are the collective work of art that DC Comics chose to represent as their publication *Animal Man.* Morrison's comments, then, are explicitly part of the comic itself, even if they become self-referential. But that is entirely the point, because Morrison is going to make a large-scale gesture of opening the question of self-referentiality into the world of the comic, and this minimal step in that direction in issue number two is a sign of what will later become his primary focus. It is telling that Morrison not only reveals the structural mechanics behind why his issues have been plotted the way they are, but he also reveals the specific structure behind why he would write that statement itself—because it's a "teaser"—in the first place.

This process of layered revelation, where symbols always take on multiple associations, yet eventually lead back only to an author with an agenda, increases with the series. The cover of issue number five reveals Animal Man lying on the ground, as if he had been hit by a car (Figure 13.1). With arms jutting outward and a bent knee, his body invokes the symbol of a cross, and he lies directly on top of a "cross" of tire tread marks. Clearly, a Christian paradigm is being invoked, but a more important element is that one-fourth of the picture is taken up by a gigantic hand, holding a paintbrush, finishing the work of coloring Animal Man's costume. The comic itself is a self-contained narrative parody of the Warner Brothers character Wile E. Coyote, as the coyote in the story, "Crafty," is given a task by his paintbrush-wielding creator. That same paintbrush, the only visible representation of the creator, is revealed at various points in the book (including the cover) as the brush that is coloring the entire text. Besides referencing the WB Coyote, Morrison is also making an homage to Chuck Jones, who directed the 1953 Warner Brothers animated cartoon "Duck

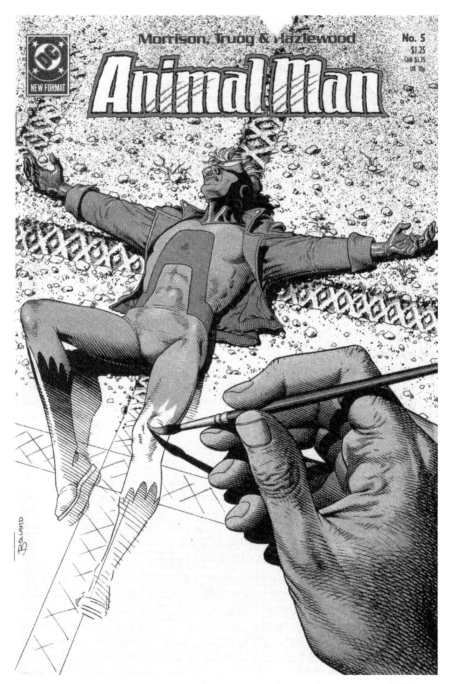

Figure 13.1 Grant Morrison's Animal Man in one of many deconstructive highlights in the *Animal Man* series, 1988. © DC Comics.

Amuck," featuring Daffy Duck as a character who is consistently provoked and humiliated by an unseen animator (eventually revealed as Bugs Bunny) throughout the piece. Crafty's narrative, which involves a good deal of suffering (falling from cliffs, having boulders land upon him, etc.) parallels the suffering of Daffy Duck and Wile E. Coyote, obviously, but also the suffering that Animal Man will endure at the hands of his creature in the forthcoming issues of the comic. Morrison's point, however, like Jones's, is less a question of allowing us to experience the suffering of his characters than it is to reveal that such suffering is a textual creation, put into a comic to achieve an effect. If that were not the explicit message, the constant inclusion of "authorial" scenes and gestures would not be necessary.

CRISIS

Thus we come to the major narrative arc of the comic. After Animal Man's family is killed, he becomes despondent, obtains a time machine, and attempts to return to the past and prevent their deaths. Time travel narratives, since people began to write them,[7] often fit a simple pattern. Either the protagonist attempts to change the past in order to eliminate some traumatic event, and fails, or the protagonist does manage to change the past, but in doing so creates an unforeseen, tragic future. The archetype of this story is Ray Bradbury's "A Sound of Thunder," where the death of a past butterfly has vast negative consequences. Bradbury's story has been influential enough to foster a new scientific term, "The Butterfly Effect," which describes the methodology of chaos theory, first proposed by meteorologist Edward Lorenz in the late 1960s, when he discovered that minuscule events within complicated systems can eventually have large, unpredictable impacts.[8] Time-travel stories are very often didactic, and they employ "The Butterfly Effect" in order to teach a moral lesson—people should not alter the past because it will inevitably have a negative impact. These texts attempt to teach us that what has happened in the past may be tragic but is "natural" and part of some necessary order. What happens in *Animal Man*, however, is a different moral lesson. Animal Man is unable to save his family, but eventually he realizes this isn't due to some "natural" and comforting order; rather, it is the result of an author constructing his history.

This authorial construction becomes direct conflict in issue twenty-four, when Animal Man encounters a group of heroes and villains who were erased in the DC *Crisis*. One character, the Psycho Pirate, contains the memory of all the lost characters, and he releases them back into the narrative of *Animal Man*. The result is a tangle of old villains and heroes, uncertain of their purpose, each attempting to understand their meaning in a new world that has place for them. Unfortunately, each of these "old" characters represents a threat to the natural order of DC Comics, at least we can presume they are a threat in the sense that the entire series of the *Crisis* had to be created in order to remove them from the narrative. In returning, these characters defy the rules of the new order, but moreover they reveal Morrison's message, that it is not so easy to write characters out of existence. Just as they exist in the "memory" of the Psycho Pirate, they still exist in the memories of readers and in the actual texts of the comics themselves that were produced prior to the *Crisis* (some of which show up as books that the characters read in the issue itself). At various points in the story, the characters reveal just how hard they are to contain and erase, by breaking the frames/panels of the very issue that contains them. The implication is that characters can change the very structure of the comics medium.

Addressing its own structure, *Animal Man* is repeating a lesson that readers had already learned from *Watchmen*, or *Batman: The Dark Knight Returns*—comics can address and rewrite their own stereotypes. However, the real innovation in *Animal Man* is that these characters are not just dangerous because they can shift the terms of the genre, nor because they represent a break in DC "continuity," but rather because their existence is a reminder of the scripts and structures of *our own* lives. Animal Man pulls one of the characters out of the panels of the book and forces him to look at the readers. As they stare at the readers of the comic, a shadowy figure in the background reveals the dangerous truth of the narrative: "There's something worse. The creators . . . They're not real either" (14). Eventually, one member of the group addresses the assembly and asserts that, whether being written out of the continuum or not, the characters are in fact more powerful and eternal than even their writers. "You can all still be seen. We can all still be seen. Our lives are replayed every time someone reads us. We can never die. We outlive our creators" (16). With this, Morrison has asserted one of the central revelations of the book, that humanity is more ephemeral than the artistic impulse that represents it.

With that revelation, the comic ends. All of the forgotten characters are reabsorbed into the mask of the Psycho Pirate and are safely tucked away again. After they are reabsorbed, two aliens, self-announced agents of the author, proclaim, "The continuum is purged at last of all inconsistencies. A foretaste of purification day, when we shall celebrate the aeonic union" (19). The comic has sealed itself up, and the loose ends of the narrative have been taken care of—each dangerous character is in its place. However, lest readers feel as if the threat is contained, and lest they think these prior stories can be truly forgotten, one of the aliens notices an insect. "Hmm. This butterfly is an Earth 14 species" (19) (Figure 13.2). With that comment, an oblique reference to chaos theory and Bradbury which is ignored by the other characters and seems otherwise irrelevant to the plot, we learn of the continued existence of a butterfly from a world that is supposed to be erased. Despite the destruction of multiple timelines and narratives of the DC Universe, these memories, tangents, and characters nonetheless

Figure 13.2 Two aliens from *Animal Man* (#39, 1989) discuss the reinstallation of order in the continuum. © DC Comics.

remain, the tiny butterflies that may one day have dire consequences on the possibility of maintaining consistency.

Issue twenty-four contains one more noteworthy revelation regarding DC's project to preserve the continuity of its creations, and that revelation comes from reading the letter column. While not typically considered part of the "comic," and never reproduced in the graphic novels that bind comic series together, the letter column is indeed part of the original work of comic art, and "forgetting" about it arguably constitutes much the same willful forgetfulness that DC enacts in its *Crisis*. A comic book, however, is not necessarily a singular vision. It is often not produced by a single artist, rather by a collective of writers, artists, inkers, and letterers. The letter-column material constitutes the artistic "work" produced by the editorial/authorial staff, who decided what letters would best represent whatever agenda they have in producing the work. In the letter column for this issue, a writer named "coreY klemoW" suggests that Morrison include one more forgotten world in the series.

> . . . you've got a chance to use one alternate world that was completely ignored during the first CRISIS, a world that was probably ignored 'cause Marv Wolfman thought he couldn't write it well enough and do justice to it . . . Are you ready for this?
>
> EARTH-H!
>
> That's right, that amazing parallel world seen so often in the 70's, where criminals could be easily distracted by throwing Hostess snacks at them! Criminals robbing the bank? Lob a Twinkie at 'em and they'll drop the loot! The Joker's getting away? Serve him a Hostess Chocolate Cupcake on a Batarang! Aliens causing havoc? Introduce them to Hostess Fruit Pies—Apple, Cherry, or Berry! (26)

While the suggestion in itself is ludicrous, put in the context of Morrison's own developing points about the nature of the comic medium, it has considerable value. Despite the restructuring that occurred in the *Crisis* series, the DC Universe is not an entity with a singular timeline, agenda, or meaning. Eventually, alternate agendas will reveal themselves. What "klemoW" reveals in his comment is one of the typically invisible, or unmentioned, goals of producing comic books—to generate advertising revenue.[9] Part of our collective fantasies of Superman, Batman, and the rest do indeed contain the lingering traces of these other agendas. The Hostess commercials that once littered comic pages in the 1970s are the perfect example of the "worlds" that will not go away once continuity has been preserved, because the commodity value that "Earth-H" represents is still a present, if often unacknowledged, element of the text itself. Those Hostess texts *were* produced, shameless as they are, and their example serves to remind us that the historical, material value of texts is always an element present both in how texts are constructed and how they are interpreted by their viewing public. Marvel Comics has its own litany of comics promoting Pizza Hut, Topps Bubble Gum, and many more, but of course the point would be the same if there were no advertisements in comics at all; as commercially available works, their meaning must be at least partially understood in terms of the network of capital in which they are distributed. One may interpret them, to take a line from Victorian cultural criticism, as "art for art's sake,"[10] but that alone is not their sole meaning. Along those same lines, Earth-H serves as a reminder that superheroes do not exist as cultural icons solely due to their appearances in the pages of actual comic books, as many heroes are known to the public solely through Saturday morning shows like *Challenge of the Superfriends* (Hanna Barbera,

1978–79), or even more recent Cartoon Network "revisions" such as *Teen Titans* (Warner Brothers, 2004–), or *Krypto the Superdog* (Warner Brothers, 2005–)—a character now reintroduced to the public after being intentionally removed in *Crisis*! DC may produce one universe as the locus of its meaning, but the collective texts of *Animal Man* reveal that no text can be purged of multiplicity and counternarrative.[11]

How important are these multiple tangles and counternarratives? Usually, they are easy to forget, with time, and some of these "changes" may seem fairly negligible, or even desirable. Think of the earliest versions of flightless Superman, where in *Action Comics* 5 (1938) he can only stop a collapsing dam by "battling like mad" (quoted in Jones 143). Today all children, and most adults, only know a vastly different and more powerful Superman, and yet many of the same elements of his character remain in place, so perhaps he hasn't changed much at all, or has changed for the better. Another reason that we do not know so much about the early history of Superman is that producers have other reasons to forget elements of that history, such as the long-standing legal battles that Superman creators Joe Shuster and Jerry Siegel underwent in order to get at least some small part of the enormous amount of money that has been made from their creation. The last thing that both producers (and even consumers) want to think about when envisioning Superman is the vast corporate mechanism that may, or may not, be equitably distributing the profits of the Superman textual history.[12]

What is at stake here isn't just a modest question of where the profits go, or even "what we think about when we think about Superman." In fact, these narratives and counternarratives, differing versions of our comics and texts, can tell us a great deal about our culture and ourselves as producers of that culture. Take, for example, Will Eisner's often celebrated and highly influential hero comic, *The Spirit* (1940–1952). Eisner is unanimously praised in the comic industry for any number of narrative and artistic techniques, yet it's worth remembering that just as Batman has been used to hawk Hostess cupcake products, so is it also true that *The Spirit* has elements that are perhaps deliberately forgotten, such as the hero's diminutive big-lipped black caricature of a sidekick, Ebony White, whose devotion to the Spirit is an obvious slave paradigm and whose dialogue consists mostly of phrases such as "Yassuh!"[13] Eisner's comic is otherwise a brilliant lesson in narrative structure and creative license, but like all artists he has created a product that different eras can read with different eyes and different agendas.

What are we to do with these narratives that we would like to forget? Often enough, we use them to support whatever purpose we have in mind at the time, and comic books in different eras have been interpreted differently. Fredric Wertham's now famous attack on the industry, his 1953 psychological "study" of comic books *Seduction of the Innocent*, is a tirade against apparent criminality and racism in comics, and shows how one man's vision of heroism may be another man's moral delinquency. *Seduction*, with scandalous and exploitative pictures and a mountain of psychological case studies (all of delinquents), is a beautiful example of misdirection and alternative interpretation. Wertham often takes passages out of context to produce meanings that are the apparent opposite of the comic's intended message (for Wertham, the villain's message is often understood as the central philosophy of the comic), and the book accuses the genre of contributing to virtually every possible tragedy or social problem (including, for example, the number of injuries to the eyes of children from the sale of air rifles—i.e., B.B. guns—advertised in comic books).[14] Wertham's text helped bring about an economic depression to the comics industry and clearly contributed to the creation, voluntary though it was, of the Comics Code Authority, which policed and censured the overall moral content of comics for the next several decades.

While today most people would agree that Wertham's vision of comics is exaggerated, or in fact downright absurd, the point is that a comic book can be, and in fact will be, understood in any number of different ways. Though Wertham's desire to legislate comics out of existence did not work, it serves as a reminder that there is a constant attempt on the part of both producers and consumers of comic book texts to either shackle them to an agenda or erase their existence entirely. Think of the great deal of trouble that Warner Brothers has gone to in order to limit the release and availability of early Bugs Bunny cartoons, such as the misogynist 1936 work "He Was Her Man," or the racist 1943 propaganda piece "Tokio Jokio."[15] A work like *Animal Man* makes clear that the DC *Crisis* is an attempt, like that of Wertham or the Warner Brothers corporation, to control and censure the production of a work. Morrison's *Animal Man*, however, reveals the impossibility of achieving that goal.

DEATH

There is one final element to *Animal Man* that clarifies Morrison's own attitudes about how agendas alter the content of a work, and that is the narrative's use of death as a structural component. *Animal Man* often faithfully reproduces traditional hero stereotypes, even when doing so with an explicit wink to the reader, and like the original stories of many heroes Animal Man's origin involves his own death. Just as Beowulf, Jesus Christ, Odysseus, and other typical epic heroes descend into the underworld, so it is revealed in issue number twelve that the explosion that gave Buddy Baker his Animal Man powers actually killed him. The aliens who caused these events explain: "You did not survive the explosion. We placed your spirit in the template and grafted onto your essence the essences of the beast avatars already there. Then we rebuilt your body, cell by cell . . . Your 'animal powers' derive from these morphogenetic grafts" (18). These heroic deaths are in some ways ubiquitous; death or loss is at the beginning of almost all fairy-tale and superhero narratives, and perhaps Animal Man belongs less to the epic tradition than he belongs to a new one being developed in the late 1980s, for just as this character is killed in order to be made anew, so were other authors at the time, such as Alan Moore (Swamp Thing) and Neil Gaiman (Black Orchid), killing their characters in order to re-create them for their own agendas.

So what is Morrison's agenda in killing his protagonist? *Animal Man* takes a turn from being a traditional hero comic as the character becomes more and more violent, and the question of death takes center stage. This focus on death and aggression occurs after Animal Man witnesses continual atrocities against animals but takes an even more fatalistic turn when his family has been killed, and he hunts down, and kills, those responsible.[16] However, his violence is eventually revealed as a staged event, in issue number twenty-six, when the author appears in the work. Upon the author's appearance, Animal Man goes into a rage and throws the Morrison character through a window, proclaiming him a murderer. The author, however, simply appears again, unharmed, and explains the situation.

> *Morrison:* I can make you do anything. I mean, you're not really violent, are you? You've never really been one of those horrible characters with a gun in every pocket and too much testosterone. You've seen the futility of violence, haven't you?
> *Animal Man:* Yes . . . Yes, I hate violence . . . I . . . Why did I do that?
> *Morrison:* I made you do it. I thought we needed some action at the start of the story, just to keep people interested. (5–6)

Morrison explains on the next page that the reason he killed Animal Man's family was equally calculated. "It added drama. All stories need drama and it's easy to get a cheap emotional shock by killing popular characters" (7). He continues by revealing that parts of the narrative in Animal Man's life were constructed because his own pet, a cat named Jarmara, died.

> And yet there was a part of me—the part that observes and writes— rubbing its hands and saying, "Well, at least if she dies, I'll be able to use it in Animal Man. It'll add a nice touch of poignancy."
> We'll stop at nothing, you see. All the suffering and the death and the pain in your world is entertainment for us. (18–19)

In the end of the comic, Morrison brings Animal Man's family back to him, as if they had never died. He then tells the readers of an imaginary friend he had when he was a child, named Foxy, whom he used to send signals to by flashlight into the dark hills. The final panels are of Morrison signaling again to Foxy. "I've come to send a signal out into the dark. In the end, it seemed like the only thing worth doing . . . Foxy, I came back.

I didn't forget. I came back" (23). In the final panel of the comic, the signal is returned. With that gesture of return, *Animal Man* reveals Morrison's relationship to text and creative production. The purpose of the work is to reveal the loose threads and forgotten products of our imagination. A work like the *Crisis* series, designed to organize and arrange our texts into singular sets of meanings, is a process of deliberate forgetfulness that will fail. Instead, the text suggests, we should devote ourselves to "the only thing worth doing," reexamining our desires, our imaginative productions, and never forgetting the gains and losses of our world, our pets, families, and loved ones, who inform upon the texts we create and the books we enjoy.

AUTHOR EX MACHINA

Since *Animal Man*, Morrison has produced a great deal more work in the comics industry, work that many would consider more critically relevant or interesting than *Animal Man*. Popular industry opinion holds that his series *The Invisibles* (1994–2000) is the central but uncredited source material for the film *The Matrix* (Wachowski, 1999), and it is hard not to see similarities between the two prorevolutionary narratives, each with hidden conspiracy theories about networks controlling the world and protagonists who test their identity/consciousness by leaping from a skyscraper. While the Morrison oeuvre contains mainstream titles—*The Doom Patrol, The New X-Men*—he has nonetheless used those titles to continue to ask questions about the nature of artistic production, and he has also written a number of comic projects where the obvious goal is to subvert traditional comic book narratives, such as the unsavory comic *The Filth* (2004), or his latest production, which may be a development of the same themes begun in *Animal Man*, DC's *Seven Soldiers*, a collection of seven four-issue miniseries (each focusing on a separate obscure character from the DC Universe), each self-contained as a narrative, but interwoven in ways that only readers, and not the protagonists of the narratives themselves, could understand, making explicit those narrative gaps and distances that open themselves in the process of reading and writing.

However, if Morrison's subsequent work has garnered more attention, in these supposedly unimportant issues of *Animal Man*, the character suffers from a number of trials and crises that reveal the heart of the Morrison agenda. While the comic may have begun with a large-scale political message on animal rights, the journey ends with Animal Man pursuing a much more intensely personal search for identity and meaning. Morrison's final arguments are that heroism is a process achieved by constant evaluation of one's self and one's motives and by constant attention to the process involved in creating, literally writing and drawing, one's own identity. The individual battles and trials are less important than the constructive process of creating oneself in relation to memory and text. And really, as the comic asserts, what else is worth doing?

NOTES

1. As Greg McCue and Clive Bloom argue in the opening pages of *Dark Knights* (1993) in response to, an analysis of the comics industry, "a medium is not a genre," asserting a useful distinction to make when considering the nature of comics. The use of the term *genre* here is accurate in the sense that Moore, Gaiman, and others, of course did not particularly change the medium of comics, but they did alter the superhero genre within it.
2. See Daniel Epstein's "Grant Morrison" interview on the Suicide Girls Web site.
3. Various accounts and summaries of the Crisis can be found throughout the Internet, but for a definitive look at the series without the polemics and agendas of the Internet coloring the presentation, see the 2005 DC Comics reprint *Crisis on Infinite Earths* (Absolute Editions), which includes a great deal of supplemental appendices and connected material, including lists of comics series whose storylines were connected to the Crisis, lists of alternate earth's, and brief discussions of the Crisis-connected series that followed the original.
4. Caliban first appears in Shakespeare's *The Tempest* (1611), but there have been subsequent attempts to explore his particular complaint, notably Robert Browning's poem "Caliban Upon Setebos; or, Natural Theology in the Island" (1864). More recently, Tad Williams has published a novel, *Caliban's Hour* (1994), elaborating Caliban's narrative even further.
5. Scott McCloud's description of comics as "sequential art" is the basis of this observation (McCloud 1994, 7–9).
6. One reader comments, on page twenty-six in the letter column of issue number five, "I just can't call him Animal Man, Buddy fits him so well."
7. H. G. Wells is often assumed the first time-travel writer for his 1895 novel *The Time Machine*, but he is preceded by several, notably Mark Twain, in 1889, with *A Connecticut Yankee in King Arthur's Court*, and L. S. Mercier's 1771 narrative *Memoirs of the Year 2500*.
8. Despite several years since its initial publication, James Gleick's 1987 work *Chaos: Making a New Science* is still considered among the best summaries of the history and implications of chaos theory.
9. See "'Holy Commodity Fetish, Batman!': The Political Economy of a Commercial Intertext," by Eileen Meehan (Meehan 1991).
10. Though not the originator of the phrase, nineteenth-century author Théophile Gautier is usually credited as the first major proponent of this ideology.
11. See "Same Bat Channel, Different Bat Times: Mass Culture and Popular Memory" (Spigel and Jenkins 1991).
12. Discussed only briefly in this paragraph, further commentary about early versions of Superman (particularly the legal battles and financial history behind the character) can be found in Gerard Jones's account of the production end of comic book history (Jones 2004).
13. This exclamation can be found in *The Spirit Archives*, Volume 2, 10 (2000), though similar language saturates the series. It is worth noting, however, that *The Spirit* used fewer stereotypes as the series developed, and Eisner eventually added a number of black characters who used standard English. To his credit as well, Eisner is less sexually exploitative than a great number of subsequent comic artists, and by being essentially the first artist to retain the copyright over his own creation, he remains a role model for aspiring writers/creators. For his own account of the early development of *The Spirit*, see the interview in Stanley Wiater and Stephen Bissette's *Comic Book Rebels* (1993) (see bibliography entry under Wiater, pp. 268–81). Another excellent source is Charles Brownstein's recent book *Eisner/Miller* (2005), published

shortly after Eisner's death. The work is a lengthy set of interviews/discussions between Eisner and Frank Miller, with their insights and opinions about the nature of the comics industry.

14. See p. 13. For a further account of the influence of Wertham's book, his claims to have met cultural critic Theodor Adorno, and his subsequent testimony at Senate subcommittee hearings on comics and juvenile delinquency, see Jones 2004, Ch.12.

15. Many younger viewers may have become aware of animation censorship only when Cartoon Network received media attention for excluding twelve controversial Bugs Bunny cartoons during a 2001 animation marathon. However, the editing and/or censorship of animated cartoons—which in their early history were often not children-oriented—has been practiced for decades. For a long treatment of censorship in animation, see Karl Cohen's *Forbidden Animation: Censored Cartoons and Blacklisted Animators in America* (2004). Dan Patanella has also written an insightful and succinct online article, "Censorship and Golden Age Animation," that reviews an animation collection and discusses the issue. See bibliography for full citation details on both.

16. He does perform an earlier, and perhaps more disturbing, "attempted murder," taking a man who has been indiscriminately killing dolphins and leaving him to drown in the middle of the ocean. The man lives, however, after a dolphin brings him back to shore.

COMIC BOOKS

Eisner, Will. 2000. *The Spirit Archives*, Vol 2. Ed. Dale Crain. New York: DC Comics.
Moore, Alan. 1987. *Watchmen*. New York: DC Comics.
Morrison, Grant. 2001. *Animal Man*. New York: DC Comics.
Morrison, Grant. 2002. *The Origin of the Species*. New York: DC Comics.
Morrison, Grant. 2003. *Deus Ex Machina*. New York: DC Comics.
"Spider-Man Meets the Home Wrecker." 1978. *Fantastic Four*. August. 31.
Wolfman, Marv. 2005. *Crisis on Infinite Earths (Absolute Editions)*. New York: DC Comics.

BIBLIOGRAPHY

Brownstein, Charles. 2005. *Eisner/Miller*. Milwaukie, OR: Dark Horse Comics.
Cohen, Karl. 2004. *Forbidden Animation: Censored Cartoons and Blacklisted Animators in America*. Jefferson, NC: McFarland & Co.
Epstein, Daniel R. 2005. "Grant Morrison." Interview. *Suicide Girls*. 15 March. http://suicidegirls.com/words/Grant+Morrison/.
Gleick, James. 1988. *Chaos: Making a New Science*. New York: Penguin Books USA.
Jones, Gerard. 2004. *Men of Tomorrow: Geeks, Gangsters and the Birth of the Comic Book*. New York: Basic Books.
McCloud, Scott. 1994. *Understanding Comics: The Invisible Art*. New York: HarperCollins.
McCue, Greg, and Clive Bloom. 1993. *Dark Knights: The New Comics in Context*. London: Pluto Press.

Meehan, Eileen. 1991. " 'Holy Commodity Fetish, Batman!': The Political Economy of a Commercial Intertext." In *The Many Lives of the Batman*, 47–65. Ed. Roberta Pearson and William Uricchio. New York: Routledge.

Pantanella, Dan. 2005. "Censorship and Golden Age Animation." *Animation—American and Japanese*. 16 March. http://www.geocities.com/d-patanella/censor.html.

Spigel, Lynn, and Henry Jenkins. 1991. "Same Bat Channel, Different Bat Times: Mass Culture and Popular Memory." *The Many Lives of the Batman*, 117–48. Ed. Roberta Pearson and William Uricchio. New York: Routledge.

Wertham, Fredric. 1972. *Seduction of the Innocent*. New York: Kennikat Press.

Wiater, Stanley, and Stephen R. Bissette. 1993. *Comic Book Rebels*. New York: Donald I. Fine.

Williams, Tad. 1995. *Caliban's Hour*. New York: HarperCollins.

14 Morrison's Muscle Mystery Versus Everyday Reality . . . and Other Parallel Worlds!

Martyn Pedler

" . . . IS THIS REAL OR ISN'T IT?"

> My big breakthrough on Superman came in 1999 when I was work-
> ing on my first proposal for the character. It was 2:00 in the morning
> and . . . at that moment, I kid you not two guys come walking across
> the rail tracks, and one of them is dressed in the best Superman suit
> I've seen. This guy looked fantastic as Superman . . . so we asked him
> if he'd answer some questions for us which he did—in the character of
> Superman! . . . He spoke to us for about an hour and a half, as Super-
> man, then went back to his lonely Fortress of Solitude at the YMCA or
> whatever. . . . (Grant Morrison, quoted in Brady 2005)

Despite my childhood wishes to the contrary, I live in the real world. It's
no Metropolis. The skyline is free of flying men or flashes of inexplicable
light. I wonder: do all comic fans, deep down, believe that superheroes
are real? As a child—and yeah, probably as a teenager too—I rationalized their absence. They were missing from the real world, but there
must have been another world in which they're as real as you or me.
A parallel world. A possible future. An 'Earth-2.' These are the same
ideas that populate the superhero comics of writer Grant Morrison. In
his work on *Animal Man* (1988–90), the *Doom Patrol* (1989–93), *Flex
Mentallo* (1996), and even the *Justice League of America* (1997–2000),
the heroes face the difficulties of these other realities that encroach upon
their own, with surreal, ludicrous, and terrifying results. They are threats
that cannot be solved with heat-vision, repulsor rays, or a swift right
hook. Worst of all—what happens when the alternative reality is actually
our reality, out here in the so-called real world? Can any hero remain
intact when faced with our mundane bodies, physics, and color scheme?
In fact, when Morrison recently wrote a world that was meant to be our
own in *Justice League Classified* #3 (2005), it was even worse than I
thought: scenes of mundane tragedy in dark colors crammed into tiny,
uniform panels. It's pathetic that our world can be captured in frames

smaller than postage stamps. Superheroes require jagged, flashy frames around them that punch right out of the page!

It's why everything would be different if, like Morrison in his earlier quote, I happened to meet a superman on the street. It would be an awkward moment for both of us. He'd look me up and down with eyes capable of seeing through everything but lead. He'd flex his muscles and his costume would ripple like a tornado under a circus tent. And he'd know in an instant that—actually—I always liked Batman best. After all, anyone could be Batman: all it requires is hard work, brutally murdered parents, and access to an enormous personal fortune. Piece of cake, right? He didn't need to be able to lift a tank over his head to be a hero. Unlike this hypothetical superman standing before me, Batman was something I could, maybe, one day, become.

But all that training? As I got older, I had to admit it was actually far more likely I would be bitten by a radioactive spider or bombarded by cosmic rays than I was to embark on a lifetime of martial arts training. It's actually the superpowered heroes who are our everymen. As the products of happy accidents, they give hope to adolescents everywhere. Failing the intervention of comic book science, my body will never transform, except to get older and weaker.

That is how Grant Morrison's *Flex Mentallo*—"Hero of the Beach!"— became my favorite superhero. His origin story is one of perfect economy. There's an old comic book advertisement that ran consistently through the 50s and 60s for the Charles Atlas bodybuilding system, titled "The Insult That Made a Man Out of Mac!" It shows a one-page comic of a boy getting sand kicked in his face, using the training system to build new muscles, and then returning to the beach to get revenge and reclaim his girlfriend. Advertisements such as these were one of the very few ways my childhood comics and the real world met—with pages of narrative and pages of ads, shuffled together. (Remember those little printed warnings when an ad was coming? "Feature continues after next page!" Like you'd think Batman was never coming back after the interruption and Mister Freeze would get away. . . .) Morrison took the primal power fantasy of Charles Atlas and transformed its star into a fully fledged superhero with great powers, great responsibility, and, mostly, a great physique—all available by mail order.

Flex's superhero costume is a pair of simple leopard-print trunks, like a circus strongman. His physique is entirely on display, which is only proper, as comic book logic holds that the superhero body is *everything*. Most other heroes might be wearing head-to-toe spandex long johns, but that's just a thin coat of primary color designed to distract the Comics Code Authority from noticing that they are practically naked. Muscles are lovingly penciled, their popping veins delicately crosshatched in ink, bodies angled forward in the frame, overshadowing any narrative caption or word balloon. (Unless, perhaps, it's with a big spiky speech bubble of Jack Kirby-style shouting.)[1]

Superhero bodies can't be scarred, marked, or pierced. They're perfectly invulnerable. In fact, the 80s revamp of Superman took on board the everyday impossibility of this kind of masculinity. Superman had to shave by reflecting his heat vision of a piece of his broken rocket ship to burn his Kryptonian whiskers off his face . . . because no earth razor could stand up to the pure testosterone of his stubble (*Man of Steel* #4, 1985). The irony is that this series was designed precisely to depower some of the some insane excesses contained in Superman's amazing body. Afterwards, he could no longer move entire planets or travel faster than light, but he still possessed super-hearing, super-vision, and—why not?—super-cold arctic breath; his costume wasn't invulnerable, but it couldn't be cut or torn so long as it was skintight, contained in the aura of his impenetrable flesh (*Man of Steel* #2, 1985).

We regular humans are pathetically fragile. I always suspected it is why Superman forces himself to stay married to Lois Lane. He has to keep touching her, holding his strength in check, to remind himself how easily we're all broken. Wouldn't it be frustrating? Why couldn't we just be built a little stronger? Couldn't we, for once, just bounce some bullets off our own chests?

There'll always be bullets. Action is the constant of comics. You can give a monologue about your evil plan so long as you do it while pounding on your archenemy. You can have a spectacular psychic battle of wills, so long as it's drawn like a regular physical confrontation—maybe just with some suitably dreamy or surreal touches to the artwork. Heroes will not throw the first punch, but they always throw the last one.[2]

Yes, sometimes superhero comics try some meaningful dialogue, or issues of so-called talking heads, but they always seem kind of embarrassed about it. *Animal Man* was some of Morrison's earliest superhero work, and it was opportunity to take a Buddy Baker, an everyday hero with everyday animal powers, and put him through the wringer of deconstruction. Poor Buddy: Morrison took him apart as a superhero, as a husband, and as a fictional character. He was ineffectual when he performed typical heroic acts; his family were brutally murdered; and, finally, famously, he sought justice by seeking out the person responsible—Morrison himself.

In the final issue of his run on *Animal Man* (#26, 1991), Morrison goes on to explain to Buddy how comics really function. He was told he was nothing special. "A generic comic book hero with blond hair and good teeth. One of hundreds." Morrison apologized for the lack of action in the comic. He spends a few pages speaking through the fourth wall, thanking his artists, editors, and loyal letter writers . . . all while putting Buddy through a bloody, pointless brawl in the background. Just to give his artists some action to draw.

It's a fine line between physical perfection and muscle-bound freak show. We saw the surreal side of usually clean-cut supermen in DC Comics' 1960s series of the *Doom Patrol*: the "world's strangest heroes." Their creator, Arnold Drake, said that he needed a team with a twist: "That was the thing that made Doom Patrol different, [that] these people hated being superheroes" (Keller 2000). More specifically, they hated their bodies.

> *Robotman:* "And you're going to tell me I've got no reason to be bitter . . . no reason to feel I'm an outcast?"
> *The Chief:* "But you forget, in your self-pity, how unique you are! You're invulnerable to most dangers—unbelievably strong—and your living brain still thrills to your five senses!"
> *Robotman:* "How do you know what it's like . . . being trapped inside this metal body?" (*My Greatest Adventure* #80, 1963)

As entertaining as superhero fisticuffs might be, audiences wanted more spectacle, and so the superhero body was forced to find new ways to dazzle. Flames fire from hands! Necks stretch two stories high! Lasers shoot from eyes! And all this energy has to be enclosed within the body.[3] The typical spandex costume must show off muscles, but it can serve another purpose: as 'containment suits' designed to keep the heroes from erupting. (Even the squeaky-clean first family of comics, the Fantastic Four, wear costumes made of 'unstable molecules' to keep up with all their bodily transformations.) For the Doom Patrol, victims of "a cruel and fantastic fate" (*My Greatest Adventure* #80, 1963), this meant their physical forms were even less predictable than those of your usual steel-skinned he-men.[4]

Negative Man must keep himself constantly wrapped in radioactive bandages. Elasti-Girl's body shrinks and grows at whim. And, as quoted earlier, Robotman's human brain is encased in a robot body that is constantly bashed, melted, and disassembled. It gets worse, too: one of their recurring villains was Animal-Vegetable-Mineral Man—"Three Threats In One!"—whose body could transform into any mismatched combination of elements. Trees for arms. Ice for hands. The legs of a dinosaur. You get the idea. It's not for nothing it used to read "The World's Strangest Heroes!" above the *Doom Patrol* logo each month.

The disruptive potential of these powers means that superbodies must be monitored closely for betrayal. The demands of serial storytelling require that something different must happen to the same character, month in and month out. This means no variation will be left unexplored, and every possible malfunction of a hero's powers will eventually occur. Sure enough, suddenly you can't turn off your heat vision, or you cyborg arm is turning against you, or your body is being perversely altered by a visiting fifth-dimensional imp . . . and not even steel skin is strong enough to hold it all inside.[5]

INFINITE EARTHS

> I've always felt that my best writing is more like channelling the voices and adventures of real characters doing this stuff in a real place—the comic as it exists in the future perhaps. Call me crazy if you like. . . .
> (Grant Morrison, quoted in Lien-Cooper 2002)

When Morrison took over the *Doom Patrol* in the late 1980s, he wrote their always odd sensibilities to new extremes. Sure, Cliff Steele (a.k.a. Robotman) was the same two-fisted, old-fashioned everyman, but now his new teammates included: Negative Man, who became a hermaphrodite that called him/herself Rebis; Crazy Jane, who suffered from Multiple Personality Disorder, each having its own superpower; and Dorothy, a facially disfigured young girl who can make her imaginary friends real. Where did this leave Cliff? Completely lost. He says: "No, I'm not complaining, but sometimes it might be nice to just stop a bank robbery or foil a criminal mastermind. You know, like the regular super-guys" (*Doom Patrol* #37, 1990).

The new *Doom Patrol* faced foes that couldn't be pummeled into submission. They had to be defeated with logic puzzles, nursery rhymes, or postmodern word games. There's the fictional city of Orquith, growing out of a metatextual book to supplant reality; the Candlemaker, one of Dorothy's imaginary childhood monsters, claiming it is real, and the Doom Patrol are not; and best of all, the Brotherhood of Evil, who renamed themselves the Brotherhood of Dada, suddenly more interested in odd, situationist art crimes and parodically running for president than taking over the world. Cliff remembers when you could just punch a villain and save the day, but here, they sometimes don't have a body at all. Mister Nobody, for example, exists in abstract space, and—best of all—Number None is a random collection of mundane objects, such as a banana peels or traffic lights. Through all of this, Cliff needs to know: "All I want is the answer to one simple question before I run screaming back to the bughouse: is this real or isn't it?" (*Doom Patrol* #21, 1989).

It's not that simple anymore. When you're under attack by imaginary villains, what guarantee is your regular reality anyway? Morrison's run on the title ends with the very *Twilight Zone* notion that his entire series might have been a delusion of teammate Crazy Jane. After fighting against these terrifying parallel worlds, she's finally thrown into hell itself—before appearing in our world. Out here. The everyday that's right outside your window. Against the bright, surreal landscapes of the superhero, this *is* hell. She finally returns to her own reality, while the narration reassures us: "There is a better world." But why is there a better world? "Well . . ." Morrison writes, " . . . there must be" (*Doom Patrol* #63, 1993).

So let's presume we've skipped past the moment where I'd be rubbing my eyes, pinching myself, and looking around for practical jokers. If there was this superman standing in front of me, I know I'd be staring. Those muscles, after all. How could you not look? He'd be embarrassed, even seething a little under his cape. The nerve of me: writing a superhero into my world, just to have him stand awkwardly so I can examine him and make the occasional self-deprecating remark. I'd be looking closer, trying to spot the pencil marks under his chest, his arms. Perhaps if I can see the drafting that went into his creation, I'll be able to pick him apart. This urge to deconstruct belongs solely to adults. A child would never do what I'd do. I'd probably point out that he couldn't possibly be real.

Saving the world is one thing, but maintaining the comic book status quo requires the Herculean effort of dedicated professionals. It mostly happens when an old character is rebooted, made young and given a more fashionable costume. Continuity isn't bulletproof; it functions more like, say, a mutant healing factor. New details are absorbed into the official storyline, and older, outdated ideas are left to fade until they eventually barely leave a scar. Morrison finds many creative moments playing within this narrative scar tissue. His Animal Man, for example, is noticeably different from the Animal Man who first appeared in the 1970s. When the modern hero faces his predecessor, the now-replaced Animal Man demands to know why he's no longer being written into new adventures. "It's not fair. Wasn't I good enough? You've taken my place! I'm not real anymore" (*Animal Man* #19, 1990).

Sometimes, however, the weight of outdated continuity becomes too much to deal with behind the scenes, and the quiet self-repair is made overt. Continuity housekeeping became the story itself in the spectacularly and hyperbolically named *Crisis on Infinite Earths*, the 'event' twelve-part series of 1985–86. Series writer Marv Wolfman explained it in his original introduction:

> We had two sets of Supermans, Batmans, Flashes, Wonder Womans, Green Lanterns, etc etc. We also had a dozen different Earths. And so on and so on and so on . . . Well, CRISIS ON INFINITE EARTHS will

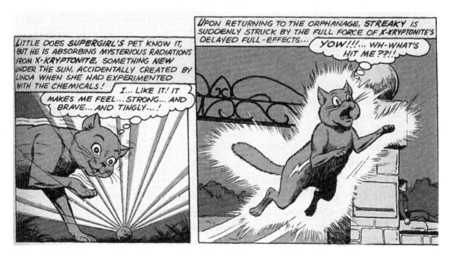

Figure 14.1 Exposed to Kryptonite, Streaky is transformed into the superpowered Streaky the Super-cat. From *Action Comics* #261, February 1960. © DC Comics.

attempt such a repair job. By series end DC will have a consistent and more easily understandable universe to play with. (*Crisis on Infinite Earths* #1, 1985)

And so all the strange, multiple worlds and antimatter twins of the DC Universe were, by issue #12, rebooted into one singular Earth—an Earth with only one Batman, one Superman, and all the rest. Their origin stories modernized and retold, too, with an eye towards something more . . . realistic? Believable? Maybe. I'd always had a special place in my childhood heart for superheroes' animal sidekicks. Superman had a whole menagerie! Krypto the Super-dog, Beppo the Super-Monkey, Streaky the Super-cat (Figure 14.1) . . . but these, and many other ridiculous characters, were gone in an instant after the *Crisis*. Now they never existed at all, paving the way for the pessimistic, so-called grim and gritty comics of the 80s and 90s.[6] It's easy for the rebooted heroes. They don't remember. It's their faithful readership, out here, outside continuity, who remember both the old and the new stories. They must willfully ignore the older adventures like they never happened—even if they have the tattered issues right there in their hands! This collector's double vision is shown in the climatic final storyline of Morrison's *Animal Man*. He uses a villain named the Psycho-Pirate, notable not really for his superpowers of emotional hypnotism or his preposterous jesterish costume, but because he is the one DC character who actually remembers the continuity reboot, and all the history that came before it. Like Morrison himself, the Psycho-Pirate can't forget these obsolete characters, and these memories spew painfully from his body—first as old pre-Crisis comic books, and then as the forgotten heroes themselves. They're determined to become real again, even if their presence threatens all reality. They're not meant to exist at all, you see.

Like the threats that faced Morrison's *Doom Patrol*, the Crisis wasn't something heroes could smash or bend or wrestle to the ground. The 'antimatter waves' of the *Crisis* are just whiteness that dissolves everything in their path. How can you fight the absence of ink? This is the true terror of the superhero. Years later, when the 'Next Issue' box of *Animal Man* #11 (1989) promised readers " . . . a fate never before seen in comics, and that's a promise!," it turned out to be a villain being erased from the comic entirely: reduced to a pencil outline, then a rough sketch, until his final speech balloon popped into nothing (*Animal Man* #12).

Now, Animal Man may have met Superman once, and was suitably awestruck; but both his title and the *Doom Patrol* remained art-house comics, as far as superheroes go. Surely the pages of the *Justice League of America* would hold some good old-fashioned fisticuffs? When Grant Morrison left his lovable freaks and took over DC's flagship superhero title, the destabilizing confusion of parallel worlds continued. In his *JLA: Earth-2* graphic novel (2000), the team face their evil twins from the antimatter dimension, the Crime Syndicate of Amerika. The twist? From the Crime Syndicate's point of view, it's *our* heroes' world that is Earth-2. The front cover might feature Superman, Batman, and Wonder Woman as we know them, but the back blurb is written from their enemies' point of view:

They are the world's gravest supervillains: ULTRAMAN, OWLMAN, SUPERWOMAN, POWER RING, and JOHNNY QUICK—the legendary CRIME SYNDICATE OF AMERIKA! Nothing has ever seriously threatened the global corruption they proudly enforce. But now a twisted mirror image of the CSA has arrived from the flip side of reality. Can anything stop this so-called "JUSTICE LEAGUE," or will the stable, perfect evil of the earth fall victim to the tyranny of law, righteousness and freedom? (*JLA: Earth-2*, 2000.)

The teams travel into each other's worlds, but it proves pointless. Decades of comic book morality have taught us that the good guys always win . . . in *our* world. In the Crime Syndicate's world, evil is always victorious. Eventually, all the teams can think to do is just go home and leave the status quo intact. For all their amazing powers, superheroes can rarely actually make a real difference in their fictional worlds. As it is with so many serialized stories, the audience is not given change but rather the illusion of change. The superhero status quo is—with apologies to the Hulk—the strongest one there is. Despite the occasional pretender, it will always be Bruce Wayne under the Bat-mask, and after half a century, Clark Kent hasn't aged a day.[7]

That's why so-called imaginary stories have enormous appeal for comic book writers. After too many cosmic crossovers that promised to CHANGE EVERYTHING! or that NOTHING WILL EVER BE THE SAME!, the superhero audience developed a skeptical immunity to supposedly earth-shattering events. It leads to desperate editorial pleading: this story is not a dream! Not a hoax! Not an imaginary story! This places the reader in much the same position as the *Doom Patrol*'s Cliff Steele, constantly demanding to know if these events 'really happened' in all-important continuity.

But in an imaginary story? Everything is open to transformation. Batman can fight Jack the Ripper (*Gotham by Gaslight*, 1989), or star in a homage to Citizen Kane ('Citizen Wayne' in *Legends of the Dark Knight Annual* #4, 1994).[8] These stories have always been a staple of comics and are most often seen under the DC 'Elseworlds' imprint, clearly labeled to keep them nicely separate from the rest of the universe. Godfather of superhero deconstruction Alan Moore famously pointed out the flaw in this logic when writing his story of Superman's possible future, *What Ever Happened to the Man of Tomorrow?* (1986). It reads: "This is an imaginary story . . . but aren't they all?"

SUPERHERO POETRY

It was always fascinating to me that Superman was so much older than me and yet I could come along and write adventures with Superman in them and add to his life story. Then I could die and Superman would keep going, with other people writing stories to keep him alive. He's more real than I am because he has a longer lifespan and more influence, so this notion of the 'real' 2-dimensional world of the comics and what it had to say to the 'real' 3-dimensional world of non-fictional people. (Grant Morrison, quoted in Epstein 2005)

How would I explain these questions of continuity to the superman in front of me? He'd know, by now, that this wasn't taking place in his regular continuity. I'm an unlikely new archvillain. So I'd just keep staring. It's amazing he still looks so good out here, especially considering that in our world, real people look pretty absurd in those skintight costumes. There have been some hugely successful superhero blockbusters lately, but we have to build our actors muscles out of rubber and strap them in tight. It's the final reminder that even the most human of superheroes aren't really human at all. No man or woman or CGI hybrid can live up to the ink on the page. Cliff Steele wonders whether he's technically human or not any more. He begins Morrison's run as a brain trapped in a robot body, and by the end of it, he isn't even that. His consciousness is stored on disk, with nothing organic remaining—just the leftover sensations of not just a phantom limb, but of his whole 'phantom' body. "There's less and less of me all the time," he says (*Doom Patrol* #60, 1992).

I felt it, too. Deep down I knew that the science of our world and the amazing fantasy of comic books would never really interact. That 'phantom body' exists as a dotted outline around the gawky adolescent form of the superhero fan. I ask you: where was *my* radioactive spider? Where were *my* cosmic rays? When did *I* finally get to transform? As a teenager, I rebelled. I decided I didn't want a body at all, and would prefer to be just a brain in a jar. Maybe some psychic powers, sure, but something subtle and sexy. It was pure coincidence that, all these years later, I discovered the Doom Patrol regularly fought a villain who *was* just a brain in a jar, and I felt strangely justified.

Looking at this hypothetical superman would make me feel like that brain in a jar all over again. He wouldn't have to use his x-ray vision to see that my body doesn't hold any secrets. I don't think I've ever managed to catch a ball, and a whole nest of radioactive spiders probably wouldn't change that fact. The real world is no place to find an origin story. There's something terribly and inescapably poignant for our lost childhoods in Alan Moore's statement about 'imaginary stories.' This superman doesn't just fail to be real out here, but also in there, on his own page. His powers, his muscles, the heroic glint in his eye . . . should I face, finally, that they've never been anything more than ink on paper?

Let's face it: in terms of real-world bodybuilding, supermuscles are untrustworthy at best. I mean, regular human weight lifters have more musclemass than Superman, but they can't pull a moon out of orbit! When Animal Man absorbs the power of flight from a passing bird . . . how come he doesn't have to flap his arms to fly?[9] Obviously, the body works differently on the comic book page. Among all the blasts and shocks and unstable molecules contained inside them, there might also be hidden their best defense against parallel worlds and antimatter twins.

The *Justice League of America* aren't the *Doom Patrol*, and they didn't fight men with clocks for heads and nursery rhyme monsters . . . but the surreal logic of superheroes still questioned the validity of the body as a way to resolve conflict. Entire issues take place in dreams, with bodies left, inert, waiting impotently for minds to return (*JLA* #8, 1997). Or in other worlds where the heroes are flattened into two dimensions, the same way we see them on the page (*JLA* #31, 1999). In one memorable scene, an enormous superbody is actually the host to an entire, miniature world, whose population has to die out of natural causes before he can be rescued (*JLA* #30, 1999).

Morrison once had the Flash remembering that " . . . with powers like ours, you have to learn to fight like a science fiction writer writes" (*Flash* #130, 1997). It might also mean rethinking conventional morality. Morrison writes Superman a new reason for refusing to kill beyond the fact that it's wrong. He berates some rookie heroes who were happy to kill their enemies, saying: "These 'no-nonsense' solutions of yours just don't hold water in a complex world of jet-powered apes and time travel" (*JLA Classified* #3, 2005). And you know? He's absolutely right.

Perhaps it's not that the overmuscled superbody is now obsolete . . . it's that it must be stronger, faster, and harder than ever before to stand up against these forces of postmodern angst. How does the Flash move smoothly between parallel dimensions? He simply runs really, really, *really* fast. In a moment of genius by Morrison, a Superman ancestor, visiting from the future, attempted to return home by virtue of his superhuman strength alone. He actually *punched* his way through time (*DC 1,000,000* #4, 1998). This pushed the boundaries of the superhuman body, and the credulity of comic fans. When asked to explain it, Morrison said: "It's superhero poetry." That readers should "bask in the audacious, absurd beauty of a man literally battering his way through the time barrier . . ." (Lien-Cooper 2002).

That's how Animal Man flies like a bird, but without wings. That's how Superman's biceps can lift an oil tanker and still be smaller than his head. Their bodies are superhero poetry. It's the wonder of Muscle Mystery.

Which brings us neatly back to Flex Mentallo, Hero of the Beach (Figure 14.2). He's too much of a man to question how his muscles function; it's enough that they do. And it's a good thing he's not bothered by these same existential questions, because his origin is more confusing than most. He was born as an imaginary friend of a young psychic boy, then brought forward into DC 'reality.' His story provides multiple points of origin: he's the childhood creation of psychic Wallace Sage; the brainchild of Morrison himself; he's the wimp from the faded Charles Atlas commercials from my childhood half-memories.[10] Does Flex whine about his reality, like Buddy

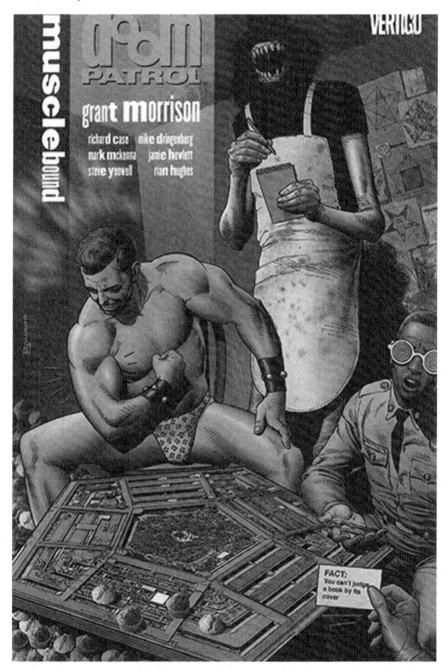

Figure 14.2 Flex Mentallo strikes a pose on the cover of the collected 4th volume edition of *Doom Patrol: Musclebound*, 2006. © DC Comics/Vertigo.

Baker? Does he spout angst about whether or not he's human, like Cliff Steele? No. "I'm a superhero," he says, and that's everything he needs to know (*Flex Mentallo* #4, 1996). In Morrison's work, it's the characters that are clearly labeled as 'imaginary' that can most easily withstand the shock of parallel worlds.

Similarly, the possibility of parallel worlds colors everything in his miniseries. Any number of dimensions are presented and explanations are given throughout the four issues: is it all a writer's delusional drug trip? An elaborate supervillain hoax? The terrifying effects of 'Black Mentallium'? A pocket universe of paper where the world's 'real' heroes have been hiding? And so on. It's all about leaving possibilities open, rather than shutting them down, and not destroying parallel worlds, but keeping them alive. Morrison writes *Flex Mentallo* as a love letter to the spectacular, ridiculous, forgotten possibilities of comics, and is much more interested in the 'infinite earths' than in the 'crisis.'

Flex Mentallo is pulled apart, put back together, and his very existence questioned again and again . . . but he never doubts himself. It's what he calls his "Muscle Mystery," you see. He's so strong that when he strikes a pose, the words "Hero of the Beach" actually appear above his head, like they did in the old Charles Atlas advertisement. He's so strong that his biceps have conceptual powers of their own. Flex narrates:

> So I summoned up the power of Muscle Mystery—activating the occult of each musclecord, each tendon. Above my head, my famous 'hero halo' shimmered into view. And I flexed, reaching out to probe the interior of the bomb with my bodymind. (*Flex Mentallo* #1, 1996)

His 'bodymind' suggests that his muscles and his heroic subjectivity are indivisible. Flex's invulnerability isn't a brittle costumed shell that might crack, allowing the disruptive energy to escape or dissipate—he's all man, through and through. By leaving his skin and muscles on display, his boy-scout morality remains absolute. When an admiring woman says to him, "Boy, I just adore all-male he-men!," he humbly answers: "And you're a fine, hardworking woman." Even when the series' villain is unmasked, Flex doesn't want revenge. He offers him the same chance we all had, reading the advertisements in those old comics, and tells the villain: "Gamble a stamp! I can show you how to be a real man!" (*Flex Mentallo* #4, 1996).

" . . . BUT AREN'T THEY ALL?"

> *Animal Man:* "Your world must be terrible. It seems so . . . grey and bleak. How can you possibly live in a world without superheroes?"
> *Grant Morrison:* "We get by." (*Animal Man* #26, 1991)

In *Flex Mentallo*, the comic book itself tells us it is 'reading' a hidden sha-
manic code locked in our DNA, and using it to free the world's heroes from
their fictional prison so they can be real again. In the final pages, we're told
to "look up!" and see that the sky is filled with these heroes, free, flying,
incredible. I read this in my copy of *Flex Mentallo* #4. I looked out my
window. In reality, there was nothing in my sky but stars.

When Morrison met Buddy in *Animal Man* #26, he explained all. "You
can't get into my world," he said, "but I can get into yours. I can fake the
real world here on the comic page." We'd previously watched Morrison wan-
der around Glasgow, illustrated in muddy browns and grays, wishing he had
better ideas for that very comic (*Animal Man* #14, 1989). In *Doom Patrol*,
our world was, simply, hell-on-earth. And in Morrison's most recent adventure with the Justice League, we saw our real world, crammed into dark,
tight panels against the spectacle of all the previous pages. In fact, this world
(here called "The Infant Universe of Qwewq") eventually reached adulthood,
became sentient, and traveled back in time to threaten the JLA as a supervillain! (*JLA Classified* #3, 2005). Seriously. Is our world really *so* bad?

I'd want to ask this hypothetical superman what he thinks. It's kind
of embarrassing he's still just standing here, static and actionless, the air
empty of word balloons around our heads. But is my imagination failing,
or is he . . . wilting? Perhaps slightly less amazing, less hyperbolic, than
when this chapter began? I think about Superman's old villain Metallo,
and his heart of Kryptonite. My body might hold a deadly, deconstructive
secret after all. The risk of depicting heroes in our sordid reality might just
be too great. Invulnerability only goes so far.

Flex's own muscle-bound self-confidence was always unshakable, but the
real world had more trouble with his interpretation. Was he pure of heart
or brutish parody? The pinnacle of the masculine ideal, or cruel mockery of
the same? His intersection with our world ensured these questions of ironic
intent were posed in a court of law, as Flex's fame finally spread to the
Charles Atlas corporation. They sued DC Comics for copyright infringement. "There has to be a limit to how far you can let someone ridicule your
trademark," said Jeffrey C. Hogue, president of Charles Atlas Inc. "They
took that character and made him into something that was not an Atlas
man. . . ." (First Amendment Center 2000).[11]

Ridicule? Flex doesn't know the meaning of the word! The court reached
a decision on April 29· 2000, with the judge failing to " . . . discern a sub-
stantive difference between 'surrealism' or 'irony' on one hand, and 'parody' on the other, much less do we find them to be mutually exclusive"
(Buchwald 2000). Charles Atlas' lawsuit against DC was dismissed, but for
Flex, it seemed a hollow victory. Perhaps because of potential future legal
issues, the court case seemed to do what Black Mentallium never could.
Flex disappeared from comics altogether.

Does our real world always have the final stamp of authority over these
fictional heroes? After Morrison appeared in his own *Animal Man* comic,

a very familiar character showed up in the pages of DC's *Suicide Squad*. In an obscure comics in-joke, he was called "The Writer" and looked suspiciously like the comic book Morrison. His power was to rewrite the universe as it happened—but since he wrote himself into his own comic, now he was fair game for *other* writers to use in their books. Later in the issue he got unexpected writer's block and was, uh, eaten by a werewolf (*Suicide Squad* #58, 1991). Morrison changed his mind after *Animal Man*, saying that he wanted more than simply to have himself drawn onto the page, to 'fake' our world. Instead, he wanted to explore " . . . the two dimensional surface of the comic itself and at the point of interface where 2-D becomes 3-D and then touches 4-D" (Epstein 2005). But perhaps Morrison lied, like superhero physiques can lie—because he said this *after* I'd seen him eaten by that werewolf.

The final issues of the original *Doom Patrol* series dealt with the power of the real world with refreshing honesty. The last page showed the artist and editor pleading at the reader, right out of the page:

"Then it is true! They are dead! The Doom Patrol will never fight again!"

"It would take a miracle to change that ending, Bruno! A tougher job than even the D.P. ever faced! And only you out there—the reader—could do it! You always wanted to be a super-hero, didn't you?" (*Doom Patrol*, Volume One #121, 1968)

I did. I did always want to be a superhero. I'm not sure their following request to buy more issues amounted to a power that would've gotten me into the Justice League, but there's something charming about being so direct about these practical links between our worlds. Increase their sales. Save their lives. Sadly, it didn't work. In time, there was another *Doom Patrol* title, and it, too, ended. Like all heroes, they continued to face deaths, disappearances, cancellations. . . .

And worse. A new *Doom Patrol* series began in 2004 that ignored all previous mentions of the team in official continuity. This meant none of Morrison's adventures ever 'really' happened, transformed with an editorial finger snap into 'imaginary stories.' By extension, it dragged Flex Mentallo down with them. And sure, there was a new Doom Patrol, still with Cliff as leader. But they weren't *my* Doom Patrol. This new model Robotman had never fought the Men from N.O.W.H.E.R.E. or the Beardhunter, had he? And so I failed to care. I couldn't help but think how disappointed Cliff would be to find out he wasn't real after all. But then I remembered the advice he was given by the Chief back in *Doom Patrol* #21 (1989): "Reality and unreality have no clear distinction in our present circumstances, Cliff. It might help to consider the Zen koan, 'First there is a mountain, then there is no mountain, then there is.' "

It does help. Now my hypothetical superhero might, hypothetically, have a distracted look in his eye. (Perhaps his teenage sidekick has activated a signal watch.) Suddenly there'd be so many things I'd want to explain to him: the term "Krypto-revisionism," for instance. It's when the comics audience simply and actively ignore certain plot twists, choosing to believe their own 'official' versions instead. And how, in a terrible and touching pun, the term is named after Superman's own ridiculous, kitsch, often out-of-continuity super-dog (Evanier 2002, 1–3). And how the court's ruling in the *Flex Mentallo* case highlighted a certain line from the background material provided: that Flex ". . . represents Morrison's argument for a space beyond critique" (Buchwald 2000).[12] These distinctions—between fact and fiction, between official and imagined, between the page and the world that sits around it, above it—might not matter.

That's no excuse for nihilism. Flex says: "Only a bitter little adolescent boy could confuse realism with pessimism" (*Flex Mentallo* #4, 1996). Morality, again, is called into question in *Flex Mentallo*—someone tries to commit suicide, reassured that somewhere out there they have an anti-matter twin who will live. This is countered, however, by Morrison refiguring parallel worlds into conscious choices. The narrator, the ex-psychic child who first created Flex, tells this story while dying of a drug overdose. At least, he might be. In one reality, the pills are killing him. In another, they're M&Ms. The choice appears to be up to him. It's not that nothing is real . . . it's that everything *might* be.

Superheroes are here to save us. That's the fundamental rule of the genre. Superman's final solution to prevent our universe (depicted as 'Qwewq') becoming self-aware, traveling back in time, and destroying us all? After panel after panel of natural disasters, wife beating, drugs, and torture . . . he injects a group of rookie heroes into our reality. They say:

"A doomed micro-earth, in an infant universe."
"With no such thing as superheroes."
"This should be interesting. . . ." (*JLA Classified* #3, 2005).[13]

These superheroes haven't appeared in our sky, but the explanation might be in Morrison's final issue of the *Justice League*—the 'antimatter twin' of the climax of *Flex Mentallo* #4. Here, Animal Man guest stars to help give all of humanity a temporary "preview of evolution" so that everyone on earth has their *own* superpowers, and can take flight to rush to Superman's rescue (*JLA* #41, 2000). Who wants to be a mild-mannered bystander or a damsel in distress? The sky is only empty because it's waiting for us to fill it. Morrison's mission isn't to deconstruct the superhero, or to fake flat simulations of different realities, or to quibble over which world might be Earth-1, and which Earth-2. It's to make *our* reality as interesting as theirs, as surreal, full of every potential and possibility.

Flex Mentallo wouldn't be bothered by Moore's statement that every story is an imaginary story. He knows perfectly well that his story isn't real, but he wouldn't see it as saying that all fiction is *just* fiction; he'd grin, knowing it meant that my story, out here, is imaginary too, and that the status quo is a little weaker for it. Appearing in each other's stories means that I've become just another in a long, long line of ridiculous narrators who will disappear from continuity the moment the page is turned. I suppose I should watch out for werewolves. Radioactive spiders. Cosmic rays. *Anything* can happen in an imaginary story.

My superman would step off the ground, hanging in front of me in the everyday air, and drift upwards as these last few sentences wipe him from further fiction; I'd look up, and think how I must look flat and two-dimensional from so far above. He'd unravel, disperse, spreading thin lines of ink and pencil and imagination through the sky, and I'd be reminded of a speech given to other ludicrous, lost characters in Morrison's *Animal Man*. From outside their reality, perhaps, their world would just look like a comic book. "Like drawings on a page. And every time someone reads our stories, we live again" (*Animal Man* #24, 1990).

EPILOGUE

Morrison was recently appointed as the DC Universe 'revamp guy': a creative consultant who helps to revise and re-vision older, out-of-date characters and attempt to bring them back to popularity (Newsarama 2005). This played into this year's *Infinite Crisis* miniseries (2005–06), a sort of sequel to the original *Crisis on Infinite Earths*. It would take all my word count so far to recount the plot permutations, but suffice to say that the last page of *Infinite Crisis* #1 (2005) was packed tight with Muscle Mystery. Here, the long-forgotten, long-overwritten Superman from Earth-2 came back into current comic book reality using his own kind of 'superhero poetry'—punching not just through space, or time, but physically shattering the continuity barrier itself!

And the effects of this blow were further felt, as the shockwaves shifted continuity for other heroes, too. There was only one that mattered to me. Continuity, you see, fragmented around a member of the current Doom Patrol in a double-page splash in a crossover issue with the *Teen Titans* (#32, 2006). It showed us all their previous incarnations: shards of the recent, rebooted 'pretenders,' pieces of the 1960s originals, all side by side with art clipped from Morrison's strange, ludicrous, heartbreaking era. And hidden amongst this mosaic? Tucked away so you can't make out a face? One thing is impossible to miss, framed with the beach as background.

Familiar, skintight, leopard-print trunks.

NOTES

1. Frank Quitely, regular Morrison collaborator and penciler of the Flex Mentallo miniseries, even provides a 'pinup' of Flex in all his muscleman glory, signed "For all my fans" and "xxooxx" (*Flex Mentallo* #1, 1996).
2. It's been pointed out that it might not be a coincidence that Morrison's origin of Flex Mentallo, presented in *Doom Patrol* #42 (1991), has his transformation taking place in 1954—the year that Frederick Werthem's *Seduction of the Innocent* was published, which declared Superman and all those like him as dangerous role models who believed in violence over democracy (Brooker 2000).
3. See Scott Bukatman's article "X-Bodies (The Torment of the Mutant Superhero)" for more on the features, both fluid and impervious, of superhero physiques (Bukatman 1994).
4. Even other heroes were disturbed by them. Morrison wrote a representative of the Justice League responding to the Doom Patrol like this: " . . . those guys give me the creeps. I mean, whose side are they on, anyway?" (*Doom Patrol* #28, 1989).
5. It's not just poor freaks like the Doom Patrol, either. In reverse order: recent *Action Comics* (#839, 2006) had Superman confused by a sudden clarity to his 'super-memory'; the revamped 80s Superman found his powers out of control back in *Superman* v.2 #10 (1987); but best of all were the surreal permutations of the Silver Age, where—for instance—Superman once was cursed with the head of a lion, but his regular costume and cape from the neck down (*Action Comics* #243, 1958).
6. See Geoff Klock's *How to Read Superhero Comics and Why* for more information on this shift towards 'darker' storylines and heroes (Klock 2002).
7. *Time Magazine*, attempting to explain comic book time with real-world timekeeping, announced in 1988 that Superman's birthday must be the 29 February, explaining how he seems to be aging at a quarter of our regular rate (Friedrich 1988).
8. See Will Brooker's *Batman Unmasked: Analyzing a Cultural Icon* (2001) for more on how Batman manages to remain (somewhat) stable through all these generic permutations.
9. This jaw-droppingly-obvious fact was finally pointed out to Buddy during writer Tom Veitch's post-Morrison run on *Animal Man*. "What's this so-called 'bird power' you talk about? The birds don't have it! The poor creatures have to flap their wings!" Buddy's response? "Uh . . . you've got a point there" (*Animal Man* #35, 1991).
10. Will Brooker, in a discussion of the ambiguous signs of Flex's sexuality, points out that these multiple origins themselves also suggest a 'queerness' present in the narrative structure itself (Brooker 2000).
11. The Charles Atlas corporation, during the case, made repeated reference to Flex 'beating' a woman in the DC parody. Certainly, during Flex's origin sequence he does shove away his would-be girlfriend, saying, "I guess I am a brute!" (*Doom Patrol* #42, 1991). It's a shame, though, that they never read on to see Flex's later adventures, and the hero that he became.
12. The background material in question was Jason Craft's "The Annotated Flex Mentallo," which is available online at http://www.earthx.org/node/153; Will Brooker's *Hero of the Beach: Flex Mentallo at the End of the Worlds* is also hosted there, and his excellent analysis deals with Flex in much more detail than I could hope to here.

13. If you want to read about the results of this superhero inoculation, they're to be found in Morrison's as-yet-uncompleted *Seven Soldiers* project for DC Comics (2005–06).

COMIC BOOKS

Augustyn, Brian, and Mike Mignola. 1989. *Gotham by Gaslight*. New York: DC Comics.

Augustyn, Brian, Mark Waid, and Joe Staton. 1994. *Legends of the Dark Knight* Annual #4. New York: DC Comics.

Binder, Otto, and Wayne Boring. 1958. *Action Comics* #243 August. New York: DC Comics.

Byrne, John, and Dick Giordano. 1985. *Man of Steel* #2. New York: DC Comics.

Byrne, John, and Dick Giordano. 1985. *Man of Steel* #4. New York: DC Comics.

Byrne, John, and Karl Kesel. 1987. *Superman* v.2 #10 October. New York: DC Comics.

Drake, Arnold, and Bruno Premiani. 1968. *Doom Patrol* v.1. #121 September. New York: DC Comics.

Drake, Arnold, Bob Haney, and Bruno Premiani. 1963. *My Greatest Adventure* #80 June. New York: DC Comics.

Johns, Geoff, Kurt Busiek, and Renato Guedes. 2006. *Action Comics* #839 July. New York: DC Comics.

Johns, Geoff, and Phil Jimenez. 2005. *Infinite Crisis* #1 December. New York: DC Comics.

Johns, Geoff, and Todd Nauck. 2006. *Teen Titans* #32 March. New York: DC Comics.

Moore, Alan, and Curt Swan. 1986. "Whatever Happened to the Man of Tomorrow? Part 1." *Superman* #423 September. New York: DC Comics.

Moore, Alan, and Curt Swan. 1986. "Whatever Happened to the Man of Tomorrow? Part 2." *Action Comics* #583. New York: DC Comics.

Morrison, Grant, and Richard Case. 1989. *Doom Patrol* v.2 #21 April. New York: DC Comics.

Morrison, Grant, and Richard Case. 1989. *Doom Patrol* v.2 #28 December. New York: DC Comics.

Morrison, Grant, and Richard Case. 1990. *Doom Patrol* v.2 #37 October. New York: DC Comics.

Morrison, Grant, and Richard Case. 1992. *Doom Patrol* v.2 #60 October. New York: DC Comics.

Morrison, Grant, and Richard Case. 1993. *Doom Patrol* v.2 #63 January. New York: DC Comics.

Morrison, Grant, and Mike Dringenberg. 1991. *Doom Patrol* v.2 #42 March. New York: DC Comics.

Morrison, Grant, and Tom Grummett. 1989. *Animal Man* #14 August. New York: DC Comics.

Morrison, Grant, and Oscar Jimenez. 1997. *Justice League of America* #8 August. New York: DC Comics.

Morrison, Grant, and Ed McGuinness. 2005. *Justice League Classified* #3 March. New York: DC Comics.

Morrison, Grant, Mark Miller, and Paul Ryan. 1997. *Flash* #130 November. New York: DC Comics.

Morrison, Grant, and Frank Quitely. 1996. *Flex Mentallo* #1 June. New York: DC/Vertigo.

Morrison, Grant, and Frank Quitely. 1996. *Flex Mentallo* #4 September. New York: DC/Vertigo.

Morrison, Grant, and Frank Quitely. 2000. *Justice League of America: Earth-2*. New York: DC Comics.

Morrison, Grant, and Frank Quitely. 2000. *Justice League of America: Earth-2*. New York: DC Comics.

Morrison, Grant, and Val Semekis. 1998. *DC 1,000,000* #4 November. New York: DC Comics.

Morrison, Grant, and Chris Truog. 1989. *Animal Man* #12 June. New York: DC Comics.

Morrison, Grant, and Chris Truog. 1989. *Animal Man* #11 May. New York: DC Comics.

Morrison, Grant, and Chris Truog. 1990. *Animal Man* #19 January. New York: DC Comics.

Morrison, Grant, and Chris Truog. 1990. *Animal Man* #24 June. New York: DC Comics.

Morrison, Grant, and Chris Truog. 1990. *Animal Man* #26 August. New York: DC Comics.

Ostrander, John, Kim Yale, and Geof Isherwood. 1991. *Suicide Squad* #58 October. New York: DC Comics.

Veitch, Tom, and Steve Dillion. 1991. *Animal Man* #35 May. New York: DC Comics.

Wolfman, Marv, and George Perez. 1985. *Crisis on Infinite Earths* #1 April. New York: DC Comics.

BIBLIOGRAPHY

Associated Press. 2000. Federal judge: Parody of Atlas man protected by First Amendment. http://www.firstamendmentcenter.org/news.aspx?id=5670 (accessed June 2, 2006).

Brady, Matt. 2005. Grant Morrison: Talking All-Star Superman. http://www.newsarama.com/DC/AS/AllStarSuperman_Morrison.htm (accessed June 2, 2006).

Brooker, Will. 2000. *Hero of the Beach: Flex Mentallo at the End of the Worlds.* http://www.earthx.org/files/flexBrooker.pdf (accessed June 2, 2006).

Brooker, Will. 2001. *Batman Unmasked: Analyzing a Cultural Icon.* New York: Continuum International Publishing.

Buchwald, J. 2000. 112 F.Supp.2d 330—Opinion and Order. www.frosszelnick.com/pdffolder/CharlesAtlasvDCC.pdf (accessed June 2, 2006).

Bukatman, Scott. 1994. "X-Bodies (The Torment of the Mutant Superhero)." In Sappington and Stalling, eds., *Uncontrollable Bodies: Testimonies of Identity and Culture.* Seattle: Bay Press.

Craft, Jason. 1999. *The Annotated Flex Mentallo.* http://www.earthx.org/node/153 (accessed June 2, 2006).

Epstein, Daniel Robert. 2005. Grant Morrison interview. http://suicidegirls.com/words/Grant+Morrison/ (accessed June 2, 2006).

Evanier, Mark. 2002. *Comic Books and Other Necessities of Life.* Raleigh, NC: TwoMorrows Publishing.

Friedrich, Otto. 1988. "Up, Up and Awaaay!!!" *Time Magazine,* March 14, 1988. Reprinted at http://theages.superman.ws/Fifty/time.php (accessed June 2, 2006).

Keller, Katherine. 2005. *This Old Drake Still Has the Fire in Him—Arnold Drake.* http://www.sequentialtart.com/archive/jan00/drake.shtml (accessed June 2, 2006).

Klock, Geoff. 2002. *How to Read Superhero Comics and Why.* New York: Continuum.

Lien-Cooper, Barb. 2002. *Punching Holes Through Time—Grant Morrison.* http://www.sequentialtart.com/archive/aug02/gmorrison2.shtml   (accessed June 2, 2006).

Newsarama. 2005. *Grant Morrison on Being the DCU Revamp Guy.* http://www.newsarama.com/dcnew/MorrisonDCU.htm (accessed June 2, 2006).

15 Enter the Aleph
Superhero Worlds and Hypertime Realities[1]

Angela Ndalianis

In issue 62 of the comic book *Swamp Thing*,[2] the protagonist, Swamp Thing, travels across the universe with the celestial being Metron by manipulating the frequencies of vibrations that make up existence. Attempting to escape the machinations of a Transmuter (a being who patrols the fringes of reality), Swamp Thing increases the vibration rate to enter a space that he believes to be "The Source" (of all knowledge and meaning of life itself). Here, he and Metron experience a plethora of images that allows them access to the universe in its entirety. The reader is later informed, however, that it wasn't the Source that they experienced but something called the Aleph (Figure 15.1). As Darkseid, the villain of the piece, explains, "Alephs are points from which one can observe all other points in time and space."[3] While television shows like *Smallville* (2004–) may not provide us with a vantage point through which to view all other points in time and space simultaneously, it does—like so many other examples of popular culture—confront its audience with multiple vantage points that expose the mythology that's constructed its main character, Kal-El/Clark Kent/Superman, across the time and space of his many media configurations. Using the Swamp Thing's experience of the Aleph as a starting point, this chapter explores some of the ways in which *Smallville,* as one of many examples of popular media, places us in the position of the Swamp Thing: the series confronts us not only with the history of Superman as a transmedia phenomenon, but also challenges *Smallville*'s audience to understand how and why it intersects with the spatiotemporal realities of many other media stories and characters. Adopting and adapting a mode of storytelling that has dominated the comics since the 1960s, *Smallville* not only participates in an intense dialogic engagement with the codes that comprise the Superman media universe, but it also becomes one of many Superman realities that occupy a multiverse of possibilities.

The Superman myth stands as one of the most successful examples of the slippery possibilities of serial and cross-media storytelling. As Roberta Pearson and William Uricchio (1991) have explained of Batman, multiple narrativisations have sprung up from, and across, a variety of media that are based on this same figure. Like Batman, the success of Superman lies very much in the capacity of the adventures of this character to branch out in a

Figure 15.1 Swamp Thing and Metron tap into the Aleph. Rick Veitch, *Swamp Thing* #62, 1987. © DC Comics.

variety of different directions. For example, in addition to the wealth of comic book serials that erupted after the first appearance of Superman in *Action Comics* in 1938 (*Action Comics, Adventures of Superman, Superman, The Kents, Man of Steel, Smallville, Superboy, Supergirl, Superman: The Man of Steel*), his story continued across film and animated serials in the 40s and 50s (*Superman, Atom Man vs. Superman, Superman and the Mole Men*), television series from the 1950s–2000s (*Adventures of Superman, Superboy, Lois & Clark: The New Adventures of Superman, Smallville*), blockbuster film sequels in the 70s and 80s (*Superman I–IV*), animated TV series (*The New Adventures of Superman, Superman, Superman: The Animated Series*) and the recent high concept manifestation (*Superman Returns*, 2006). Supported by a densely conglomerated entertainment industry with transmedia economic interests,[4] these examples barely scratch the surface in mapping the layered and intersecting narrative dimensions that comprise the Superman mythos.[5] In all these variations, the Superman narrative is expanded and extended beyond the confines of a single comic book or a single television series. With each Superman addition across a variety of narrative-series and media, the phenomenon that is the tale of Superman is transformed, altered, and often contradicted. As such, the story is never stable and closed but is more like a delicate yet indestructible web that extends its sinewy narrative threads ever outwards.

Drawing upon the writings of Umberto Eco, Jim Collins (1991) has argued that the complexity of current popular culture (as played out, in his case, across the example of the Batman story) is revealed in the "negotiation of the array" of what's already been said; in this case, what's already been said about Superman, his origins, and adventures. The density, complexity, and originality are reflected in the way the new addition to the story positions itself in relation to this intertextual array. This phenomenon is freely acknowledged within the comic book community, and is accepted (and, at times, vehemently rejected) in processes such as retconning ('retroactive continuity'), which alters details—sometimes minor, sometimes dramatic—about aspects of a character's mythology, or rebooting, which more dramatically rewrites the origins and mythological traits of a superhero. Multiple versions of 'stories' can—and *do*—coexist, somehow creating their own space and time to contain the history of their superhero. The idea of competing discourses within the array of the larger Superman narrative is not only limited to the comic book medium; it's seen frequently, in fact, in *Smallville*. So much so that the process of the "negotiation of the array" has, especially since Season 4, become an integral part of the series' production of meaning and mode of engagement.[6]

SUPERHEROES AND THE SPATIOTEMPORAL PARADOX

In his essay "The Myth of Superman" (1972), Umberto Eco makes a further clarification about the uniqueness of the narrative phenomenon that the superhero comics introduced into popular culture. Traditional heroes like Hercules and Roland, he argues, have stories that have already been told. The mythic status of these characters attains its aura and archetypal value *because* the events have already happened. Like some colossal sculpture, mythic heroes remain frozen in time, occupying the realm of the "already said." The modern novel and the era of mass production it ushered in, however, introduced "a story in which the reader's main interest is transferred to the unpredictable nature of *what will happen* . . . The event has not happened *before* the story; it happens *while* it is being told. . . ." And further, he continues, "This new dimension of story sacrifices for the most part the mythic potential of the character" (1972, 15). The comic book form of storytelling introduced with the appearance of Superman complicated these two models in that it combined both: superhero stories present archetypal characters and events whose tales have been already told (and have a presence in public memory), but they also participate in the more episodic, serial narrative actions that are in the process of being told and fall prey to the dictates of time. For Eco, while the two coexist, they retain their independence: the mythic or archetypal can't succumb to the novelistic, serial tellings that are left for individual crimes, everyday happenings, and general superhero hijinx (for example, Superman is lured into another Lex Luthor trap that exposes him to kryptonite; Superman saves a train from derailing and killing its passengers; Superman again thwarts Lois Lane's efforts to expose his true identity, etc.). Superman's origin story—his arrival from Krypton, his adoption by Martha and Jonathan Kent, his unrequited love for Lois Lane, his weakness when exposed to kryptonite, his relationship to his nemesis Lex Luthor, in short, his epic dimension—can't change and "must remain static in time because, having been told, it is something that exists in the past."[7]

In order to disguise the temporal paradox that so many superhero stories display, Eco explains that "The stories develop in a kind of oneiric climate—of which the reader is not aware at all—where what has happened before and what has happened after appear extremely hazy. The narrator picks up the strand of the event again and again as if he had forgotten to say something and wanted to add details to what had already been said" (Eco 1972, 17). For Eco, critical awareness and reflexive reading and viewing experiences were (in the early 70s) relegated to the realm of modernist, or what he calls 'superior' art. But a great deal has changed since the early 1970s. Like *Finnegan's Wake* and Robbe-Grillet's *Into the Labyrinth* (examples that Eco introduces as a point of difference to those of Superman), now "the breakdown of familiar temporal relations happens in a conscious manner" (1972, 19) across examples of popular culture. The temporal paradox, which, according to Eco, "should not be obvious to the reader," now *is* obvious and, in fact, becomes an integral part of a narrative game that the audience is invited to engage with.

Smallville relies on the nostalgic desire of fans who have decades of memories of Superman stories to draw upon. Part of the desire generated by the series is the anticipation and arrival of the canonized myth of Superman: the adoption of his costume and role as savior of humanity (particularly, those inhabiting the United States), his move to Metropolis and work as a reporter at the *Daily Planet*, his growing love for Lois Lane, his destructive relationship with his archnemesis Lex Luthor. Audience desire is for the realization of the Superman metanarrative according to their past experience of it. The viewer is continuously and mercilessly teased for our nostalgia for something from the past which can, within the boundaries of the series, only be found in the future (because Clark is not yet Superman). According to the Cambridge dictionary, the etymology of the word "nostalgia" comes from the Greek *nostos*, meaning "a return home, or a feeling of pleasure and sometimes slight sadness at the same time as you think about things that happened in the past," and -*algia*, meaning "pain or grief."[8] To be nostalgic for something evokes a sensation akin to homesickness; a longing for a return to something from the past that is beyond our grasp in the present and which, as a result, brings with it feelings of pain. In the case of *Smallville,* this nostalgic desire, which is inseparable from our past memories and experiences of 'Superman' (whether the Golden, Silver or post-80s comics versions, the animated, live-action television shows, or the blockbuster movies), is to witness him coming into his full, mythological potential.

Smallville's writers turn to specific manifestations of the Superman myth, selecting from combinations within an assortment of past media in order to fulfill (or not) our nostalgic desires. The audience is repeatedly teased with mise-en-scène that echoes the colors of the Superman costume that Tom Welling's Clark Kent has yet to adopt: red, blue, and yellow. The corridors and classrooms of Smallville High School, the décor of the *Daily Planet*, the interior and exterior surroundings of the Kent farm; the clothing of the characters who populate the series, all have nostalgic reverberations for the thing that is yet to be: Superman. The lack or absence of Superman is also reflected in the color combinations: where there is yellow and blue, there is often no red. Where there is red and yellow, there is no blue. And, as in the case with Clark's shirts and T-shirt combinations, where there is blue and red, there is no yellow. The episode "Vengeance" (5:13) is typical of the way the show's writers play with audience nostalgia for a thing that's yet to come. In the episode, Andrea, the bumbling *Daily Planet* journalist (who wears thick-framed spectacles), transforms into the fearless Angel of Vengeance when mayhem strikes, thus echoing Clark Kent and Superman's future at the *Daily Planet* and as savior of Metropolis (at the end of the episode, the empty desk in the office, which presumably awaits the yet-to-be reporter Clark Kent, drives this home even further). The Angel of Vengeance's iconic traits—her long coat/cape, her use of a telephone booth to change into her costume, her thick-rimmed glasses, her ability to fly, her burning desire to save the weak, her origin story—all conjure feelings of longing in the audience for Superman's superhero beginnings. The episode is loaded with allusions to Superman's own origins, with one dramatic difference: the Angel of Vengeance kills the evildoers she captures. Yet, it's this very difference that further triggers our longing for a Superman brand of justice, a justice that's fair and forgiving, a longing that's driven home again at the end of this episode when Clark stands in a cemetery in front of the statue of an angel. Here, the viewer is left yearning for the appearance of Clark's own wings in the form of the bright red billowing cape of Superman.[9]

The presence of nostalgic longing is ever-present given that Clark Kent's mythic past still awaits him and the audience. Its future state, and the fact that in this reality it has not yet been told, implies that it can undergo changes, a fact that threatens to destabilize Eco's insistence on the static myth that has already been told. The introduction of changes and differences becomes an important game with and for the viewer who is literate in the Supermanverse. Drawing selectively on the vast pool of Superman origin details, the creators of *Smallville* tweak, alter, and very often dramatically rewrite or refuse to acknowledge some 'official' versions of the myth. For example, Clark's parents Martha and Jonathan Kent play an integral role, but not the elderly versions familiar to many fans. Chloe Johnson is an altogether new addition to Clark's early playmates, even though Pete Ross and Lana Lang were Clark's childhood friends in many post-50's versions of the Superman story. But even here we have twists: Pete Ross is of African-American rather than Anglo-Saxon descent and, far from hanging around to become Lana Lang's husband, and vice president of the United States (to Luthor's president), Pete exits Clark's world in Season 3. Like the 1960 comic book retcon of the Lex Luthor story (*Adventure Comics,* Siegel, #271), Lex lives in Smallville as a teenager and befriends Superboy. 'Superboy,' however, is rejected as a 'reality' of the Superman mythology. Unlike the Golden Age Superman who was given a backstory as the young Superboy (with his own iconic costume and his own adventures), *Smallville*'s version owes more to John Byrne's reboot in *The Man of Steel* (1986). In Byrne's version, rather than possessing his powers immediately, Clark's abilities developed gradually as he entered his teen years, culminating eventually with his ability to fly. Because it took until his late teen years for all of his powers to develop, Clark only adopted the Superman identity in adulthood, and was never Superboy. In the Byrne's reboot, Superboy never existed. All of these features clearly impact on the mythology of *Smallville*. This remythologizing of the teen years of Clark Kent has gained ground as an alternative mythology to the equally valid and accepted earlier renditions. Drawing on *Smallville*, which drew on *The Man of Steel,* in the 2006 November issue of *Superman* (#656), it's revealed that Smallville had been protected by someone called 'Super-Boy' years earlier; however, this hero's[10] existence was confirmed to be an urban legend that sprang up in response to the presence of a young Clark Kent—minus spandex tights and chevron—in Smallville during his teen years.

In his 1986 reboot, John Byrne also revised Lex's background by having him grow up in the Suicide Slum area of Metropolis with his abusive father and mother. Taking an insurance policy out on his parents, Lex has both parents killed by 'fixing' their car brakes, a fact that is exposed years later by Lex's unauthorized biographer Peter Sands. Needless to say, Lex has Sands killed and his findings die with him. However, due to the immense popularity of the actor John Glover, who plays Lionel Luthor, Lex's father, the writers of *Smallville* adapted this history of Lex's Suicide Slum upbringing by transforming it into the history of Lionel Luthor in the series. [11] In another reboot, *Superman: Birthright,* published in 2004 and written by Mark Waid, many of the changes introduced in *Smallville,* including the emphasis on father/son relationships, the younger Kents, and the absence of a Superboy history, are adopted into the comic book world, revealing the extent of slippage between media that can occur. Much to the chagrin of Waid, *Smallville*'s popularity with viewers warranted acceptance of its version of the myth.[12]

In episode after episode, our expectations are set up so that they may be toyed with and undermined as well as fulfilled. In one episode, a dog that we're set up to believe is Krypto, Superboy's dog, not only makes an appearance but becomes a regular ("Krypto," 4:14).[13] While the name 'Krypto' is suggested by Clark, it's eventually rejected by Lois as 'stupid' and replaced by the name 'Shelby.' The quasi-Krypto 'Shelby' also has a different heritage. Shelby's superpowers are the result of an aborted LexCorp experiment, whereas Krypto was sent to Earth by Jor-El in a prototype rocket that would test the technology before sending Kal-El.[14] Similarly, the central role played by the Native American Kawatche Caves as source of truth for Clark's origins undermines the traditional myth's Fortress of Solitude—that is, until that mythic trope is introduced later in the series. Even so, the central role of the caves has caused a partial reboot of the metanarrative, becoming a first stage of Kal-El's access to his Superman origins. Lois appears in Smallville and meets Clark *before* they meet at the *Daily Planet*(the order of telling that occurs in the comics, the *Superman* films, and the *Lois and Clark* television series). "*Before* causally determines *after,* and the series of these determinations cannot be traced back" otherwise, says Eco; the myth is disrupted, falters, or is radically revised and undermined (Eco 1972, 16). *Smallville* continually confronts the audience with this possibility. It daringly threatens to affect (and, at times, does affect) the causality of the myth *after* it has happened and, while often it only teases and reverts back to the authority of an original myth contained within the memory of the audience, at other times it stubbornly offers alternative versions of the Superman mythology. In *Smallville,* the anticipated metanarrative—Eco's mythic layer—is *both* worshipped as static entity *and* revealed to always be in a state of process, an interplay that problematizes Eco's distinction between the mythic and the serial. In the case of *Smallville,* it's the mythic level that shifts and is retold, and the mythic begins to succumb to a serial logic.[15] In doing so, the series reflects a further shift in the narrative practices of popular culture 'texts' to those articulated by Eco in his article in 1972.

Smallville's relationship with the first two Ilya Salkind–produced *Superman* blockbuster films of the 1970s–80s is especially telling in this respect. The negotiation of the mythology as depicted in these films runs heavily throughout the series. Aside from the fact that Annette O'Toole, who is Martha Kent (Clark's mother) in *Smallville,* and played the role of Lana Lang (Clark's girlfriend) in *Superman II* (let's not go there . . .), Christopher Reeve (who played Superman) and Margot Kidder (who was Lois) appear in numerous episodes as Dr. Swann and his assistant Bridgette Crosby, as does the John Williams theme music from the films. The first time we hear the music is in Season 4 when Clark meets the character Dr. Swann, who is played by Christopher Reeve. Dr. Swann is the wealthy and eccentric keeper of many Kryptonian secrets that allow Clark access to his alien heritage. Reeve's star persona functions forcefully as a legitimizing presence, one that audiences still associate with the Superman role he played in blockbuster films. The Williams theme music is first heard when Reeve and Welling confront one another, and when the secret of Kal-El is unlocked by Swann. It's difficult to explain to a non-Superman aficionado the level of emotion that wells up during this exchange and, while the diegetic layer of the episode functions to open Clark's eyes to his nature as the Kryptonian Kal-El, on another more potent level, the scene is imbued with a mythological potency that is only possible because of the preexistence of this character in another media manifestation. Through a combination of theme music and star presence, just as the character Dr. Swann tells Clark of his Kryptonian origins, it's as if the actor Reeve also passes on the Superman mantle to the actor Tom Welling, who will be the new Superman.[16] The epic quality of the exchange reaches feverish pitch when Kal-El finally finds his way to the Fortress of Solitude, which uncannily resembles the vast, arctic cavern in *Superman: The Movie* (Richard Donner, 1978)—complete with Williams' theme music.

Such combinations of repetitions, variations, and rewritings of the Superman mythology run rampant in the series, and, as mentioned above, often expectations are introduced so that they can be overturned. For example, the voice of Jor-El (Kal-El's Kryptonian father) is that of Terence Stamp. But, in *Superman: The Movie* and *Superman II,* Stamp played the ultimate Kryptonian bad guy, General Zod, who (along with his two accomplices, Ursa and Non) had been imprisoned in the Phantom Zone by the *Superman: The Movie* Jor-El for crimes against Krypton. In the TV series, this fact becomes an important strategy, serving to emphasize the questionable motivations of Jor-El; in fact, *Smallville* Jor-El and his possibly malevolent intentions persist well into Season 5. By collapsing the preestablished star presence of Terence Stamp as Zod (which itself has attained mythic cult status) into his altered role as the *Smallville* version of Jor-El, the series imbues the Jor-El character with additional and altered meaning. In the first episode of Season 5 ("Arrival"), two (supposed) Kryptonians arrive in Smallville. Not only do they possess characteristics that recall Zod's fellow inmates from *Superman: The Movie* and *Superman II*, but the absence of their general—Zod—adds further doubt to Jor-El's character, the implication being that he may be the third figure and missing leader. In "Solitude" (5:08), this comes to a head when it's finally revealed that the actual third figure is the synthetic being Brainiac (alias Professor Fine, Clark's university professor), who is attempting to both destroy the Fortress of Solitude and cut off Kal-El's link to his father, and orchestrate the release of the real General Zod from the Phantom Zone.[17]

FLASH OF TWO WORLDS AND THE MULTIVERSE

Smallville is not alone in its delivery of a dynamic fictional universe that's filled with intertextual exchanges and spatiotemporal paradoxes that confuse prior continuities of its superhero's narrative. The comic book world has been immersed in this phenomenon for decades. In 1961, for the first time in DC history, the DC comic *Flash of Two Worlds* attempted a more sophisticated and reflexive explanation of problematic continuities which had been plagued by a confusing web of connections that, more than not, failed to connect. Prior to *Flash of Two Worlds,* Superman's origins as experienced by readers of the early Golden Age were different from those experienced by later generations. Early on, Superman's powers were attributed to his alien origin. Kryptonians were simply a superior race of people, both physically and intellectually, and, while he was strong and invulnerable, Kal-L (his Kryptonian name was changed to Kal-El later) couldn't fly, even though he could jump really high. As time went on, not only could Superman fly, but his power was given an alternative source: it was Earth's gravity and (later) the rays of the sun that gave him his superpowers. In early versions of his childhood, John and Mary Kent, Clark's adopted parents, sold their farm and opened a general store in Smallville. In later versions, not only did John and Mary become Jonathan and Martha, but the Kents never sold their farm (this being the version audiences are most familiar with today).

Lex's tale also shifted. In some versions Lex Luthor was a mad but genius scientist, while in others he was a power- and money-hungry businessman. In some versions he had lived in Smallville as a youth and had known Superboy; in others, he met Clark Kent when Clark moved to Metropolis. *Flash of Two Worlds* opened the way to, partially, rationalizing the contradictions and conflicts that had been created over many decades of tellings and retellings of superhero stories across the DC Universe. Here, the revamped Silver Age Flash, Barry Allen,[18] was transported to the world of Jay Garrick, the Golden Age Flash. Not only did this story explain the existence of Earth-One (which includes most of the DC superhero story realities between the 1950s–80s, the so-called Silver and Bronze Ages) and Earth-Two (home to DC's Golden Age era beginning with Superman in 1938 up until the mid to late 1950s when the Silver Age begins), but it also established the presence of other parallel universes: Earth-One was the Earth inhabited by Silver Age characters; Earth-Two, by Golden Age 'originals'; Earth-Prime was the 'real' world in which most DC characters existed only in comic books; Earth-Reality was the actual world of the reader; and post-*Flash of Two Worlds* there were many others. Taking this into account, Eco's superhero narrative model can be understood as beginning to come apart as early as the 1950s (if not earlier).

Following this issue of *Flash*, the concept of the multiverse opened the way to the possibility of multiple story continuities, which could then be rationalized as belonging to alternate worlds. Like *Smallville,* each continuity, especially those dealing with mythic dimensions of the superhero story, wrote itself over the previous versions. The myth-as-serial manifests itself not as the linear continuation that is typical of the serial but rather as a multilinear serial that often retells the same story in an alternative way. Instead of refusing to acknowledge the existence of the other story, each new story thread acknowledges those that lie beneath it even if it is in order to reject it. Like the shifting continuities and the intertextual web of narrative threads that connect, or fail to connect, them, as more stories entered the arena the continuities (and the multiverse system that contained them) became far more elaborate. *Crisis on Infinite Earths* was a twelve-issue crossover comic book series that was devised by DC Comics and published in 1985 in order to simplify the convoluted and, frequently, contradictory plotlines, events, and characters that inhabited the DC Universe's fifty-year-old continuity. Written by Marv Wolfman and illustrated by George Pérez, the series eliminated (or, at least, attempted to) the Multiverse from the DC Universe. In addition, it resulted in the demise of characters such as Supergirl and the (second) version of the Flash, Barry Allen. The Anti-Monitor, once ruler of the antimatter universe, initiated the 'crisis of infinite earths' by destroying positive-matter universes. Absorbing them into his antimatter world, he succeeded until only a few universes survived. The Monitor (of positive-matter universes) gathered superheroes from the surviving five earths (Earth-One, Earth-Two, Earth-Four, Earth-S, and Earth-X) in an attempt to put an end to the destruction. Thwarted, and intent on altering the origin point of creation, the Anti-Monitor traveled back to the beginning of time, causing major disturbances in the fabric of reality. The Anti-Monitor was finally destroyed by Kal-L (the Earth-Two Superman), Alexander Luthor (of Earth-Three), and Superboy-Prime, who, in addition to Earth-Two Lois Lane, were transported by Alexander to a paradise reality. The result was that the history of the multiverse as it had been known within the comic book world of DC Comics—and to its comic book readers—was transformed into one in which only a single universe existed.[19]

In DC's attempts to clean up loose ends, other continuity-fixers—*Infinite Crisis* and *Zero Hour*[20]—followed but the premise remained the same: to create a single continuity. Because the Anti-Monitor had gone back to the beginning of time in an attempt to rewrite creation, the end result—the existence of a singular universe—had wiped any memory of other Earths and superheroes.[21] In fact, because the origin point of creation itself had been tampered with, these alternate worlds and individuals had never existed in the first place. But how can entire fictional histories and the characters who participated in them be wiped from the memories of readers who had experienced them? Comic book readers aren't like characters in soap operas whose minds can easily be wiped clean at the whim of a charismatic, yet evil, genius.

HYPERTIME AND PROBLEMS WITH THE LINEAR MEN

Hypertime was officially given a name in 1999 with the publication of *The Kingdom* (DC). Written by Mark Waid of *Kingdom Come* (1996) fame, the concept of Hypertime had actually appeared earlier in the writings of Grant Morrison, in particular during his stint as writer on *Animal Man* (1988–1990). In an attempt to resolve continuity problems in the DC Universe, Morrison and Waid elaborated on the 'reality' of 'Hypertime.' Refusing to accept the singular reality imposed by DC, and adapting the multilinear and multiverse reality of the pre-*Crisis* DC Universe, Morrison and Waid created parallel, yet self-contained, worlds and punctured exit and entrance passageways between them. In *The Kingdom,* which is both sequel and prequel to *Kingdom Come*, linear time is threatened because Gog (previously known as William, and sole survivor of the nuclear destruction of Kansas[22]), with the help of the Quintessence (Shazam, Zeus, Ganthet, Izaya Highfather, and—to a lesser degree—the Phantom Stranger), who resent the fact that humanity no longer worships them, is granted incredible powers and the ability to travel across time. Gog uses his new talents to travel backwards and forwards in time and repeatedly kill Superman—always in inventive and gruesome new ways. The Linear Men, who protect time and ensure that time paradoxes are resolved, fear that Gog's actions are generating ruptures in the space-time continuum; however, Rip Hunter (one of the Linear Men) discovers an alternative reality. Time is not singularly linear—a fact supported by the existence of multiple dead Supermen (at the hands of Gog) from across time and space within the one spatiotemporal reality. In the words of Rip Hunter, Hypertime is "The vast, interconnected web of parallel timelines which comprise all reality." When Wonder Woman points out that the Linear Men have "told us over and over again that alternate timelines are a myth" (reflecting the way DC Comics would insist on a singular reality in the post-*Crisis* period), Rip Hunter counters that "the problem with the Linear Men is that they're too linear . . . They think orderly, catalogued continuity is preferable to a kingdom of wonder" (226). Approaching a model akin to the many-worlds interpretation of quantum theory, Hypertime encompasses a "central timeline," but "events of importance often cause divergent 'tributaries' to branch off the main timestream" and form their own realities. But unlike the DC multiverse or many-worlds interpretation, these realities frequently intersect:

> On occasion, those tributaries return—sometimes feeding back into the central timeline, other times overlapping it briefly before charting an entirely new course. An old friend is suddenly recalled after years of being forgotten. A scrap of history becomes misremembered, even reinvented in the common wisdom.

> Then, within a panel that reveals one version of Superman gazing upwards at another version of himself, Rip Hunter's words continue: "These Hypertime fluxes . . . these carryovers from one kingdom to another . . . let them simply be a reminder . . . that the lives we lead are forever part of a greater legend." (227)

Like the multiple media and serial variations of superhero 'kingdoms' that exist in our reality, within the diegetic universe, multiple versions of a superhero cumulatively work to create the version that eventually becomes the legend. While not using the term 'Hypertime,' in *Animal Man,* Morrison not only develops the concept of Hypertimelines within the story but applies the concept reflexively to comment upon the post-*Crisis* phenomenon and its impact on the followers of the DC Universe. Rather than refusing to acknowledge the existence of past DC characters and realities, Morrison persistently insists—as do characters within the *Animal Man*-verse—that past continuities can never be erased. In fact, on a reflexive level, Morrison's stint on *Animal Man* reinforced that DC's attempted enforcement of a singular time line was becoming undone.

In an interview, Morrison explained that 'Hypertime' theory "allowed every comic story your ever read to be part of a larger-scale mega-continuity, which also include other comic book 'universes' as well as the 'real world' we living in and dimensions beyond our own" (2005, n.p.). Drawing attention to the parallels between Hypertime theory and "current cosmological ideas emerging from the field of superstring research and M-Theory," significantly, Morrison states that:

> It was also about how the world of fiction relates literally and geometrically to the world of 'reality' . . . We all live in Hypertime—in our 3-Dimensional level of Hypertime, which can be seen as CUBE TIME in relation to the DCU's LINE TIME, we can pick up comics and leaf through them, flipping in any direction—'time travelling' back and forward through the 'continuity' like some new Doctor Who! . . . And

think about the emotional experience of reading comics. Nothing but ink on paper, right? Yet people fall in love with Jean Grey and threaten to commit murder in her name! People cry when Ted Kord gets shot dead! As we all know, inert drawings and words on a page can produce an absorbing, often addictive, unfolding illusion of life. (Morrison in Offenberger 2005, n.p.)

What Morrison 'gets' that the DC Comics' *Infinite Crisis* production team didn't is the integral role played by the audience in the continuity structure, in particular the integral role that memory serves as a databank of complex, interconnected, and retrievable chunks of information. Wiping out Supergirl and Superboy can't mean that they no longer exist because they still live in the memory and experiences of their readers. Morrison explores the way the reader's memory functions like the version of Hypertime that he explores in his story world. No matter that the *Infinite Crisis* wiped out entire characters and universes; the fact that they existed in the memory of their readers meant that they were real.

SUPERMAN MEETS THE DUKES OF HAZZARD

The writers of *Smallville* also understand the central role played by the audience in the renegotiation of codes and conventions. Like many other superhero stories, *Smallville* recognizes the way it's playfully altered and reshaped the signs that comprise its main character's history but not only in relation to the Superman mythology but also to other examples of popular culture. Recalling the film strategies of the French New Wave, these new breeds of superhero media are as much about the *process* of meaning construction as they are about the stories they deliver. Aside from the more fleeting allusions to examples of popular culture (for example, "Void" [5:17] presents a version of the film *Flatliners*, "Mercy" [5:19] injects *Saw*'s gory games into the world of Lionel Luthor, and Professor Fine/Brainiac frequently pays homage to the liquid terminator the film *Terminator 2*), other codes from television series history are regularly introduced and threaten to collapse the fictional reality of the Supermanverse. The episode "Exposed" (5:6) acknowledges John Schneider's (Pa Kent) more famous role as Bo Duke, one of *The Dukes of Hazzard*, when the actor Tom Wopat (Luke Duke) makes an appearance as Jonathan's senator friend Jack Jennings. To drive home the reference further, Jennings not only arrives at the Kent farm in one of the Dodge Chargers from *The Dukes of Hazzard*, but he zips in doing wheelies to boot! In the episode 'Thirst' (5:05), the rewriting of signs drawn from superhero mythology creates in the viewer an intense desire for the arrival of the signs that give meaning to the Superman mythology. But this occurs in a media-layered way that involves myth codes being represented in order to be aligned with unexpected meanings. The presence of James Marsters (Spike in *Buffy the Vampire Slayer*) in the episode (as Professor Milton Fine of Smallville University but actually one of Superman's nemeses, Brainiac[23]) triggers a vampire story. To add to the collision with Buffy the Vampire Slayer mythology, a character called Buffy *Saunders* is introduced, but rather than being a slayer she's a vampire. But because the Buffy codes are placed within the Superman universe, the real villain turns out not to be Buffy Saunders the vampire but Lex Luthor, whose experiments on bats created her and other vampires in the story. A fancy dress party that takes place in the episode teases the audience with the possibility of Clark's transformation into Superman, but Clark comes dressed as Zorro, a mythic hero who impacted on Batman's origins. Taking the Batman allusions further, Lana comes to the party as a "Catwoman," and we're told that, like Bruce Wayne as a boy, Buffy Saunders experienced a bat attack in a cave. Then, merging the signs of vampires, bats, and bat-men during the party the Bauhaus song *Bela Lugosi's Dead* (which was also theme to the vampire movie *The Hunger*) can be heard thumping in the background. To cap it off, the episode writer is Steven S. De Knight, one of the writers on *Buffy the Vampire Slayer* and *Angel*—the *Buffy* spin-off. Through these collisions, the theme of the invincibility or immortality of the superhero is visited through the iconic image of the vampire's immortality. Finally, having traveled a journey through these bat-heavy mythologies, the episode finally refers nostalgically to *Smallville*-Clark's future through a reference to a representation of another Superman from the past when Chloe's final words there's "no place to go but up, up and away" recall the George Reeves series of the 50s, which, in turn, harks back to the radio series of 1940–1951. Extending on *Smallville*'s intertextual interplay with Superman codes derived from a variety of media, *Smallville* therefore repeatedly establishes dialogic exchanges with systems of signification that are drawn both from within and outside the Supermanverse. At times, the heteroglossic exchange reaffirms our desire for the Superman mythos, while at others, the external signs—of vampires, Batmen and terminators—threaten to overpower the more familiar codes of the Superman story.

The question of authenticity is not an issue when dealing with these examples because once entering the Superman array you have no lesser or greater claim to authenticity; each new form simply creates its own variation out of previous signs in the Superman universe. What *Smallville* does is to take the basic signs that comprise the myth of Superman and alter their meaning by placing them in the new context of its television format. But what's important to recognize, and is something missing from Eco's explanation, is that story concerns aren't necessarily the primary or only drive for viewers. The insertion of other media examples or other versions of the Superman story are just as integral to

Figure 15.2 Clark Kent and his sometimes not so arch enemy Lex Luthor from the *Smallville* television series. © Warner Bros. TV/The Kobal Collection.

the viewer's involvement with and interpretation of *Smallville*'s version of the myth. Citation becomes a way of engaging the audience in a game that is about a homage to and renegotiation of the past. This "hyper-consciousness" permits viewers to become engrossed in the narration in a more conventional sense, with the story and themes unraveling along syntagmatic lines; but they're also encouraged to participate with the work on the paradigmatic level through the multilayered, intertextual references (Collins 1991, 173), in the process watching and unpicking the creative process that *has* and *is* creating an alternative Superman universe. In other words, a mythology that is *both* already said *and* which is in the process of being said; this is not only something that unsettles Eco's schema but it also calls into question his assertion that the myth value of the superhero collapses when the myth layer succumbs to serial logic. The primary reason that no such collapse takes place is made clear in Morrison's *Animal Man*: the reader is always an integral part of the superhero genre. Through their immediate experience and, later, their memory of the experience of reading a comic book, the reader becomes as embedded in the hypertimelines of a superhero's story.

Discussing generic process, Mikhail Bakhtin explained that

> A genre is always the same yet not the same, always old and new simultaneously. Genre is reborn and renewed at every new stage in the development of literature and in every individual work of a given

genre. This constitutes the life of the genre . . . A genre lives in the present, but always remembers its past, its beginning. (1984, 106)

This holds all the more true for the superhero genre and the mythological (re)tellings that cross multiple serial texts and multiple media formats. The continuities that the superhero genre attempts to contain actually serve to expand the genre's parameters. While containing the past, it must also make way for the present and look towards its future. However, for a genre to achieve this it requires an audience that's familiar with its conventions and rules and that, to apply Bakhtin's own term, engages in a dialogic relationship with its processes of construction. In his book *Film Language: A Semiotics of the Cinema*, Christian Metz (1974) provides an evocative explanation for the creative process that is film language and how we engage with and understand it as spectators. As is the case with any language, the simpler structures—letters, words, sentences—become, through repeated use and increasing numbers of users, more complex structures that continue to grow. As a language's vocabulary grows over time, it multiplies the methods through which like-minded patterns of meaning may be expressed. Sometimes, words are introduced that even undermine, multiply, or complicate the signification of prior meanings. Being integral to the narratives of popular culture, genres function in precisely the same way. The superhero genre, like any genre, isn't only a static language that remains frozen in time; it's a dynamic, formal structure that plunges itself into repeated, ongoing conversations with its creators, other creations, and its audiences across time. And given the prevalence and multiplication of media technologies as disseminators of generic 'language,' fans are being incorporated into conversations with these texts all the more aggressively. As Bakhtin explains about the process of speech:

In the actual life of speech, every concrete act of understanding is active . . . To some extent, primacy belongs to the response, as the activating principle . . . it prepares the ground for an active and engaged understanding. Understanding comes to fruition only in the response. Understanding and response are dialectically merged and mutually condition each other; one is impossible without the other. (1981, 282)

Superhero comic book readers, like the audience of *Smallville,* actively participate in a gamelike conversation that's about the construction of the rules of the superhero genre across media: its various points of origin, its points of divergence, and its radical transformations—in other words, the content of its various hypertimelines. In fact, the fan's own voice is at times so strong that it actually impacts on the language of the generic text.[24] For Eco the stories take place in a perpetual present that excludes all notions of change and development . . . If Superman actually married Lois Lane or became elderly, this would indicate an irreversible progression in character development that would necessarily implicate him in the temporal flux of events . . . Superman comes off as a myth only if the reader loses awareness of the temporal relationships in the story . . . When events no longer have a structure such that one event follows another in a linear sequence, concepts like causality, which presupposes a sense of temporality, also collapse. (Andrae 1987, 136)

The superhero narratives are aware of a process that elides Eco: genres and the audiences that engage with them can never be removed from the temporalities that contain them: they are hyper-spatiotemporal creations that are intimately entwined with the memories of their audience. Where for Eco it is impossible for Clark Kent/Superman to marry Lois Lane (because it would be an irreversible act that seeks to rewrite the archetype myth established at some origin point in the past), in the world of comic books this *did* happen in the late 90s—the myth of Superman participated in temporal progression yet the mythology *wasn't* destroyed as a result. Not only does *Smallville* add more signs into the array that is the Superman universe, making it one of many authentic variations of the story, but it also generates a parallel time line in the array that begins its own variation of the previous mythology. Sometimes, as if passing through a portal, the mythic realities coexist; at other times *Smallville* follows its own spatiotemporal continuum, aware of the other's existence but refusing to cross into its universe.

Shows like *Smallville* inform us of changes in audience reception. New storytelling practices (and modes of consuming them) have been developing because of the multiplication of access to media technologies through which we, as audiences, gain access to these universes. Television, mobile phones, cable, the Internet, DVD technology—all amplify our access to and understanding of these media texts. They multiply our exposure to them. Our home entertainment environments—or our pop media worship rooms are *our* Aleph. The Swamp Thing temporarily lost his sanity when confronted with the universe in its entirety.[25] While confronted with our media Aleph (which maps out the expansive and growing intertextual web that is media culture), we may not lapse into insanity (well, maybe, if we lived through the tangled web that was the first three seasons of *Alias*), but we are expected to stand before this media world like all-knowing celestial beings who have access to all fictional knowledge at their fingertips. The representations of the mythology (the examples that exist within the array and are visible to our Swamp Thing viewer within the media Aleph) have become part of the mythology and, as such, the *telling* of the myth has become *as* important as the myth that is told.

COMIC BOOKS

Jurgens, Dan. 1994. *Zero Hour: Crisis in Time!* September. New York: DC Comics.

Kesel, Karl. 1999. *Superboy.* March–August. New York: DC Comics.

Morrison, Grant, Frank Quitely, and Jamie Grant. 2005–. *All Star Superman.* New York: DC Comics.

Waid, Mark. 1999. *The Kingdom.* New York: DC Comics.

Waid, Mark, and Brian Augustyn. 1999. "Chain Lightning, Finale: Finish Line." *The Flash.* July. New York: DC Comics.

Wolfman, Marv, and George Pérez. 1985. *Crisis on Infinite Earths.* January–December. New York: DC Comics.

Wolfman, Marv, George Pérez, and Dick Giordano. 1985–1986. *Crisis on Infinite Earths.* April–March. New York: DC Comics.

BIBLIOGRAPHY

Adkins, Cecil. "The History of Hypertime" and "The Original Hypertime Theory." *The Unofficial Hypertime Website 5.0.* http://www.geocities.com/Hypertime2000/features/index.html.

Andrae, Thomas. 1987. "From Menace to Messiah: The History and Historicity of Superman." In *American Media and Mass Culture: Left Perspectives,* 124–38. Ed. Donald Lazare. Berkeley: University of California Press.

Bakhtin, Mikhail. 1981. "Discourse in the Novel." The Dialogic Imagination: Four Essays. Ed. Michael Holquist. Austin: University of Texas Press.

Bakhtin, Mikhail. 1984. *Problems of Dostoevsky's Poetics.* Minneapolis: University of Minnesota Press.

Collins, Jim. 1991. "Batman: The Movie, Narrative: The Hyperconscious." In *The Many Lives of the Batman: Critical Approaches to a Superhero and His Media,* 64–181. Eds. Roberta E. Pearson and William Uricchio. New York: Routledge.

Eco, Umberto. 1972. "The Myth of Superman." *Diacritics,* 2(1): 14–22.

Gordon, Ian. 2001. "Nostalgia, Myth, and Ideology: Visions of Superman at the End of the 'American Century.' " In *Comics & Ideology,* eds. Matthew McAllister, Edward Sewell, and Ian Gordon. New York: Peter Lang Publishing.

Gordon, Ian. 2003. "Superman on the Set: The Market, Nostalgia and Television Audiences." In *Quality Popular Television: Cult TV, the Industry and Fans.* Eds. Mark Jancovich and James Lyons. London: British Film Institute & Berkeley: University of California Press.

Metz, Christian. 1974. *Film Language: A Semiotics of the Cinema.* Translated by Michael Taylor. Chicago: University of Chicago Press.

Ndalianis, Angela. 2004. *Neo-Baroque Aesthetics and Contemporary Entertainment.* Cambridge, MA: MIT Press.

Ndalianis, Angela. 2005. "Television and the Neo-Baroque." In *The Contemporary Television Series,* 83–101. Eds. Lucy Mazdon and Michael Hammond. Edinburgh: University of Edinburgh.

Offenberger, Rik, n.d. "Uniquely Original: Grant Morrison" (interview with Grant Morrison). *Silverbullet Comic Books.* http://www.silverbulletcomicbooks.com/features/112602239631900.htm.

Pearson, Roberta E., and William Uricchio, eds. 1991. *The Many Lives of the Batman: Critical Approaches to a Superhero and His Media.* New York: Routledge.

Veitch, Rick. 1987. "Wavelength." *Swamp Thing* (July). New York: DC Comics.

Vibber, Kelson. "Time and Hypertime." *The Flash: Those Who Ride the Lightning.* Available at: http://www.hyperborea.org/flash/Hypertime.html.

NOTES

1. My thanks to Jim Collins, Ian Gordon, Simon McLean, and Martyn Pedler for their valuable feedback on this chapter.
2. 'Wavelength,' DC, July 1987, Rick Veitch.
3. "The Aleph" is also a short story by the writer Jorge Luis Borges. It is one of the stories in the book *The Aleph;* first published in 1949, and revised in 1974, it clearly influences both Alan Moore and Rick Veitch, the writers of the revamped *Swamp Thing* series. As is the case in the 'Wavelength' episode of *Swamp Thing,* in Borges's story, the Aleph is a point in space that contains all other points. Anyone who gazes into it can clearly see everything in the universe from every angle simultaneously.
4. For further discussion of the economic and conglomerate drive of the entertainment industry, see Ndalianis 2004.
5. Or the innumerable traumas that Superman has lived through (and died through) in the comic book stories, including the cloned and cyborg versions, as well as crossover series that has the caped crusader battle the acid-bleeding Aliens who first appeared in the blockbuster films.
6. This playful and reflexive negotiation of the array is, by no means, limited to *Smallville* and the Superman mythology. For a further discussion of popular culture's recent and playful engagement with meaning construction, see Ndalianis 2004, Chs. 1 & 2, and Ndalianis 2005.
7. Superman, therefore, "possesses the characteristics of timeless myth, but is accepted only because his activities take place in our human and everyday world of time" (Eco 1972, 16).
8. For a detailed analysis of the role of nostalgia in the Superman mythos, see Ian Gordon's chapter "Nostalgia, Myth, and Ideology: Visions of Superman at the End of the 'American Century,'" in McAllister, Sewell, and Gordon (2001). Gordon updates Umberto Eco's "The Myth of Superman," arguing that Superman must constantly be reinvented in order to appeal to a new audience across a diverse range of media. See also Gordon (2003).
9. A similar nostalgia for the villain, Lex Luthor, is at play. The episode "Scare" (4:10) includes a glimpse into Lex's future where, as president (he became president of the United States in 2000 in the comics), he instigates the destruction of Earth in apocalyptic proportions. Here (and in other sequences that recur in the series), Lex wears the iconic leather glove familiar to the comic book audience: in the comics, Luthor gets a sample of kryptonite from the cyborg Metallo and creates a ring that's lethal for Superman. The only problem is, the kryptonite's radiation ends up giving Lex cancer and his hand is amputated and replaced with a fake appendage that he keeps gloved.
10. A new, cloned Superboy (Kon-El) was introduced in 1993 in the wake of the 'dead' Superman. This Superboy was the product of secret government genetic experiments (known as Project Cadmus). It was later revealed that Superboy was, in fact, made up of a combination of the DNA of Superman and Lex Luthor. A quasi love child, perhaps?
11. Kal-El's arrival on Earth is built up to more epic proportions in the series. The meteor shower that caused the destruction of Krypton and plunges to Earth with Kal-El's rocket ship has major ramifications for the people of Smallville and nearby districts, generating many strange events that Clark is continually called upon to rectify. The biblical elements of the Superman story are developed to the max by the writers. Pummeled by the rain of meteorites, a young, red-haired Lex Luthor curls up in terror in the cornfields, finally emerging with his hallmark bald head. The cornfield is also the place where Clark is 'crucified' on a scarecrow post and tormented like the Savior

Jesus Christ himself (1:1). The father and son relationships are also deliberately given a biblical touch in the series. The audience hears the booming, godly voice of Jor-El, Clark's mysterious otherworldly father, only when he needs to impart information that will have grand ramifications. Not to be outdone, Lionel Luthor's mass of hair not only counters Lex's lack of hair, but it calls up connotations of Samson-like power: Lionel initially had power but gained it through corrupt means. When his hair was shaved in prison, the corrupt power migrated to Lex, the son. Instead, Lionel, like Samson, gained humility and true wisdom (i.e., insight into the mysteries of Kal-El).

12. One of the most recent reboots is *All Star Superman* (Grant Morrison, Frank Quitely, Jamie Grant). First published in 2005, the comic aims at introducing a version of the Superman origin myth to a new generation of readers.

13. Superboy may have first appeared in 1944 (*More Fun Comics* #101), but his dog Krypto wouldn't make an appearance until 1955 in Adventure Comics (#210).

14. Similarly, because of their nostalgic desire, when a Supergirl-like character makes an appearance in the show, our expectations make us believe that she's the 'real' thing, until she's exposed as a fake.

15. For more on serial form and contemporary television, see Ndalianis 2005 and 2004 (Ch.1).

16. The popularity of John Glover, the actor who plays Lionel Luthor, prompted the writers to provide him with a backstory. Originally, Glover was to appear in Season One of the series, but his role has continued into the current sixth season.

17. Clark captures them in The Phantom Zone, the alternate prison dimension that the Clark/Superman of *Superman II* also propels the evil Kryptonians into.

18. A version of the Flash appears in the *Smallville* episode "Run" (4:5). His name is Bart Gallner; however, the allusions to other historical versions of Flash's identity are driven home in the false identifications he carries with him—these include Jay Garrick, Barry Allen, and Wally West, the three Flashes of the DC Universe.

19. Several characters from the pre-Crisis era, including Kara Zor-El/Supergirl and Barry Allen/Flash, were killed during *Crisis*, the intention being to erase them from DC continuity history.

20. In 1994, the miniseries *Zero Hour* attempted to fill some of the continuity gaps generated by *Crisis* by again altering the DC Universe. And again in 2005, the series *Infinite Crisis* tried to redress further problems and fan concerns which included the return of Earth-Two's Superman Kal-L, Earth-Three's Alexander Luthor, Jr., and Earth-Prime's Superboy. A version of Superboy was created in 1985—before *Crisis on Infinite Earths*. This version came from a parallel Earth known as Earth-Prime, where Superman and the other DC superheroes only existed as fictional characters. At the end of the Crisis, Superboy joined Alexander Luthor of Earth-Three and the Lois Lane and Superman of Earth-Two in a "paradise dimension." In DC's *Infinite Crisis* miniseries, Superboy-Prime, Alex Luthor, and Superman and Lois Kent of Earth-Two were revealed to have been watching the DC Universe since they entered the "paradise dimension."

21. Of course, the 'solution' proved more confusing than the problem, and gaps began to emerge in the post-Crisis universe.

22. *Kingdom Come* was set some decades into the future of the 1996 reality in which it was published and a decade after Superman's retirement following the coming into power of a new generation of vigilante-style superheroes and supervillains. Most of the 'old school' superheroes have either disappeared, are in hiding, or are operating in secrecy. During a major battle led by Magog

(leader of the new superheroes' group Justice Battalion), Captain Atom is destroyed, his body causing a nuclear holocaust that wipes out Kansas. Coming out of retirement, Superman wages war against the new generation renegades and the battle that follows mirrors that between the Greek Olympian gods and the Titans: in this case, however, it's the old guard who return to their former glory. A little boy, William, is rescued from the Kansas horror by Superman and, in *The Kingdom*, he establishes a religion that worships Superman. Early in this series, however, he discovers that the Kansas disaster may have never happened if Superman had not withdrawn from human society. Incapable of dealing with the knowledge of Superman's fallibility, he loses his sanity, adopts the name Gog, and travels back in time repeatedly killing Superman.

23. *Smallville*'s Brainiac is more aligned with the humanoid computer which appears in the animated series *Superman: The Animated Series* and *Justice League*.

24. A classic example in the superhero comic book is the input that fans had on the fate of Jason Todd, who became the second Robin in 1983. Fan hatred of Jason was voiced loud and clear, so much so that, in 1988, DC Comics introduced a telephone poll that decided the fate of Robin. Coinciding with the four-part story "A Death in the Family" (*Batman* #426–429, 1988), at the conclusion of *Batman* #427, Jason was beaten by the Joker and left to die in an explosion. This issue also provided the phone numbers fans could call to vote for Jason's survival or demise. And the rest, as they say, is history.

25. Swamp Thing's memory of the Aleph was wiped from his mind so that he could continue to function.

Contributors

Paul Atkinson is a lecturer in communications and writing in the School of Humanities, Communications and Social Sciences at Monash University (Gippsland Campus, Churchill) in Australia.

Jason Bainbridge is a lecturer in journalism and media studies at the University of Tasmania, Hobart. He has published on celebrity, merchandising, and representations of law in popular culture and is currently working on the book *Media, Journalism and the Modern World: From Theory to Practice* (Oxford University Press). He is also an avid (some would say rabid) comic collector.

Scott Bukatman is an associate professor in the Film and Media Studies Program in the Department of Art and Art History at Stanford University. He is the author of *Terminal Identity: The Virtual Subject in Postmodern Science Fiction* (Duke University Press), *Blade Runner* (British Film Institute), and *Matters of Gravity: Special Effects and Supermen in the 20th Century*. His writing highlights the ways in which popular media (film, comics) and genres (science fiction, musicals, superhero narratives) mediate between new technologies and human perceptual and bodily experience. His latest project is a book-length study of Winsor McCay, an early innovator in both newspaper comics and animated film.

Jennifer Dowling's master's work (Ohio State) concentrated on Yiddish riddles, and doctoral thesis (Oxford) discussed the characterization of the feminine in eighteenth-century Yiddish chapbooks. In 1997, she was appointed as the inaugural lecturer in Yiddish language and culture at the University of Sydney. She has presented papers on Yiddish studies in Australia, Yiddish literature, *Buffy the Vampire Slayer*, and *Angel*. Jennifer's present research projects include Yiddish chivalric romances, the digitization of Yiddish archives, TimeMaps, and for sanity's sake, the representation of Jews in modern culture.

Karen Healey is a PhD candidate at the University of Melbourne, Australia, and is currently writing her dissertation on superhero comics and fandom. She graduated from the University of Canterbury, New Zealand, with a BA in classics, and BA (Hons) and MA in English. She is a founding member of feminist comics fan organization *Girl-Wonder.org* and the writer of the blog *Girls Read Comics (And They're Pissed).* In her next life, she would like to be Power Girl.

Henry Jenkins is professor and head of the Comparative Media Studies Program at MIT. He has published numerous books dealing with film, television, and popular culture, including *Textual Poachers: Television Fans and Participatory Culture, What Made Pistacchio Nuts? Early Sound Comedy and the Vaudeville Aesthetic,* and *Science Fiction Audiences: Watching Dr. Who and Star Trek* (coauthored with John Tulloch). He has also published widely in journals and book anthologies on topics that deal with a range of his research interests, including superheroes, television, computer games, and fan culture. His Web site is available at http://web.mit.edu/21fms/www/faculty/henry3/.

Angela Ndalianis is head of cinema studies in the School of Culture and Communication at Melbourne University. Her research interests in special effects cinema, computer games, theme parks, comic books, and media history are reflected in publications which include the book *Neo-Baroque Aesthetics and Contemporary Entertainment* (MIT Press, Cambridge, MA 2004) and coedited anthologies *Super/Heroes: From Hercules to Superman* (New Academia Publishing 2006), and *Stars in Our Eyes* (Praeger 2002). She is currently completing a book on the history and cultural significance of theme parks.

Martyn Pedler is a Fitzroy writer of all kinds of pop and pulp fiction. He completed his master's in creative writing at the University of Melbourne with a novella about how disappointed we all were when the world failed to end on New Year's Eve 1999. His fairly terrifying comic book collection is stored safely in long, white boxes under his bed, and no, you can't touch them.

Clare Pitkethly is a PhD media studies candidate at La Trobe University, Melbourne. Her research topic is "Reinventing the Amazon," which focuses on female superheroes like Wonder Woman.

Vanessa Russell is completing a PhD in the School of Culture and Communication at the University of Melbourne. Her research interests range from the comic books of Joe Sacco, Chris Ware, and Art Spiegelman to literary deconversion narratives.

Sallye Sheppeard is a retired professor of English and former chair of the Department of English and Modern Languages at Lamar University in Beaumont, Texas. She holds an MA degree in American literature from Texas Christian University, a PhD in sixteenth- and early seventeenth-century British literature and rhetoric from Texas Woman's University, and an MA in mythological studies from Pacifica Graduate Institute in California. She continues teaching, writing, and participating in professional organizations.

Greg M. Smith is associate professor of communication and graduate director of the Moving Image Studies program at Georgia State University. He is author of *Film Structure and the Emotion System* (Cambridge University Press), *Passionate Views: Film, Cognition, and Emotion* (Johns Hopkins University Press), and *On a Silver Platter: CD-ROMs and the Promise of a New Technology* (New York University Press). His latest book, *Beautiful TV: The Art and Argument of Ally McBeal*, is forthcoming from the University of Texas Press.

Saige Walton is a postgraduate student in the Cinema Studies Program at Melbourne University, and is writing her dissertation on the neo-baroque logic of the cinematic experience. She is also a researcher with the Australian Centre for the Moving Image.

Steven Zani is an assistant professor of English at Lamar University. Besides his history of work in multiple comic book stories, he has a PhD in comparative literature from the State University of New York in Binghamton.

Index

CPSIA information can be obtained
at www.ICGtesting.com
Printed in the USA
LVOW13s0605161216

517557LV00005B/21/P

9 780415 878418